Victimisation in a Digitised Society

Safety & Security Studies

The Safety & Security Studies are an initiative of the network of Collaborating Institutions for Security (in Dutch: *Samenwerkende Kennisinstellingen voor Veiligheid* (SKV network)) that comprises the Avans University of Applied Sciences, University of Applied Sciences Windesheim, The Hague University of Applied Sciences, Inholland University of Applied Sciences, Utrecht University of Applied Sciences, Zeeland University of Applied Sciences, Catholic University of South-west Flanders, Netherlands Institute for Physical Security *Nibra*, NHL University of Applied Sciences, Saxion University of Applied Sciences Enschede and the Police Academy of the Netherlands.

The editors of the series are Evelien De Pauw MSc (Coordinator Research centre and lecturer in public safety and security, KATHO University College), W.K.F. Rodenhuis MSc (lecturer risk management at the Saxion University of Applied Sciences), Prof. Dr W.Ph. Stol (lecturer cyber safety at NHL University of Applied Sciences and the Police Academy of the Netherlands, professor police studies at the Open University) and Dr J. Timmer (lecturer security and social cohesion at Windesheim University).

Previously published works in the Security Studies include:

- E.R. Leukfeldt, K.W.C. van der Straten, M.P. Kruis & W.Ph. Stol, *Ter plaatse. Alledaagse samenwerking tussen de primaire hulpdiensten* [On the spot. Everyday cooperation between primary care services] (2007)
- J. Kerstens, M. Toutenhoofd & W.Ph. Stol, *Wie niet weg is, is gezien. Gevalstudie over een proef met cameratoezicht in de Leeuwarder binnenstad* [In full view. Case study about an experiment using cameras in the center of Leeuwarden] (2008)
- W.Ph. Stol, H.W.K. Kaspersen, J. Kerstens, E.R. Leukfeldt & A.R. Lodder, *Filteren van kinderporno op internet. Een verkenning van technieken en reguleringen in binnen- en buitenland* [Filtering child pornography on the Internet. An exploration of techniques and regulations at home and abroad] (2008)
- L. Symons, J. Deklerck, D. Gelders & S. Pleysier, *Inbraakpreventief advies in België. De mening van de burger* [Advise about preventing break-ins in Belgium. The citizens' opinions] (2010)
- E.R. Leukfeldt, M.M.L. Domenie & W.Ph. Stol, *Verkenning cybercrime in Nederland 2009* [Investigating cybercrime in the Netherlands 2009] (2010)
- T. van Ham, E.R. Leukfeldt, B. Bremmers, W.Ph. Stol & A.Ph. van Wijk, *The art of the Internet. A study of illegal online trading in cultural goods* (2011)
- T. van Ham, E.R. Leukfeldt, B. Bremmers, W.Ph. Stol en A.Ph. van Wijk, *De kunst van het internet. Een onderzoek naar de online illegale handel in cultuurgoederen* (2011)
- J. Kerstens & W.Ph. Stol, *Jeugd en cybersafety. Online slachtoffer- en daderschap onder Nederlandse jongeren* [Youth and cybersafety: Online victimization and perpetration among Dutch Youth] (2012)
- M.M.L. Domenie, E.R. Leukfeldt, J.A. van Wilsem, J. Jansen & W.Ph. Stol, *Victimisation in a digitised society* (2013)
- W.Ph. Stol & J. Jansen, *Cybercrime and the Police* (2013)

Victimisation in a Digitised Society

A Survey Among Members of the Public Concerning E-fraud, Hacking and Other High Volume Crimes

M.M.L. Domenie

E.R. Leukfeldt

J.A. van Wilsem

J. Jansen

W.P. Stol

eleven
international publishing

Published, sold and distributed by Eleven International Publishing
P.O. Box 85576
2508 CG The Hague
The Netherlands
Tel.: +31 70 33 070 33
Fax: +31 70 33 070 30
e-mail: sales@budh.nl
www.elevenpub.com

Sold and distributed in USA and Canada
International Specialized Book Services
920 NE 58th Avenue, Suite 300
Portland, OR 97213-3786, USA
Tel: 1-800-944-6190 (toll-free)
Fax: +1-503-280-8832
orders@isbs.com
www.isbs.com

Eleven International Publishing is an imprint of Boom uitgevers Den Haag.

ISBN 978-94-6236-068-6
ISBN 978-94-6094-798-8 (E-book)

Printed in The Netherlands

Preface

This publication is about what is happening in society in the sphere of crime victimisation with a digital component. This kind of victimisation includes various punishable acts, such as hacking and spreading malware, but also e-fraud and stalking on the internet.

The Dutch government is giving priority to investigating and combating cybercrime, and is adopting legal and organisational measures in that area. The objective is to enable the criminal justice system to combat cybercrime effectively. Investigative policy demands that the police and judicial authorities set priorities. The most serious problems deserve to be addressed first. The gravity of a problem is determined by its nature as well as its extent. In the case of cybercrime, less is known about its extent than about its nature. Now and then experts and those directly involved announce that a certain type of crime is alarmingly on the increase, but systematic and thorough research into the extent of cybercrime is conspicuously absent.

To this end, the Dutch Central Unit, formerly known as the Netherlands Police Agency [Korps Landelijke Politiediensten (KLPD)] and the Programme Against Cybercrime [Programma Aanpak Cybercrime (PAC)] commissioned a national victim survey and the development of a standardised method that will enable future mapping of this kind of victimisation. This publication reports on that research.

A survey of this kind relies on the cooperation of many. First and foremost we would like to thank the consultative group that gave us their valuable comments throughout the process. We would also like to thank Statistics Netherlands for their close collaboration during data collection and analysis. It goes without saying that we also thank all the experts who participated in interviews during the preliminary phase. Without their input, we would never have been able to complete the research. We are grateful to all of these people.

Reader's guide

Chapter 1 gives the context of the research. Chapter 2 gives an account of the methodology used. In Chapters 3, 4 and 5 we explore various kinds of cybercrime in greater depth. In Chapter 3, we discuss malware and hacking; in Chapter 4 financial offences (fraud via auction or retail sites, advance fee fraud and identity abuse); and in Chapter 5 offences in the private sphere (stalking and threats). In these chapters, we discuss the prevalence of each offence; the perpetrators' modi operandi; the relationship between perpetrators and victims; what the material and immaterial damage to victims encompasses; how often members of the public report this kind of crime; and police response to it. In each chapter, we examine risk factors.

In Chapter 6 we focus on multiple victimisation. Here we make it clear who the victims of numerous offences are. Chapter 7 brings the subject matter together; in it we reveal what members of the public feel the role of the police should be, and how taking down statements affects citizen satisfaction levels vis-à-vis the police. In Chapter 8 we present our conclusions and recommendations. The appendices include a detailed account of the methodology and questionnaire used. All these subjects are covered in the comprehensive executive summary.

May 2013

Miranda Domenie
Rutger Leukfeldt
Johan van Wilsem
Jurjen Jansen
Wouter Stol

Contents

Summary

Cybercrime as a concept under discussion

This publication is about victimisation from offences with a digital component, also known as 'cybercrime'. We understand cybercrime to mean crime in which information and communication technology (ICT) plays a significant role in the committing of the offence. Within this definition, two categories can be distinguished: cybercrime in the narrow sense and cybercrime in the broader sense. Offences in which ICT is both the means and the end fall into the first category. Examples of these include hacking and the spreading of viruses. The second category relates to offences that are carried out with the aid of ICT. These include classic offences in which ICT is significant for their execution. Examples of these are crimes committed by fraudsters using websites to scam people, by paedophiles spreading child pornography on cyber networks, and by stalkers who also use the internet to harass their victims.

A question under discussion within the criminal justice system is whether cybercrime in the broader sense of the word should be defined as cyber criminality. The issue is whether there is evidence of a new kind of crime that demands new methods of criminal prosecution – which is not uncommon in cases of cybercrime in the narrow sense – or whether this category merely refers to pre-existing kinds of crime that are being committed using new means. The latter do not call for significant changes to the criminal justice system. The discussion about the definition to be used has not yet ended. For the purposes of this research we reserve judgment on the issue, and for that reason opt for the customary distinctions found in the literature.

Cybercrime: a relatively unknown phenomenon that needs to be given priority

The Dutch government is giving priority to the investigation and combating of cybercrime and is adopting various legal and organisational measures to this end. According to the 'Freedom and Responsibility' coalition agreement drawn up by the Rutte cabinet (2010 to 2012), an *integrated approach to cybercrime* is being developed (Regeerakkoord, 2010, p. 42). According to the Rutte cabinet's coalition agreement, investment is going into the tracking of cyber criminals. The objective is to enable the criminal justice system to combat cybercrime effectively. The Dutch police force is also giving high priority to cybercrime. In the wake of the 2007 coalition agreement, in which cybercrime was designated as a serious crime, the Board of Chief Commissioners instituted the Programme Against Cybercrime and the Team High Tech Crime was established within the Dutch Central Unit. At the same time, the Public Prosecution Service initiated the Intensification Programme on Cybercrime, and, for the judicial system, the Cybercrime Centre of Expertise was established.

Investigative policy demands that the police and judicial authorities set priorities because they simply do not have the capacity to deal with every offence that is reported to the police. The most serious problems deserve to be addressed first. The gravity of the problem is determined by both its nature and its extent. For investigative policy, the police and the judicial authorities must have information at their disposal about the nature and extent of cybercrime. This implies that they must have a method in place for acquiring this knowledge. Less is known about the extent of cybercrime than about its nature. At present, there is no nationwide instrument in the Netherlands to monitor the extent of cybercrime. On occasion, experts and those directly involved make known that a certain type of crime is increasing alarmingly, but systematic and thorough research into the extent of cybercrime is conspicuous by its absence. This research aims to fill that gap.

In addition to insights into the nature and extent of victimisation, it is important for policy development to know who has a heightened risk of becoming a victim. If victimisation were limited, for instance, to a very specific section of internet users, taking general preventative measures would not be effective. In terms of preventing crime, it is also useful to know whether certain internet behaviour leads to an increased risk of victimisation or whether certain behaviour rather acts as a shield.

Research objective and questions

This publication is about victimisation relating to offences with a digital component among members of the public in the Netherlands. We are not basing this study on a theoretical definition of the concept 'cybercrime' that we subsequently operationalise. The research investigates offences to which people fall victim in which ICT plays a significant role at the time, and for which the police and judicial authorities are confronted by a lack of knowledge about victimisation.[1] The study relates to both cybercrime in the narrow sense (hacking and malware) and cybercrime in the broader sense (fraud via auction and retail sites, identity theft, identity fraud, advance fee fraud, stalking and threats).

Cybercrime victimisation is measured by first assessing what the person being interviewed says on the matter. During these interviews, several verification questions were posed to get an indication of how certain it was that the person was in fact a victim. Two themes are central to this. First, we want to know the extent of cybercrime victimisation is. In this context factors that increase or reduce the chances of victimisation are important. We also explored what people using the internet consider to be the role of the police when it comes to security on the internet, as well as whether victims report these crimes to the police and whether they are satisfied with the police response to this reporting.

1 A detailed explanation for the selection is given in Chapter 2.

This publication reflects the state of affairs in 2011 and is not intended to be used to make predictions. The authorities and the police may use the research findings when determining new policies. Policy areas for which the research results may be useful include prioritising prevention and investigation, conducting criminality analyses, developing a national threat assessment, and answering parliamentary questions regarding the nature, extent and strategies for tackling cybercrime. The results can also be used to design further research, particularly in-depth research into the field of cybercrime. The research also produced a questionnaire that can be used in repeat studies. Part of the questionnaire has already been included by Statistics Netherlands (*Centraal Bureau voor de Statistiek* (CBS)) in their Safety Monitor. In due course this will give some insight into developments in the nature and extent of victimisation.

Research methodology

The research comprised a development phase and an implementation phase. The development phase commenced with a study of the literature. Books, articles and reports were found using online media libraries. This provided insight into what is known about cybercrime victimisation in the Netherlands and abroad. Based on the literature study, a topic list was compiled for interviews with key figures in the police and justice departments, at both at policy and operational levels. The interviews focussed on gleaning insights into the priorities set by the police, judiciary and government regarding cybercrime in the Netherlands as it stands now and in the immediate future. We also asked what precisely it is that the police, judiciary and government specifically need to know about cybercrimes. Three group interviews were then held with small groups of internet users. The primary objective of these group interviews was to seek clarification about how best to question members of the public about cybercrime victimisation. Cybercrime is, after all, a relatively new phenomenon that is unfamiliar to many people and that is not as easily defined as bicycle theft, for example.

A pilot questionnaire was compiled on the basis of the literature study, interviews with experienced experts and group interviews. That questionnaire was distributed to a sample of 1,000 Dutch members of the public. The pilot study was conducted as far as possible in line with the Safety Monitor. Phrasing of the questions was aligned with questions about offline crime, and the interviewing method was largely the same as the Safety Monitor. The objective of the pilot study was primarily to uncover errors in the questionnaire with a view to optimising the surveying of cybercrime, i.e. does the questionnaire provide answers to the research questions?

During the implementation phase (2011), the amended questionnaire was distributed to 21,800 people aged 15 years and older on the basis of a representative sample drawn by the CBS from municipal personal records [*Gemeentelijke Basisadministratie* (GBA)]. The response rate was 10,314 (47%). The CBS used background characteristics to assign weighting factors to each individual respondent on the basis of their representativeness in the sample. The analyses for the study were carried out on the responses of the 9,163 respondents who indicated that they used the internet (89% of the respondents). Where we refer to respondents in this study, we are therefore referring to this group of 9,163 respondents. In order to develop a monitoring methodology for victimisation, we worked closely with the CBS during this research.

Hacking

In this publication we define hacking, in line with Section 138ab of the Dutch Criminal Code [*Wetboek van Strafrecht, henceforth Sr*], as gaining access intentionally and unlawfully to a computerised work or part thereof. According to the law, a computerised work is a system that is intended to store, process and transfer information using electronic means, for instance a computer, a database or a server on which websites are hosted (Section 80e Sr). If someone gains access to the account of another without permission, this is known as hacking, even if that person guesses the password, and even if that person could have gained access anyway.

Hacking is difficult offence to investigate. Hacking is often not the objective per se, but rather a means to commit another kind of crime. For this reason, we measured hacking victimisation in our study in various ways. First, respondents were asked directly and on the basis of three questions whether they had been hacked. Second, in the sections on identity theft and stalking, we asked respondents whether hacking was part of the perpetrator's modus operandi.

In total, 4.3 per cent of the respondents had been victims of at least one kind of hacking in the twelve months prior to the research: 1.5 per cent were victims of defacing (changing a website or profile page without permission); 0.7 per cent had their computers hacked; 2.9 per cent had their email accounts hacked; and perpetrators hacked 0.3 per cent of the respondents' computers or changed websites or profiles as part of their modi operandi for stalking and/or identity theft.

Bivariate analyses show that the younger internet users are, the more likely they are to fall victim to hacking. The percentage for victimisation is particularly high in the 15 to 24 years age group (10.1%). Furthermore, we noted that the risk of victimisation is greater for those who live alone, and for those whose highest level of completed education is primary school. The bivariate analysis did not reflect differences between men and women, between ethnic groups or those with many or few hours of paid work.

We subsequently carried out multivariate analysis. Introducing internet activity as a predictor of hacking shows that age still has a negative and significant effect. A considerable factor in the reason why younger people are likely to be hacked more often is because they undertake more internet activities that increase the risk of being hacked. According to this model, the specific activities that increase the risk of being hacked are: the frequency with which one surfs the internet, a high level of exposure (visibility on the web), and not using virus scanners. For the rest, we noted a lower risk of being hacked among people who are conscious of the risks that accompany internet usage. An unexpected finding of this model is that the risk of getting hacked drops as the frequency of downloading increases.

Finally, as interaction effects[2] were added, it emerged that the risk of being hacked increases with age with respect to both activity (emailing and targeted searching for information on the internet) and exposure (untargeted surfing, downloading, using MSN, skyping, chatting, visiting forums and social media sites and using Twitter). In other words, younger people are not at increased the risk of being hacked the more exposed they are and the more they take part in activity on the internet, whereas for older people this is indeed the case. That is, the risk that young people take does not increase when they increase their activity on the web. This as opposed to older people, whose relatively low risk does increase as their internet activity increases.

Malware

Malware is a generic name for malicious software. Examples include viruses, worms, Trojan horses and spyware. Of all the respondents that indicated that they use the internet, 16.7 per cent noticed that they had had malware on their own computers during the previous twelve-month period. The percentage of internet users whose computers had been infected by malware is in all probability higher because not all users will have noticed malware. Those who were more likely to notice malware were more highly educated people, men, people between the ages of 35 and 54, and people with paid employment.

Respondents who had noticed malware were asked how this malware got on to their computer. Almost four out of ten respondents who had spotted malware were not aware of how it had got on to their computer (38.4%). According to just over a quarter of these, the malware got on to their system via email; a similar number blamed a link on a website; and more than a fifth said they were infected via a download.

Of the respondents who noticed malware, 16.1 per cent stated that they had suffered financial loss. This means that 2.7 per cent of all internet users suffered financial loss through malware, for example by having to have their computer fixed as a consequence. Of those who had suffered loss through malware, 78.2 per cent could specify the extent of the damage. More than half of the known losses amounted to 100 euros or less, and 7.9 per cent amounted to 501 euros or more. Of the respondents who noticed the malware, 11.9 per cent (equivalent to 2.0 per cent of all internet users) lost files or software.

Fraud via auction and retail sites

Fraud via auction and retail sites generally takes place as follows: the buyer pays the agreed price (or part thereof) in advance, but the seller does not deliver the goods as agreed. In most cases, the buyer is therefore the victim. The reverse is also possible. The seller delivers the goods, but the buyer fails to pay the price (or part thereof).

2 This explores whether the influence of certain online behavioural clusters (activity and exposure) differs for people of varying ages and with different levels of education.

Of the internet users who took part in the survey, 73.2 per cent had made at least one purchase via the internet in the previous twelve-month period. Of the buyers during that period, 3.1 per cent had paid for a product or service that was never provided. This equates to 2.4 per cent of all the internet users interviewed.

Of all internet users, 32.8 per cent had sold a product or service via the internet in the previous twelve-month period. Of this group, 1.0 per cent had provided a product or service for which no payment was received. This equates to 0.3 per cent of all internet users.

There is only a sufficient number of victims of the 'bought but never received' variety of this kind of fraud to warrant further analyses. If we look at the influence of background characteristics on victimisation, we see that the chances of falling victim to this kind of fraud decreases with age. If we add internet activity as a predictor of fraud, we see that the age effect becomes insignificant, which indicates that the reason for the increased risk of fraud among younger people lies in their higher levels of risky internet behaviour. This is related in particular to their increased activity (emailing and searching for information on the internet). Finally, when interaction effects are included, it emerges that the more educated the user, the less likely activity is to increase risk on the internet. In other words, activity increases the risk of fraud for everyone, but particularly those with lower education qualifications. For the rest, there are no significant interaction effects.

In 19.2 per cent of all cases, contact with the seller came via foreign countries. In other words, in a fifth of all cases, the perpetrator operated abroad or through foreign countries. If more of these cases are reported to the police, the international character of their workload will increase even more.

Fraud has consequences for the trust that people have in trading on the internet. Half of the victims (50.7%) lost faith in trading on the auction or retail site on which they were swindled, and for 27.4 per cent trust in any form of trade on the internet also decreased. For more than a quarter (26.0%) of the victims, their general sense of security on the web diminished.

Identity fraud

Identity fraud is the committing of fraud using a fabricated/assumed identity. Preparations for identity abuse of this kind can be made by creating a fictitious identity, assuming the identity of an existing person with their permission, or by stealing the identity of an existing person (identity theft). Identity theft can be done by stealing digital personal details, for instance, through phishing or using spyware.

In the questionnaire we used the following description: 'Identity fraud is when someone uses your personal or financial details without your permission in order to make money. For instance, it is when someone withdraws money from your account, buys products in your name or applies for official documents in your name. Identity fraud is generally a consequence of identity theft, but in some cases you may have provided your identity details yourself.'

In total, 0.9 per cent of internet users had fallen victim to identity fraud. The identity information of 0.5 per cent of internet users was stolen using ICT. According to the respondents, skimming was the method most often used to access their identity details. Respondents also often put their information on a website or an online form themselves.

If we look at the influence of background characteristics on victimisation, we see that the risk of identity fraud is divided equally among, for example, men and women, young and old, and those with higher versus those with lower education. Certain internet activities do seem to contribute to the risk of online identity fraud. These are activities (emailing and searching for information on the internet) and participating in paid contact or dating sites. We established earlier that internet activity increases risk. It also emerged that the more PCs there were in the household, the lower the risk. It is not clear how to interpret this finding. We did not find any significant interaction effects.

Six of the ten victims suffered financial loss, which amounted to 1,000 or more euros for more than a third of these. Ten of the 63 victims suffered loss that was not compensated. A third of the victims contacted their banks as a consequence of the incident. Twelve of the 63 victims (19.0%) also contacted the police.

For more than a third of victims, their general sense of security (also on the internet) diminished as a consequence of falling victim to identity theft and/ or fraud.

Advance fee fraud

Advance fee fraud is a kind of fraud whereby victims are promised large sums of money if they first deposit a relatively small amount to so-called defray expenses or if they invest a small amount of money; the victims are subsequently not paid out. For instance, the potential victims are asked to pay legal fees to access the inheritance of an unknown family member in Africa.

Of the 9,163 internet users interviewed, 18 fell victim to advance fee fraud. This equates to 0.2 per cent of the respondents. We considered someone to be a victim of advance fee fraud if they had actually suffered loss. It is not possible to draw generalising conclusions due to the limited number of victims.

Stalking

Cyberstalking is the generic name for the systematic and relentless online harassment and/or threatening of a person by making provocative statements and/ or placing provocative messages on online forums and bulletin boards, and in chat rooms, by spying on the person using spyware or by continuously sending unsolicited emails and spam. It also includes posting offensive pages with photos of and information about the victim on the internet. In addition to this, other internet users may be incited to harass or threaten the victim.

Among internet users, 1.1 per cent fell victim to cyberstalking in the 12 months leading up to the research. If we look at the influence of background characteristics, we see that the risks are higher for younger respondents and respondents without partners. We discovered no differences in risks between, for instance, men and women, or between people from different ethnic backgrounds.

If we add internet activities as a predictor of stalking, we see that the effects of age and the presence of a partner disappear. The differences between younger and older people and those with and without partners can therefore be ascribed to the various internet activities that they undertake. This model shows us that activity and exposure coincide with a higher risk of online stalking. Additional analysis (not shown) does in fact show that younger people and people living alone do tend to take part in such activities more often. Interaction effects were not significant.

The above indicates that prevention and information must not be directed exclusively at the young, but also at people with high exposure in cyberspace. Privacy by default may well be a protective software-based measure for this group; information about the risks of online exposure also presents itself as a possible effective strategy for this group.

Perpetrators use a range of ways to stalk victims, of which email, mobile phone and chat programmes are those used most frequently. In more than half the cases, the victim knew the perpetrator. Our analysis did not demonstrate how this correlates with the finding that the extent of the victim's internet activity is related to victimisation. Almost one in three victims go to the police.

Threats

For a threat in the criminal sense, there must be evidence of the threat of murder, rape, committing overt violence in association with others in the private sphere or property, aggravated assault, kidnapping or arson (Sect. 285 Sr). It is not a requirement that the victim actually feels threatened: it is sufficient that the threat is of the kind and takes place under such circumstances that 'reasonable fear can arise' in the person being threatened that the threat will be carried out. If someone threatens someone else with death on a chat programme such as MSN, this threat constitutes a crime according to Section 285 Sr. This is therefore the same as a crime that takes place on the street.

Among internet users, 0.7 per cent fell victim to cyber threats. Around three quarters of these respondents were threatened more than once. A similar proportion knew who the perpetrator was. Four respondents suffered financial loss as a consequence of threats.

If we look at the influence of background characteristics on victimisation, we note that there is an increased risk for young people and for unemployed respondents (or those with part-time work of less than twelve hours a week). If we include internet activities as a predictor of threats, it emerges that the age effect decreases considerably and that the unemployment effect is no longer significant. Part of the difference in risk linked to age can therefore be attributed to the fact that younger people undertake internet activities that increase risk. It accounts entirely for the difference between the employed and the unemployed. In addition, it emerges that the greater one's exposure, the higher the risk of threat: the more one engages in exposure-increasing activities, the higher the risk of threats. Finally, when interaction effects are included, no interaction effects are found for exposure, while they are for activity. In other words, exposure is equally likely to increase risk for both young and old as well as for those with higher or lower education. For activity, the risk of threats increases among those with lower levels of education and this is significantly less likely to be the case as levels of education increase.

Multiple victimisation

Annually, 8.5 per cent of internet users fall victim to one or more kinds of the offences with a digital component that we researched. There is a group of victims that falls victim more than once. This group is interesting because interventions directed at this group could be more effective than interventions aimed at other internet users. As a small group, they are victims of a relatively large share of the offences.

Multiple victimisation means that the respondent became a victim of various offences in the previous twelve months. The question with this group of victims is: who are they and why were they victims of various offences? When determining whether a respondent was a multiple victim, we did not take malware into account because respondents were only asked whether they noticed malware. And we did not take hacking as a modus operandi into account because a victim who was hacked for identity theft, for example, was actually only a one-off victim.

Of the internet users in our research, 1.5 per cent were multiple victims. The percentage of multiple victims was particularly high in the age group 15 to 34 years. Internet users without partners were also relatively more likely to be victims.

Relations between the police and the public

Among internet users, 29.0 per cent believe that the police have a responsibility to safeguard security on the internet. However, the respondents lay most of the responsibility at the feet of financial institutions and website owners.

The percentage of victims who had contacted the police was 13.4 per cent on average, but varied according to the offence: from 4.1 per cent (hacking) to 30.4 per cent (stalking). Police response to the various reports from victims varies. For fraud via auction or retail sites and for advance fee fraud and identity fraud – in short: offences targeting the victim's money – police took statements for more than half of the cases reported. For offences aimed at the person or for the suspect's private purposes (hacking, stalking, threats and so on), the percentage is lower at 28.6 per cent.

Victims from whom statements were taken tend to be more satisfied with the police response than victims whose statements were not taken. But it is not simply a question of deducing that if the police take statements more often, members of the public will be more satisfied. This is because even though the police tend to take statements more often for offences aimed at taking money than they do for offences in the private sphere or for private purposes, victims of offences directed at money are in general not more satisfied about the police than victims of offences in the private sphere or for private purposes. This indicates that there are more factors influencing the satisfaction of members of the public: these may be related to the capacity of the police to give the right kind of positive attention in offences that impact on privacy aspects or the victim's person. How this exactly works is the subject of further study.

Conclusion: prevalence

As far as prevalence is concerned, our findings show that, in the twelve months preceding the survey, 8.5 per cent of all internet users were victims of at least one of the offences with a digital component that were surveyed. The key figures for crime policy that emerge from our survey, taken on an annual basis, indicate that 4.3 per cent of all Dutch internet users fall victim to hacking and 3.5 per cent fall victim to e-fraud (fraud via an retail or auction site, identity fraud, advance fee fraud).

The figures show that, in terms of prevalence, cybercrime is a serious factor in the daily lives of the public. We compared cybercrime victimisation (i.e. crimes with a digital component) and some victim data from the CBS's national Safety Monitor 2011. Traditionally, the Netherlands is the land of bicycle theft (4.8%) because this offence normally scores the highest in classic victimisation surveys. The findings from our research show that the Netherlands can now be characterised as the country of bicycle theft (4.8%) and hacking (4.3%). Cybercrime has taken on the character of high volume crime: ordinary crime interwoven with daily life. This means that knowledge about how to handle reports of cybercrime, and then how to tackle it, must be present across the breadth of the police organisation. This is not the case at present. The dark number is high. Reporting of cybercrime may increase significantly if, for instance, the public decide that cybercrime is a matter for the police.

Given the interrelatedness of cybercrime with daily life that is reflected in the figures, the question arises of whether the offences discussed here should be labelled as 'cybercrime', a term suggesting it is a separate kind of offence. The fact that hacking is almost as widespread as bicycle theft means that this 'cybercrime in the narrow sense' has shifted from being a specialist offence to an offence under general criminal law. Much of what we have so far labelled cybercrime has outgrown the status of specialist crime and can therefore be treated as nothing less than 'crime in the digital society'.

Conclusions: factors that play a role in victimisation

Across all the offences, it is apparent that age and levels of internet activity are the most important predictors of victimisation. For prevention policy, the findings taken as a whole indicate that attention should focus on young people and the activities they undertake on the internet, because activities on the internet not only bring them closer to their objectives, but also to risks. The findings call for attention to be paid to the question of how active internet use can go hand in hand with limited levels of exposure. In this, the focus could be on user awareness as well as on the option of using rules and aids to design user environments so that their activities lead as little as possible to unintended (automatic) follow-up actions and/or unintended visibility.

It is noteworthy that limited self-control is not a predictor of victimisation, except in the case of hacking. This is not in line with earlier victim research findings. Further research is required in this respect.

Conclusions: internationalisation of high volume crime

For fraud involving paying for but not receiving a product or service (2.4% of all internet users were victims of this), one fifth of the cases (19.2%) involved contact with a seller in a foreign country, according to the victims. Therefore, a significant portion of the e-fraud cases that the police have to handle has an international character. For the police, this introduces a new aspect to their workload because, in the pre-internet era, police teams were hardly ever confronted with reports involving suspects from outside the country. If such cases did arise, they were exceptional, and were soon passed on to regional detective teams. Through the internet, the police now regularly get reports about relatively minor cases involving suspects from abroad. This is a new phenomenon that could be labelled 'international high volume crime'. The police organisation is not designed to handle such crime and international police collaboration is not geared to it.

1 Introduction

This publication discusses what is happening in Dutch society in the field of victimisation from offences with a digital component. These include punishable acts like hacking and the spreading of malware, but also e-fraud and stalking on the internet. These kinds of offence are referred to as 'cybercrime'. Because this term is contested in police and judicial circles, we will first discuss the debate as it currently stands.

1.1 Context: cybercrime as a term under discussion

The arrival of the internet has brought with it new options for committing crime, and these are frequently used. To start with, there are the 'classic' types of crime that are now also committed on the internet. Examples of these are fraud on websites, the spreading of child pornography using cyber networks, and stalking on the internet. These are examples of old wine in new bottles, as it were – old crimes that are committed using new (digital) means. This is crime in which ICT plays a significant role as a means to commit the offence, but in which the punishable act in itself is not directed against ICT. These are also kinds of crime that can be carried out without the help of ICT (fraud, child pornography, stalking and so on). Until recently, the opinion prevailing in police and judicial circles was that while such crime needed to be differentiated from hard-core cybercrime, such as hacking and the spreading of viruses, this 'familiar crime in a new guise' does belong to the cybercrime family. This 'familiar crime in a new guise' is generally called 'cybercrime in the broad sense' (KLPD, 2010; Leukfeldt, Domenie & Stol, 2010). What we have conveniently called hard-core cybercrime is 'cybercrime in the narrow sense' – its essential characteristic being that it cannot be committed outside the digital world because this crime is not only committed *using* ICT but also *against* ICT (i.e. it has ICT as its target).

When referring to cybercrime in the broad sense, Van der Hulst and Neve (2008) use the term 'cybercrime', and use 'computer crime' for cybercrime in the narrow sense. The Dutch Central Unit (KLPD, 2010) also refers to category A cybercrime (narrow sense) and category B (broad sense). A range of concepts can be found in the literature, and Van der Hulst and Neve (2008, p. 19) note in their literature study: 'There is no common definition and consistent terminology for this field of crime. An entire arsenal of terminology is used, sometimes in combination with cyber, computer, e-, internet, digital or information. … Terms are adopted whether they are relevant or not, they are applied randomly, some overlap and some reflect important gaps in meaning.' There is, however, one constant factor in the discourse: a separate category comprising crime that is not only committed using ICT, but is also used against ICT – referred to above as cybercrime in the narrow sense.

For more than ten years, the indications in the discussion about cybercrime have been that 'cybercrime in the broad sense' is best not included in the cybercrime family (e.g. Stol, Treeck & Van der Ven, 1999). According to this view, crime should not be characterised by the means with which the offence is committed. This would mean that for each new technology, criminal law and criminal procedure terminology would need to be redefined. Whenever the police and judicial authorities are of the opinion that they are being confronted with a new class of offences, the discussion quickly arises as to whether they need to create new procedures and organisational structures to address them, and whether new experts need to be trained for this. This discussion can be avoided if 'cybercrime in the broad sense' is not considered to be a new class of crime, but rather as crime that has always been around but is being committed in new ways. This means that it is not necessary to change much in the criminal justice system. The criminal justice system was traditionally set up to address changes in the way criminals operate. Since the 1950s, for example, the police have been working with a 'modus operandi system' (MO system, later known as the Identification System) in which they keep track of the way crimes are committed (Buissant des Amorie, 1960; Stol, 1996). Should new methods arise among criminals, whether or not they are based on new technology, the police gather information about them and develop strategies to combat them. What they do not do is develop new departments and procedures. Traditionally, the police combat new MOs within existing structures.

If the police and judicial authorities construe 'cybercrime in the broad sense' as a new type of crime, and go on to set up new departments, specialists and procedures to tackle it, then a division will arise in the criminal justice system: one pillar that addresses crime in which ICT does not play a significant role, and another pillar that targets crime in which this is the case. It is not difficult to see that all kinds of problems will arise, including those to do with coordinating operations. Moreover, the first pillar will not be able to ignore ICT because the police and judicial authorities will still need to investigate what the victim and the perpetrator undertook in the digital world, even when they are dealing with classic offences that take place in the real world, such as murder and assault. A more obvious approach would be for the existing organisation and people to learn to deal with the new MO: the MO of a digitally skilled criminal in a digital society. Dealing with this MO requires a digitally skilled criminal justice system.[3]

It is clear to the police and judicial authorities that cybercrime in the narrow sense is a new kind of crime (crime using and directed at ICT). Examples of this would be hacking, destroying computer data, spreading viruses and so

3 We will not discuss here whether every police officer and public prosecutor needs to be computer literate. Everyone will need to have certain basic skills. For the current state of affairs within the police force, see Stol, Leukfeldt and Klap (2012).

on. In this respect, it is pertinent that specific sections of the law have been introduced (for the three crimes mentioned, respectively Sect. 138ab, 350a/350b and 350a/139d Sr). Part of 'cybercrime in the narrow sense' is the work of high-tech criminals, which requires a response from high-tech police officers and public prosecutors; a considerable portion, however, is carried out by 'normal members of the public' (Leukfeldt et al., 2010) and by all accounts quite often by young people harassing one another (Kerstens & Stol, 2012).

If we link developments in crime to the criminal justice system, we see that the police and judicial authorities have taken special measures against 'cybercrime in the narrow sense'. The police force has a Team High Tech Crime (THTC) for advanced cybercrime in the narrow sense that has an international and innovative character. So far, the THTC has dealt with a few cases per year.[4] All other cybercrime in the narrow sense is handled by the normal investigation teams (there are no special cybercrime detectives in the police forces) and these teams can get the support of digital specialists (compare Stol et al., 2012; Leukfeldt, Veenstra, Domenie & Stol, 2012a). The Public Prosecution Service has appointed special cybercrime public prosecutors for cybercrime in the narrow sense.

The situation is different for cybercrime in the broad sense. As far as the Public Prosecution Service is concerned, all cybercrime in the broad sense is classified as old crime with a modern MO and is therefore dealt with by the public prosecutor who would handle the old crime as part of his portfolio. For instance, internet fraud is dealt with by the fraud officer, who must become familiar with the new MO. Within the police force, the normal teams also deal with cybercrime in the broad sense.[5]

The discussion about how the organisation can best be structured to tackle the developments is undoubtedly still ongoing. We mentioned earlier that some cybercrime in the narrow sense is committed by normal people, quite often young people, who are bent on harassing one another (Leukfeldt et al., 2010; Kerstens & Stol, 2012). What happens regularly is that young people hack one another's computers or email accounts and then do things that place the other in a bad or strange light (uploading embarrassing images, defacing the other's profile, send offensive emails from the other person's account and so on).

This raises the question of whether we should still be talking about cybercrime in the narrow sense: crime with ICT and *directed against* ICT. In such cases, the perpetrator is not really directing the attack against ICT, but is instead using the ICT in an everyday and non-technical way to harass another person. Making another person's life difficult or making oneself popular is the objective; hacking (cribbing a password and logging in) is no more than a means. Predictably, therefore, the police and judicial authorities will not view some 'cybercrime in the narrow sense' (hacking, defacing) as hard-core cybercrime – and will there-

4 The THTC is being expanded and the number of cases it handles increased (Stol et al., 2012).

5 For insights into how cybercrime cases are dealt with by the criminal justice system, see Leukfeldt, Kentgens, Frans, Toutenhoofd, Stol and Stamhuis (2012b).

fore probably not feel that it needs to be dealt with by cybercrime specialists. In other words: perhaps not all cybercrime that falls within the definition of 'cybercrime in the narrow sense' (such as hacking) can actually be earmarked as real cybercrime.

In this research, we do not make any statements about how the criminal justice system should ideally be organised. This research is primarily about what is taking place in society in the field of victimisation relating to specific offences with a digital component. This encompasses both cybercrime in the narrow sense, such as hacking, and cybercrime in the broad sense, such as e-fraud. The offences that we specifically researched are discussed in Section 1.3. First we will consider the priority that the topic cybercrime has.

1.2 Context: cybercrime as a relatively unknown phenomenon that needs to be given priority

The Dutch government is giving priority to the investigation and combating of cybercrime and is adopting various legal and organisational measures to this end. According to the 'Freedom and Responsibility' coalition agreement drawn up by the Rutte I cabinet (2010 to 2012), an *integrated approach to cybercrime* is being developed (Regeerakkoord, 2010, p. 42). According to the Rutte II cabinet's coalition agreement, investment is being targeted at the tracking of cyber criminals. The objective is to enable the criminal justice system to combat cybercrime effectively. The Dutch police force is also giving high priority to cybercrime. In the wake of the 2007 coalition agreement, in which cybercrime was designated as a serious crime, the Board of Chief Commissioners instituted the Programme Against Cybercrime and the Team High Tech Crime was established within the Dutch Central Unit. At the same time, the Public Prosecution Service initiated the Intensification Programme on Cybercrime, and, for the judicial system, the Cybercrime Centre of Expertise was established.[6]

Investigative policy demands that the police and judicial authorities set priorities because they simply do not have the capacity to deal with every offence that is reported to the police. The most serious problems deserve to be addressed first. The gravity of the problem is determined by both its nature and its extent. For investigative policy, the police and the judicial authorities must have information at their disposal about the nature and extent of cybercrime. This implies that they must have a method in place for acquiring this knowledge. Less is known about the extent of cybercrime than about its nature (see among others Van der Hulst & Neve, 2008; Leukfeldt et al., 2010). On occasion, experts and those directly involved make known that a certain type of crime is increasing at an alarming rate, but systematic and thorough research into the extent of cybercrime is conspicuous by its absence. Until 2009, no attention of any kind was

6 www.rechtspraak.nl/Organisatie/Gerechtshoven/DenHaag/OverHetGerechtshof/Organisatie/Pages/Kenniscentrum-Cybercrime.aspx. Last consulted on 23 February 2012.

given to victimisation relating to cybercrime in the Safety Monitor of Statistics Netherlands (CBS). Since then, some questions about cybercrime have been included in the Safety Monitor in a few regions, and Statistics Netherlands has experimented at national level with questions about cybercrime victimisation. At present, however, there is no national instrument for monitoring the extent of cybercrime in the Netherlands.[7]

Although less is known about the extent of cybercrime than about its nature, some information is available. Research commissioned by the PAC into the registered workload relating to cybercrime showed that cybercrime in 2007 constituted less than 1 per cent of the overall registered workload in two police regions (Domenie, Leukfeldt & Stol, 2009). However victim research conducted in 2009 into cybercrime in Haaglanden showed that victimisation was significantly higher than 1 per cent, while the reporting percentage was extremely low (Hesseling, 2010). A national sample taken from the LISS panel shows that a further 2.2 per cent of the Dutch population had experienced an online threat during the previous year (Van Wilsem, 2010b).[8] For comparison purposes, here are figures relating to some classic offline offences: 3.5 per cent fell victim to threats, 1.7 per cent to pickpocketing and 1.5 per cent to burglary (CBS, 2012). Only bicycle theft occurs more frequently (4.8%). This research shows that victimisation relating to offences with a digital component is significant, and that knowledge on the subject is fragmentary.

Alongside insight into the nature and extent of victimisation, it is also important for policy development to know who has an increased risk of becoming a victim. Were victimisation to be limited, for instance, to a very specific section of internet users, taking general preventative measures would not be effective. In terms of preventing crime, it is also useful to know whether certain internet behaviour leads to an increased risk of victimisation or whether certain behaviour acts rather as a shield.

1.3 Research subject

This publication reports on research into victimisation from offences with a digital component conducted among members of the public in the Netherlands. Crime is defined in various ways. Bonger (1932, cited in Lissenberg, 2001) defines crime as 'serious antisocial acts to which the state responds with penalty (punishment or measures). That is: crime is the committing of offences, as Ferwerda (2008) describes it. This present research defines crime in line with Ferwerda's approach as behaviour that legislators deem to be punishable.

7 In the spring edition of the 2013 Safety Monitor, questions about cybercrime have been added. The questions are based on this study.

8 LISS stands for Longitudinal Internet Studies for Social Sciences (www.lisspanel.nl. Last consulted on 22 May 2012).

We are not basing this study on a theoretical definition of the concept 'cybercrime' which we subsequently operationalise. The study is based on offences to which people fall victim in which ICT plays a significant role at the time, and which confront the police and judicial authorities with a lack of knowledge about victimisation.[9] It involves:

- cybercrime in the narrow sense:
  - hacking and malware;
- cybercrime in the broad sense:
  - in the financial sense via auction or retail sites, identity theft, identity fraud, advance fee fraud;
  - offences in the private sphere: stalking, threats.

These are the actual offences that were investigated in this research. From now on, we will no longer be using the terms cybercrime in broad or narrow sense. However, for convenience we will still use the term cybercrime to refer in general to the offences that we researched.

In this research we measured cybercrime victimisation by first assessing what the person being interviewed said on the matter. During these interviews, several verification questions were posed to get an indication of how certain it was that the person was in fact a victim.

Hidden victimisation falls outside the scope of this research. For instance we cannot trace how often computers are included in botnets without the users being aware of this. This problem also occurs in offline crime, for example in pickpocketing and intrusions that are not noticed. But the problem is more pervasive in cybercrime because users are not always aware of what is going on in their computers. It is also not possible for us to measure victimless cybercrime with this research. Victim surveys are unsuitable for that purpose.

1.4 Research questions

This publication has two main themes. First we wanted to establish the extent of cybercrime victimisation. For this purpose it is important to know which factors increase and which decrease the risk of victimisation. The following research questions are pertinent here:

1. What is the extent of cybercrime victimisation among internet users?
2. Which factors increase or decrease the risk of cybercrime victimisation?

We also investigated what the role of the police is, according to internet users, when it comes to security on the internet, whether victims report cases to the police and whether they are satisfied with the police response to reporting. The research questions relating to this were:

9 Chapter 2 contains a more detailed explanation of the selection.

3. What is the role of the police in safeguarding security on the internet, according to internet users?
4. Who among cybercrime victims are likely to contact the police when they fall victim to cybercrime?
5. To what extent are victims satisfied with the police response to reporting cybercrime?

1.5 Potential for use in practice

This publication reflects the state of affairs in 2011 and is not intended for use in making predictions. The authorities and the police may use the research findings when determining new policies. Policy areas for which the research results may be useful include prioritising prevention and investigation, conducting criminality analyses, developing a national threat assessment, and answering parliamentary questions regarding the nature, extent and strategies for tackling cybercrime. The results can also be used to design further research, particularly in-depth research into the field of cybercrime. The research also produced a validated questionnaire that can be used in repeated measurements. Part of the questionnaire has already been included by CBS in their Safety Monitor. In due course, this will give insight into developments in the nature and extent of victimisation. That will help in the evaluation of policy measures. Given the limited space available in the Safety Monitor, no questions relating to risk models were included. In order to gain insights into the developments in this field, research will have to be repeated in course of time.

2 METHOD

Cybercrime and victimisation

In this publication, cybercrime is used as an overarching concept for all kinds of crime in which ICT plays a significant role when it is committed (PAC, 2008; Van der Hulst & Neve, 2008; KLPD, 2007; Leukfeldt et al., 2010).

This research is based on self-reporting. Victimisation is a problematic concept in cybercrime because people do not always realise that they are victims. In this research, we measured cybercrime victimisation by first assessing what the person being interviewed had to say on the matter. This means that we did not get any insight into cybercrime to which people were unaware that they had fallen victim, for instance, where their computer had been hacked and had been included in a botnet.

Research methods

The research comprised a development phase and an implementation phase. The development phase started with a study of the literature. Books, articles and reports were found using online media libraries. This provided insight into what is known about cybercrime victimisation in the Netherlands and abroad. Based on the literature study, a topic list was compiled for interviews with key figures in the police and justice departments, both at policy and operational levels. The interviews focused on gleaning insights into the priorities set by the police, judiciary and government regarding cybercrime in the Netherlands as it stands now and in the immediate future. We also asked what the police, judiciary and government precisely need to know about cybercrimes. Three group interviews were then held with small groups of internet users. The primary objective of these group interviews was to clarify how members of the public can best be questioned about cybercrime victimisation. Cybercrime is after all a relatively new phenomenon that is unfamiliar to many people and not as easily defined as bicycle theft, for example. A pilot questionnaire was compiled on the basis of the literature study, interviews with experiential experts and group interviews. This questionnaire was distributed among a sample of 1,000 Dutch members of the public. The pilot study was conducted as far as possible in line with the Safety Monitor. Phrasing of the questions was aligned with questions about offline crime, and the interviewing method was largely the same as the Safety Monitor. The objective of the pilot study was primarily to uncover errors in the questionnaire so that the surveying of cybercrime could be optimised, i.e. does the questionnaire provide answers to the research questions?

During the implementation phase (2011), the amended questionnaire was distributed among 21,800 people aged 15 years and older on the basis of a representative sample drawn by Statistics Netherlands (CBS) from the municipal personal records database [*Gemeentelijke Basisadministratie* (GBA)]. The response rate was 10,314 (47%). The CBS used background characteristics to assign weighting factors to each individual respondent on the basis of their representativeness in the sample. The analyses for the study were carried out on the responses from 9,163 respondents who indicated that they used the internet (89% of the respondents). Where we refer to respondents in this study, we are therefore referring to this group of 9,163 internet users.

In order to develop a monitoring methodology for victimisation, we worked closely with the CBS during this research. A detailed explanation of the methodology used in this research, in which validity, usability and areas for improvement are discussed, is given in Appendix 1.

Weighted and unweighted data

Where statements about all internet users are made in this publication, the results are weighted (see Appendix 6 for an explanation). This applies to victimisation prevalence among internet users and to the bivariate analyses that measure whether victims differ from non-victims in their personal background characteristics. Follow-up analyses are unweighted because these were calculated on the basis of a (often small) subpopulation that differed in terms of background characteristics from the overall population.

Excluded offences

Not all the offences that we investigated are included in this publication. It emerged that the questions about fraud linked to the sale of fake goods were too vague. The analysis of the open answers showed that the respondents who had not in fact been swindled indicated that they had been victims of this kind of fraud, for instance because an order had not entirely met with their expectations. For that reason the offence was not taken into consideration. It also emerged that questions about blackmail/extortion were not well formulated. From the open answers it was clear that some people considered spam to be blackmail. Because victimisation related to this kind of offence also did not happen often, it was decided not to include this offence. Finally, it emerged that questions about libel/defamation were also too vague. For this reason, these offences were also excluded.

3 Hacking and malware

This section deals with offences in which ICT is not only the means used to commit an offence, but also the target. In Section 3.1, we discuss hacking at greater length. In Section 3.2, we discuss malware.

3.1 Hacking

The term 'hacking' used in combination with technology dates back to the 1960s. It was a description with positive connotations and used to refer to someone who was skilled in the development of elegant, creative and effective solutions for technical problems (Yar, 2006). In those days, hacking was the innovative use of technology aimed at the right to gather information and knowledge freely. These hackers 'investigated' other people's computer systems out of a sense of curiosity. Information that they found was shared with others. Corrupting other systems during their search operations was considered to be unethical and a sign of incompetence (Stol et al., 1999; Yar, 2006).

It is often claimed in the literature and reports published by commercial antivirus companies that, since those somewhat romantic times, the motives of hackers have shifted from hacking for fame to hacking for fortune (see among others Van der Hulst & Neve, 2008; KLPD, 2007; McAfee, 2006). Cyber criminals are apparently much more interested in financial gain. This may seem likely but there is no sound empirical underpinning for this assumption. Leukfeldt et al. (2010) analysed 665 police files and concluded that, while there is a group of hackers who commit offences for money, there is another dominant phenomenon: hacking is no longer the preserve of advanced software engineers. Hackers may have a range of motives, and financial gain is part of this, but personal relationships are often at their root. In many cases ex-lovers are involved, for instance, or young people trying to harass each other and using technological means to do so. This is a development that is in keeping with the image of a digital society sketched in the introduction and the digitisation of everyday crime.

In this research, we define 'hacking' in line with Section 138ab of the Dutch Criminal Code as gaining access intentionally and unlawfully to a computerised work or part thereof. According to the law, a computerised work is a system that is intended to store, process and transfer information using electronic means, for instance, a computer, a database or a server on which websites are hosted (Sect. 80e Sr). If someone gains access to the account of another without permission, this is known as hacking, even if that person guesses the password, and even if that person could have gained access anyway (for a detailed analysis, see Leukfeldt et al., 2012b).

Hacking is a problematic offence to research because it is often not the objective per se, but rather a means to commit another kind of crime. Leukfeldt et al. (2010) found in their study based on 655 police files that hacking is linked to numerous other kinds of crime and is often used as a means to commit other offences. For this reason, victimisation relating to hacking was measured in various ways in our study. First, respondents were asked whether they had been hacked by responding with 'yes' or 'no' to the following three statements.

1. Someone changed your web page and/or profile (Hyves, Facebook and so on) without your permission (defacing).
2. Someone hacked your computer and destroyed, changed or stole data.
3. Someone hacked your email or logged on to your email account without permission.

Second, for identity theft and stalking, respondents were asked whether hacking was part of the perpetrator's modus operandi.

Prevalence

In total, 4.3 per cent of the respondents had been victims of at least one of the abovementioned kinds of hacking in the twelve months prior to the research. With a 95 per cent confidence interval and during the previous twelve-month period, between 3.9 and 4.7 per cent of Dutch internet users fell victim to hacking: 1.5 per cent were victims of defacing (changing a website or profile page without permission); 0.7 per cent had their computers hacked; 2.9 per cent had their email accounts hacked; and perpetrators hacked 0.3 per cent of the respondents' computers or changed websites or profiles as part of their modi operandi for stalking and/or identity theft.

Risk groups

To find out which internet users were most at risk of being hacked, we carried out bivariate analysis (see Table 3.1).

Table 3.1 shows that internet users without a partner are more likely to fall victim to hacking than internet users with partners (column 'Total Hacking'). There is also a link between victimisation and education and age. This table shows that internet users in the 15 to 24 age category are particularly prone to falling victim to hacking, as are those whose highest level of completed education is primary school. These findings may be related to each other. After all, respondents in the 15 to 24 age group are probably more likely to be without a partner and are probably more likely to have not yet completed more than primary school.

Table 3.1 Hacking victimisation according to background characteristics (weighted, bivariate)

	Defacing	Hacking PC	Hacking email	Hacking as MO	Total Hacking
Level of education[10]					
No education	1.2	1.8	1.3	0.0	2.9
Primary education	3.3	1.1	5.0	0.2	7.8
Lower vocational schooling	0.1	0.4	1.9	0.2	2.1
VMBO/MAVO	2.0	1.0	2.1	0.6	4.0
HAVO/VWO	2.4	1.1	4.4	0.5	6.7
MBO	1.3	0.4	2.8	0.1	3.9
HBO	1.5	0.6	2.6	0.3	3.7
WO	0.9	0.5	3.3	0.1	4.5
$\chi^2(7)$	*33.53***	*13.24*	*23.99***	*9.41*	*42.50***
Age category					
15-24	4.7	1.3	5.9	0.7	10.1
25-34	1.7	0.7	4.9	0.3	5.9
35-44	0.7	0.6	1.8	0.2	2.8
45-54	1.0	0.6	1.6	0.3	2.5
55-64	0.6	0.6	1.9	0.4	2.6
65+	0.2	0.3	1.2	0.0	1.4
$\chi^2(5)$	*140.11***	*11.98**	*105.91***	*11.05*	*195.60***
Employment status					
<12 hours paid work	1.9	0.6	2.5	0.4	4.1
12+ hours paid work per week	1.3	0.7	3.1	0.3	4.3
$\chi^2(1)$	*5.36**	*0.52*	*2.27*	*0.53*	*0.26*
Partner					
No partner	2.3	0.7	3.9	0.4	5.9
Partner	0.7	0.6	1.8	0.2	2.5
$\chi^2(1)$	*39.93***	*0.21*	*36.32***	*3.15*	*68.74***
Ethnic origin					
Native Dutch	1.3	0.6	2.8	0.3	4.0
1st generation	2.4	1.3	2.6	0.0	4.7
2nd generation, 1 parent	1.6	0.8	4.1	0.6	6.0
2nd generation, both parents	3.2	1.2	4.1	0.0	5.9
$\chi^2(3)$	*12.48***	*8.83**	*4.55*	*5.47*	*7.07*
Gender					
Male	1.5	0.8	2.8	0.2	4.2
Female	1.5	0.6	2.9	0.4	4.3
$\chi^2(1)$	*0.98*	*0.99*	*0.08*	*3.33*	*0.11*
Total	**1.5**	**0.7**	**2.9**	**0.3**	**4.3**

* p<0.05, ** p<0.01.

10 VMBO: pre-vocational secondary education; MAVO: junior general secondary education; HAVO: senior general secondary education; VWO: pre-university education; MBO: senior secondary vocational education; HBO: university of applied sciences degree programme; WO: university education.

In order to ascertain whether the bivariate links hold, we carried out a multivariate analysis (see Table 3.2). First we introduced respondent background characteristics into the model. In addition, we formulated assumptions about variables that would influence victimisation on the basis of the literature. These variables were also included in the model. We discuss the underlying assumptions below.

On the basis of the routine activities theory (Cohen & Felson, 1979; Felson & Clarke, 1998) a link can be expected between victimisation and the kinds of activities that a person undertakes. For this reason we introduced the variables activity and exposure. Activity comprises emailing and targeted searching for information on the internet. Exposure comprises untargeted surfing, downloading, using MSN, skyping, chatting, visiting forums and social media sites and using Twitter.[11] In addition to this, the expectation is that downloading is a risky activity in connection with hacking. The more one downloads, the greater the chance of getting infected with malware.

According to the rational choice theory (Coleman, 1973, 1990), criminals constantly weigh up the costs versus the benefits when committing crimes. The aim is to have as few costs as possible (chances of getting caught, degree of difficulty and so on) with as many benefits as possible (victim's money). Frequently used software is an attractive target for criminals; a large number of victims can be reached with one hit (one flaw in the software ensures that all its users can be attacked and infected electronically with malware, for instance). Weak security is also attractive: it makes it easy to infect a computer and it means the costs will be low. For this reason, we looked at the users' operating systems and web browsers in our risk model, as well as at the use of virus scanners.

Risk awareness possibly also plays a role in victimisation. Internet users who are aware of the risks they are exposed to online are in a better position to respond to them, and this means they reduce their risk of becoming a victim. Incidentally, we do not know what the cause and effect are. It could be that internet users become more aware of risks once they have been victims. Another possibility is that people who think that they have covered themselves for all the risks are more likely to fall victim because they behave more recklessly (I can download that, my security is fine, after all). We do, however, assume that people who are digitally skilled, and are aware of the risks, fall victim less frequently. To assess whether risk awareness influences victimisation, we compiled a risk awareness variable.[12]

11 For a detailed explanation of the methodology used, see Appendix 1.

12 For the composition of this and other variables, see the account of the methodology used in Appendix 1.

Table 3.2 Logistic regression of hacking on respondent characteristics

	Model 1		Model 2		Model 3	
	B	S.E.	B	S.E.	B	S.E.
Intercept	-1.347**	0.347	-5.313**	1.350	-1.694	1.710
Gender (male=ref)	-0.096	0.114	-0.056	0.121	-0.050**	0.121
Age	-0.040**	0.004	-0.022**	0.005	-0.105	0.022
Ethnicity (native population=ref)						
1st generation	0.274	0.199	0.179	0.209	0.111	0.211
2nd gen., parent foreign	0.424	0.219	0.380	0.223	0.386	0.222
2nd gen., both parents foreign	0.056	0.354	0.048	0.360	-0.020	0.361
Partner	-0.452**	0.144	-0.461**	0.153	-0.474**	0.153
Level of education	0.022	0.034	0.003	0.038	0.049	0.178
Work (12 hours per week or more)	-0.016	0.129	0.053	0.134	-0.018	0.138
Degree of internet usage			0.482*	0.241	0.341	0.243
# of PCs in household			0.056	0.058	0.049	0.058
Mobile most used app. for internet			0.343	0.254	0.381	0.256
Operating system (Windows=ref)						
Mac OS			-0.252	0.335	-0.271	0.334
Linux			-0.660	1.043	-0.670	1.044
Mobile system (e.g. Android)			0.100	0.362	0.048	0.365
Other			-1.034	1.037	-1.065	1.034
Don't know			-0.283	0.522	-0.329	0.522
No virus scanner			0.415*	0.211	0.434*	0.212
Browser						
Internet Explorer			-0.272	0.150	-0.279	0.150
Google Chrome			0.111	0.140	0.131	0.139
Firefox			-0.089	0.157	-0.072	0.157
Opera			-0.327	0.537	-0.272	0.534
Safari			-0.226	0.279	-0.230	0.277
Activity			0.154	0.097	-0.258	0.287
Exposure			0.606**	0.143	-0.058	0.371
Buying via the internet			-0.144	0.149	-0.169	0.149
Download			-0.144	0.068*	-0.130	0.067
Computer skill			-0.005	0.143	-0.028	0.143
Risk awareness			-0.259*	0.110	-0.281*	0.111
Paid email subscription			-0.160	0.172	-0.189	0.173
Paid subscription for webhosting			0.030	0.223	-0.007	0.233
Paid gaming or gambling sites.			-0.149	0.304	-0.146	0.303
Paid download sites			0.293	0.180	0.296	0.180
Paid contact or dating sites			0.146	0.385	0.071	0.386
Computer sharing			0.229	0.156	0.220	0.156
Activity x education					-0.025	0.049
Activity x age					0.016*	0.006
Exposure x education					0.016	0.057
Exposure x age					0.017*	0.008
Nagelkerke R^2	7.9		11.0%		11.7%	
N	9.123		8.957		8.957	

* p<0.05, ** p<0.01 (two-sided).

Alongside risk awareness, knowledge of the devices with which one is online (and is therefore communicating and making payments) can also influence victimisation. We assume that people who do not know anything about the devices also know less about the risks that they are running. Here we are referring to knowledge about operating systems, internet connections and browsers, and virus scanners. For this purpose we compiled a computer knowledge variable.

Other high-risk behaviour is allowing other people to use one's computer. The owner then has less control over devices and is not always aware what the other person is doing on the computer. We therefore also assessed the effect of sharing a computer with others.

Self-control is also used to explain victimisation. According to Gottfredson and Hirschi (1990, p. 90) people with low self-control are more likely to be 'impulsive, insensitive, physical (as opposed to mental), risk-taking, short-sighted, and nonverbal'. Research shows that low self-control is linked to offending (see Pratt & Cullen, 2000). Indications have also been found of a relationship between victimisation and low self-control (see Jansen, 2012; Schreck, Stewart & Fisher, 2006; Van Wilsem, 2010b). Because the statements about self-control were not presented to all respondents, (see Appendix 1), we assessed separately whether it had any effect.

The threat model comprises three models (see Table 3.2). In the first model, we only looked at the influence of background characteristics on victimisation. The second model maps the influence of respondent attitude and behaviour on victimisation. These models are useful for interpreting the overall Model 3. In this model, all the variables are included, together with four interaction variables. Using Models 1 and 2, it is possible to determine more accurately why certain variables act as predictors and others do not, and, for instance, why some can be explained away (see also Appendix 1).

In Model 1 of the threat model, we see that the younger the users, the higher the risks of hacking; risks are also higher for those who live alone. We did not find differences between men and women, between ethnic groups or those with high or low levels of education, or between people with or without paid work.

In Model 2, internet activities were introduced as predictors of hacking. Here we see that age still has a negative and significant effect – young people are more likely to be victims of hacking – but, in terms of extent, the age effect is almost halved in comparison to Model 1 (B coefficient from -0.040 to -0.022). This means that a considerable part of the reason why younger people are likely to be hacked more often is because they undertake more internet activities that increase the risk of being hacked. According to this model, the specific activities that increase the risk of being hacked are: the frequency with which one surfs the internet, a high level of exposure,[13] and not using virus scanners. For the

13 Reminder: activity comprises emailing and targeted searching for information on the internet. Exposure comprises untargeted surfing, downloading, using MSN, skyping, chatting, visiting forums and social media sites and using Twitter. For a detailed explanation of the methodology used, see Appendix 1.

rest, we noted a lower risk of being hacked among people who are conscious of the risks that accompany internet usage. An unexpected finding of this model is that the risk of being hacked declines as the frequency of downloading rises. In addition to this, it emerged in this model that the operating system (e.g. Windows) is not related to risk of being hacked, nor are browsers.

In Model 3 incorporates interaction effects. This enabled us to investigate whether two kinds of internet use (activity and exposure) have differing effects for people from different age groups and people with different levels of education. The results show that this is to some extent the case. It emerged that the older the respondent is, the more both activity and exposure heighten the risk of falling victim to hacking. Younger people, on the other hand, do not run a greater risk of being hacked the more exposed they are and the more they take part in activities on the internet.

Finally, additional analyses carried out on a sub-sample (not shown) show that low self-control is linked to a higher risk of being hacked.[14]

Conclusions

Of all internet users, 4.3 per cent fell victim to hacking. Hacking of email accounts occurred most frequently (2.9%).

The bivariate analyses (see Table 3.1) show that the younger internet users are, the more likely they are to fall victim hacking. The percentage for victimisation is particularly high among those in the age group 15 to 24 years (10.1%). Furthermore, we noted that the risk of victimisation is greater for those who live alone, and for those internet users whose highest level of completed education was primary school. These finding are presumable linked: internet users in the age category 15 to 24 years are more likely than average to live alone and are more likely than average to have primary school as their highest level of completed education. In the bivariate analysis, we found no differences between men and women, between ethnic groups or between people with a lot of paid work and those with less paid work.

When we include internet activities as predictors of hacking (see Table 3.2), the age effect remains negative and significant. This means that a considerable part of the reason why younger people are likely to be hacked more often is because they undertake more internet activities that involve a greater risk of being hacked. According to this model, the specific activity factors that increase the risk of being hacked are: the frequency of surfing the internet, a high level of exposure, and not using virus scanners. For the rest, we noted a lower risk of being hacked among people who are aware of the risks that accompany internet usage. An unexpected finding of this model is that the risk of being hacked declines as the frequency of downloading rises. This model also revealed that operating systems (e.g. Windows) are unrelated to the risk of being hacked, as are browsers.

---

14 For an explanation concerning this sub-sample, see the explanation of the methodology in Appendix 1.

Finally, once interaction effects are introduced, it emerges that the older the respondent is, the more both activity and exposure increase the risk of falling victim to hacking. Younger people, on the other hand, do not run a greater risk of being hacked the more exposed they are and the more they take part in activities on the internet.

3.2 Malware

Malware is a generic name for malicious software. Examples include viruses, worms, Trojan horses and spyware:

- Virus: software that can spread itself and can, for instance, destroy a computer system or send files to someone who has malicious intentions.
- Worm: software that can spread itself via the internet and can damage computers and network connections.
- Trojan horse: software that allows the infringer to gain access to the computer without the knowledge of the user.
- Spyware: software that sends the user's information to another without the user's permission. The kind of information could be keystrokes, screenshots, email addresses, surfing behaviour or personal information, such as credit card numbers.

Under Section 350a paragraph 3 Sr, it is a punishable offence to intentionally and unlawfully make available or to spread data, such as computer viruses, that are intended to damage computerised works. The objectives of the malware determine what other penalty provisions apply. If the malware is intended to copy data, or to tap or store data (e.g. to record passwords using a keylogger), this constitutes theft. In this case, Sections 139d Sr and 139e apply. Malware also destroys digital data. This is a punishable offence according to Sections 350a and 350b Sr. If malware causes disruptions, Sections 138b, 161e and/or 161f Sr apply. Leukfeldt et al. (2012b) give a detailed description of the penalisation of these crimes.

Malware infection is a type of victimisation that is difficult to measure. It is not always clear to users whether there is malware on their computers. Spyware is a kind of malware that users do not necessarily know they have until, for instance, their virus scanner indicates that they are infected with malware, or when money disappears out of their bank account (after their login information has been stolen). Also victims do not always know why their computers are no longer functioning properly. It could be due to malware, but it could also be something the user is doing incorrectly.

For this reason, we asked users whether they *had noticed* that they had had malware on their computer during the previous twelve months. This is thus not an indication of the actual prevalence of malware; it cannot be measured accurately in victim research (for this the victim would have to be certain that they have had malware on their computer). It is an indication of the number of people who were aware that their computers were infected.

Prevalence

Of all the respondents who indicated that they use the internet, 16.7 per cent had noticed malware during the previous twelve-month period (with a 95% confidence interval, that is between 15.9% and 17.5% of all internet users). The percentage of internet users whose computers had been infected by malware is probably higher because not all users will have noticed malware.

Modus operandi

Respondents who had noticed malware were asked how this malware got on to their computer. Multiple answers were possible for this question. Table 3.3 shows that almost four out of ten respondents who had spotted malware were unaware of how it got on to their computer (38.4%). According to just over a quarter, the malware got on to their system via email; a similar number blamed a link on a website; and more than a fifth said they were infected via a download.

The respondents who chose 'other' as an answer were then given the option of specifying how the malware got on to their computer. The response mentioned most frequently (33 times) was through an application (e.g. Skype, Limewire) or a website. External data carriers, such as USB sticks, were also occasionally mentioned.

Table 3.3 Ways in which malware got on to computers, according to respondents (multiple answers possible, unweighted)

	Number *	% of victims (n=1,512)
Don't know	581	38.4
Via a link on a website	399	26.4
Via an email	385	25.5
Via a download	321	21.2
Other	64	4.2
Via an MSN message	54	3.6
Via a Twitter message	2	0.1

* Because multiple answers per victim were possible, the total in this column is greater than the number of victims.

Losses

Of the respondents who had noticed malware, 16.1 per cent stated that they had suffered financial loss (see Table 3.4). This means that 2.7 per cent of all internet users suffered financial loss through malware, for example through having to have their computer fixed as a consequence. Of those who had suffered loss through malware, 78.2 per cent knew what the extent of the damage was. More than half of the known losses amounted to 100 euros or less, and 7.9 per cent of the damages amounted to 501 euros or more. Of the respondents who noticed the malware, 11.9 per cent – which equates to 2.0 per cent of all internet users – lost files or software.

Table 3.4 Loss through malware (unweighted)

	Number	% of victims (n=1,512)	% of known loss	% of internet users (n=9,163)
No losses/losses				
No losses	1,246	82.4		
Not known	23	1.5		
Losses	243	16.1		2.7
Extent of loss (in euros)				
Not known				0.8
1-100			57.4	1.2
101-200			20.5	0.4
201-500			14.2	0.3
501-1,000			6.8	0.1
1,001 or more			1.1	0.0

Who notices malware?

To find out which internet users noticed malware, we carried out bivariate analyses (see Table 3.5). The analyses showed that men notice malware more frequently than women, and that people with a paid job of at least twelve hours per week notice malware more frequently than people who have paid work for fewer than twelve hours per week. There is also a link between education level and age. Table 3.5 shows that more highly educated respondents were more likely to notice malware than those with lower education, and that internet users between the ages of 35 and 54 were more likely to notice malware than those outside this age group. No logistic regression analysis was carried out for malware. No threat model was created for malware because this is a group who themselves had noticed malware on their computers.

Conclusions

Of the internet users surveyed, 16.7 per cent stated that they had noticed malware on their own computers during the previous twelve-month period; 2.7 per cent suffered financial loss through this and 2.0 per cent lost files and/or software through malware. Those most likely to notice malware were highly educated people, men, people aged between 35 and 54, and people with a paid job.

Table 3.5 Malware noticed according to background characteristics (weighted)

Have you noticed malware on your computer?	% yes
Level of education[15]	
No education completed	8.8
Primary education	14.6
Lower vocational education	10.7
VMBO/MAVO	14.4
HAVO/VWO	17.5
MBO	17.3
HBO	19.5
WO	19.0
$\chi^2(7)$	*54.70***
Age category	
15-24	16.7
25-34	17.4
35-44	20.0
45-54	19.6
55-64	13.5
65+	9.4
$\chi^2(5)$	*78.87***
Employment status	
<12 hours paid work per week	14.1
12+ hours paid work per week	18.1
$\chi^2(1)$	*25.40***
Partner	
No partner[3]	16.3
Partner	17.1
$\chi^2(1)$	*1.07*
Ethnic origin	
Native Dutch	16.6
1st generation	17.1
2nd generation, 1 parent	18.5
2nd generation, both parents	14.3
$\chi^2(3)$	*2.45*
Gender	
Male	19.6
Female	13.6
$\chi^2(1)$	*59.86***
Total	**16.7**

* p<0.05, ** p<0.01.

15 VMBO: pre-vocational secondary education; MAVO: junior general secondary education; HAVO: senior general secondary education; VWO: pre-university education; MBO: senior secondary vocational education; HBO: university of applied sciences degree programme; WO: university education.

16 Living alone, widowed or divorced, according to GBA municipal records.

4 Financial offences

This section covers crimes where the perpetrator's objective is financial gain. In Section 4.1 we discuss fraud via auction and retail sites. We then discuss identity fraud and advance fee fraud (Sections 4.2 and 4.3 respectively).

4.1 Fraud via auction and retail sites

In the Netherlands, many consumers use the internet to purchase goods or services. A lively trade between private individuals is conducted on websites like Marktplaats.nl, Speuders.nl and Ebay.nl. Marktplaats.nl, currently the largest online retail site in the Netherlands, has more than 6.5 million advertisements, 277,000 new advertisements per day and 6.1 million unique visitors.[17] According to the Dutch Home Shopping Monitor, online consumer spending exceeded € 8 billion in 2010 (Blauw Research, 2010).

Of all internet users who took part in the research, 73.2 per cent had made at least one purchase via the internet during the previous twelve months. Almost 80 per cent of buyers paid for their purchase using iDEAL, while almost half paid through an internet banking transfer, and over one third used a credit card. More than 6 per cent paid in cash (see Table 4.1).

Table 4.1 Payment methods for goods bought on the internet (unweighted, multiple answers possible)

	Number	% of buyers
iDEAL	5,295	79.3
Internet banking	3,323	49.8
Credit card via the internet	2,342	35.1
PayPal	995	14.9
Offline via the bank (acceptance giro/transfer)	977	14.6
Automatic authorisation	840	12.6
Cash	405	6.1
Other	68	1.0
Don't know/would not say	46	0.7

17 http://statisch.marktplaats.nl/html/about_us.html. Last consulted on 1 September 2012.

Fraud via auction and retail sites generally takes place as follows (Leukfeldt et al., 2012b; Taylor, Caeti, Loper, Fritsch & Liederbach, 2006; Van der Hulst & Neve, 2008). The buyer pays the agreed price (or part thereof) in advance, but the seller does not deliver the goods as agreed. In most cases, the buyer is therefore the victim. However the reverse may also occur: the seller delivers the goods, but the buyer fails to pay the price (or part thereof). Sometimes the buyer may transfer more than was agreed. The buyer then asks the seller to pay back the excess via a money transfer. It then turns out that the first money transfer was fraudulent and the banking institution then asks the seller to reverse the payment. The goods are then generally not collected.

In both of these cases (the seller not delivering the goods and the buyer not paying in full), Section 326 Sr (fraud) applies. This section makes fraud with a view to enjoying or providing another with unlawful benefits a punishable offence. Among other things, Section 326 Sr covers fraud that leads to the delivery of goods (including money transfers and notes and coins), the provision of services or making information available. The application of this article in cases of fraud via auction and retail sites does not differ to its application in cases of offline fraud. For a detailed analysis, see Leukfeldt et al. (2012b).

A complicating factor in this kind of fraud is that it is not always easy to determine whether fraud has been committed, or whether it is in fact a dispute under civil law, if the offender only has one victim. Because of this, the police sometimes turn victims away, telling them it is impossible to report the incident because it involves a civil case (Leukfeldt et al., 2012a; Toutenhoofd-Visser, Veenstra, Domenie, Leukfeldt & Stol, 2009). Fraudsters may however have victims in various police regions, who are all trying to report their cases individually. It is not always possible to have an overview when a fraudster has swindled several people.[18] For that reason the police are advised always to take statements (Leukfeldt et al., 2012b). Given that this is victim research, we refer to victimisation if the respondents themselves indicate that they are victims. We mentioned explicitly in the question that the incident must involve fraud.[19]

4.1.1 Prevalence

Paid but not received: prevalence

As noted previously, 73.2 per cent of all internet users who took part in the research had made at least one purchase via the internet during the previous twelve months. We asked the group of 'buyers' the following question: 'Have you bought a product or a service via the internet and made at least a part

18 The police acknowledge this and in October 2010 they set up an Internet Fraud Hotline [Meldpunt Internetoplichtingen] at national level where reports about fraud are analysed, aggregated and disseminated to regional police forces (see www.mijnpolitie.nl/if.shtml).

19 We stipulated this to avoid respondents claiming to be victims when the quality of product they received did not meet expectations, for instance, rather than actual fraud. We did not manage to completely filter out fraud linked to the sale of fake goods; for a description of this, see the account of the methodology used.

payment, and then never received the product or service because the seller swindled you?'

In the twelve months prior to the research, 3.1 per cent of the buyers had paid for a product or service that was never delivered. This equates to 2.4 per cent of all internet users who were surveyed. With a 95 per cent confidence interval, between 2.1 and 2.7 per cent of internet users had fallen victim to this kind of fraud during the previous twelve-month period. This percentage is in line with the LISS panel finding (Van Wilsem, 2010b) that in 2007, 2.5 per cent of Dutch internet users were swindled in this way. Of the victims of this kind of fraud, 11.4 per cent had fallen victim twice and a further 4.0 per cent three times during the previous twelve months.

Sold but no payment received: prevalence

We asked all internet users who had sold a product or service in the twelve months prior to the research the following question: 'As a private individual, have you sold a product or service via the internet, but not received payment from the buyer after having supplied the product or service because the buyer swindled you?'

In the twelve months prior to the research, 32.8 per cent of internet users had sold a product or service via the internet. One per cent of that group had sold a product or service in the previous twelve months for which they had never received payment. This equates to 0.3 per cent of all internet users. With a 95 per cent confidence interval, we ascertained that between 0.2 and 0.4 per cent of internet users had not received payment for products or services sold during the previous twelve-month period.

Of the victims, 8.0 per cent had fallen victim to this kind of fraud twice during the previous twelve months (2 out of 25). Given that the number of victims of this kind of fraud found in this research is small (n=25), we use unweighted figures rather than percentages when referring to the group 'sold but no payment received' in the rest of this section. Caution should be exercised when interpreting these results.

4.1.2 Modus operandi

Paid but not received: modus operandi

In 37.7 per cent of the cases the fraud involved consumer goods; in 26.5 per cent of the cases it involved electronic products. For the rest, a lot of fraud involved DVDs, films, books, games, toys, collectors' items and holidays.

In 45.6 per cent of the cases contact with the fraudster came about via an online retail site where private individuals buy and sell goods; in 23.0 per cent via a (registered) webshop; and in 21.6 per cent in some other way.

In 19.2 per cent of the cases (n=34), contact with the seller was made via a foreign country: eight times via China, seven times via the United States, five times via Germany, three times via Belgium, and three times via the United Kingdom. A number of other countries were each mentioned once. Leukfeldt et al. (2010) found in their study on the basis of police files that in 14.5 per cent of e-fraud cases the perpetrators operated from abroad.

Sold but no payment received: modus operandi

The products or services involved in the fraud varied widely: in eight cases consumer goods were involved, in four cases electronic goods, twice services were mentioned, and for the rest a horse blanket, toys and so on.

In 17 of the 25 cases, contact came about because the fraudster responded to the victim's advertisement, in four cases the victim responded to the fraudster's advertisement and four times contact came about in another way, namely via the victim's website, via email and by telephone.

In seven of the 25 cases the buyer was abroad: twice in Italy, once in China, once in Belgium, once in Spain, once in the United Kingdom and in one case it was not known what country was involved.

4.1.3 Material losses

Paid but not received: material losses

Financial loss was suffered by 85.3 per cent of the victims. Of the 29 victims who did not suffer financial loss as a result of the fraud, almost half (13) indicated that they eventually got their money back from the seller. How the remaining sixteen got their money back is not known.

Table 4.2 shows that, of the people who were able to specify how much they had lost, almost three quarters lost 100 euros or less and that 5.2 per cent of the victims lost more than 500 euros.

Sold but no payment received: material loss

Of the 25 victims, 22 knew the extent of the loss. For most of them the loss was 100 euros or less; a small number lost more than 1,000 euros (see Table 4.2).

Table 4.2 Loss through retail site fraud (unweighted)

	Paid but not received				Sold, no payment
	Number	% of victims (n=204)	% of known loss	% of internet users (n=9,163)	Number
No losses/losses					
No losses	29	14.2			0
Not known	1	0.5			3
Losses	174	85.3			22
Extent of loss (in euro)					
Not known				0.0	
1-100			74.1	1.6	15
101-200			16.1	0.4	1
201-500			4.6	0.1	4
501-1,000			2.9	0.1	0
1,001 or more			2.3	0.0	2

4.1.4 *Groups at risk*

Paid but not received: risk groups
We carried out bivariate analyses to establish which internet users were more at risk of falling victim to this kind of fraud (see Table 4.3). The findings of these analyses form the basis for the multivariate analyses (see Table 4.4).

The bivariate analyses (column 3) show that internet users without a partner are more likely to fall victim than internet users with partners, and that internet users with twelve hours or more of paid work are more likely to fall victim than internet users with less or no paid work. This link disappears, however, when we calculate it for the internet buyers group – this indicates that people with paid work are more likely to fall victim because they make more frequent use of the internet for buying goods. Furthermore, there is a link between victimisation and education and victimisation and age, as was the case with malware and hacking. Table 4.3 shows that internet users aged 55 years and older are less likely to fall victim, both among internet users in the general (column 3) as among internet buyers specifically (column 4). For level of education, the findings are less clear-cut. It looks as if the risks are more concentrated in the middle groups for internet users in the general (HAVO/VWO/MBO/HBO),[20] but the differences are not more pronounced once the focus is moved to internet buyers specifically. The differences relating to level of education that we mentioned earlier seem to be linked to online buying activity. In short, this analysis shows that the younger age groups are more likely to fall victim than the older age groups, and that those who live alone are more likely to fall victim than people with a partner. Presumably the two are connected because people from the younger (youngest) age group are more likely to live alone than those from the older age group.

As we did with hacking, we carried out multivariate analysis to investigate whether the bivariate links held (see Table 4.4). We only carried out multivariate analyses on the 'Paid but not received' group of victims. The other group was too small to carry out these analyses. First we introduced respondent background characteristics into the model. In addition, we formulated assumptions about variables that would influence victimisation on the basis of the literature. As was the case with hacking, we expected to find a link between victimisation and the kinds of activities undertaken. For this reason we introduced the variables activity and exposure into the model. We also included payment method as a possible predictor of victimisation. We furthermore assessed whether victimisation is influenced by risk awareness, knowledge of the devices with which one is online (and is therefore communicating and making payments) and self-control influence victimisation.[21,22]

20 See footnote 10 for an explanation of abbreviations.

21 Because the statements about self-control were not presented to all respondents (see Appendix 1), we assessed separately whether it had any effect.

22 For more information about the choice of the variables, see Appendix 1.

Table 4.3 Fraud victimisation via auction or retail sites according to background characteristics (bivariate)

	Purchases made via the internet (% internet users, weighted)	Fraud victimisation via auction or retail sites, purchase not received (% internet users, weighted)	Fraud victimisation via auction or retail sites, purchase not received (% buyers, weighted)
Level of education[21]			
No education completed	37.1	1.8	4.8
Primary education	49.5	1.1	2.9
Lower vocational education	54.9	2.3	3.7
VMBO/MAVO	60.6	1.8	2.6
HAVO/VWO	75.1	2.6	3.2
MBO	76.6	2.9	3.7
HBO	83.3	3.0	3.2
WO	89.0	1.0	1.3
$\chi^2(7)$	*808.65***	*19.98***	*13.03*
Age category			
15-24	71.2	2.8	4.0
25-34	85.2	3.2	3.6
35-44	83.2	2.9	3.2
45-54	76.2	2.8	3.6
55-64	66.2	1.5	2.2
65+	47.2	0.5	1.0
$\chi^2(5)$	*629.38***	*30.59***	*17.32***
Employment status			
<12 hours paid work per week	60.0	1.8	2.9
12+ hours paid work per week	80.7	2.7	3.1
$\chi^2(1)$	*461.95***	*7.85***	*0.42*
Partner			
No partner*	73.1	2.8	3.7
Partner	73.3	2.0	2.6
$\chi^2(1)$	*0.08*	*6.81***	*7.58***
Ethnic origin			
Native Dutch	75.0	2.4	3.0
1st generation	62.3	2.5	3.5
2nd generation, 1 parent	73.9	2.2	3.2
2nd generation, both parents	62.1	2.0	3.9
$\chi^2(3)$	*88.40***	*0.35*	*0.55*
Gender			
Male	74.6	2.5	3.1
Female	71.1	2.3	3.0
$\chi^2(1)$	*10.43***	*0.18*	*0.09*
Total	**73.2**	**2.4**	**3.1**

* p<0.05, ** p<0.01.

23 VMBO: pre-vocational secondary education; MAVO: junior general secondary education; HAVO: senior general secondary education; VWO: pre-university education; MBO: senior secondary vocational education; HBO: university of applied sciences degree programme; WO: university education.

In Model 2, internet activities were introduced as predictors of fraud. The age effect then becomes insignificant, which indicates that the reason for the increased risk of fraud is linked to increased levels of risky internet behaviour.

Table 4.4 Logistic regression of fraud via auction or retail sites (paid but not received) on respondent characteristics (among online buyers)

	Model 1		Model 2		Model 3	
	B	S.E.	B	S.E.	B	S.E.
Intercept	-2.264**	0.477	-5.559**	1.160	-7.342**	2.183
Gender (male=ref)	-0.071	0.144	0.112	0.152	0.089	0.153
Age	-0.011*	0.006	-0.005	0.006	-0.017	0.030
Ethnicity (native population=ref)						
1st generation	0.179	0.275	0.096	0.280	0.064	0.282
2nd gen., parent foreign	0.072	0.317	0.034	0.320	0.048	0.320
2nd gen., both parents foreign	0.105	0.519	0.131	0.524	0.097	0.526
Partner	-0.213	0.167	-0.240	0.169	-0.252	0.168
Level of education	-0.067	0.044	-0.133**	0.048	0.346	0.250
Work (12 hours per week or more)	0.109	0.167	0.065	0.170	-0.019	0.175
Activity			0.409**	0.172	1.437**	0.518
Exposure			0.312	0.186	-0.607	0.569
Download			0.009	0.087	0.012	0.086
Computer skill			0.393	0.225	0.377	0.225
Risk awareness			-0.205	0.143	-0.228	0.144
Payment						
Offline via bank			0.236	0.198	0.224	0.198
Via internet banking			0.448**	0.157	0.434**	0.156
Via automatic authorisation			-0.477	0.246	-0.477	0.246
Via PayPal			0.614**	0.176	0.604**	0.176
Via iDEAL			0.065	0.188	0.045	0.188
With credit card via the internet			0.175	0.164	0.190	0.164
Cash			0.672**	0.238	0.662**	0.238
Activity x education					-0.147*	0.071
Activity x age					-0.007	0.008
Exposure x education					0.011	0.079
Exposure x age					0.018	0.010
Nagelkerke R^2	1.2%		4.9%		5.5%	
N	6,660		6,650		6,650	

* $p<0.05$, ** $p<0.01$ (two-sided).

Once again, the threat model comprises three models (see Table 4.4). In the first model, we only looked at the influence of background characteristics on victimisation. The second model maps the influence of respondent attitude and behaviour on victimisation. These models are useful for interpreting the overall Model 3, which includes all the variables, together with four interaction variables. Using Models 1 and 2 it is possible to determine more accurately why certain variables act as predictors and others do not, and, for instance, why some can be explained away.

In the first model we see that the older the respondent is, the smaller becomes the risk of victimisation from this kind of fraud. There was no correlation between this kind of fraud and the other background characteristics, such as gender, ethnicity and level of education.

This model shows that high levels of risky activity are involved.[24] In addition to this, there is also increased risk of online fraud among respondents who had paid cash or used internet banking or PayPal for online purchases in the previous year. However it is impossible to give unequivocal interpretations of these payment method effects. Given the phrasing of the questions, we do not know whether the payment method used was linked to the purchase involving fraud, but only that all these people had used this payment method recently. In addition to this, the question arises of whether the payment method itself is risky or whether it is used for purchases that are more risky. For instance, it may well be the case that PayPal is used more frequently for purchasing certain products that are in any event linked to increased risk of fraud (e.g. importing of products from abroad). This would then entail a selection effect that we cannot adequately assess. Finally, it is noteworthy that education has a significant effect in Model 2, which was not evident in Model 1: respondents with higher levels of education were less likely to be swindled. This is probably a so-called suppressor effect.[25] Additional analyses show that people with higher levels of education participate in activities on the internet more frequently (emailing and searching for information). Because these activities increase risk, it is to be expected that those with higher levels of education run more risks. Yet despite this we see in Model 1 that this is not the case: there are no differences relating to level of education. Model 2 reveals the underlying correlations: activity *increases* risk (and this is an activity that is undertaken more frequently among those with higher levels of education) and level of education *reduces* risk (lower risks among those with a higher level of education). There are therefore two opposing effects that cancel each other out, and this means that people with higher and people with lower levels of education run the same risk of being swindled online.

In Model 3 interaction effects are introduced. This reveals that the more educated one is, the less one's activity on the internet increases the risk of fraud. In other words, activity increases the risk of fraud for everyone, but particularly for those with lower levels of education. Other than these, there were no significant interaction effects.

24 Reminder: activity comprises emailing and searching for information on the internet. Exposure comprises untargeted surfing, downloading, using MSN, skyping, chatting, visiting forums and social media sites and using Twitter. For a detailed explanation of the methodology used, see Appendix 1.

25 The suppressor effect is the phenomenon whereby a correlation between two variables does not appear to exist initially but then becomes significant when the effects of a third variable are assessed.

Additional analyses on the sub-sample show that self-control is unrelated to online fraud victimisation. This is not in line with earlier research into fraud victimisation; in this study, low self-control was a predictor of victimisation (Van Wilsem, 2010b).

Sold but no payment received: risk groups
The number of victims of this kind of fraud in the present research is too small to be able to identify risk groups.

4.1.5 Actions undertaken by the victim

Paid but not received: actions undertaken by the victim
Of the 204 victims, 11.3 per cent had not taken any action as a consequence of the fraud (see Table 4.5). The majority of the victims had attempted to get their money back. The ways in which victims tried to get their money back included repeatedly approaching the seller (56.4%) and contacting their own or the fraudster's bank (19.6% and 5.9% respectively). After being swindled, 36.8 per cent of the victims also searched the internet for information about the fraudster, while 19.6 per cent contacted the police (see Section 7 for more information).

Other action undertaken by the victims included trying to get their money back in other ways, for instance through PayPal or a credit card company, or trying to stop the fraudster from victimising other people. These latter attempts took the form of taking out an advertisement on the retail site warning people about the fraudster, putting high bids on fraudster's advertisements or describing the fraudster on websites like opgelicht.nl [*opgelicht* is Dutch for swindled].

Sold but no payment received: action undertaken by victims
Of the 25 victims, fifteen made an attempt to get their money back (see Table 4.5). Thirteen victims did this by relentlessly approaching the seller; two tried to get their money back by contacting the fraudster's bank. A further six victims reported the incident to the retail site or webshop where the fraud had taken place, and seven victims searched for information about the buyer. Four victims did nothing at all and two contacted the police. Victims mentioned under 'other actions' that the fraudster did not respond to their requests to contact them.

Table 4.5 Actions undertaken by victims of fraud via auction or retail sites 'paid but not received' (unweighted)

	Number	% of victims (n=204)	n=25
Nothing	23	11.3	4
Reported to online retail site or webshop	80	39.2	6
Tried to get money back by continuing to contact the seller	115	56.4	13
Tried to get the money via my bank	40	19.6	0
Tried to get the money via the seller's bank	12	5.9	2
Looked for information about the seller on the internet	75	36.8	7
Contacted the police	40	19.6	2
Other action	26	12.7	4

4.1.6 Immaterial losses

Paid but not received: immaterial losses

We presented ten statements to the victims to determine what consequences the offence had had for them. Possible answers ranged from 'disagree completely' to 'agree completely'. A total of 201 of the 204 victims chose answers to the statements (see Figure 4.1). Half of the victims (50.7%) lost trust in trading via the auction or retail site where they were swindled. Among a further 27.4 per cent, trust in any kind of trade via the internet declined, and among more than a quarter of the victims (26.0%), their sense of security on the internet in general declined. Eight per cent suffered financial problems and 5.5 per cent suffered psychological problems as a result of the fraud.

A further 6.4 per cent of the victims indicated that the offence had had other consequences for them. Victims indicated, for instance, that immediately after the offence they felt stressed, but that this had since passed. Other consequences that victims mentioned were feelings of helplessness because nobody could or wanted to catch the perpetrator, or that they found it incomprehensible that anyone would be capable of doing such a thing. Victims also mentioned changing their own behaviour: they are now more alert when buying items via the internet.

Figure 4.1 Consequences for the victim (n=201)

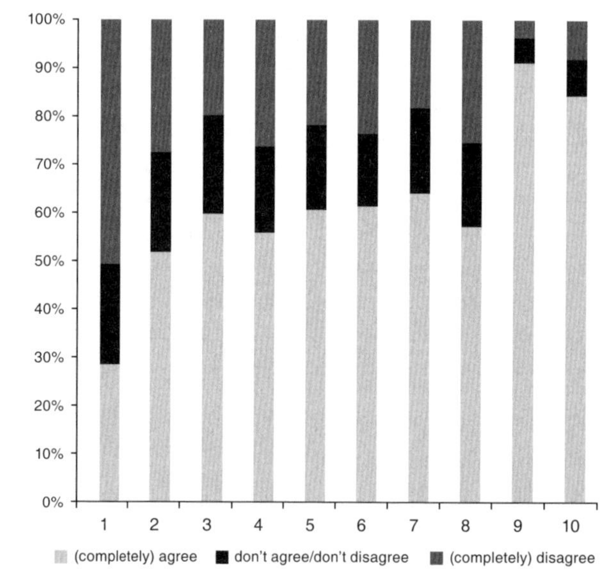

1. Trust in trading on that particular retail site or webshop declined.
2. Trust in trading on that any retail site or webshop declined.
3. Trust in any kind of trade on the internet declined.
4. General sense of security on the internet declined.
5. General sense of security declined.
6. Trust in humankind in its entirety declined.
7. Trust in the Dutch police declined.
8. Trust in the Dutch rule of law declined.
9. Suffered from psychological problems.
10. Suffered from financial problems.

Sold but no payment received: immaterial loss

We presented the ten statements shown in Figure 4.1 to the victims to determine what consequences the offence had had for them. Because there were no more than 25 victims, we did not create a figure showing the percentages. Possible answers ranged from 'disagree completely' to 'agree completely'. All 25 victims chose answers to the statements. Eight victims had lost trust in trading on the retail site where they were swindled. Nine victims had lost faith in humankind, and for five of them their sense of security on the internet had declined. A further four of the victims indicated that the offence had had other consequences for them. Victims had had feelings of helplessness and could not understand how anyone could do such a thing.

4.1.7 Conclusions

Paid but not received: conclusions

Of all internet users, 2.4 per cent fell victim to e-fraud of the kind 'paid but not received'. If we look at the influence of background characteristics on victimisation, we see that the risk of this kind of fraud decreases with age. If we include internet activities as predictors of fraud, we see that the age effect becomes insignificant, which indicates that the reason for the increased risk of fraud among young people is linked to their increased levels of risky internet behaviour. This is linked in particular with high levels of activity (searching for information on the internet and emailing).[26]

Finally, once interaction effects were introduced, it emerged that activity on the internet is less likely to increase risk of fraud among those with higher levels of education. In other words, activity increases the risk of fraud for everyone, but particularly for those with lower levels of education. Other than these, there were no significant interaction effects. Additional analyses show that self-control is unrelated to online fraud victimisation.

In 19.2 per cent of all cases, contact with the seller took place through a foreign country. In other words: in a fifth of all these cases, the perpetrator operated from abroad. If the police receive more reports of this kind of crime, their workload will become more international in nature.

Fraud has consequences for people's confidence in trading on the internet. Half of the victims (50.7%) lost trust in trading via the auction or retail site where they were swindled, and among a further 27.4 per cent, trust in any kind of trade on the internet also declined. Among more than a quarter of the victims (26.0%), their sense of security on the internet in general declined.

Sold but no payment received: conclusions

In the twelve months prior to the research, 32.8 per cent of internet users had sold a product or service via the internet, of which 1 per cent had received no payment for a product sent or service provided at least once. This equates to 0.3 per cent of all internet users.

---

26 Reminder: activity comprises emailing and searching for information on the internet. Exposure comprises untargeted surfing, downloading, using MSN, skyping, chatting, visiting forums and social media sites and using Twitter. For a detailed explanation of the methodology used, see Appendix 1.

4.2 Identity fraud

Identity fraud is the committing of fraud using a fabricated/assumed identity (De Vries, Tigchelaar, Van der Linden & Hol, 2007; Finch, 2007). Preparations for identity abuse of this kind can take the form of creating a fictitious identity, assuming the identity of an existing person with their permission, or stealing the identity of an existing person (identity theft). Identity theft can be carried out by stealing digital personal details, for example through phishing or using spyware. The theft need not necessarily take place on the internet; it is also carried out using old fashioned methods, such as raking through waste paper recycling bins, also known as dumpster diving. Misusing other people's identities has always been popular among criminals; by assuming someone else's identity, a criminal can conceal his own identity and thus hamper investigations (Ollman, 2004).

According to Leukfeldt et al. (2010) determining whether identity theft has been committed can be difficult in practice. In cases of illegal use of credit cards for ordering goods via the internet, it is not always clear who has the stolen identity. It may be that the son or daughter used the credit card to buy things on the internet without saying anything. It is even more difficult to establish how the identity was stolen: deceit through social engineering manipulations, computer hacking, using spyware, via a phishing site, skimming, or dumpster diving. In the questionnaire we used the following description: 'Identity fraud is when someone uses your personal or financial information without your permission for his or her own financial gain. For instance, it is when someone withdraws money from your account, buys items in your name or applies for official documents in your name. Generally identity fraud is a consequence of identity theft, but in some cases you may have provided your identity information yourself.'

We first asked whether the respondent had fallen victim to identity fraud, regardless of whether it was online or not. Of all surveyed internet users, 0.9 per cent had fallen victim to identity fraud. We then wanted to establish whether ICT played a significant role in the committing of the offence and whether it therefore qualified as cybercrime (as defined in Section 1.1). We did so by establishing how the fraudster obtained the identity information, and by establishing whether the fraudster used the internet to commit the fraud. We refer to identity fraud cybercrime (in short 'identity fraud') if:

- the fraudster obtained the identity information using ICT (identity theft using e.g. skimming of phishing), and/or:
- the fraudster used the internet to commit the fraud.

Of the internet users who took part in the research, a total of 18 fell victim to identity theft alone, 22 to identity fraud alone and 23 to both identity theft and identity fraud. There were therefore altogether 63 victims of identity fraud, of whom 41 were victims of identity theft. The remainder of this section relates to the 63 internet users who were victims of either or both of the crimes described above.

Of all respondents who use the internet, 0.8 per cent (n=63) indicated that they had fallen victim to identity fraud in the twelve months leading up to the research. With a 95 per cent confidence interval, between 0.6 and 1.0 per cent of internet users had therefore fallen victim to identity fraud during the previous twelve-month period. The percentage of victims is in all probability higher because not all users will know that their identity information has been obtained *via ICT*, and because they do not always know whether the fraud was committed *via the internet*.

We will now look separately at the 41 victims of identity fraud who indicated that the perpetrator obtained the identity information using ICT (in short: 'identity theft'). We will then present an analysis of all 63 victims of identity fraud.

Prevalence

We asked the respondents who indicated that they were victims of identity fraud how the fraudster had obtained their identity information. We subsequently categorised those respondents whose identity was stolen using ICT as victims of identity theft. In total, 0.5 per cent of the respondents had fallen victim to identity theft in the twelve months prior to the research (n=41). With a 95 per cent confidence interval, between 0.4 and 0.6 per cent of internet users had fallen victim to identity theft during the previous year.

Modus operandi

We presented the respondents with seven ways in which ICT may have been used to commit identity theft (see Table 4.6). Multiple answers were possible; a fifth of the respondents ticked more than one answer, which shows that victims are not always certain how the identity theft was committed. According to the results, skimming is the modus operandi most often used to obtain the identity information (31.7%). In addition to this, 31.7 per cent of the victims indicated that they had entered information for a lottery or survey on a website, and 19.5 per cent had entered data on a hacked website.

Of the 41 victims of identity theft, some (seven) knew and some (four) suspected that they knew who the perpetrator was (26.8%). In five cases, they knew the person; in three cases it was someone they did not know personally; in two cases it was an ex-partner and in one case it was someone from work.

Table 4.6 Ways in which the identity information was stolen (unweighted)

	Number	% of victims
Skimming	13	31.7
Information entered for lottery, survey and so on	11	26.8
Hacking and/or virus	8	19.5
Information entered on a hacked website	8	19.5
Personal information entered on a website	6	14.6
Information given after an email request	2	4.9
Phishing	1	2.4

Material losses

We will now look at all 63 victims of identity fraud. Material losses were suffered by 60.3 per cent of the victims. The amounts varied from 1 to 112,500 euros. More than a third of the victims who suffered loss, lost more than 1,000 euros (see Table 4.7).

Table 4.7 Loss through identity fraud (unweighted)

	Number	% loss
No losses/losses		
No losses	25	39.7
Losses	38	60.3
Extent of loss (in euros)		
1-100	6	15.8
101-200	4	10.5
201-500	6	15.8
501-1,000	8	21.1
1,001 or more	14	36.8

Ten of the 38 victims with loss (26.3%) were not compensated. For four of these ten, the loss was less than 35 euros. The other losses that were not compensated involved amounts of 250, 800, 3,000, 5,000, 10,000 and 20,000 euros. In 19 cases, the bank compensated the loss. We did not ask in the questionnaire who compensated the other nine losses, and that is therefore not known.

Risk groups

Internet users who are in paid work comprising twelve hours or more per week are more likely to fall victim to identity fraud than other internet users (see Table 4.8).

Table 4.8 ID fraud victimisation according to background characteristics (weighted, bivariate)

	Identity fraud victims (% internet users)
Level of education[28]	
No education completed	0.0
Primary education	0.2
Lower vocational education	0.6
VMBO/MAVO	0.7
HAVO/VWO	0.9
MBO	0.7

27 VMBO: pre-vocational secondary education; MAVO: junior general secondary education; HAVO: senior general secondary education; VWO: pre-university education; MBO: senior secondary vocational education; HBO: university of applied sciences degree programme; WO: university education.

	Identity fraud victims (% internet users)
HBO	0.9
WO	1.0
χ^2(7)	*5.30*
Age category	
15-24	0.5
25-34	0.9
35-44	1.0
45-54	0.6
55-64	0.8
65+	0.7
χ^2(5)	*3.63*
Employment status	
<12 hours paid work per week	0.4
12+ hours paid work per week	0.9
χ^2(1)	*6.71***
Partner	
No partner	0.9
Partner	0.6
χ^2(1)	*2.23*
Ethnic origin	
Native Dutch	0.7
1st generation	0.8
2nd generation, 1 parent	1.4
2nd generation, both parents	0.8
χ^2(3)	*3.04*
Gender	
Male	0.9
Female	0.6
χ^2(1)	*3.15*
Total	**0.8**

* p<0.05, ** p<0.01.

A multivariate analysis was carried out in order to ascertain whether the bivariate links hold (see Table 4.9). First we introduced respondent background characteristics into the model. We also formulated assumptions, on the basis of the literature, about variables that would influence victimisation. These variables were also included in the model. We discuss the underlying assumptions below.

Because hacking may be a means of obtaining identities for committing fraud, the variables that were relevant for hacking were also included in the threat model for identity fraud. Below we briefly reiterate the assumptions underlying these variables.

On the basis of the routine activities theory (Cohen & Felson, 1979; Felson & Clarke, 1998) a link can be expected between victimisation and the kinds of activities that a person undertakes. For this reason we introduced the variables activity and exposure.[28] Downloading can also be expected to be a risky activity in connection with hacking. The more one downloads, the greater the chance of being infected with malware.

According to the rational choice theory (Coleman, 1973, 1990), criminals constantly weigh up costs versus benefits when committing crimes. The aim is to the lowest possible costs (chances of getting caught, degree of difficulty and so on) with as many benefits as possible (victim's money). Frequently used software is an attractive target for criminals: a large number of victims can then be reached with one hit (one flaw in the software ensures that all its users can be attacked and infected electronically with malware, for instance). Weak security is also attractive. It makes it easy to infect a computer and it means the costs will be low. For that reason we looked at operating systems and web browsers in our risk model, as well as the use of virus scanners.

Risk awareness possibly also plays a role in victimisation. Internet users who are aware of the risks that they are exposed to online are in a better position to respond to these, and this means that they reduce their risk of becoming a victim.

Alongside risk awareness, knowledge of the devices with which one is online (and is therefore communicating and making payments) can also influence victimisation. We assume that people who know nothing about the devices also know less about the risks that they are running. Here we refer to knowledge about operating systems, internet connections and browsers, and virus scanners. For this factor we compiled a computer knowledge variable.[29]

Other high-risk behaviour is allowing other people to use one's computer. The owner then has less control over devices and is not always aware what the other person is doing on the computer. We therefore also assessed the effect of sharing a computer with others.

Self-control is also used to explain victimisation (Gottfredson & Hirschi, 1990). Because the statements about self-control were not presented to all respondents, (see Appendix 1), we assessed separately whether it had any effect.

Once again, the threat model comprises three models (see Table 4.9). In the first model, we looked only at the influence of background characteristics on victimisation. The second model maps the influence of respondent attitude and behaviour on victimisation. These models are useful for interpreting the overall Model 3, which incorporates all the variables from Models 1 and 2, together with four interaction variables. Using Models 1 and 2, it is possible to determine more accurately why certain variables act as predictors and others do not, and, for instance, why some can be explained away.

Model 1 shows that there are no background characteristics that are related to identity fraud. Largely in line with the findings from the descriptive analyses, the risks of falling victim to this offence are equally divided between, for example, men and women, young and older people, and those with higher and lower levels of education.

28 For a detailed explanation of the methodology used, see Appendix 1.
29 For the composition of these, see the account of the methodology used in Appendix 1.

Table 4.9 Logistic regression of identity abuse via ICT on respondent characteristics

	Model 1		Model 2		Model 3	
	B	S.E.	B	S.E.	B	S.E.
Intercept	-5.239**	0.844	-8.377**	2.567	-5.849	4.407
Gender (male=ref)	-0.436	0.262	-0.212	0.275	-0.220	0.276
Age	0.012	0.010	0.014	0.012	-0.072	0.051
Ethnicity (native population=ref)						
1st generation	0.160	0.472	-0.011	0.487	-0.049	0.490
2nd gen., parent foreign	0.432	0.474	0.436	0.482	0.427	0.484
2nd gen., both parents foreign	0.608	0.732	0.563	0.744	0.544	0.745
Partner	-0.516	0.277	-0.383	0.290	-0.411	0.291
Level of education	0.121	0.080	0.035	0.088	0.442	0.474
Work (12 hours per week or more)	0.680**	0.344	0.666	0.344	0.588	0.352
Degree of internet usage			-0.275	0.335	-0.399	0.335
# of PCs in household			-0.311*	0.127	-0.296*	0.127
Mobile most used app. for internet			-0.274	0.764	-0.283	0.765
No virus scanner			0.461	0.458	0.461	0.462
Browser						
Internet Explorer			-0.100	0.341	-0.104	0.342
Google Chrome			0.134	0.325	0.155	0.326
Firefox			0.155	0.343	0.169	0.345
Opera			0.217	1.052	0.198	1.053
Safari			0.135	0.535	0.141	0.537
Activity			0.714**	0.246	0.794	1.055
Exposure			0.376	0.351	-0.697	1.253
Buying via the internet			0.253	0.473	0.199	0.473
Download			-0.136	0.168	-0.134	0.168
Computer skill			0.622	0.447	0.591	0.446
Risk awareness			-0.005	0.246	-0.022	0.248
Paid email subscription			-0.459	0.356	-0.463	0.356
Paid subscription for webhosting			0.205	0.448	0.195	0.449
Paid gaming or gambling sites.			-0.107	0.752	-0.113	0.755
Paid download sites			0.037	0.439	0.060	0.438
Paid contact or dating sites			1.258*	0.566	1.217*	0.565
Payment						
Offline via bank			-0.457	0.540	-0.448	0.541
Via internet banking			-0.233	0.308	-0.230	0.308
Via Automatic authorisation			-0.831	0.624	-0.823	0.625
Via PayPal			0.483	0.355	0.478	0.355
Via iDEAL			-0.254	0.361	-0.231	0.362
With credit card via internet			0.329	0.321	0.320	0.322
Cash			-1.013	1.020	-1.009	1.021
Activity x education					-0.194	0.136
Activity x age					0.023	0.014
Exposure x education					0.152	0.156
Exposure x age					0.005	0.017
Nagelkerke R^2	3.2%		8.5%		9.2%	
N	9,123		8,958		8,958	

* p<0.05, ** p<0.01 (two-sided).

Model 2 shows that there are a number of internet activities that contribute to risk of online identity fraud. These are: activities on the internet and participation in paid contact or dating sites. For the rest, the more PCs in the household, the lower the risk.

The interaction effects introduced in Model 3 are all insignificant. This means that activity and exposure have the same effects on younger as on older respondents and on those with higher as on those with lower levels of education.

Analyses of the sub-sample show that low self-control does not influence the risk of being experiencing online identity fraud.

Actions undertaken by the victim

Table 4.10 shows that after falling victim to identity theft and/or fraud, 33.3 per cent of the victims attempted to get their money back via the bank, 15.6 per cent contacted the police and 11.1 per cent took no action.

Table 4.10 Action undertaken by victims (n=63)

Action	Number	%
Other action	34	54.0
Tried to get the money back via the bank	21	33.3
Contacted the police	12	15.6
No action	7	11.1
Tried to get the money back via insurance	2	3.2
Appealed to Identity Fraud Hotline	1	1.6
Appealed to website/victims association	0	0.0

The victims described various actions in the 'Other actions' category. Twelve victims contacted the medium with which or where the identity fraud was committed. Four victims were informed by the company that was used in the fraud. Three victims changed their login details so that the fraudster could no longer use it. Three victims tried to approach the perpetrators themselves.

Immaterial losses

We presented seven statements to the victims to determine what consequences the offence had had for them. Possible answers ranged from 'disagree completely' to 'agree completely'. All the victims chose answers to the statements (see Figure 4.2). Of these, 34.9 per cent indicated that their general sense of security on the internet had declined. The same percentage indicated that their general sense of security had declined. A further 25.4 per cent indicated that their trust in humankind in its entirety had declined, and 15.9 per cent said that they had suffered from psychological problems.

Figure 4.2 Consequences for the victim (n=63)

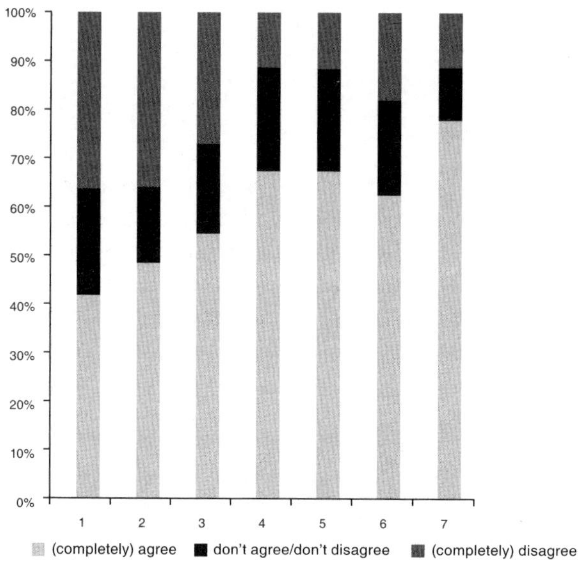

1. General sense of security on the internet declined.
2. General sense of security declined.
3. Trust in humankind in its entirety declined.
4. Trust in the Dutch police declined.
5. Trust in the Dutch rule of law declined.
6. Suffered from psychological problems.
7. Suffered from financial problems.

Conclusions

The identity information of 0.5 per cent of internet users was stolen using ICT. Of all internet users surveyed, 0.9 per cent had fallen victim to identity fraud. Skimming was mentioned most often as the way in which identity information was obtained. Entering data on a website or an online form was also mentioned quite often.

If we look at the influences of background characteristics on the risks of falling victim, we see that the risks of falling victim to this offence are equally divided between, for instance, men and women, young and older people, or between those with higher and lower levels of education. Certain internet activities do seem to contribute to the risk of online identity fraud. These are: activities on the internet (emailing and searching for information on the internet) and taking part in paid contact or dating sites. We have already noted that internet activities increase risks. For the rest, the more PCs there are in the household, the lower the risk. It is unclear how we are to interpret this finding. We found no significant interaction effects. That means that activity and exposure have the same effects on younger and older people and on those with higher and lower levels of education. Analyses of the sub-sample show that low self-control does not influence the risk of being confronted with online identity fraud.

Six of the ten victims suffered financial loss, of which more than one third amounted to 1,000 euros or more. Ten of the 63 victims who suffered loss were not compensated. One third of the victims contacted their bank in consequence of the incident. Twelve of the 63 victims (19.0%) contacted the police.

General sense of security (including on the internet) declined for more than a third of the victims as a consequence of identity theft and/or fraud victimisation.

4.3 Advance fee fraud

Advance fee fraud is a kind of fraud where victims are promised large sums of money provided they first pay a relatively small amount to defray expenses; the victims are subsequently not paid out. For instance, the potential victims are asked to pay legal fees to access the inheritance of an unknown family member in Africa. One type of advance fee fraud is committed via dating sites. 'According to the fraud helpdesk, loss due to dating fraud is on the increase. Precisely how many victims are involved is unclear because not everyone is prepared to report it. Last year 45 reports were submitted. On average, the victims lost 2,250 euros, according to Fraud Hotline's Fleur van Eck' (*de Volkskrant*, 7 June 2012). Perpetrators first attempt to gain their victims' trust by presenting themselves as interesting candidates for a relationship. The perpetrator then asks for money, for example for an airline ticket to come over, or to open a shop or for a family member who is in trouble. Once the victim realises that they have been swindled after paying the prospective partner, the perpetrator disappears from the scene.

Advance fee fraud is punishable on the basis of Section 326 Sr (fraud). This section makes fraud with a view to enjoying or providing another with unlawful benefits a punishable offence. Among other things, Section 326 Sr covers fraud that leads to the delivery of goods, including money transfers and notes and coins. The application of this article in cases of advance fee fraud is no different to its application in cases of other kinds of fraud, including offline fraud. Forgery of documents can also play a role in this kind of e-fraud. This is a punishable offence pursuant to Section 225 Sr. On the grounds of Section 225 paragraph 1 Sr, it is punishable to forge or counterfeit ('to prepare falsely') any document that is intended to serve as proof of any fact. Forging and counterfeiting is only a punishable offence if the perpetrator intends to use the document as 'genuine and unfalsified' for him- or herself, or for others to use.[30] For a detailed analysis, see Leukfeldt et al. (2012b).

30 The term 'document' is interpreted broadly. Computer data that are readable or can be rendered readable relatively easily, and have been recorded in a relatively fixed way (i.e. with the intention of being stored, temporarily or not) constitute a document (Supreme Court, 15 January, Dutch Law Reports 1991, 668; more generally: Parliamentary Paper II 2002/03, 29 025, no. 3, p. 3). This applies, for instance, to emails, web pages and most computer files. This does not mean that they necessarily fall under Section 225 Sr; for this the requirement is that they also have to serve as evidence ('that according to generally accepted standards usually serve as evidence of any fact' (Supreme Court 30 September 1980, Dutch Law Reports 1981, 70; Supreme Court 20 April 2004, 681)).

Prevalence

Of the 9,163 internet users surveyed, 18 fell victim to advance fee fraud (four times via a dating site, 14 times in some other way). This equates to 0.2 per cent of all internet users surveyed. We considered a respondent to have been the victim of advance fee fraud if that person had actually suffered loss.

Material losses

The losses varied from 7 to 8,000 euros. In more than half of the cases, the loss was less than 100 euros (see Table 4.11).

Table 4.11 Loss through advance fee fraud (unweighted)

Euros	Number
1-100	11
101-200	2
201-500	1
501-1,000	0
1,001 or more	4

Risk groups

The number of victims of this kind of fraud in this present research is too small to be able to identify risk groups.

Action undertaken by the victim

Six victims tried to get their money back by approaching the fraudster(s). Four victims took no action. One victim contacted the police (see Table 4.12).

Table 4.12 Action undertaken by victims (n=18)

Action	Number
Nothing	4
Looked for information about the fraud on the internet	4
Tried to contact fellow victims	2
Carried on approaching fraudster	6
Sought legal assistance	2
Contacted the police	1
Other action	3

Immaterial losses

We showed the victims the seven statements shown in Figure 4.2 about the consequences of the offence. All 18 victims chose answers to the statements. Eight victims indicated that their general sense of security on the internet had declined. Eight victims also indicated that their general sense of security had declined. For the rest, two victims indicated that they had suffered from financial problems.

Conclusions

Advance fee fraud does not happen often. Only 0.2 per cent of all internet users surveyed fell victim to this kind of fraud. This amounts to a total of eight victims. Due to the limited number of victims, it is not possible to draw generalised conclusions.

5 OFFENCES IN THE PRIVATE SPHERE

In this section we will discuss offences that are also referred to as interpersonal crimes. These involve digital kinds of punishable behavioural offences in which personal privacy is violated. In this, perpetrators use ICT as a (one way) means of communicating with the victim (Van der Hulst & Neve, 2008). First we discuss stalking (Sect. 5.1) and subsequently threats (Sect. 5.2).

5.1 STALKING

Cyberstalking is the generic term for the systematic and relentless online harassment and/or threatening of a person by making provocative statements and/or placing provocative messages on online forums and bulletin boards and in chat rooms, by spying on the person using spyware or by continuously sending unsolicited emails and spam (Van der Hulst & Neve, 2008). It also includes posting offensive pages on the internet with photos of and information about the victim. In addition to this, other internet users may be incited to harass or threaten the victim (Van der Hulst & Neve, 2008). The respondents were presented with the following definition of stalking: stalking is the conscious and repeated pursuing of a person with the intention of making that person do something or scaring them. Stalking may be done through repeatedly doing the same thing or through various actions, such as following and spying on someone, making threats, making unwanted phone calls or damaging property, including electronic devices.

In the Dutch Criminal Code, stalking is called '*belaging*' and is made punishable in Section 285b Sr. This provision applies to both offline and online stalking (cyberstalking). It is a punishable offence to unlawfully, systematically and intentionally violate the personal privacy of another person with the aim of coercing that person to do something, to stop them from doing something or to tolerate something or to frighten them. Stalking is an offence that is only subject to prosecution on complaint, on the grounds of Section 285b, paragraph 2 Sr. Prosecution therefore follows after the victim has filed a complaint with the police. On the grounds of Section 164, paragraph 1 of the Dutch Code of Criminal Procedures (*Wetboek van Strafvordering, henceforth* Sv), a complaint comprises a police report with a request for prosecution.

Cyberstalking may involve the perpetrator in using stolen digital data, such as digital photographs, or spying on the victim using spyware. Leukfeldt et al. (2012b) give a detailed description of the penalisation of these crimes.

Prevalence

Respondents were asked whether they had fallen victim to stalking during the previous twelve-month period. In the twelve months prior the research, 1.3 per cent of internet users had fallen victim to stalking. In 82.9 per cent of the cases, ICT had also been used for stalking purposes. This means that, in total, 1.1 per cent of the respondents who used the internet had fallen victim to cyberstalking in the twelve months prior to the research (n=92). With a 95 per cent confidence interval, between 0.9 and 1.3 per cent of internet users fell victim to cyberstalking during the previous twelve-month period.

Modus operandi

We asked the victims what means stalkers used to do their stalking. Multiple answers were possible. On average, stalkers used more than two of the means cited (see Table 5.1). Sending email messages (52.2%), sending mobile phone messages (46.7%), and sending chat messages (44.6%) were the means most often used by the stalkers.

Table 5.1 Means used by cyberstalkers (unweighted)

Means used by cyberstalkers	Number	% of victims
Unsolicited emails	48	52.2
Message via mobile phone	43	46.7
Unsolicited chat messages	41	44.6
Other method via the internet	28	30.4
Embarrassing photographs/stories via the internet	19	20.7
Hacked email	12	13.0
Changes to profile, web pages	8	8.7
Hacked computer	5	5.4
Total means	**204**	
Total number of victims	**92**	**100**

Victims were then asked whether they knew who the stalker was (see Table 5.2). In 62.0 per cent of the cases the victim knew who the perpetrator was. If the victim ticked 'Other known', the victim was not asked how they knew the perpetrator. In those cases, it is not known whether the perpetrator and the victim knew each other in the real world or only via the internet.

Table 5.2 Relationship perpetrator-victim of cyberstalking (unweighted)

Relationship perpetrator-victim	Number	% of victims
Perpetrator not known	35	38.0
Ex-partner	18	19.6
Colleague	7	7.6
Someone from the neighbourhood	6	6.5
Family member	4	4.3
Other known	25	27.2
Total	**92**	**100**

Material losses

Of the 92 victims (10.9%), ten suffered material loss as a consequence of stalking; four of them also knew the extent of the loss: 20, 50, 1,000 and 15,000 euros.

Risk groups

We carried out bivariate analysis to establish which internet users fall victim to stalking, (see Table 5.3). Table 3.1 shows that internet users without a partner are more likely to fall victim than internet users with partners. As was the case with malware, hacking and e-fraud, there were differences in levels of victimisation between the various education levels and between the various age groups.

In order to ascertain whether the bivariate differences hold, a multivariate analysis was conducted (see Table 5.4). First we introduced respondent background characteristics into the model. We then formulated assumptions about variables that would influence victimisation, based on the literature, as is also done for the other offences. These variables were also introduced in the model. We discuss these underlying assumptions below.

Table 5.3 Cyberstalking victimisation according to background characteristics (weighted, bivariate)

	Cyberstalking victimisation (unweighted) % internet users
Level of education[31]	
No education completed	0.0
Primary education	2.2
Lower vocational schooling	0.3
VMBO/MAVO	1.8
HAVO/VWO	1.2
MBO	1.3
HBO	0.9
WO	0.5
$\chi^2(7)$	*21.51***
Age category	
15-24	2.5
25-34	0.9
35-44	0.8
45-54	1.1
55-64	0.8
65+	0.5

31 VMBO: pre-vocational secondary education; MAVO: junior general secondary education; HAVO: senior general secondary education; VWO: pre-university education; MBO: senior secondary vocational education; HBO: university of applied sciences degree programme; WO: university education.

Table 5.3 (continued)

	Cyberstalking victimisation (unweighted) % internet users
$\chi^2(5)$	*35.96***
Employment status	
<12 hours paid work per week	1.4
12+ hours paid work per week	1.0
$\chi^2(1)$	*3.50*
Partner	
No partner	1.6
Partner	0.7
$\chi^2(1)$	*16.29***
Ethnic origin	
Native Dutch	1.1
1st generation	0.9
2nd generation, 1 parent	1.6
2nd generation, both parents	1.6
$\chi^2(3)$	*2.01*
Gender	
Male	1.1
Female	1.1
$\chi^2(1)$	*0.01*
Total	**1.1**

*p<0.05, **p<0.01.

On the basis of the routine activities theory (Cohen & Felson, 1979; Felson & Clarke, 1998) a link can be expected between victimisation and the kinds of activities that a person undertakes. For this reason we introduced the variables activity and exposure.[32]

Risk awareness may also play a role in victimisation. Internet users who are aware of the risks that they are exposed to online are in a better position to respond to them, and that means they reduce their risk of becoming a victim.

Alongside risk awareness, knowledge of the devices with which one is online (and is therefore communicating) can also influence victimisation. We assume that people who know nothing about the devices also know less about the risks that they are running. Here we refer to knowledge about operating systems, internet connections and browsers, and virus scanners. For this factor we compiled a computer knowledge variable.[33]

Self-control is also used to explain victimisation (Gottfredson & Hirschi, 1990). Because the statements about self-control were not presented to all respondents, (see Appendix 1), we assessed separately whether it had any effect.

32 For a detailed explanation of the methodology used, see Appendix 1.

33 For the composition of these, see the account of the methodology used in Appendix 1.

Once again, the threat model comprises three models (see Table 5.4). In the first model, we looked only at the influence of background characteristics on victimisation. The second model maps the influence of respondent attitude and behaviour on victimisation. These models are useful for interpreting the overall Model 3, which incorporates all the variables together with four interaction variables. Using Models 1 and 2, it is possible to determine more accurately why certain variables act as predictors and others do not, and why, for instance, some can be explained away.

Table 5.4 Logistic regression of online stalking on respondent characteristics.

	Model 1		Model 2		Model 3	
	B	S.E.	B	S.E.	B	S.E.
Intercept	-8.871	1051.501	-11.761	1159.496	-14.687	1149.367
Gender (male=ref)	0.074	0.214	0.159	0.225	0.161	0.225
Age	-0.022**	0.007	-0.004	0.009	-0.005	0.037
Ethnicity (native population=ref)						
1st generation	-0.336	0.464	-0.462	0.472	-0.360	0.475
2nd gen., parent foreign	0.011	0.465	-0.072	0.469	-0.091	0.471
2nd gen., both parents foreign	-0.137	0.726	-0.097	0.730	-0.098	0.734
Partner	-0.549*	0.265	-0.515	0.273	-0.508	0.276
Level of education	0.007	0.063	-0.017	0.068	0.566	0.351
Work (12 hours per week or more)	-0.436	0.233	-0.359	0.238	-0.222	0.250
Degree of internet usage			-0.077	0.336	-0.154	0.348
# of PCs in household			-0.009	0.106	-0.024	0.107
Mobile most used app. for internet			-0.156	0.479	-0.228	0.482
Computer skill			-0.239	0.224	-0.229	0.229
Risk awareness			0.145	0.213	0.170	0.216
Activity			0.382*	0.193	0.521	0.567
Exposure			0.831**	0.257	2.070**	0.607
Buying via the internet			0.135	0.288	0.171	0.287
Download			-0.022	0.123	-0.037	0.127
Activity x education					-0.108	0.101
Activity x age					0.012	0.010
Exposure x education					-0.097	0.093
Exposure x age					-0.021	0.013
Nagelkerke R^2	3.9%		6.7%		7.5%	
N	9,123		9,056		9,056	

* p<0.05, ** p<0.01 (two-sided).

The first model shows that the risk of online stalking is higher for younger internet users and for internet users without partners. No differences were discovered in degree of risk between, for instance, men and women, or between people from various ethnic backgrounds.

In Model 2, the effects of age and presence of a partner disappeared. That means we can attribute the differences between young people and older and between people with and without partners to the various internet activities that they undertake. For example, we see in this model that activity and exposure are linked to a higher risk of online stalking. Additional analyses (not shown) do in fact show that young people and those who live alone undertake these activities more frequently.

For the rest, Model 3 shows that the interaction effects are insignificant. This means that conduct and exposure have the same effect on people from various age categories and with various levels of education. For exposure the risk increases, and for conduct there is no effect.

Additional analyses on the sub-sample show that self-control is unrelated to online stalking.

Action undertaken by the victim

The majority of the victims did not take any action as a consequence of this offence (58.7%). Almost one third of the victims (30.4%) contacted the police. Other victims contacted their GP (3.3%), Victim Support (2.2%) or the Regional Institute for Outpatient Mental Healthcare [Riagg] (1.1%) (see Table 5.5).

In addition to this, 17.4 per cent of the victims indicated that they had contacted other authorities. The authorities mentioned most often were KPN (the Dutch landline and mobile telecommunications company) (3.3%), school (3.3%) and Hyves (2.2%). For the rest, victims contacted various organisations, such as Tros Radar (a Dutch TV show), the mayor and a housing association.

Table 5.5 Action undertaken by victims (n=92)

Action	Number	%
None	54	58.7
Contacted the police	28	30.4
Contacted GP	3	3.3
Contacted Victim Support	2	2.2
Contacted Riagg	1	1.1
Contacted Anti-stalking Foundation	0	0.0
Contacted fellow victims association	0	0.0
Contacted the Criminal Injuries Compensation Fund	0	0.0
Contacted Stichting M. (Report Crime Anonymously)	0	0.0
Contacted another authority	16	17.4

Conclusions

Of all internet users, 1.1 per cent fell victim to *cyber*stalking in the course of a year. If we look at the influence of background characteristics on victimisation, we see that risks are higher for young people and for respondents without partners. No differences were discovered in the degree of risk between, for example, men and women, or between people from various ethnic backgrounds.

After internet activities were introduced as predictors of stalking, it emerged that the effects of age and the presence of a partner disappear. This means we can attribute the differences between young people and older and between people with and without partners to the various internet activities that they undertake. For instance, we see in this model that conduct and exposure activities are linked to a higher risk of online stalking. Additional analyses (not shown) do indeed show that young people and those who live alone do in fact undertake these activities more frequently. Interaction effects were not significant. Activity and exposure have the same effect on people from various age categories and with various levels of education. For exposure the risk increases, and for activity there is no effect. Additional analyses on the sub-sample show that self-control is unrelated to online stalking.

The foregoing means that prevention and information must not be directed solely at young people, but at people with high exposure in cyberspace. Privacy by default may well be a protective software-based measure for this group; information about the risks of online exposure also presents itself as a potential effective strategy for this group.

Perpetrators use a range of ways to stalk victims, of which email, mobile phone and chat programmes are those most frequently mentioned. In more than half of the cases, the victim knows the perpetrator. Almost one in three victims goes to the police.

5.2 Threats

For a threat in the criminal sense, there must be evidence of the threat of murder, rape, committing overt violence in association with others against persons or property, aggravated assault, kidnapping or arson (Sect. 285 Sr). Incidentally, it is not a requirement that the victim actually feels threatened: it is sufficient that the threat is of the kind and takes place under such circumstances that 'reasonable fear can arise' in the person being threatened that the threat will be carried out.[34] If someone threatens someone else with death on a chat programme such as MSN, this threat constitutes a crime according to Section 285 Sr. This is therefore the same as a crime that takes place on the street.

Threatening someone with digital offences may also fall under Section 285 Sr. Among other things, it is a punishable offence to threaten anyone 'with any crime in which danger to the general security of persons or property or from which collective danger to the provision of services arises'. This includes the crimes that fall under Section 161e Sr and Section 161f Sr. These sections criminalise, for instance, the causing of disruptions in a computerised work, provided there is evidence of the consequence: 'collective danger for the provision of services'. For a detailed legal analysis, see Leukfeldt et al. (2012b).

To assess whether a respondent had been a victim of a threat, we first presented respondents with the following definition: 'a threat is to threaten – in most cases – a person or his/her property with physical violence or death'.

34 Supreme Court 18 January 2005, National Case-Law Number AR7062; Supreme Court 11 December 2007, National Case-Law Number BB7701.

Prevalence

Respondents were asked whether they had fallen victim to threats during the previous twelve-month period. Of all internet users, 1.2 per cent had been victims of a threat, whereby in 54.8 per cent of the cases the internet was also used to make the threat. This means that 0.7 per cent of the internet users surveyed had fallen victim to *cyber* threats in the twelve months prior to the research (n=54). With a 95 per cent confidence interval, between 0.5% and 0.9 per cent of internet users fell victim to cyber threats during a one-year period. Of the 54 victims, 40 (74.1%) had been threatened more than once in the twelve months prior to the research. It is not known whether one perpetrator or various perpetrators were responsible.

Modus operandi

We asked the victims of cyber threats what means the perpetrator had used to make the threats. Multiple answers were possible. Table 5.6 shows that on average just under two means were used to make the threats. It emerged that around four of the ten perpetrators had used all the means cited when threatening their victims.

Table 5.6 Means used by cyber threateners (unweighted)

Means used by cyber threateners	Number	% of victims
Mobile phone	24	44.4
Chat messages	23	42.6
Emails	21	38.9
Social media sites	21	38.9
Other way via the internet	8	14.8
Total number of victims	**54**	**100**

Victims were then asked whether they knew who had threatened them. In 72.0 per cent of the cases the victim knew who the perpetrator was. If the victim ticked 'Other known', the victim was not asked how they knew the perpetrator. In those cases, it is not known whether the perpetrator and the victim knew each other in the real world or only via the internet. If the victim indicated that they knew who it was who threatened them, they could indicate this by ticking more than one answer; two victims did this (see Table 5.7).

Table 5.7 Relationship perpetrator-victim cyber threats (unweighted)

Relationship perpetrator-victim	Number	% of victims
Other known	20	37.0
Perpetrator not known	15	28.0
Ex-partner	10	18.5
Someone from the neighbourhood	4	7.4
Colleague	4	7.4
Family member	2	3.7
Partner	1	1.9
Total number of victims	**54**	**100**

The final question was: 'Do you think that the reason for the threat lay in the fact that you belong to a specific group (e.g. ethnic minority, sexual preference or a public position such as a police officer or politician?' Two-thirds (n=36) of the victims said that they did not belong to a specific group (see Table 5.8). Of the 18 victims who belonged to a minority group, half (nine) said that the reason was indeed the fact that they belonged to a specific group, and another four said that that could have been the cause.

Table 5.8 Reason for cyber threats (unweighted)

	Number	% of victims
Does not belong to a specific group	36	66.7
Belonging to a specific group is not the reason	5	9.3
Belonging to a specific group may be the reason	4	7.4
Belonging to a specific group is the reason	9	16.7
Total	**54**	**100**

Material losses

Four of the 54 victims suffered material loss as a consequence of threats; two of them also knew the extent of the loss: 1,000 and 12,000 euros.

Risk groups

To find out which internet users fall victim to threats, we carried out a bivariate analysis. From Table 5.9 it can be deduced that – similar to what we saw earlier with malware, hacking, e-fraud and cyberstalking – those most vulnerable to cyber threats are internet users between 15 and 24 years of age, internet users who have not (yet) completed primary school, internet users who have less than twelve hours per week paid work and internet users without partners.

From a study into traditional and cyber threat victimisation by Van Wilsem (2011) among more than 6,000 households in the Netherlands, it also emerged that on average less than 1 per cent of internet users fall victim to threats, but that this percentage is significantly higher among internet users aged up to 25 years, namely above 5 per cent.

Table 5.9 Cyber threat victimisation according to background characteristics (weighted, bivariate)[35]

	Cyber threat victims % internet users
Level of education[35]	
No education completed	0.6
Primary education	1.7
Lower vocational education	0.4
VMBO/MAVO	1.1
HAVO/VWO	1.1
MBO	0.6
HBO	0.5
WO	0.2
$\chi^2(7)$	*18.80***
Age category	
15-24	2.2
25-34	0.7
35-44	0.5
45-54	0.3
55-64	0.1
65+	0.2
$\chi^2(5)$	*63.50***
Employment status	
None or <12 hours paid work per week	1.0
12 hours or more paid work per week	0.5
$\chi^2(1)$	*7.14**
Partner	
No partner	1.0
Partner	0.4
$\chi^2(1)$	*10.48***
Ethnic origin	
Native Dutch	0.7
1st generation	0.8
2nd generation, 1 parent	0.4
2nd generation, both parents	1.6
$\chi^2(4)$	*3.90*
Gender	
Male	0.6
Female	0.7
$\chi^2(1)$	*0.27*
Total	**0.7**

* p<0.05, ** p<0.01 (two-sided).

35 VMBO: pre-vocational secondary education; MAVO: junior general secondary education; HAVO: senior general secondary education; VWO: pre-university education; MBO: senior secondary vocational education; HBO: university of applied sciences degree programme; WO: university education.

A multivariate analysis was carried out in order to ascertain whether the bivariate differences hold (see Table 5.10). First we introduced respondent background characteristics into the model. As we did with stalking, we formulated some general assumptions on the basis of the literature.

On the basis of the routine activities theory (Cohen & Felson, 1979; Felson & Clarke, 1998) a link can be expected between victimisation and the kinds of activities that a person undertakes. For this reason we introduced the variables activity and exposure.[36]

Risk awareness possibly also plays a role in victimisation. Internet users who are aware of the risks that they are exposed to online are in a better position to respond to them, and this means that they reduce their risk of becoming a victim.

Alongside risk awareness, knowledge of the devices with which one is online (and is therefore communicating and making payments) can also influence victimisation. For this factor we compiled a computer knowledge variable.[37]

Self-control is also used to explain victimisation (Gottfredson & Hirschi, 1990). Because the statements about self-control were not presented to all respondents, (see Appendix 1), we assessed separately whether it had any effect.

Once again, the threat model comprises three models (see Table 5.10). In the first model, we looked only at the influence of background characteristics on victimisation. The second model maps the influence of respondent attitude and behaviour on victimisation. These models are useful for interpreting the overall Model 3, which incorporates all the variables together with four interaction variables. Using Models 1 and 2, it is possible to determine more accurately why certain variables act as predictors and others do not, and why, for instance, some can be explained away.

With respect to threats, in Model 1 we found increased risks for young people and respondents without work (or only a small job comprising less than twelve hours per week).

In Model 2, where internet activities were introduced, we see that the age effect has declined and that the effect of not being employed is no longer significant. This means that a considerable part of the risk-related age differences for threats can be attributed to the fact that younger people more often undertake internet activities that increase risks. Differences in internet activities explain the significant difference between the employed and the unemployed. This model also shows that exposure is the core risk-increasing activity: the more exposed one is, the more likely one is to be subjected to threats.

36 For a detailed explanation of the methodology used, see Appendix 1.
37 For the composition of these, see the account of the methodology used in Appendix 1.

Table 5.10 Logistic regression of online threats on respondent characteristics

	Model 1		Model 2		Model 3	
	B	S.E.	B	S.E.	B	S.E.
Intercept	-2.569**	0.696	-7.387*	3.014	-11.137*	4.311
Gender (male=ref)	0.022	0.278	0.143	0.289	0.157	0.290
Age	-0.062**	0.013	-0.044**	0.014	-0.059	0.056
Ethnicity (native population=ref)						
1st generation	0.265	0.478	0.026	0.494	0.109	0.503
2nd gen., parent foreign	-1.103	1.015	-1.208	1.019	-1.183	1.021
2nd gen., both parents foreign	0.106	0.734	0.002	0.748	-0.116	0.757
Partner	0.084	0.395	0.225	0.401	0.233	0.407
Level of education	-0.015	0.081	-0.035	0.087	0.830	0.487
Work (12 hours per week or more)	-0.671*	0.311	-0.613	0.313	-0.515	0.318
Degree of internet usage			0.008	0.537	-0.026	0.554
# of PCs in household			-0.134	0.137	-0.125	0.138
Mobile most used app. for internet			0.760	0.412	0.695	0.416
Computer skill			0.283	0.335	0.255	0.338
Risk awareness			0.125	0.275	0.150	0.276
Activity			0.404	0.240	1.736*	0.759
Exposure			1.026**	0.318	0.742	0.810
Buying via the internet			-0.259	0.322	-0.165	0.333
Download			-0.053	0.151	-0.061	0.154
Activity x education					-0.384**	0.136
Activity x age					0.018	0.015
Exposure x education					0.204	0.124
Exposure x age					-0.025	0.018
Nagelkerke R^2	9.8%		13.9%		15.4%	
N	9,123		9,056		9,056	

* p<0.05, ** p<0.01 (two-sided).

Finally, Model 3 shows that no interaction effects are found for exposure. In other words, exposure increases risk across the board, i.e. regardless of age and level of education. However a significant interaction effect was found for activity: it increases risks for those with lower levels of education in particular, and considerably less so for those with higher levels of education. It should be noted that we have no information about the way in which the various groups of respondents make themselves apparent on the internet. Activity comprises emailing and searching for information on the internet. We did not investigate whether 'emailing and looking for information' had different connotations for the various groups. If group A is looking for a different kind of information (and therefore visits a different location on the internet) or sends a different kind of email to group B, it may mean that this activity exposes group A more than group B.

Additional analyses on the sub-sample show that self-control is unrelated to threats. As in the case of fraud victimisation, this was not in line with expectations since earlier research had revealed a link between self-control and victimisation from online threat (see Van Wilsem, 2010a).

Actions undertaken by the victim

Fifty-four respondents fell victim to threats; of these, 38.9 per cent took no action as a consequence of the offence (see Table 5.11) while 27.8 per cent contacted the police. In addition, 37.0 per cent of the victims indicated that they had undertaken other steps. The most frequently cited actions were 'approached the perpetrator to try to stop the threats' (11.1%), 'contacted those responsible for the medium where the threat was made' (9.3%) and 'contacted the perpetrator's school' (5.6%). Other victims avoided the offender, 'laughed at the perpetrator' or contacted the parents or the Youth Care Office.

Table 5.11 Action undertaken by victims (n=54)

Action	Number	%
Nothing	21	38.9
Contacted the police	15	27.8
Other action	20	37.0
Total number of victims	**54**	**100**

Conclusions

Of the internet users surveyed, 0.7 per cent fell victim to cyber threats. Around three quarters of these respondents were threatened more than once. The same number knew the person who had threatened them. Four respondents suffered financial loss as a consequence of the threat.

If we look at the influence of background characteristics on victimisation, we see that risks are higher for young people and for respondents without work (or those with a job comprising less than twelve hours per week). After internet activities as predictors of threats were introduced, we saw that the age effect declines considerably and that the effect of not being employed is no longer significant. Part of the age-related increase in risk can be attributed to the fact that younger people more often undertake internet activities that increase risks. It accounts entirely for the differences in risk exposure between the employed and the unemployed. This model also shows that exposure is the core risk-increasing activity: the more exposed one is, the more likely one is to be subjected to threats.[38]

Finally, once interaction effects were introduced, no interaction effects were found for exposure, but some were found for activity. In other words, exposure increases risk across the board, i.e. regardless of age and level of education.

38 Reminder: activity comprises emailing and searching for information on the internet. Exposure comprises untargeted surfing, downloading, using MSN, skyping, chatting, visiting forums and social media sites and using Twitter. For a detailed explanation of the methodology used, see Appendix 1.

Activity increases risks for those with lower levels of education in particular, and to a considerably lesser extent for those with higher levels of education.

6 Multiple victimisation

6.1 Determining multiple victimisation

Annually, 8.5 per cent of internet users fall victim to at least one of the kinds of offences with a digital component that we investigated. There is a group of people who are likely to fall victim more than once. This group is interesting because interventions directed at this group could be more effective than interventions aimed at other internet users. As a small group, they are victims of a relatively large share of the offences.

Victimology distinguishes between repeated victimisation and multiple victimisation. Repeated victimisation means that a respondent falls victim to the same offence more frequently than once in a period of twelve months. Multiple victimisation means that a respondent falls victim to various offences in the same period of time. The questions that arise about the latter group of victims are: Who they are? And why are they victims of various crimes? So far we have discussed our research into the following incidents:

1. Malware: respondents have noticed malware on the computer they use to go on to the internet.
2. Hacking, defacing: a profile page or website was changed against the owner's wishes.
3. Hacking, mail hacked: someone broke into or logged on to an email account without the respondent's permission.
4. Hacking, PC hacked: someone hacked the computer and destroyed, changed or stole data.
5. Hacking as modus operandi: the respondent fell victim to hacking as part of another offence.
6. Fraud via auction or retail sites: 'paid but not received'.
7. Fraud via auction or retail sites: 'sold but no payment received'.
8. Identity theft: the respondent's identity was stolen using ICT.
9. Identity theft: the respondent's identity was abused for financial gain using ICT.
10. Advance fee fraud: the respondent paid advanced fee for a non-existent investment a contact on the internet.
11. Stalking: ICT was used to stalk the respondent.
12. Threats: ICT was used to threaten the respondent.

When determining whether a respondent was a multiple victim, we did not take malware into account because respondents were only asked whether they noticed malware. We also did not take hacking as a modus operandi into account because a victim who was hacked for identity theft, for example, was actually only a one-off victim. For the purpose of this research respondents are therefore only considered to be multiple victims of offences with a digital component if they were victims of two or more of the above crimes numbered 2, 3, 4, 6, 7, 8, 9, 10, 11 and 12.

6.2 Prevalence and risk groups

Of the victims, 17.6 per cent were victims of two or more different types of crimes, which equates to 1.5 per cent of internet users. Of the internet users surveyed, 7.0 per cent fell victim to one kind of crime. Overall, therefore, 8.5 per cent fell victim to one or more crimes.[39]

Table 6.1 shows that internet users without partners are at greater risk of becoming multiple victims. Furthermore, the distribution of victimisation across the various age groups is not coincidental. The table shows that the percentage of multiple victimisation is particularly high in the 15- to 34-year-old age group. We saw this prevalence in this younger age group in previous sections. We also saw in a study of police files that cybercrime is apparently linked to young people (Leukfeldt et al., 2010; Leukfeldt & Stol, 2011). In-depth analysis revealed that younger internet users are a group who require special attention.

6.3 Multiple victimisation: conclusions

Over a one-year period, 8.5 per cent of internet users fall victim to at least one of the offences with a digital component that we list in Section 6.1. Multiple victimisation refers to the victimisation of an internet victim related to more than one of these crimes. Of the internet users in our research, 1.5 per cent were subjected to multiple victimisation. The percentage of multiple victimisation is particularly high in the 15- to 34-year-old age group. Internet users without partner are also more likely to fall victim, relatively speaking. In additional in-depth analysis, special attention should be paid to younger internet users.

39 This refers to the crimes mentioned in Section 6.1, i.e. 2, 3, 4, 6, 7, 8, 9, 10, 11 and 12.

Table 6.1 Multiple victimisation according to background characteristics (weighted, bivariate)

	Multiple victimisation % internet users
Level of education[40]	
No education completed	1.2
Primary education	2.2
Lower vocational schooling	0.4
VMBO/MAVO	1.8
HAVO/VWO	1.5
MBO	1.6
HBO	1.6
WO	0.9
$\chi^2(7)$	*11.74*
Age category	
15-24	3.1
25-34	2.3
35-44	1.1
45-54	1.0
55-64	0.6
65+	0.5
$\chi^2(5)$	*53.21***
Employment status	
None or <12 hours paid work per week	1.5
12 hours or more paid work per week	1.4
$\chi^2(1)$	*0.07*
Partner	
No partner	2.0
Partner	0.9
$\chi^2(1)$	*18.22***
Ethnic origin	
Native Dutch	1.3
1st generation	1.9
2nd generation, 1 parent	1.4
2nd generation, both parents	3.2
$\chi^2(3)$	*7.41*
Gender	
Male	1.3
Female	1.6
$\chi^2(1)$	*2.01*
Total	**1.5**

*p<0.05, **p<0.01.

40 VMBO: pre-vocational secondary education; MAVO: junior general secondary education; HAVO: senior general secondary education; VWO: pre-university education; MBO: senior secondary vocational education; HBO: university of applied sciences degree programme; WO: university education

7 Police

This section is about the role of police in the context of offences with a digital component, seen through the eyes of internet users. Do they think the police are responsible for their security in the digital world? And if a victim reports an offence with a digital component, do the police take statements? And to what extent are victims satisfied with the police response to reporting cybercrime?

7.1 Responsibility

Do members of the public think that the police are the appropriate organisation to safeguard security on the internet? There are, after all, also other actors who should shoulder responsibility: for instance, financial institutions (regarding digital payments), website owners, internet service providers and the internet users themselves.

Figure 7.1 Responsible for security on the internet according to members of the public

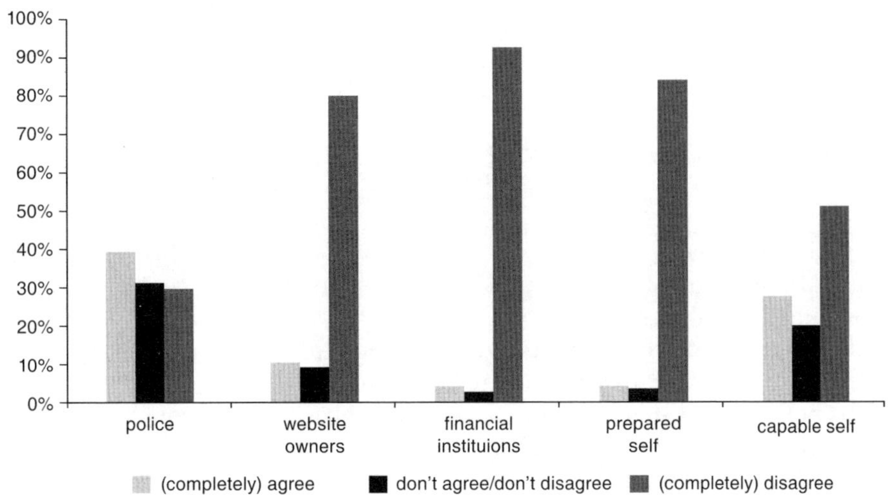

Figure 7.1 gives the answers to the question of who ought to safeguard security on the internet. According to internet users, it is financial institutions (93.4%) and website owners (79.9%) in particular who are responsible for security on the internet. Of all the internet users surveyed, 85.1 per cent indicated that they

themselves were also prepared to do something about their security on the internet. However, over a quarter of internet users (27.1%) felt that they were unable to fully safeguard their own security. Almost three out of ten internet users (29.0%) felt that the police also have a responsibility to safeguard security on the internet.

7.2 Relationship between police and members of the public

Contact with the police

In Sections 3 to 5 we discussed which organisations the victims contacted in response to offences, according to the kind of crime they fell victim to. In this section we examine contact with the police more closely.

On average, 13.4 per cent of the victims contacted the police. Table 7.1 shows that this percentage is relatively high for stalking and threats (30.4 and 27.8% respectively). Fraud via auction or retail sites followed at 19.6%. The percentages are small for victims who contacted the police as a consequence of advance fee fraud and hacking (in this case: defacing, or hacking a computer or email account) (5.6 and 4.1% respectively).

Table 7.1 Contact with the police as a consequence of victimisation, unweighted

	Number of individual victims	Respondents who contacted the police at least once (n)	%
Stalking	92	28	30.4
Threats	54	15	27.8
Paid but not received	204	43	21.1
Identity fraud and/or theft	63	12	15.6
Sold but not paid	25	2	8.0
Advance fee fraud	18	1	5.6
Hacking (specifically asked)	339	14	4.1
Total	**876**	**117**	**13.4**

The police response

We asked the victims how the police had responded to being contacted about these crimes. Possible answers were:

1. The police took a statement and traced or tried to trace the perpetrator.
2. The police took a statement and are still trying to trace the perpetrator.
3. The police took a statement and haven't heard back from them.
4. The police recorded the crime but did not take a statement.
5. The police gave advice, but did not record the crime or take a statement.
6. The police said that there was nothing they could do about it.
7. The police did not take the person making the report seriously.
8. Other response from the police.

In order to analyse the police response further, we defined three separate categories:

1. the police took a statement (responses 1, 2 and/or 3);
2. the police recorded the crime or gave advice (response 4 or 5, and not response 1, 2, 3, 6, 7 or 8);
3. the police did not undertake any criminal action (response 6, 7 or 8, and not response 1, 2, 2, 3, 4 or 5);

We asked about the police response in three places in the questionnaire, which gave us information about their responses to three groups of crimes:

- when respondents contacted the police because they had fallen victim to one or both kinds of fraud via auction and/or retail sites;
- because there was contact as a consequence of advance fee fraud and/or identity fraud;
- because there was contact as a consequence of stalking, threats, defacing, computer hacking and/or email account hacking.

Table 7.2 shows the police responses cited by the respondents for the three groups of offences with a digital component.

Table 7.2 The police response (unweighted)

Response	Took a statement		Recorded it or gave advice		No criminal action	
	Number	%	Number	%	Number	%
(€) Fraud via auction or retail sites (n=45)	26	57.8	7	15.6	12	26.7
(€) Advance fee fraud and identity fraud (n=13)	7	53.8	3	23.1	3	23.1
(P) Stalking, threats, defacing, computer hacked, email hacked (n=63)	18	28.6	33	52.4	12	19.0

(€): crimes targeting money; (P): crimes against the victim's person or personal privacy.

When respondents contacted the police in connection with fraud via auction or retail sites, the police took statements in 57.8 per cent of the cases. Police statements were taken in 53.8 per cent of cases involving advance fee fraud/identity fraud; and for hacking and personal offences, the police took statements in 28.6 per cent of the reported cases. In the case if personal offences, the police were more likely to record the crime or give advice (52.4%).

Looking at the first two groups together 'crimes targeting the victim's money' and comparing them to the last group (stalking etc.) – which we can characterise as 'crimes directed in the private sphere or the victim's privacy' –

we see that the percentages for statements taken are 56.9 per cent and 28.6 per cent respectively. The difference between the two is significant.[41]

Satisfaction with police response

We also assessed whether victims were satisfied with the response they got from the police. Victims could indicate their level of satisfaction on a 5-point scale, ranging from extremely dissatisfied (1) to extremely satisfied (5). Satisfaction with police response was covered in the same place in the questionnaire as police response, and can thus not be attributed with certainty to any one particular offence. We therefore once again report findings for levels of satisfaction in the three crime clusters (see Table 7.3). Average satisfaction levels for police response to fraud via auction or retail sites are 2.7. Handling of advance fee fraud and/or identity abuse scores 3.4, and handling of crimes against privacy 3.0.

Table 7.3 Victim's satisfaction levels regarding the police response (5-point scale)

	Satisfaction on average	Took a statement (A)	Did not take a statement (G)	Significance (A versus G)
(€) Fraud via auction or retail sites	2.7	3.2	2.0	(n=45, p<0.001)
(€) Advance fee fraud, Identity fraud and/or theft	3.4	4.0	2.7	(n=13, p=0.083)
(P) Stalking, threats, defacing, computer hacked, email hacked	3.0	3.6	2.8	(n=63, p=0.022)

(€): crimes targeting money; (P): crimes against the victim's person or personal privacy.

Because victim satisfaction may be related to police response, we investigated whether satisfaction differed among victims according to whether the police did or did not take a statement. For fraud via auction and retail sites, for hacking and crimes against privacy, we discovered that victims from whom the police did take a statement were more satisfied with the response than those from whom the police did not take a statement. The number of victims who went to the police because of advance fee fraud and/or identity abuse is small, which means that the difference between 4.0 and 2.7 is not significant.

From Table 7.3 (columns A and G) it can be deduced that taking statements contributes to higher levels of satisfaction among victims. But this is not the whole story. For crimes targeting the victim's person or their privacy (P), the police are less likely to take statements than for crimes targeting the victim's money (€) (28.6% versus 56.9% – see Table 7.2). But there is very little difference between the two groups in terms of average satisfaction towards the police (see Table 7.3, column 2). So merely taking down statements is not the only factor

41 P<0.01; z score for proportions.

that influences the public's levels of satisfaction. Apparently the police are not given to taking statements about crimes targeting persons or their privacy ((P) see Table 7.2); yet victims leave in a reasonably satisfied frame of mind (see Table 7.3). This may be related to the positive attention that the police give to the victim (compare Van der Vijver, 1993). Our research findings therefore do not warrant the conclusion that the police can satisfy the public by simply taking statements. For crimes in the private sphere or privacy, the police demonstrate that they can also satisfy the victims without necessarily taking down statements. Precisely how the type of offence, the police response and the public's satisfaction are interrelated (what leads to what) should be the subject of further study.

Role of the police: conclusion

Twenty-nine per cent of internet users felt that the police, too, have a responsibility to safeguard security on the internet. However, the respondents were more inclined to place responsibility with financial institutions and website owners.

The percentage of victims who contact the police is not high: it varies from 4.1 per cent (hacking) to 30.4 per cent (stalking): on average 13.4 per cent. The police response to the different kinds of reports varies. For fraud via auction or retail sites and for advance fee fraud and identity fraud – in short: crimes targeting the victim's money – the police took statements in more than half of the cases reported. For crimes targeting persons or privacy (hacking, stalking, threatens etc.), the percentage is considerably lower at 28.6 per cent. Victims from whom statements were taken were considerably more satisfied about the police response than victims for whom this was not done. Yet it is not simply a case of deducing that if the police take statements more readily, members of the public will be more satisfied. After all, even though the police are more inclined to take statements relating to crimes targeting money than to crimes in the private sphere (see Table 7.2), the former are not more satisfied about the police than the latter (see Table 7.3). This indicates that there are more factors that influence the satisfaction of members of the public: these may be related to the capacity of the police to give the right kind of positive attention in offences that impact on privacy aspects or the victim's person. Exactly how this works is the subject of further study.

8 Conclusions

8.1 Victimisation

Key figures victimisation

In the introduction to this publication, we presented the figures from the few studies relating to the volume of offences with a digital component. On the basis of these figures, the expectation was that victimisation would be significant. In terms of prevalence, our victim research shows that, in the twelve months prior to the survey, 8.5 per cent of all internet users fell victim to at least one of the offences with a digital component that we surveyed (see Table 8.1). The table also gives the prevalence figures for the individual crimes. Finally, 16.7 per cent of the respondents noticed malware their computer.

The key figures for crime that were revealed by our research show that, on an annual basis, of all Dutch internet users:

- 4.3 per cent fall victim to hacking;
- 3.5 per cent fall victim to e-fraud (fraud via retail or auction sites, identity fraud, advance fee fraud).

Table 8.1 Prevalence of victimisation relating to offences with a digital component

Offence	Prevalence (% of internet users)	Confidence interval (95%)
Hacking: defacing	1.5	1.3 – 1.7%
Hacking: computer hacked	0.7	0.5 – 0.9
Hacking: email hacked	2.9	2.6 – 3.2
Hacking: as MO	0.8	0.6 – 1.0
Hacking: total	*4.3*	*3.9 – 4.7*
Paid but not received	2.4	2.1 – 2.7
Sold but not paid	0.3	0.2 – 0.4
Identity theft and/or fraud	0.8	0.6 – 1.0
Advance fee fraud	0.2	0.1 – 0.3
Financial offences: total	*3.5*	*3.1 – 3.9*
Stalking	1.1	0.9 – 1.3
Threats	0.7	0.5 – 0.9
Offences in the private sphere: total	*1.5*	*1.3 – 1.7*
Crimes: total excl. malware	*8.5*	*7.9 – 9.1*
Malware noticed	16.7	15.9 – 17.5

We did not survey all crimes with a digital component in this research. There are simply too many to cover.[42] Also, not all offences can be surveyed through victim research because people do not always realise that they are victims (e.g. that they are part of a botnet, or that they have malware on their computer), or are not aware that there is a digital component to their victimisation (e.g. cases involving theft of personal details using hacking and subsequent misuse of this information in the offline world). The prevalence of victimisation relating to offences with a digital component is in all probability higher than the overall percentage given in Table 8.1.

Table 8.2 compares victimisation from offences with a digital component with some other victimisation percentages, such as those found in the national Integrated Security Monitor 2011 (CBS, 2012). Traditionally, the Netherlands is the land of bicycle theft (4.8%) because it is the offence that normally gets highest scores in classic victim research. The findings from our research show that the Netherlands can now be characterised as the country of bicycle theft (4.8%) and hacking (4.3%).

The figures show that, in terms of prevalence, cybercrime is a serious presence in the daily lives of the public. Cybercrime has taken on the character of high volume crime: ordinary crime interwoven with daily life. This means that knowledge about how to handle reports of cybercrime, and then how to tackle these, must be present across the breadth of the police organisation. This is not the case as it stands now (Stol et al., 2012). The dark number is high. Reporting of cybercrime may increase significantly if, for instance, the public decide that cybercrime is a matter for the police.

The interrelatedness of cybercrime with daily life that is reflected in the figures raises the question of whether the offences discussed here should be labelled 'cybercrime', which suggests that it is a separate kind of offence (see Sect. 1.1). The fact that hacking is almost as widespread as bicycle theft means that this 'cybercrime in the narrow sense' has moved from being a specialist offence to an offence under general criminal law. Much of what we have labelled cybercrime thus far has outgrown the status of specialist crime and can therefore be treated as nothing less than 'crime in a digital society'.

42 See for instance the *Guide to offences with a digital component [Handreiking voor delicten met een digitale component]*, which alone deals with 28 different crimes (Leukfeldt et al., 2012b).

Table 8.2 Victimisation relating to offences with a digital component and classic crime in the Netherlands

Type of offence	% of victims	N (sample size)*
Digital offences: earlier research #		
Threats	2.2	6,900
Fraud	2.5	6,200
Digital offences: this research		
Hacking	4.3	9,000
E-fraud retail and auction sites	2.7	9,000
Stalking	1.1	9,000
Identity fraud and/or theft	0.8	9,000
Threats	0.7	9,000
Advance fee fraud	0.2	9,000
Classic crime ^		
Bicycle theft	4.8	220,000
Threats	3.5	220,000
Pickpocketing	1.7	220,000
Domestic burglary	1.5	220,000
Assault	1.0	220,000

* Rounded off; # Van Wilsem, 2010a, 2010b; ^ CBS, 2012.

Multiple victimisation

Multiple victimisation occurs when someone falls victim to more than one kind of offence. Of internet users, 1.5 per cent were multiple victims of at least one of the kinds of offences with a digital component that we investigated. The percentage of multiple victimisation is particularly high in the 15- to 34-year-old age group.

Factors that play a role in victimisation

Age is a factor that plays a role in several types of offence with a digital component. Young people (particularly those aged between 15 and 34 years) have an increased risk of being victimised. This is apparent for all the crimes. For the rest, victimisation is particularly linked to the internet activities that are undertaken and to high-risk internet behaviour – activities and behaviour, incidentally, that are undertaken and occur among young people in particular. These findings may be an indication that young people run an above average risk of falling victim because of their age and related behaviour. As one becomes older, one's behaviour changes and the risk of victimisation diminishes, a trend that is parallel to the fact that young people run an above average risk of becoming the victim of a traffic accident. There is another possibility. It could be that the young people in our research will continue to behave differently on the internet compared to the preceding generation (the older people in our research). In which case, victimisation will not diminish with age. Our research, however, does not give a definitive answer to this because it is a synchronic study: it reflects the situation at a specific point in time.

The activities and behaviour that increase the risk of victimisation differ per offence:

- For hacking the frequency with which one surfs the internet, a high level of exposure[43] and not using a virus scanner are determining factors. For the rest, we noted a lower risk of being hacked among people who are conscious of the risks that accompany internet usage.
- For victimisation from fraud via auction and retail sites (the type where payment was made but nothing received), increased risk levels are linked to higher levels of risky internet behaviour. This is linked in particular to high levels of activity (searching for information on the internet and emailing).
- For identity fraud, it emerged that risk is increased by activities on the internet (emailing and searching for information on the internet) as well as participating in paid contact or dating sites. For the rest, the more PCs in the household, the smaller the risk. However, our research does not offer an answer to the question of why this should be.
- For stalking, we see that activity and exposure are linked to an increased risk of victimisation. Additional analyses show that young people and those who live alone undertake these activities more frequently.
- The same applies to threats: exposure increases the risk of victimisation. Young people in particular are vulnerable to online threats through their exposure, and their exposure probably gives rise to threats. Exposure increases risk across the board, i.e. regardless of age and level of education. Activity increases risks for those with lower levels of education in particular, and to a considerably lesser degree for those with higher levels of education.

In summary, age and internet activities are therefore the most important predictors of victimisation. For prevention policy, the findings taken as a whole indicate that attention should focus on young people and the activities that they undertake on the internet, because activities on the internet not only bring them closer to their objectives, but also to risks. The findings call for attention to be paid to the question of how active internet use can go hand in hand with limited levels of exposure. In that context the focus could be on caution among users, but also on the option of using rules and aids to design user environments such that user activities do not lead to unintended (automatic) follow-up actions and/or unintended visibility.

It is noteworthy that limited self-control is not a predictor of victimisation, except in the case of hacking. This is not in line with the findings of Van Wilsem (2010b), who did find this link. Further research is required in this respect. A hypothesis for such research could be: the more information there is on the internet about a large group, the less relevant self-control is as a protection

43 Reminder: activity comprises emailing and searching for information on the internet. Exposure comprises untargeted surfing, downloading, using MSN, skyping, chatting, visiting forums and social media sites and using Twitter. For a detailed explanation of the methodology used, see Appendix 1.

factor. In other words: more and more information about people with high levels of self-control will gradually also become available on the internet – which means that they will also be running greater risks of becoming victims, with the result that those with low self-control will no longer be the prime target.

Internationalisation

For fraud involving paying for but not receiving a product or service (2.4% of all internet users were victims of this), one fifth of the cases (19.2%) involved contact with a seller in a foreign country, according to the victims. On the basis of a study of police files, Leukfeldt et al. (2010) found that in 14.5 per cent of e-fraud cases the perpetrators operated from abroad. Therefore, a significant portion of the e-fraud cases that the police have to handle has an international context. For the police, this introduces a new aspect to their workload because, in the pre-internet era, police teams scarcely ever had to deal with reports involving suspects from outside the country. If such cases did arise, they were exceptional and were soon passed on to regional detective teams. Because of the internet, the police now regularly get reports about relatively minor cases involving suspects from abroad. This is a new phenomenon that could be labelled 'international high volume crime'. The police organisation is not designed to handle this and international police collaboration is not geared to it. Investigation teams cannot take on all minor cases involving suspects from abroad. The basic teams are not in a position to handle international cases. This international component is not expected to diminish in time. It is more likely to increase, for instance as members of the public begin to report these cases more frequently because they see that the police are actively engaging in this field of crime. The question arises of how the police can organise an adequate response to this new international component in its workload.

8.2 The role of the police

The role of the police in safeguarding security in cyberspace

Most respondents consider financial institutions and website owners to be responsible for security on the internet. 29.0 per cent of internet users felt that the police, too, have a responsibility to safeguard security on the internet.

Contact with the police

There were 786 victims (weighted). Of these, 117 contacted the police on at least one occasion, i.e. 14.9 per cent. This percentage is lower than the average percentage that was measured in the Integrated Security Monitor with regard to the offline crimes it surveyed. Only the percentage of *statements taken* is significantly higher (26.3%) in the Safety Monitor; the percentage for *reporting* offline crimes is even higher at 34.5 per cent (CBS, 2012). In other words, the dark number for offences with a digital component is significantly larger than the dark number for classic crime. We can undoubtedly find part of the explanation for this in the finding that internet users do not immediately think of the police when they are asked who is responsible for security on the internet, but are more likely to think of financial institutions and website owners instead (see Sect. 7.1).

For offences with a digital component, percentages for crimes reported to the police are between 4.1 per cent (hacking) and 30.4 per cent (stalking) (on average 14.9%). The police response to the different kinds of reports varies. The police took statements in more than half of the cases reported relating to fraud via auction or retail sites, and for advance fee fraud and identity fraud. For hacking and crimes against privacy, the reporting percentage is significantly lower at 28.6 per cent.

Once the police become more active in combating cybercrime, members of the public can be expected to turn to the police more frequently and the police will be more inclined to take statements. Both the percentage reported and the percentage of statements taken will rise as a result.

Satisfaction with the police

On a scale of 1 to 5, the handling of fraud via retail sites scores 2.7, the handling of identity fraud and advance fee fraud, 3.4 and the handling of crimes in the private sphere, 3.0. In our analysis, taking down statements is linked to satisfaction levels with regard to police response. But merely taking down statements may not necessarily enhance levels of satisfaction among members of the public. When it comes to the police, satisfaction levels among members of the public do not increase in quite such a mono-dimensional fashion (compare Van der Vijver, 1993). This was also reflected in our research.

For crimes targeting the victim's person or their privacy, the police are less likely to take statements than for crimes targeting the victim's money (see Table 7.2). Yet there is very little difference between the two groups in terms of satisfaction with the police (see Table 7.3, column 2). So merely taking down statements is not the only factor that influences the public's levels of satisfaction. Apparently the police are not given to taking statements about crimes targeting persons or their privacy (see Table 7.2), yet victims leave in a reasonably satisfied frame of mind (see Table 7.3). This satisfaction may be related to the positive attention that the police give to the victims. Exactly how the type of offence, the police response and the public's satisfaction are interrelated is the subject of further study.

References

Bethlehem, J.G. (1999). Cross-sectional Research. In: H.J. Ader & G.J. Mellenbergh (Eds.), *Research Methodology in the Social Behavioural and Life Science*. London: Sage Publications.

Bethlehem, J.G. (2006). *Representativiteit van web-surveys – Een illusie?* Voorburg: Centraal Bureau voor de Statistiek.

Bethlehem, J.G. (2007). *Reducing the bias of web survey based estimates*. Voorburg/Heerlen: Centraal Bureau voor de Statistiek.

Blauw Research (2010). *Online thuiswinkelen in Nederland. Essential Facts*. Rotterdam: Blauw Research.

Brecko, B.N. & R. Carstens (2006). *Online data collection in SITES 2006: Paper versus web survey – Do they provide comparable results?* Proceedings of the 2nd IEA International Research Conference, Washington, DC.

Buelens, B.A.H. & J.A. van den Brakel (2011a). *Inference in surveys with sequential mixed-mode data collection* (CBS discussion paper). Heerlen: Centraal Bureau voor de Statistiek.

Buelens, B.A.H. & J.A. van den Brakel (2011b). *Weging integrale veiligheidsmonitor 2010* (CBS-nota, BPA-nr. DMK-2011-03-02-BBUS). Heerlen: Centraal Bureau voor de Statistiek.

Buissant des Amorie, C. (1960). Kan een MO-systeem ons bij de oplossing van gepleegde misdrijven helpen? *Tijdschrift voor de Politie*, 109 (3), 43-45.

CBS (2009). *De digitale economie*. Voorburg/Heerlen: Centraal Bureau voor de Statistiek.

CBS (2012). *Integrale veiligheidsmonitor 2011. Landelijke Rapportage*. Den Haag/Heerlen: CBS.

Cohen, L. & M. Felson (1979). Social change and crime rate trends: a routine activity approach. *American Sociological Review*, 44, 588-608.

Coleman, J. (1973). *The mathematics of collective action*. London: Heinemann.

Coleman, J. (1990). *Foundations of social theory*. Cambridge (MA): Harvard University Press.

Denscombe, M. (2006). Web-based questionnaires and the mode effect: An evaluation based on item nonresponse rates and data contents of near-identical questionnaires delivered in different modes. *Social Science Computer Review*, 24 (2), 246-254.

Denscombe, M. (2008). Item non-response rates: a comparison of online and paper questionaires. *International Journal of Social Research Methodology*, 11 (3), 1-10.

Domenie, M.M.L., E.R. Leukfeldt & W.Ph. Stol (2009). *Werkaanbod cybercrime bij de politie. Een verkennend onderzoek naar de omvang van het geregistreerde werkaanbod cybercrime*. Leeuwarden: Noordelijke Hogeschool Leeuwarden.

Domenie, M.M.L., E.R. Leukfeldt & W.Ph. Stol (2011). *Verantwoording pilot slachtofferonderzoek cybercrime*. Leeuwarden: Noordelijke Hogeschool Leeuwarden.

Elias, N. & J.L. Scotson (1965). *The Established and the Outsiders: a Sociological Enquiry Into Community Problems*. London: Cass.

Felson, M. & R.V. Clarke (1998). Opportunity makes the thief: Practical theory for crime prevention. In: B. Webb (Ed.), *Police Research Series* (paper 98). London: Home Office.

Ferwerda, H. (2008). Theorie over criminaliteit. In: W.Ph. Stol & A.Ph. van Wijk (red.), *Inleiding criminaliteit en opsporing*. Den Haag: Boom Juridische uitgevers.

Finch, E. (2007). The problem of stolen identity and the Internet. In: Y. Jewkes (Ed.), *Crime Online*. Uffculme: William Publishing.

Gottfredson, M.R. & T. Hirschi (1990). *A general theory of crime*. Stanford: Stanford University Press.

Hesseling, R. (2010) Vooral vermogensmisdrijven bepalen cybercrime. *Secondant*, 24 (5) 6-13.

Hulst, R.C. van der & R.J.M. Neve (2008). *High-tech crime: Inventarisatie van literatuur over soorten criminaliteit en hun daders.* Den Haag: WODC.

Jansen, J. (2012). Online financieel-economische criminaliteit. In: J. Kerstens & W.Ph. Stol (red.), *Jeugd en cybersafety: Online slachtoffer- en daderschap onder Nederlandse jongeren.* Den Haag: Boom Lemma uitgevers.

Kerstens, J. & W.Ph. Stol (red.) (2012). *Jeugd en cybersafety: Online slachtoffer- en daderschap onder Nederlandse jongeren.* Den Haag: Boom Lemma uitgevers.

KLPD (2007). *Cybercrime - Focus op High Tech Crime: Deelrapport Criminaliteitsbeeld 2007.* Rotterdam: Thieme Media Center.

KLPD (2010). *High Tech Crime, criminaliteitsbeeldanalyse 2009.* Driebergen: KLPD.

Leukfeldt, E.R. & W.Ph. Stol (2011). *Internetoplichters uitgelicht. E-fraudeurs en klassieke fraudeurs vergeleken.* De Bilt/Leeuwarden: Programma Aanpak Cybercrime/NHL Hogeschool.

Leukfeldt, E.R., M.M.L. Domenie & W.Ph. Stol (2010). *Verkenning Cybercrime in Nederland 2009.* Den Haag: Boom Juridische uitgevers.

Leukfeldt, E.R., A. Kentgens, B. Frans, M. Toutenhoofd, W.Ph. Stol & E. Stamhuis (2012b). *Alledaags politiewerk in een gedigitaliseerde wereld. Handreiking voor delicten met een digitale component.* Den Haag: Boom Lemma uitgevers.

Leukfeldt, E.R., S. Veenstra, M. Domenie & W.Ph. Stol (2012a). *De strafrechtketen in een gedigitaliseerde samenleving. Een onderzoek naar de strafrechtelijke afhandeling van cybercrime.* De Bilt/Leeuwarden: PAC/NHL.

Lissenberg, E. (2001). Definities van criminaliteit. In: E. Lissenberg, S. van Ruller & R. van Swaaningen (red.), *Tegen de regels 4. Een inleiding in de criminologie.* Nijmegen: Ars Aequi Libri.

Lozar Manfreda, K., M. Bosnjak, I. Haas & V. Vehovar (2006). Web surveys versus other survey modes. A meta-analysis comparing response rates. *International Journey of Market Research,* 50 (1), 79-104.

McAfee (2006). *Virtual Criminology Report. Organised Crime and the Internet.* www.mcafee.com. Laatst geraadpleegd op 19 april 2008.

McAfee (2007). *Virtual Criminology Report: Cybercrime The Next Wave.* www.mcafee.com. Laatst geraadpleegd op 19 april 2008.

Nieuwenbroek, N. & H.J. Boonstra (2002). *Bascula 4.0 Reference Manual.* Heerlen: Centraal Bureau voor de Statistiek.

Noordelijke Hogeschool Leeuwarden (2011). *Vragenlijst onderzoek naar (on)veiligheid in de digitale wereld* (digitale publicatie). Leeuwarden: NHL Hogeschool.

Ollmann, G. (2004). *The Phishing Guide (Part 1) Understanding and Preventing Phishing Attacks.* NGSSoftware Insight Security Research: www.ngsconsulting.com.

PAC (2008). *Definities van Cybercrime. Een onderzoek naar en toetsing van diverse bestaande definities van Cybercrime, om te komen tot één werkbare, herkenbare en gedragen definitie voor intern en extern gebruik door het PAC.* De Bilt: interne notitie.

Pratt, T.C., & Cullen F.T. (2000). The empirical status of Gottfredson and Hirschi's General Theory of Crime: A meta-analysis. *Criminology, 38,* 931-64.

R Development Core Team (2011). *R: A language and environment for statistical computing.* Wenen: R Foundation for Statistical Computing. www.R-project.org/.

Regeerakkoord (2010). Vrijheid en verantwoordelijkheid. Regeerakkoord VVD-CDA. www.rijksoverheid.nl/documenten-en-publicaties/rapporten/2010/09/30/regeerakkoord-vvd-cda.html.

Särndal, C.-E., B. Swensson & J. Wretman (1992). *Model Assisted Survey Sampling.* New York: Springer Verlag.

Schreck, C.J., E.A. Stewart & B.S. Fisher (2006). Self-control, victimization, and their influence on risky lifestyles: A longitudinal analysis using panel data. *Journal of Quantitative Criminology,* 22, 319-340.

Sikkel, D. (2010). *Opzet enquête financieel-economische criminaliteit en computercriminaliteit.* Leidschendam: WODC.

Stol, W.Ph. (1996). *Politie-optreden en informatietechnologie*. Lelystad: Koninklijke Vermande.

Stol, W.Ph., E.R. Leukfeldt & H. Klap (2012). Cybercrime en politie. Een schets van de Nederlandse situatie anno 2012. *Justitiële Verkenningen*, 38 (1), 25-39.

Stol, W.Ph., R.J. Treeck & A.E.B.M. van der Ven (1999). *Criminaliteit in cyberspace – een praktijkonderzoek naar aard, ernst en aanpak in Nederland*. Den Haag: Elsevier.

Taylor, R.W., T.J. Caeti, D.K. Loper, E.J. Fritsch & J. Liederbach (2006). *Digital crime and digital terrorism: The criminology of computer crime*. New Jersey: Pearson Prentice Hall.

Tennekes, M., E. de Jonge & P.J.H. Daas (2011). *Visual profiling of large statistical datasets* (CBS-discussion paper, BPA-nr DMK-2011-02-15-MTES). Heerlen/Den Haag: Centraal Bureau voor de Statistiek.

Toutenhoofd-Visser, M.H., S. Veenstra, M.M.L. Domenie, E.R. Leukfeldt & W.Ph. Stol (2009). *Politie en Cybercrime. Intake en Eerste Opvolging. Een onderzoek naar de intake van het werkaanbod cybercrime door de politie*. Leeuwarden: NHL.

Vijver, C.D. van der (1993). *De burger en de zin van strafrecht*. Lelystad: Koninklijke Vermande.

Vries, U.R.M.Th. de, H. Tigchelaar, M. van der Linden & A.M. Hol (2007). *Identiteitsfraude: een afbakening: Een internationale begripsvergelijking en analyse van nationale strafbepalingen*. Utrecht: Universiteit Utrecht.

Wilsem, J.A. van (2010a). Digitale en traditionele bedreiging vergeleken. Een studie naar risicofactoren van slachtofferschap. *Tijdschrift voor Criminologie*, 52 (1), 73-87.

Wilsem, J.A., van (2010b). Gekocht maar niet gekregen. Slachtofferschap van online oplichting nader onderzocht. *Tijdschrift voor Veiligheid*, 9 (4), 16-29.

Wilsem, J.A. van (2011). Worlds tied together? Online and non-domestic routine activities and their impact on digital and traditional threat victimization. *European Journal of Criminology*, 8 (2), 115-127.

Yar, M. (2006). *Cybercrime and Society*. Gateshead: Athenaeum Press.

Appendix 1: Methodology explanation

This appendix gives a detailed explanation of the methodology used. We used various methods for this victim research. Section 1.1 describes how the literature research, interviews with experts and group interviews were designed and carried out. Section 1.2 describes the questionnaire structure. How the questionnaires were administered is presented in the two subsequent sections: Section 1.3 discusses the pilot study (for the purposes of the development phase) and Section 1.4 the final measurements (for the purposes of the implementation phase). Finally, in Section 1.5 we discuss the data analysis. For those who wish a brief overview of how the research was carried out, we refer to Section 2 of this publication.

Organisation of the research

The Investigation Board of the Board of Chief Commissioners commissioned this research. The project was managed on behalf of the Board by a steering committee comprising a representative from the Dutch Central Unit and the Programme Against Cybercrime. The Central Unit is an 'adoption corps' [*adoptiekorps*] and acted on behalf of the steering committee as a first point of contact for the researchers. The steering committee was supported by a consultative group.[44] The following organisations were represented in the consultative group:

- three allied northern police regions;
- six allied southern police regions;
- Amsterdam-Amstelland police region;
- Dutch Central Unit;
- PAC;
- CBS;
- Ministry of Security and Justice;
- Ministry of the Interior and Kingdom Relations;
- University of Tilburg.

44 The consultative group met at the start of the research, during the development phase, at the end of the development phase, during the implementation phase and on completion of the research.

1.1 Preliminary research

Literature research
Books, articles and reports about the various manifestations of cybercrime, explanations for victimisation and so on were found using online media libraries. We used both Dutch and English search words in this. This provided insight into what is known about cybercrime victimisation in the Netherlands and abroad.

Interviews with experts
Based on the literature research, we compiled a topic list for the interviews. This was based primarily on the inventory of cybercrimes that occur which was compiled by the Research and Documentation Centre [*Wetenschappelijk Onderzoek- en Documentatiecentrum*] (Sikkel, 2010) and the questionnaire that is used for the Safety Monitor. The interviews had two functions: to gather information and to assess needs. During the interviews, knowledge was gleaned about cybercrime and about how to frame questions about cybercrime in victim research. Second, we investigated which cybercrimes have priority and which aspects of victimisation are relevant according to staff at the police and judicial authorities, at both a policy and operational level. In the period from November 2009 to January 2010, a total of 23 interviews were conducted with key figures within the police and judicial authorities. The list of people interviewed can be found in Appendix 2.

Group interviews
To clarify how members of the public can best be questioned about cybercrime victimisation and how familiar they are with the various cyber terms, we held two group interviews with 16 members of the public. These interviewees were recruited via the vraaghetdevries.nl consumer panel. This panel comprises around 1,400 residents of Friesland province who are interviewed six times a year by first year students from the Institute of Economics and Management at the NHL University of Applied Sciences.

1.2 Questionnaire

Based on the literature research, interviews with experts and group interviews, we compiled a list of cybercrimes and aspects of victimisation that deserve the most attention, according to those working in this field. This list was presented to the members of the consultative group who, together with the researchers, decided on the questionnaire content. The questionnaire comprised the following aspects:[45]

45 In the final assessment, some of the subjects were not covered separately. Instead the information was obtained from CBS data.

a. personal background characteristics:
   - gender;
   - age;
   - ethnicity;
   - live with or without a partner;
   - level of education;
   - have or do not have paid work;
b. security level of computer used most in the home;
c. internet behaviour;
d. risk awareness;
e. victimisation (previous five years and twelve months):
   - spam;
   - malware;
   - cyber marketplace fraud;
   - advance fee fraud;
   - identity fraud;
   - stalking;
   - libel/slander;
   - threats;
   - blackmail/extortion;
   - hacking.

If someone was a victim of one or more crimes, we asked them questions about:
a. the perpetrator's modus operandi;
b. international components;
c. relationship perpetrator-victim;
d. victim's reaction, including willingness to report and satisfaction regarding police response;
e. material and immaterial losses.

The questionnaire also included an optional section with statements to measure self-control, attitude to life and compulsive internet use. In the end, self-control was the only aspect used as a possible explanatory factor for the risk models (see Sect. 1.5). The questions about attitude to life and compulsive internet use were scrapped to save space and because internet behaviour proved to be a more relevant variable than compulsive internet use. We measured self-control using nine statements. Reliability for self-control is high (α=0.77):[46]
- I have trouble stopping bad habits.
- I am lazy.
- I make improper remarks.

46 Reliability is a measure of the extent to which various questions measure the same phenomenon (internal consistency). Reliability is reflected using Cronbach's alpha (α). It ranges between negative infinity (unreliable) to 1 (very reliable). A sound level of reliability is an alpha of 0.70.

- I sometimes do things that are bad for me if I enjoy them.
- I wish I had more self-discipline.
- Having fun sometimes stops me from finishing my work.
- I have difficulty concentrating.
- Sometimes I can't stop myself from doing something, even when I know it's wrong.
- I often do things without thinking properly about possible alternatives.

In order to test hypotheses using regression analysis, it was necessary to combine separate variables into constructs. These constructs were also included in the regression models that were set up for the various kinds of cybercrime (see also Sect. 1.5). The following constructs were assessed:
- Activity (emailing and searching (targeted surfing) for information on the internet); α=0.64.
- Exposure (untargeted surfing, downloading, using MSN, skyping, chatting, visiting forums and social media sites and using Twitter); α=0.71.
- Computer skills (knowledge about operating system, internet connection and browser and virus scanner).
- Risk awareness:
  - I open emails from senders I don't know.
  - I open files or attachments from senders I don't know.
  - I download via Torrent applications (e.g. Bittorrent or Vuze) and/or peer-to-peer systems (e.g. Gnutella, Kazaa or Limewire).
  - I look out for the padlock when I pay online.
  - I look out for the 's' after 'http' when I pay via the internet or when I do internet banking.
  - If I buy things on the internet, I try to find out whether the seller is reliable.
  - I am careful about the information that I leave on the internet about myself.
  - I use strong passwords that are difficult to guess consisting of at least eight characters and including both figures and letters.
  - I use different passwords for different accounts.
  - I change my password for security reasons.

The list of subjects was converted into a draft questionnaire. This questionnaire was presented to the consultative group. Their comments were taken into account and resulted in a second draft. This draft was discussed with a smaller group of consultative group members. The final changes were made and the questionnaire was put into digital format for testing. This test was carried out by around thirty people from our own network, by both researchers and by the survey target group. The online questionnaire was programmed by ISIZ, a company that specialises, among other things, in online questionnaire design. The questionnaire (without the optional section) is included in Appendix 4.

1.3 Pilot study design

The objective of the pilot study was twofold. First we wanted to gain insight into the extent and the representativeness of the response rate for the methodology used. For the research, we aimed at a response rate of 10,000 respondents whose background characteristics would be representative for internet users aged 15 years and above. The second objective of the test was to improve the questionnaire.

Design

Traditionally, population surveys are conducted using written, telephone and face-to-face interviews. Nowadays, data for many surveys is gathered via the internet. There is an ongoing discussion among researchers about the error sources that can influence the quality of victim survey research findings. According to Bethlehem (2006), *undercoverage* in particular is a major problem in online surveys. People who do not have an internet connection obviously cannot take part in research that is done entirely online. In addition to this, *sampling errors* through self-selection may occur, according to Bethlehem, because in many online surveys the respondents are not approached by the researchers. Instead they participate in response to an invitation to do so on the internet. This means that researchers have very little influence on the representativeness of the sample. Finally, the non-response rate, a problem that applies to all kinds of research, can be even more of an issue because of technical problems, slow modems and out-dated browsers that cannot render online surveys properly.

Problems with sampling errors through self-selection were overcome in this research by not conducting all the interviews digitally. Respondents were selected randomly from the Municipal Personal Records Database [*Gemeentelijke Basisadministratie* (GBA)] and those selected were sent an invitation by surface mail to take part by completing an online questionnaire (see Appendix 5). This means that no self-selection took place, which would have been the case had the respondents been recruited digitally on websites. So we reduced problems related to undercoverage by approaching respondents with an invitation letter. We also approached people who did not have internet connections in this way. People who do not use the internet were also asked to complete the questionnaire about cybercrime victimisation because they can also fall victim to cybercrime: their identity information may be stolen offline, for instance, at an ATM, and then misused online when it is used to buy things on the internet. The letter gave the research team's telephone number and email address where people could unsubscribe for the research or request a written questionnaire. This enabled people without an internet connection to take part; it also gave us insight into reasons for not wishing to participate.

Those who did not respond were sent a reminder letter in which they were told that they would be approached directly by telephone. Telephone numbers were sought for those people who also did not respond to the reminder. They were subsequently called. During the telephone conversation, they were once again given the option of completing the questionnaire online, on paper, directly by telephone or to refuse participation altogether. Combining all these methods in this way was the obvious approach. The Safety Monitor was conducted using this method for the first time in the autumn 2008, and all subsequent measurements were carried out in the same way. The CBS carried out the research using the 'old method' parallel to this method. In this, the interviews were conducted in writing and verbally only. The differences in research findings were significant for victimisation. Victimisation figures in the online survey were higher.

Sample

Nine municipalities were sent a letter requesting a sample for the purposes of the research. National legislation obliges municipalities to supply samples on request; a municipal by-law stipulates that refusing to supply samples is illegal. Using density of addresses in the vicinity, the CBS divided municipal urbanisation into five levels: extremely urbanised, strongly urbanised, moderately urbanised, hardly urbanised and not urbanised. We chose a sample from Leeuwarden Municipality based on contacts we had with them. Leeuwarden Municipality falls into the category 'strongly urbanised'. For the remaining four categories, we wrote to two municipalities for each, spread over the whole of the Netherlands. Five of the eight municipalities we approached reacted positively and undertook to send a sample. One municipality refused 'on the basis of bad experiences in the past'. Two municipalities did not respond at all. We selected four of the five municipalities that responded positively, which meant that we were able to write to members of the public from all urbanisation categories. The municipalities that took part in the pilot study were: Leeuwarden, Soest, Zeevang, Hilvarenbeek and Beverwijk.

From three municipalities, we received random samples of 500 inhabitants and from two municipalities random samples of 499 inhabitants aged between 15 and 70 years. The overall sample size therefore came to 2,498 members of the public.

Digital questionnaire

The questionnaire was available online between 6 October 2010 and 3 January 2011 on www.cybercrime-onderzoek.nl. The questionnaire could only be accessed using a login code. A login code was created for each respondent and comprised a five or six digit and letter combination. The respondents had the option of interrupting the questionnaire and returning to it at a later stage. Once the respondent clicked 'send' at the end of the questionnaire, that login code could no longer be used to access the questionnaire. This ensured that the questionnaire could not be completed more than once. There was no progress bar visible because the first half of the questionnaire took much longer to complete than the second half. A progress bar may have discouraged respondents. Completing the questionnaire online took on average twenty minutes, including the optional questions that were filled in by 70% of the respondents.

Design

Given that establishing the extent and representativeness of the response rate was a primary objective of the assessment, we decided to write to half of the sample on behalf of the Dutch Central Unit and half on behalf of NHL University of Applied Science. The Dutch Central Unit format of the letter (see Appendix 5) was virtually the same as the NHL format. A Dutch Central Unit representative signed the Dutch Central Unit letters; the NHL letters were signed by the NHL research project leader.

Per municipality, 250 randomly selected members of the public were sent a Dutch Central Unit letter; the rest were sent an NHL letter. The exception to this was the Municipality of Zeevang, a very small municipality with 4,500 people in the age group 15 to 70, spread across about 2,000 households. On average, one in four households were sent a letter and sometimes more than one person in the household was included in the sample. Given that we expected that people would be surprised and suspicious if members of the same family received letters in both the Dutch Central Unit and NHL formats, we decided in the case of Zeevang Municipality to send all letters to the same street in the same format.

Invitation for online questionnaire

In the invitation letters, people were addressed by name (initials and surname). The letter invited respondents to participate in the research by logging in on the website using a unique code given in the letter. Respondents were not given an incentive to take part. After logging in on a neutral login screen, respondents were directed to a website which had the same layout as the letter. First instructions were given on how to complete the questionnaire, after which the respondent could proceed to fill in the questionnaire. At the end of the questionnaire, respondents were asked whether they were prepared to answer a number of additional questions (optional questions). If the respondent refused, the questionnaire was considered to be 'completed in full'.

After about a fortnight, a reminder was sent to the respondents who had not as yet responded. All respondents received a letter in the same format as the invitation letter. The reminder letter was also signed.

Call-backs

It was our intention to do call-backs for respondents who had not responded to the invitation and the reminder letter. Because the response rate was not as high as we had hoped, and we had budgeted for call-backs, we contacted a sample of respondents by telephone. We estimate that in the 75 hours that were available, we processed 800 telephone calls. First we looked for telephone numbers for the surplus addresses that we had been given. In the case of academic research (as opposed to market research) it is permissible to approach people on the 'don't call me' register.[47] Members of the public can also indicate that they would prefer not to be approached for academic research, but only a few are registered in this way. We found telephone numbers that we could use for 76 per cent of the addresses. Per format, we drew a sample of 400 respondents randomly from the numbers that we found. At some of the addresses, particularly in Zeevang, the same number was found more than once because several respondents lived at the same address.

The telephone interviewers knew from which samples the telephone numbers were drawn. They introduced themselves as follows: 'Good day Mr or Mrs <name>, I am <name>, I am calling you on behalf of <Dutch Central Unit or NHL University of Applied Science>'. They then asked to speak to the person who was mentioned in the file. If more than one person in the household was in the sample, both people were surveyed. Each number was called six times at most. It took 68.5 hours to process all the telephone calls. As previously noted, respondents were given a choice: complete an online questionnaire, a written questionnaire, be interviewed by telephone, or refuse altogether. Given the limited time available, we instructed the interviewers to encourage respondents to take the first option, then the second, and so on. If respondents agreed to complete the questionnaire online, they were asked to give an email address. Overall, 141 of the 244 (57.8%) respondents who undertook to complete the questionnaire online gave their email addresses. None of the email addresses was invalid. We sent them an email with a link to the questionnaire and their personal login code. After about three weeks, we sent a reminder to the respondents who had been sent an email but had not responded. No one opted to be interviewed by telephone.

Written questionnaire

The written questionnaire differed from the online questionnaire in two ways as we did not discourage respondents with a thick wodge of paper. First, the follow-on questions about victimisation at the end of the questionnaire were only asked once instead of for each kind of victimisation. Respondents could indicate which kind of cybercrime they had last fallen victim to and answer the questions relating to that kind of victimisation. Second, the additional questions were not included in the written questionnaire.

Research findings from pilot study

The approach we used resulted in a response rate of 35.4 per cent for the Dutch Central Unit format and 20.8 per cent for the NHL format. Overall (NHL and Dutch Central Unit together), 533 respondents filled in the questionnaire, which equates to a response rate of 21.3 per cent.

47 The 'don't call me' register ['bel me niet' register] is a register that Dutch consumers can put their names on to avoid being approached for unsolicited telemarketing and similar exercises.

The pilot study led to several conclusions. In terms of urbanisation, age, ethnicity and employment situation, the response rate deviated significantly from the population, but not to the extent that we could not weight the results in line with the background characteristics used by the CBS. In terms of internet usage, there were also differences between response rate and population, but these could not be explained on the basis of the pilot study results. As variables, gender and education were representative in the pilot study. A decision will still be needed on whether a correction will be required for the baseline measurement. Finally, the under-represented group in the 30 to 39 age group proved to be sensitive to telephone call-backs. Older people are more likely to respond to letters. Other background variables did not have a significant influence on which method respondents were inclined to choose.

For a detailed overview of the pilot study results, we refer readers to the pilot study report on cybercrime victimisation by Domenie, Leukfeldt and Stol (2011).

1.4 Main research design

In terms of design, the main survey was broadly similar to the pilot study (see Sect. 1.3). However, the pilot study did lead to some adjustments to the questionnaire and the way in which the research was conducted. We will discuss these first. We will then discuss the response rate and representativeness of the main research that is the subject of this publication.

Adjustments to the questionnaire

Determining identity fraud victimisation on the basis of the data we gathered in the pilot study proved to be problematic. For this reason, we changed the phrasing of the questions. Advance fee fraud victimisation (inheritance, lottery etc.) had not occurred among the respondents in the pilot study. Advance fee fraud via dating sites occurred twice. These types of fraud were included in 'advance fee fraud'.

Overall there were seven individual victims of crimes relating to relationships (1.3%). Two victims indicated that they had fallen victim to several kinds of inter-personal (relational) crimes, in both cases at the hands of the same perpetrator. In the research, we asked victims of all kinds of relational crime about their relationship with the perpetrator and the modus operandi for each case. We asked questions about material and immaterial losses and willingness to report only once, even if the victim had been the target of more than one kind of relational crime.

Because the CBS uses a unique CBS code to enrich the data with all kinds background characteristics, such as income and socio-economic status, we were able to use fewer background characteristics in the research. Questions about background characteristics were put at the end of the questionnaire. Matrices with more than six statements were spread across more than one page. In addition, minor changes were made on the basis of comments from the respondents and insights into how the questionnaire could be improved. We also deleted response categories that were not ticked.

Adjustments to the way the research was conducted

Despite the fact that a Dutch Central Unit letter would probably be more appealing to victims than a neutral format, we opted for the Dutch Central Unit format because we wanted a high response rate. Our motivation in this regard was that there would in any event be a change in methodology if a new method was to be used after the baseline measurement to measure the extent of victimisation (e.g. in a module in the Safety Monitor). The other research questions (related to risk factors, protection factors and the consequences of victimisation) are crucial to those working in this field.

For the baseline measurement, a random sample of the Dutch population was drawn in order to reduce local influences from the region where the respondents lived as far as possible. The CBS supplied the sample. We did not impose an age limit for the baseline measurement; instead Dutch citizens over the age of 15 were approached, in line with the Safety Monitor. Those aged 15 were approached via their parents because informed consent is a statutory requirement for persons aged 16 and under. To ensure that the response rate was as high as possible, we took the following measures:

- Communications
  - The questionnaire was made available on www.politie.nl/klpd/internetonderzoek. The spokesperson for the Dutch Central Unit issued a press release about the research, which was also posted on the police website. Information about the organisations involved was also posted on the website, as well as a link to the cybersafety lectorate where there was a description of the research.
  - The invitation letter included the statement concerning protection of privacy used by CBS.
  - The research was presented as an investigation into security in the digital world and not as victim research: the words 'victim' and 'cybercrime' were not used in the letter or on the website and only appear half way through the questionnaire.
  - The letter was given a more professional layout.
- Ease of finding the login screen
  - During the pilot study, it became apparent that quite a few respondents typed www.cybercrime-research.nl in Google's search bar, for instance. The police website was easy to find, also via Google. 'Internet research' was mentioned in large red letters on every page on the police website, and this provided a link to the login screen. Due to the large number of visitors to the research, after a few days the login screen then became the first search result to appear after entering the web address in Google. None of the respondents called to say that they could not find the login screen.
- Technical security
  - An https connection was used for the research.

Sample

The CBS provided the sample for the research from the national personal records database. Individuals in the sample were given a unique login code to ensure that only people from the sample could access the questionnaire. In addition, to this, the CBS provided a CBS code so that, after data capture, the data could be enriched with data from the Social Statistical Database (SSB) and the GBA, and so that the CBS could weight the data. This also meant that, of the 21,800 invited to take part in the study, we could gain insight into how people responded, who they were and whether they had been victims of cybercrime.

Response rate

We approached 283 parents and asked them to allow their 15-year-old children to complete an online questionnaire. A total of 158 15-year-olds completed the questionnaire (55.8%). In addition to this, 21,517 Dutch citizens aged 16 years and older were invited by letter. Of these, 10,122 responded (47.0%). The overall response was 10,280, which equates to a response rate of 47.2 per cent.

Questionnaires were completed through telephone interviewers and online by the respondents themselves. Contrary to the pilot study, the budget for the research was sufficient to call-back all those people who had not responded to the invitation letter and the reminder, and to encourage people to undertake a telephone interview during call-backs. Respondents were also given the option of completing a written questionnaire. We will discuss our approach and the response rate for each method in the following sections.

Response to the invitation letters

The invitation letters were sent on 15 April 2011. The letters were printed on Dutch Central Unit stationery and signed using the chief officer's digital signature. In the letter, respondents were asked to visit www.politie.nl/klpd/internetonderzoek and to log in using a unique login code. The letter gave the research team's telephone number and email address where people could unsubscribe for the research or request a written questionnaire. The respondents were also given the option of unsubscribing via a link on the police website or requesting a written questionnaire. On 6 May 2011, we sent a reminder letter to respondents who had not responded to the invitation letter. In the reminder we mentioned that respondents would be approached by telephone if they did not respond, either by participating or refusing to participate.

Table B1.1 shows that 2,887 people went to the website and completed the questionnaire in response to the first invitation letter. A further 2,723 did the same in response to the reminder. Together this equates to 25.7% of the sample. In addition to this, 1,346 people unsubscribed for the research by telephone or via the website (6.2%). This mainly happened by telephone after receiving the second letter. A further 306 people requested a written questionnaire by telephone or via the website. A total of 73 respondents were not reachable by post either because TNT could not deliver the letter or because those living at the address indicated that the person in question no longer lived at that address and the letter was returned. Thirty-five people responded in some other way.

They requested, for instance, a written questionnaire as well as turning down participation in the research, or completed the questionnaire online. In the end, there were no respondents who responded both online and on paper.

Table B1.1 Online response to invitation letters

	N	%
First letter	21,800	100.0
Response 1st letter	2,887	13.2
Response 2nd letter	2,723	12.5
Undeliverable	73	0.3
Unsubscribed in response to letters	1,346	6.2
Requested written questionnaire	306	1.4
Overlap in processing	35	0.2
Outstanding addresses for call-backs	14,500	66.5

A total of 33.5 per cent of the sample were processed in response to the two invitation letters, leaving 14,500 addresses remaining.

Accessed by telephone

EMD Data BV looked up telephone numbers for the remaining 14,500 addresses. They have a computerised system for this. They looked for landline and cell numbers using names and addresses. Possible results were no numbers, one number or two numbers. After all the telephone numbers had been called once, the firm Companen once again looked for the telephone numbers for all those in the sample for whom no numbers were found or for whom the number that was found was incorrect. At least one telephone number was found for a total 82.4 per cent of the names.

Companen interviewers called all the telephone numbers during the period 23 May to 2 July 2011. Of the remaining persons in the sample for whom at least one number was found, it emerged that in 13.0 per cent of the cases the number was incorrect. A further 7.9 per cent of these people were not reached after a minimum of nine attempts to call them. The login code was no longer usable for 1.5 per cent of the remaining people. To save time, we looked up telephone numbers quite soon after sending the reminder; the respondents either completed the questionnaire online during the time that the telephone interviews were being prepared or they unsubscribed for the research in this period. Overall 59.2 per cent of the persons who did not respond to the invitation letters were reached by telephone.

Table B1.2 Accessed by telephone

	N	% of total	% of remaining sample
Outstanding addresses for call-backs	14,500	66.5	100.0
Telephone numbers looked up	14,496	66.5	100.0
Telephone numbers found	11,946	54.8	82.4
Incorrect number	1,889	8.7	13.0
Login code not usable	333	1.5	2.3
Not reached in 9 attempts	1,144	5.2	7.9
Reached by telephone	8,580	39.4	59.2

Of the 14,500 persons remaining in the sample, 8,580 were reached by telephone. Of these, 44.3 per cent were prepared to answer the questions by telephone, but 0.3 per cent stopped answering the questions half way. This means that 44.0 per cent of the persons reached by telephone participated in the research, which equates to 17.3 per cent of the sample. The optional questions were not asked during telephone interviews. Of the persons who were reached, 42.0 per cent refused to cooperate at all, 7.6 per cent undertook to complete the questionnaire online and 1.4 per cent asked the interviewer to send a written questionnaire.

Table B1.3 Response rate approached by telephone

	N	% of total	% reached by telephone
Reached by telephone	8,580	39.4	100.0
Response rate telephone	3,777	17.3	44.0
Refusals	3,606	16.5	42.0
Undertook to complete online	652	3.0	7.6
Other non-response	374	1.7	4.4
Requested written questionnaire	122	0.6	1.4
Broke off half way	55	0.3	0.6
Overlap in processing	6	0.0	0.1

Overall response rate

The letters resulted in 2,887 and 2,723 fully completed online questionnaires, amounting to 25.7 per cent of the sample. A total of 3,777 respondents were surveyed by telephone, which amounts to 17.3 per cent of the sample.

A total of 428 written questionnaires were sent, 306 in response to the invitation letters and a further 122 after call-backs. In total, 248 of these questionnaires were returned after completion (57.9%), which equates to 1.1 per cent of the sample. During the call-backs, 652 people from the sample undertook to complete the questionnaire online; 221 of these went on to do so (33.9%). This equates to 1.0 per cent of the sample.

'Other response' came about in two different ways. During the call-back period, there were respondents who completed the questionnaire themselves before they were called. Since the telephone interviewers were working with the same software as the respondents, it is impossible to tell precisely how many this entailed. Secondly, after data capture it turned out that a number of questionnaires were not completed because they hung on the final screen or in the optional questions section. If the questions were completed up to the obligatory question, the questionnaire was included in the response rate. A total of 424 questionnaires fell into this category (1.9% of the sample).

Table B1.4 Overview of overall response rate

Response rate	N	% of total	% of response
Response 1st letter	2,887	13.2	28.1
Response 2nd letter	2,723	12.5	26.5
Response rate telephone	3,777	17.3	36.7
Written questionnaire response rate	248	1.1	2.4
Online response rate after telephone call	221	1.0	2.1
Other response	424	1.9	4.1
Overall response rate	10,280	47.2	100

The overall response rate in the database was actually 10,314. This difference arose from a difference in the manual and digital administration. The response rate was therefore not 47.16% but 47.31%. We cannot establish with any certainty where this deviation of 0.15% arose (34 questionnaires). The data analysis, however, is restricted to internet users, which means that this deviation does not influence the overall result (see below).

Representativeness

Of 10,314 respondents, 1,150 respondents (12%) never use the internet. The reporting is based on the 9,163 respondents who did use the internet. In this publication, prevalence is referred to as a percentage of 'internet users'.

The CBS enriched the data with data from the GBA and the SSB. The CBS subsequently calculated weighting factors across all 10,314 respondents. An account of this weighting is included in Appendix 6.

Validation

Questions about the sale of fake goods were not phrased properly: not used. Questions about blackmail were also not phrased properly (spam was interpreted as blackmail) and, in addition to this, blackmail occurred very infrequently: not included in the reporting. In questions about libel/slander, these terms were defined too broadly; while libel was included in this publication, it was not considered to be an offence.

1.5 Data analysis

The data were analysed using SPSS, a statistics program. Where statements about all internet users are made in this publication, the results are weighted. This applies to victimisation prevalence among internet users and to the bivariate analyses that measure whether victims differ from non-victims in terms of their background characteristics. Follow-up analyses are unweighted because these were calculated on the basis of a (often small) subpopulation that differed in terms of background characteristics from the overall population. For example, a respondent who suffered losses because of an offence and who at the same time has a relatively high weighting factor (because he belongs to an under-represented group) may influence the outcome inordinately and therefore skew the results.

Various logistic regression analyses were carried out to test hypotheses. Logistic regression analysis was chosen because the dependent variables were coded as dichotomous (0=no, 1=yes) variables (victim or not). In this way it is possible to identify those variables that influence the likelihood of people falling victim to certain kinds of cybercrime. B-coefficients were included in the regression models. These coefficients reveal the direction of the relationship between variables. However, they do not reveal anything about causality; the cause-event sequence is not known. The Nagelkerke R^2 is also presented in the models. This parameter lies between 0 and 1 and measures the explained variance. The closer it is to 1, the better the statement.

A potential problem for logistic regression analysis that includes several explanatory variables is so-called multicollinearity. We checked for this during the analyses. We did not find any VIF values above 4 in any of the models. For the models with interaction variables, we carried out these collinearity tests on centred variables.

The regression models were developed in three phases. In the first phase, we only looked at the influence of background characteristics on victimisation. The second phase involved mapping the influence of respondent attitude and behaviour on victimisation. In this way it is possible to see to what extent differences between people with various background characteristics (e.g. men and women) are a consequence of varying behaviour on the internet. In a scenario such as this, the effect of a background characteristic from Model 1 would be smaller in Model 2 where certain online behaviour is taken into account. In phase three, interaction variables were introduced to assess whether the influence of certain online behaviour clusters (activity and exposure) differs according to age and education.

Finally, we assessed the regression analyses for the variable 'self-control'. As mentioned previously, the questions about self-control were in the optional questions section. 5,032 respondents completed this section. For this reason, the models were not based on all internet users (more than 9,000), but on a subsample of these.

We looked at significance levels for all statistical analyses. A significance level of 95 per cent was used throughout this publication, unless otherwise indicated. This means that, where there are significant differences within the sample, we can state with a 95 per cent confidence interval that such differences also exist in reality.

Appendix 2
People interviewed

Brigitte Bloem, fraud researcher, IPOL team, Dutch Central Unit

Erik Boerboom, acting team head FO – Digital Police Flevoland

Jolanda Boorsma, Amsterdam-Amstelland Vice Squad

Stef Cusiel, TDE of the NRE

Rob van Dalen, head of TDE of the National Investigation Service

Nural Orucu, Cybercrime Hotline

Hans Doevendans, TDE of the NRE

Ruud Elderhorst, head of digital expertise Haaglanden police

Barend Frans, former project leader of quality incentive initial processing and investigation and deputy team leader, TDE Amsterdam-Amstelland

Simon van de Geer, Ministry of Security and Justice;

René Hesseling, senior researcher Haaglanden police

Gerard Hofstede, Flevoland police

John van Kesteren, researcher at Intervict, University of Tilburg

Chantal Malfeyt, Marktplaats

Dick Meuldijk, Security Monitor Bureau

Hans Pijnenburg, BR Southeast

Cees Schep, fraud researcher, IPOL team, Dutch Central Unit

Michael van de Velde, PWC consultant, Identity Fraud Hotline

Marjolein Viersma, digital investigator Amsterdam-Amstelland police

Wim Wensink, PWC consultant, Identity Fraud Hotline

Peter Zinn, Team High Tech Crime consultant

Lodewijk van Zwieten, public prosecutor High Tech Crime, National Office of the Public Prosecution Service

Appendix 3
Consultative group

Bert-Jaap Koops (chairman), professor of technology regulation, University of Tilburg

Danielle Lahey, public prosecutor cybercrime

Elke Moons, Statistics Netherlands

Frank Willemsen, member of staff at EWB, Research and Documentation Centre [WODC]

Henri José, head of Supraregional Investigation Forum South Six

Hugo van Klaveren, head of Northern Investigation Unit

Jan ter Mors, programme manager NIM

John van Kesteren, University of Tilburg

Joost Bruinsma, Ministry of the Interior and Kingdom Relations

Karolien Lammerts van Bueren, digital expertise team, regional police Amsterdam-Amstelland

Katja van Hoever, Programme Against Cybercrime

Rudie Neve (secretary), senior researcher Dutch Central Unit

Simon van de Geer, cybercrime policy officer, Ministry of Security and Justice

Thijs van der Wel, Strategic Analysis team leader at Dutch Central Unit

Tjeerd ten Brink, Intel Programme

Wieteke Verwijk, policy & development consultant, cybercrime coordinator, Dutch Central Unit

Appendix 4
Questionnaire

Research into security in the digital world questionnaire

Questionnaire structure The questionnaire consisted of three parts: 1. Internet use 2. Incidents on the internet: fraud via online retail sites and webshops; advance fee fraud and identity fraud; incidents in the private sphere. 3. Personal background characteristics Even if you have never experienced any of these incidents, your answers are extremely important to the research! Answering the questions Normally, you can give one answer per question. If you have the option of choosing more than one answer, this will be indicated and the place to be ticked will be square and not round. Red printing in the questionnaire is an indication that you can skip certain questions. Depending on your answers, completing the questionnaire should take between 10 to 20 minutes. Returning the questionnaire You can return the questionnaire back using the enclosed envelope. No postage stamp is required!

Internet use

1. How often do you use the internet?

☐ never →	go to question 20
☐ less than once a month	
☐ at least once a month but not weekly	
☐ at least once a month but not weekly	
☐ (almost) daily	

2. How many computers, laptops, mobile phones or other devices with an internet connection (for instance, iPod, iPad, Nintendo, Xbox etc.) are in use in your household?

☐ 0 →	go to question 19
☐ 1	
☐ 2	
☐ 3	
☐ more than 3	

3. How many of the computers, laptops, mobile phones or other devices <u>in your household</u> do you yourself use to go on the internet?

☐ 0 →	go to question 19
☐ 1	
☐ 2	
☐ 3	
☐ more than 3	

4. Who else uses these computers, laptops and/or other mobile devices that you yourself use to go on the internet <u>regularly</u> more than you do? *You can tick more than one option*

☐ no one
☐ partner
☐ parent(s)
☐ child(ren)
☐ other family members
☐ other members of the household
☐ friends/acquaintances
☐ others

5. Is the device in your household that <u>you use the most</u> to go on the internet a desktop computer, a laptop, a telephone or another kind of device?

☐ desktop computer
☐ laptop
☐ telephone (mobile phone, smartphone, PDA, etc.)
☐ other devices (iPod, iPad, Nintendo DS, PS3, Xbox360, etc.)

6. *In the rest of this questionnaire, other devices, including all mobile devices and laptops, will be referred to as 'computer' for simplicity.*
What kind of internet connection(s) does the computer in your household have that <u>you yourself use the most to go on the internet</u>? *You can tick more than one option*

☐ ADSL
☐ Cable
☐ mobile (GPRS, UMTS, HSDPA etc.)
☐ analogue (dial up)
☐ ISDN
☐ satellite (via a dish)
☐ fibre optic
☐ other
☐ don't know

7. Is this computer part of a local network, for instance, in your house, neighbourhood or city? *You can tick more than one option*

☐ no →	go to question 9
☐ yes, part of a network in my house	
☐ yes, part of a network in my neighbourhood	
☐ yes, part of a public/city network	
☐ don't know→	go to question 9

8. Is this network and/or the network router secure (protected)?

☐ no
☐ yes
☐ don't know

9. What operating system does this computer have?

☐ Windows →	go to question 11
☐ Mac OS (Apple/Macintosh)	
☐ Linux	} go to question 12
☐ mobile system (Android, IOS, Windows Mobile, Symbian etc.)	
☐ other, namely ____________________	
☐ don't know	

10. Which Mac version do you use on this computer?

☐ MAC OSX 10.*	} go to question 12
☐ Leopard	
☐ Snow Leopard	
☐ other, namely ____________________	
☐ don't know	

11. Which Windows version do you use on this computer?

☐ old: 3.11 / 95, 98, ME, NT4
☐ 2000
☐ XP
☐ Vista/Longhorn
☐ 7
☐ other, namely ____________________
☐ don't know

12. Which web browser or internet browser do you use on this computer? *You can tick more than one option*

☐ Internet Explorer (Microsoft/Windows)
☐ Google Chrome
☐ Mozilla Firefox
☐ Opera
☐ Safari
☐ other, namely ____________________
☐ don't know

13. Has a virus scanner been installed on this computer?

☐ no →	go to question 19
☐ yes	
☐ don't know →	go to question 19

14. a Did you buy this virus scanner or was it free?

☐ paid for the virus scanner (with or without free trial period)
☐ free virus scanner
☐ don't know

15. How often do you switch off the virus scanner and/or firewall?
For instance, to make the computer work faster or because the virus scanner or firewall does not permit certain kinds of data traffic.

☐ never
☐ seldom
☐ sometimes
☐ often
☐ very often

16. How often do you stop the virus scanner manually while it's scanning?
For instance, because the computer slows down while it's scanning or because it makes a lot of noise.

☐ never
☐ seldom
☐ sometimes
☐ often
☐ very often

17. How often are files scanned to check for viruses and so on without the scanner requesting this?

☐ daily
☐ weekly
☐ monthly
☐ less frequently than monthly
☐ never
☐ don't know

18. How often are virus scanner updates installed on this computer?

☐ never
☐ sometimes if the virus scanner requests them
☐ always if the virus scanner requests them
☐ always if the virus scanner requests them and someone installs additional updates
☐ the virus scanner does it automatically
☐ don't know

19. What do you use the internet for?

	never	*less than 1 hour per week*	*1 → 2 hours per week*	*more than 2 hours per week*
to email	☐	☐	☐	☐
looking for information (targeted)	☐	☐	☐	☐
surfing (untargeted)	☐	☐	☐	☐
music, films, downloading software *(combine the hours spent surfing and downloading)*	☐	☐	☐	☐
MSN/Skype	☐	☐	☐	☐
chatting online via chat sites	☐	☐	☐	☐
online gaming	☐	☐	☐	☐
actively participating in internet forums	☐	☐	☐	☐
communicating on social network sites such as Hyves, Facebook and LinkedIn (looking at profiles, adding texts, reading messages, sending messages)	☐	☐	☐	☐
Twittering	☐	☐	☐	☐
making and/or maintaining websites	☐	☐	☐	☐

20. Do you use a computer for internet banking?

☐ no
☐ yes

If you never use the internet, you can skip to question 70.

21. Which paid online services have you used in the previous 12 months? *You can tick more than one option*

☐ email (paid subscription)	
☐ webhosting (paid subscription)	
☐ paid gaming or gambling sites	
☐ paid download sites (iTunes, audio, video, ringtones, software etc.)	
☐ paid contact or dating sites	
☐ other paid online services	
☐ would rather not say	
☐ I have not used any paid online services →	go to question 24

22. Have you used any of these paid online services with the computer in your household that you yourself use the most to go on the internet?

☐ no
☐ yes

23. Have you used a credit card for these paid online services during the previous 12 months?

☐ no
☐ yes
☐ don't know

24. The following statements are about your personal opinion of security on the internet. To what extent do you agree or disagree you with the following statements?

	completely disagree	*disagree*	*do not disagree/ or agree*	*agree*	*completely agree*	*don't know/ no opinion*
I think it's safe to buy things on the internet	☐	☐	☐	☐	☐	☐
Compared to buying things in other ways, buying things on the internet is risky	☐	☐	☐	☐	☐	☐
The police should safeguard my security on the internet	☐	☐	☐	☐	☐	☐
Website owners should safeguard my security on the internet	☐	☐	☐	☐	☐	☐
Banks and financial institutions should safeguard my security on the internet	☐	☐	☐	☐	☐	☐
I am prepared to do something to safeguard my security on the internet	☐	☐	☐	☐	☐	☐
I am capable of doing something to safeguard my security on the internet	☐	☐	☐	☐	☐	☐

25. To what extent do the following statements apply to you?

	never	*seldom*	*some-times*	*often*	*not applica-ble/don't know*
I open emails from senders I don't know	☐	☐	☐	☐	☐
I open files or attachments from senders I don't know	☐	☐	☐	☐	☐
I download applications via Torrent (*e.g. Bittorrent or Vuze*) and/or peer-to-peer systems (*e.g. Gnutella, Kazaa or Limewire*)	☐	☐	☐	☐	☐
I look out for the padlock 🔒 when I pay online	☐	☐	☐	☐	☐
I look out for the 's' after 'http' when I pay via the internet or when I do internet banking	☐	☐	☐	☐	☐
If I buy things on the internet, I try to find out whether the seller is reliable	☐	☐	☐	☐	☐
I am careful about the information that I leave on the internet about myself	☐	☐	☐	☐	☐
I use strong passwords that are difficult to guess consisting of at least eight characters and including both figures and letters	☐	☐	☐	☐	☐
I use different passwords for different accounts	☐	☐	☐	☐	☐
I change my password for security reasons	☐	☐	☐	☐	☐

Incidents on the internet: spam and malware

26. *Spam* refers to emails that you receive even though you didn't ask for them. You don't know the sender personally. The email may have been sent from an email address belonging to someone or an organisation that you do know, so that you do initially think you know who the sender is.
    Have you received spam in the 'post box' or 'inbox' of any of your email addresses during the previous 12 months?

☐ no →	go to question 28
☐ yes	
☐ don't know →	go to question 28
☐ n/a I don't use email →	go to question 28

27. Have you read any emails (briefly) during the previous 12 months?

☐ no
☐ yes
☐ don't know

28. *Malware* is malicious software that is unsolicited and is generally installed on your computer without you noticing it. Examples of malware are viruses, Trojan horses, worms and spyware.

During the previous 12 months, have you noticed that you had malware on the computer in your household that you yourself use the most to go on the internet?

☐ no →	go to question 33
☐ yes	
☐ don't know →	go to question 33

29. How did this malware get on to your computer? *You can tick more than one option*

☐ via an email
☐ via an MSN message
☐ via a link on a website
☐ via a download
☐ via a Twitter message
☐ other, namely ____
☐ don't know

30. During the previous 12 months, have you suffered any financial loss because you had to replace or restore the computer as a consequence of malware?

☐ no →	go to question 32
☐ yes	
☐ don't know →	go to question 32

31. What was the overall amount that you lost because of malware during the previous 12 months?
If you do not know precisely, you can also give an estimate.

☐ ______ euro
☐ don't know

32. During the previous 12 months, have you lost any software, photographs, text, audio, video or other files because you had malware on this computer?

☐ no
☐ yes
☐ don't know

Incidents on the internet: fraud via online retail sites and webshops

Via the internet, you can buy products such as clothing, books, electronics, plane tickets and other tickets. You can also buy services, such as those offered by painters and beauticians. You can buy things directly from private individuals via so-called online retail sites or via webshops.

Have you bought any products or services via the internet <u>during the previous 5 years</u>?

no →	go to question 53
yes	

Have you bought any products or services via the internet <u>during the previous 12 months</u>?

no →	go to question 53
yes	

How did you pay for the products or services that you bought via the internet <u>during the previous 12 months</u>? *You can tick more than one option*

☐ offline via the bank (acceptance giro/transfer)
☐ via the internet banking (acceptance giro/transfer)
☐ automatic authorisation
☐ via PayPal
☐ via iDEAL
☐ with a credit card via the internet
☐ cash
☐ other
☐ don't know/would rather not say

33. Have you bought a product or a service via the internet, and made at least a part payment, and then the product or service was never supplied **because the seller swindled you**?

☐ no →	go to question 43
☐ yes	
☐ don't know →	go to question 43

34. Was this during the previous 12 months?

☐ no →	go to question 43
☐ yes	
☐ don't know →	go to question 43

35. How often did this happen this during the previous 12 months?

☐ ______ times
☐ don't know

36. Did you lose any money because of this <u>during the previous 12 months</u>?

☐ no →	go to question 38
☐ yes	
☐ don't know (yet) →	go to question 39

37. What was the overall amount that you lost because of this fraud <u>during the previous 12 months</u>?
If you do not know precisely, you can also give an estimate.

______ euro→	go to question 39

38. How come you didn't lose any money because of this? *You can tick more than one option*

☐ I had the money returned to my account myself
☐ I got the money back from the seller
☐ I got the money back from insurance
☐ for another reason, namely____

39. *If you were swindled in this way more than once, answer the following questions on the basis of the last time that it happened.*
How did you come into contact with the fraudster (the last time it happened)?

☐ via an advertisement on an online retail site
☐ via a webshop
☐ via a link in an email
☐ in another way, namely ____
☐ don't know

40. Was the contact with the seller from abroad in any way? For instance, was a foreign web address, email address, postal address, telephone number and/or bank account number involved?

☐ no
☐ yes, namely via this country: ____________________
☐ yes, but don't know which country
☐ don't know

41. What kind of product or service was it?

☐ consumer items (clothing, shoes, accessories etc.)
☐ electronics
☐ subscription
☐ ticket
☐ other, namely ____________________

42. What did you do when you discovered that someone had swindled you in this way? *You can tick more than one option*

☐ nothing
☐ reported it to the online retail site or webshop
☐ tried to get the money back by continuing to contact the seller
☐ tried to get the money via my bank
☐ tried to get the money via the seller's bank
☐ looked for information about the seller on the internet
☐ contacted the police
☐ other, namely ______________________________

43. Have you bought a product or a service via the internet <u>during the past 5 years</u>, and made at least a part payment, and then the product turned out to be fake or of a much worse quality than expected **because the seller swindled you**?

☐ no →	go to question 53
☐ yes	
☐ don't know →	go to question 53

44. Was this during the previous 12 months?

☐ no →	go to question 53
☐ yes	
☐ don't know →	go to question 53

45. How often did this happen <u>during the previous 12 months</u>?

☐ ______ times
☐ don't know

46. Did you lose any money because of this <u>during the previous 12 months</u>?

☐ no →	go to question 48
☐ yes	
☐ don't know (yet) →	go to question 49

47. What was the overall amount that you lost because of this fraud <u>during the previous 12 months</u>?
If you do not know precisely, you can also give an estimate.

______ euro →	go to question 49

48. How come you didn't lose any money because of this? *You can tick more than one option*

☐ I had the money returned to my account myself
☐ I got the money back from the seller
☐ I got the money back from insurance
☐ for another reason, namely_______________________________________

49. *If you were swindled in this way more than once during the previous 12 months, answer the following questions on the basis of the last time that it happened.* How did you find the website where you bought the product or service in question?

☐ via an advertisement on an online retail site
☐ via a webshop
☐ via a link in an email
☐ in another way, namely _______________________________________
☐ don't know

50. Was the contact with the seller from abroad in any way? For instance, was a foreign web address, email address, postal address, telephone number and/or bank account number involved?

☐ no
☐ yes, namely via this country: ____________________
☐ yes, but don't know which country
☐ don't know

51. What kind of product or service was it?

☐ consumer items (clothing, shoes, accessories etc.)
☐ electronics
☐ subscription
☐ ticket
☐ other, namely ____________________

52. What did you do when you discovered that someone had swindled you in this way? *You can tick more than one option*

☐ nothing
☐ reported it to the online retail site or webshop
☐ tried to get the money back by continuing to contact the seller
☐ tried to get the money via my bank
☐ tried to get the money via the seller's bank
☐ looked for information about the seller on the internet

☐ contacted the police	
☐ other, namely ____	

53. As a private individual, have you <u>sold</u> any products or services via the internet <u>during the previous 5 years</u>?

☐ no →	go to question 65
☐ yes	

54. Have you <u>sold</u> any products or services as a private individual via the internet <u>during the previous 12 months</u>?

☐ no →	go to question 65
☐ yes	

55. <u>During the previous 5 years</u>, have you as a private individual sold a product or service via the internet, but not received money from the buyer after having supplied the product or service **because the buyer swindled you**?'

☐ no →	go to question 65
☐ yes	
☐ don't know →	go to question 65

56. Was this during the previous 12 months?

☐ no →	go to question 65
☐ yes	
☐ don't know →	go to question 65

57. How often did this happen this <u>during the previous 12 months</u>?

☐ ______ times	
☐ don't know	

58. Did you lose any money or goods because of this <u>during the previous 12 months</u>?

☐ no →	go to question 60
☐ yes	
☐ don't know (yet) →	go to question 61

59. What was the overall amount that you lost because of this fraud <u>during the previous 12 months</u>?
If you do know not precisely, you can also give an estimate.

______ euros →	go to question 61

If you were swindled in this way more than once during the previous 12 months, answer the following questions on the basis of the last time that it happened.

60. How come you didn't lose any money or goods because of this? *You can tick more than one option*

☐ I had the money returned to my account myself
☐ I got the money back from the buyer
☐ I got the money back from insurance
☐ for another reason, namely_______________________________________

61. How did you come into contact with the buyer?

☐ the buyer responded to my advertisement on an online retail site
☐ I responded to the buyer's advertisement on an online retail site
☐ other, namely ____

62. Was the contact with the buyer from abroad in any way? For instance, was a foreign web address, email address, postal address, telephone number and/or bank account number involved?

☐ no
☐ yes, namely via this country: ____________________
☐ yes, but don't know which country
☐ don't know

63. What kind of product or service was it?

☐ consumer items (clothing, shoes, accessories etc.)
☐ electronics
☐ subscription
☐ ticket
☐ other, namely ____

64. What did you do when you discovered that someone had swindled you in this way? *You can tick more than one option*

☐ nothing
☐ reported it to the online retail site or webshop
☐ tried to get the money back by continuing to contact the seller
☐ tried to get the money via my bank
☐ tried to get the money via the seller's bank
☐ looked for information about the seller on the internet
☐ contacted the police
☐ other, namely ____

If you have never been swindled via an online retail site or webshop, you can skip to question 70.

65. Please indicate to what extent you agree with following statements <u>with regard to fraud via online retail sites or webshops.</u>

	com-pletely disagree	disagree	do not disagree/ or agree	agree	completely agree
My trust in trading on that/those particular retail site(s) or webshop(s) has declined	☐	☐	☐	☐	☐
My trust in trading on any online trading site or webshop has declined	☐	☐	☐	☐	☐
My trust in any kind of trade on the internet has declined	☐	☐	☐	☐	☐
My general sense of security on the internet has declined	☐	☐	☐	☐	☐
My general sense of security has declined	☐	☐	☐	☐	☐
My trust in humankind in its entirety has declined	☐	☐	☐	☐	☐
My trust in the Dutch police has declined	☐	☐	☐	☐	☐
My trust in the Dutch rule of law has declined	☐	☐	☐	☐	☐
I have suffered psychological problems	☐	☐	☐	☐	☐
I have suffered financial problems	☐	☐	☐	☐	☐

66. Have you suffered any other consequences because of what happened, other than the ones mentioned above?

☐ no
☐ yes, namely

If you have never contacted the police because you have been swindled via an online retail site or webshop, you can skip to question 70.

67. What was the police response? *You can tick more than one option*

☐ the police took a statement and traced or tried to trace the perpetrator
☐ the police took a statement and are still busy tracing the perpetrator
☐ the police took a statement
☐ the police recorded it but did not take a statement (the police recorded the incident but did not make a police report; you were not given a signed document)
☐ the police gave advice, but did not record it or take a statement
☐ the police said that there was nothing they could do about it.
☐ the police did not take me seriously
☐ other, namely ________________________________

68. Were you satisfied with the police response?

☐ extremely satisfied
☐ satisfied
☐ neutral
☐ dissatisfied
☐ extremely dissatisfied

69. Please comment on why you were satisfied/dissatisfied with the police response:

Incidents on the internet: identity fraud and advance fee fraud

70. The following questions are about *identity fraud*. Identity fraud is when someone uses your personal or financial information without your permission for their own financial gain. For instance, it is when someone withdraws money from your account, buys items in your name or applies for official documents in your name. Generally identity fraud is a consequence of identity theft, but in some cases you may have provided your identity information yourself.
Has anyone committed identity fraud with your identity information <u>during the previous 5 years</u>?

☐ no →	go to question 83
☐ yes	
☐ don't know →	go to question 83

71. Was this during the previous 12 months?

☐ no →	go to question 83
☐ yes	
☐ don't know →	go to question 83

72. *If your identity has been misused more than once, answer the following questions on the basis of the last time that it happened.*
Did the perpetrator use the internet to commit the identity fraud?
For instance, to take money out of your account, to buy things, to apply for loans or to forge papers?

☐ no
☐ yes
☐ don't know

73. Do you know who misused your identity?

☐ no →	go to question 75
☐ I have a suspicion	
☐ yes	

74. Who (do you suspect) misused your identity?

☐ partner
☐ ex-partner
☐ family member
☐ someone from the neighbourhood
☐ someone at work
☐ other known person
☐ someone who I do not know personally

75. How did the perpetrator obtain your identity information?

	yes	no	don't know
I gave the person the information myself	☐	☐	☐
My credit card or bank card was copied at an ATM (skimming)	☐	☐	☐
I entered my identity information on an electronic form that I received by email and that turned out later to be fake (phishing)	☐	☐	☐
I entered my data on a website (survey, lottery, webshop or something similar)	☐	☐	☐
Via an email, I was promised money or something else in exchange for personal details	☐	☐	☐
My computer was hacked and/or malware (virus, keylogger or something similar) was installed on my computer	☐	☐	☐
I entered information on a known website, that I later found out was hacked, to which criminals had access	☐	☐	☐
Someone put my personal information on the internet	☐	☐	☐
Documents were stolen from my waste paper or letter box, or someone intercepted my post somewhere	☐	☐	☐
A copy was made of a document of mine at a company or government department	☐	☐	☐

76. Did the identity theft take place in another way?

☐ no/don't know
☐ yes, namely ______________________________

77. If you indicated in question 75 that your computer was hacked and/or that malware was installed on your computer: was this the computer <u>in your household that you yourself use most often to go on the internet</u>?

☐ no
☐ yes

78. What did you do when you discovered your identity had been misused?
You can tick more than one option

☐ nothing
☐ tried to get the money via my bank
☐ tried to get the money via my insurance
☐ turned to the website/association for victims
☐ turned to the Identity Fraud Hotline
☐ contacted the police
☐ other, namely____

79. What was the overall amount that you estimate you lost because of identity fraud <u>during the previous 12 months</u>?
By this we mean the overall loss, so before you were compensated for any loss.

______ euros → if you didn't suffer any financial loss, go to question 83

80. Which part of the loss (do you estimate) was not compensated?

______ euros

81. Did you get the money back or an undertaking from your bank that you would get the money back from them?

☐ no
☐ yes
☐ don't know

82. Did you get the money back or an undertaking from your insurance company that you would get the money back from them?

☐ no
☐ yes
☐ don't know

If you never use the internet, you can skip to question 133.

83. *Advance fee fraud* is a kind of internet fraud. The way advance fee fraud works is that victims are promised a large sum of money provided they pay an advance. The money would be from a so-called inheritance, an investment or a lottery, for instance.

During the previous 5 years, have you been **swindled because you transferred money** to someone who approached you via email or the internet with stories about making money quickly through an inheritance, investment, lottery or something similar?

☐ no →	go to question 85
☐ yes	

84. Was this during the previous 12 months?

☐ no
☐ yes
☐ don't know

85. A specific kind of advance fee fraud is when fraudsters (generally from abroad) win people's trust via contact or dating sites. They then ask for money so that they can meet you or to solve so-called personal problems that they or their families have.

During the previous 5 years, have you been **swindled because you transferred money** to someone who you met on a contact or dating site?

☐ no
☐ yes

86. Was this during the previous 12 months?

☐ no	
☐ yes	
☐ don't know	

You were a victim of advance fee fraud	go to question 87
You were a victim of identity fraud but not advance fee fraud	go to question 89
You were not a victim of identity fraud or advance fee fraud	go to question 94

87. What was the overall amount that you estimate you lost because of **advance fee fraud** during the previous 12 months?
If you do know not exactly, you can give an estimate.

______ euros

88. *If you were swindled by advance fee fraud more than once, answer the following questions on the basis of the last time that it happened.*

What did you do when you discovered you had fallen victim to advance fee fraud?
You can tick more than one option

☐ nothing
☐ looked for information about the fraud on the internet
☐ tried to contact fellow victims
☐ tried to get the money back by continuing to contact the fraudster
☐ sought legal assistance
☐ contacted the police
☐ other, namely ___

89. Please indicate to what extent you agree with following statements with regard to identity fraud or advance fee fraud.

	completely disagree	disagree	do not disagree/ or agree	agree	com-pletely agree
My trust in any kind of trade on the internet has declined	☐	☐	☐	☐	☐
My general sense of security on the internet has declined	☐	☐	☐	☐	☐
My general sense of security has declined	☐	☐	☐	☐	☐
My trust in humankind in its entirety has declined	☐	☐	☐	☐	☐
My trust in the Dutch police has declined	☐	☐	☐	☐	☐
My trust in the Dutch rule of law has declined	☐	☐	☐	☐	☐
I have suffered psychological problems	☐	☐	☐	☐	☐
I have suffered financial problems	☐	☐	☐	☐	☐

90. Have you suffered any other consequences because of identity fraud or advance fee fraud happened, other than the ones mentioned above?

☐ no
☐ yes, namely:

If you have never contacted the police because you fell victim to identity fraud or advance fee fraud, you can skip to question 94.

91. What was the police response? *You can tick more than one option*

☐ the police took a statement and traced or tried to trace the perpetrator
☐ the police took a statement and are still busy tracing the perpetrator
☐ the police took a statement

☐ the police recorded it but did not take a statement (the police recorded the incident but did not make a police report; you were not given a signed document)
☐ the police gave advice, but did not record it or take a statement
☐ the police said that there was nothing they could do about it
☐ the police did not take me seriously
☐ other, namely ____________________

92. Were you satisfied with the police response?

☐ extremely satisfied
☐ satisfied
☐ neutral
☐ dissatisfied
☐ extremely dissatisfied

93. Please comment on why you were satisfied/dissatisfied with the police response:

Incidents on the internet: incidents in the private sphere

94. *Extortion* is the use of threats of physical violence or computer attacks for financial gain. *Blackmail* is threatening to disclose personal information, secrets or sensitive material for financial gain.

Sometimes the extortionist or blackmailer doesn't ask for money but for personal information instead, such as a pin code or password.

Has anyone extorted something from you or blackmailed you <u>during the previous 5 years</u>?

☐ no →	go to question 105
☐ yes	

95. Was this during the previous 12 months?

☐ no →	go to question 105
☐ yes	
☐ don't know →	go to question 105

96. Did the perpetrator use any of the following means to blackmail you or extort something from you?

	no	yes
Unwanted chat messages via MSN or an online chat site, for instance	☐	☐
Unsolicited emails sent	☐	☐
Embarrassing photographs, stories or rumours spread via the internet	☐	☐
Changes made to your personal profile(s), web pages etc.	☐	☐
Computer hacked	☐	☐
Email hacked	☐	☐
(Multimedia) messages sent via mobile phone	☐	☐

97. If the extortionist/blackmailer hacked your computer: was this the computer that you yourself use at home the most to go on the internet?

☐ n/a
☐ no
☐ yes

98. Did the extortionist or blackmailer use the internet in any other ways to harass you?

☐ no
☐ yes, namely

99. *If you were a victim of extortion or blackmail more than once, answer the following questions on the basis of the most recent incident.*

Did know you the perpetrator one of the perpetrators?

☐ no →	go to question 101
☐ yes	

100. Where did know you the perpetrator(s) from? *You can tick more than one option*

☐ partner
☐ ex-partner
☐ family member
☐ someone from the neighbourhood
☐ someone at work
☐ other known

101. Do you think the reason for the extortion or blackmail lay in the fact that you belong to a specific group (e.g. ethnic minority, sexual preference or a public position such as a police officer or politician)?

☐ no, I don't belong to one of those groups
☐ no, the fact that I belong to one of those groups had nothing to do with the extortion or blackmail
☐ perhaps
☐ yes
☐ don't know

102. What did you do in response to the extortion or blackmail? *You can tick more than one option*

☐ nothing
☐ contacted the police
☐ other, namely ___________________________

103. Did you suffer any material loss through the extortion or blackmail?

☐ no →	go to question 105
☐ yes	

104. What was the overall amount that you estimate you lost because of extortion or blackmail?

☐ ______ euros
☐ don't know

105. *Stalking* is the conscious and repeated pursuing of a person with the intention of making that person do something or scaring them. Stalking may be done through repeatedly doing the same thing or through various actions, such as following and spying on someone, making threats, making unwanted phone calls or damaging property, including electronic devices.

Has anyone stalked you during the previous 5 years?

☐ no →	go to question 115
☐ yes	

106. Was this during the previous 12 months?

☐ no →	go to question 115
☐ yes	
☐ don't know →	go to question 115

107. Did the stalker use any of the following means?

	no	yes
Unsolicited chat messages sent via MSN or an online chat site, for instance	☐	☐
Unsolicited emails	☐	☐
Embarrassing photographs, stories or rumours spread via the internet	☐	☐
Changes made to your personal profile(s), web pages etc.	☐	☐
Computer hacked	☐	☐
Email hacked	☐	☐
(Multimedia) messages sent via mobile phone	☐	☐

108. If the stalker hacked your computer: was this the computer that you yourself use at home the most to go on the internet?

☐ n/a
☐ no
☐ yes

109. Did the stalker use the internet in any other way to harass you?

☐ no
☐ yes, namely

110. Did you know the stalker or one of the stalkers?

☐ no →	go to question 112
☐ yes	

111. Where did know you the stalker(s) from? *You can tick more than one option*

☐ partner
☐ ex-partner
☐ family member
☐ someone from the neighbourhood
☐ someone at work
☐ other known

112. Did you turn to any authorities because you were stalked? *You can tick more than one option*

☐ no
☐ the police
☐ GP
☐ Riagg [Regional Institute for Outpatient Mental Healthcare]
☐ Victim Support

☐ Anti-stalking Foundation
☐ an association of fellow victims
☐ the Criminal Injuries Compensation Fund
☐ Stichting M. (Report Crime Anonymously)
☐ another authority namely ______________________________

113. Stalking can bring with it material losses such as having to move house, applying for a new telephone number, restoring damage or even losing a job.

Did you suffer any material loss through stalking?

☐ no →	go to question 115
☐ yes	

114. What was the overall amount that you estimate you lost because of stalking during the previous 12 months?

☐ ______ euros
☐ don't know

115. A *threat* is to threaten – in the most cases – a person or his/her property with physical violence or a person with death.

Has anyone threatened you <u>during the previous 5 years</u>?

☐ no →	go to question 125
☐ yes	

116. Was this during the previous 12 months?

☐ no →	go to question 125
☐ yes, ______ times in the previous 12 months	
☐ don't know →	go to question 125

117. Did the person who threatened you use any of the following means <u>during the previous 12 months</u>?

	no	yes
Chat message(s) sent via MSN or an online chat site, for instance	☐	☐
Email(s) sent	☐	☐
Message(s) sent via social media sites (Facebook, Hyves, etc.)	☐	☐
(Multimedia) messages sent via mobile phone	☐	☐

118. Did the perpetrator use the internet in any other ways to threaten you?

☐ no
☐ yes, namely

119. *If you were threatened more than once via chat, email, and social media sites or in some other way on the internet, answer the following questions on the basis of the last time that it happened.*

Did know you the perpetrator one of the perpetrators?

☐ no →	go to question 121
☐ yes	

120. Where did know you the perpetrator(s) from? *You can tick more than one option*

☐ partner
☐ ex-partner
☐ family member
☐ someone from the neighbourhood
☐ someone at work
☐ other known

121. Do you think that the reason you were threatened lay in the fact that you belong to a specific group (e.g. ethnic minority, sexual preference or a public position such as a police officer or politician)?

☐ no, I don't belong to one of those groups
☐ no, the fact that I belong to one of those groups had nothing to do with the threats
☐ perhaps
☐ yes
☐ don't know

122. What did you do in response to the threats? *You can tick more than one option*

☐ nothing
☐ contacted the police
☐ other, namely ____________________

123. Did you suffer any material loss through threats?

☐ no →	go to question 125
☐ yes	

124. What is the overall amount that you estimate you have lost because of the threats (up until now)?

☐ ______ euros
☐ don't know

125. In the following table, *other incidents related to privacy and in the private sphere* that happen on the internet are described. Did any of these incidents happen to you as far as you know <u>during the previous 12 months?</u>

	no	yes
Someone changed your web page and/or social networking site profile (Hyves, Facebook and so on) without your permission	☐	☐
Someone posted an embarrassing web page and/or social networking profile (Hyves, Facebook and so on) about you without your permission	☐	☐
Someone spread stories, gossip, videos or photographs about you via email or the internet without your permission	☐	☐
Someone hacked your computer and destroyed, changed or stole data	☐	☐
Someone hacked your email or logged on to your email account without permission	☐	☐

126. If someone hacked your computer and destroyed or changed information: was this the computer that you yourself use at home the most to go on the internet?

☐ n/a
☐ no
☐ yes

127. Did you contact the police because of any of these incidents?

☐ n/a
☐ no
☐ yes

If you were not a victim of extortion/blackmail (question 98), stalking (question 109), threats (question 119) or an incident related to privacy/personal relationships (question 128), you can now skip to question 133.

128. Please indicate to what extent you agree with the following statements with regard to extortion/blackmail, stalking, threats or any other incidents to do with privacy or relationships.

	completely disagree	disagree	do not disagree/or agree	agree	completely agree
My general sense of security on the internet has declined	☐	☐	☐	☐	☐
My general sense of security has declined	☐	☐	☐	☐	☐
My trust in humankind in its entirety has declined	☐	☐	☐	☐	☐
My trust in the Dutch police has declined	☐	☐	☐	☐	☐
My trust in the Dutch rule of law has declined	☐	☐	☐	☐	☐
I have suffered psychological problems	☐	☐	☐	☐	☐
I have suffered financial problems	☐	☐	☐	☐	☐

129. Have you suffered any other consequences because of what happened, other than the ones mentioned above?

- ☐ No
- ☐ yes, namely

If you have never contacted the police because you fell victim to extortion/blackmail, stalking, threats or any other incidents to do with privacy or relationships, you can skip to question 133.

130. What was the police response? *You can tick more than one option*

- ☐ the police took a statement and traced or tried to trace the perpetrator
- ☐ the police took a statement and are still busy tracing the perpetrator
- ☐ the police took a statement
- ☐ the police recorded it but did not take a statement (the police recorded the incident but did not make a police report; you were not given a signed document)
- ☐ the police gave advice, but did not record it or take a statement
- ☐ the police said that there was nothing they could do about it
- ☐ the police did not take me seriously
- ☐ other, namely ______

131. Were you satisfied with the police response?

☐ extremely satisfied
☐ satisfied
☐ neutral
☐ dissatisfied
☐ extremely dissatisfied

132. Please comment on why you were satisfied/dissatisfied with the police response:

Personal background characteristics

133. What is your gender?

☐ male
☐ female

134. How old are you?

_____ years old

135. How many people are there in your household (including yourself)?

_____ people

136. How many of these people are younger than 15 years old?

_____ people

137. How many hours do you work in a normal working week, excluding unpaid work?
Working for short periods should be included, as should freelance work.

☐ I do not do paid work
☐ on average ____ hours

138. What is your highest level of education for which you obtained a diploma?

☐ no education completed
☐ primary education
☐ Lower vocational schooling (e.g. LTS, LEAO, domestic science school)
☐ VMBO, MAVO (MULO)
☐ HAVO/VWO (HBS, MULO-B, Lyceum)
☐ MBO (e.g.. MTS, MEAO, UTS)
☐ HBO (e.g. HTS, HEAO, College for Social Work , Teachers Training College, PABO, HAS)
☐ Academic level (university)

Please enter your login code from the letter here: ☐☐☐☐☐

This is the end of the questionnaire. Thank you very much for taking part in our survey! You can send the questionnaire back using the enclosed envelope. **No postage stamp is required!**

Appendix 5
Letter used in research

Netherlands Police Agency
c/o P.O. Box 1080
8900 CB Leeuwarden

Leeuwarden, 15 April 2011

<Mr/Mrs/Ms> <initials> <name>
<address>
<postal code> <town>

Ref: Research into security in the digital world

Dear <Mr/Mrs/Ms> <name>,

By way of this letter we would like to invite you to participate in countrywide research into security in the digital world. Computerisation has offered people in the Netherlands many new possibilities in the recent past. Via the internet, people can now shop, keep in touch with one another, do their banking, listen to music, look for information and so on. But the digital world, just like the 'real world', is not always safe.

The Open University of the Netherlands (OU) and the Cybersafety Lectorate of the NHL University of Applied Sciences are conducting this research in order to gain insight into how Dutch citizens are using this digital world and how they are dealing with unsafe situations on the internet, The research project was commissioned by the Dutch Central Unit. The Ministry of Security and Justice, the Ministry of the Interior and Kingdom Relations and Statistics Netherlands (CBS) are also closely involved.

Why have you received this invitation?

It goes without saying that it would impossible to survey everyone in the Netherlands. For this reason, the CBS drew a sample for this research from the personal records databases of Dutch municipalities. Your name was drawn as part of this sample.

How can you take part?

We would like you to complete a questionnaire about security in the digital world. Completing the questionnaire should take between 15 to 20 minutes. The questions are about how you use the digital options available to you, how you deal with unsafe situations on the internet and incidents that you may have experienced in the digital world. Even if you don't use the internet or have never experienced any of these incidents, your answers are extremely important to the research! You can complete the questionnaire either via the internet or on paper.

To complete the questionnaire on the internet, you need to do the following:
- Open your web browser (for instance, Internet Explorer, Firefox or Google Chrome);
- Enter 'www.politie.nl/klpd/internetonderzoek' in the web browser's search bar (at the top of your screen);
- you will be directed to the police website;
- click on the link 'complete the questionnaire'. You will then be sent to the questionnaire through a protected connection. You will be able to recognise this protected connection by the letters 'https' instead of 'http';
- you can log in using this login code: <**login code**>;
- after logging in, you will be given more information about how to fill in the questionnaire.

If you cannot or would prefer not to complete the questionnaire on the internet, you can request a written questionnaire either by telephone at 058-2511700, or by sending an email to internetonderzoek@klpd.politie.nl, or via the website www.politie.nl/klpd/internetonderzoek. If you would rather not take part, you can also unsubscribe for the research in the same way; you will then no longer be approached for this research.

Privacy

Your privacy will be fully safeguarded in this research project. Your personal details will be destroyed on completion of the research. Once the internet questionnaire has been completed, the answers are sent to the CBS, where the CBS Privacy Guarantee applies. You can read more on the subject of privacy at the bottom of this page.

Finally

Should you have any questions about the project or about privacy safeguards, or if you have difficulty filling in the questionnaire, you can contact the research team. You can do this by sending an email to internetonderzoek@klpd.politie.nl or by calling 058-2511700. The research team is available from Monday to Friday between 9 am and 5 pm. You can find out more about the research on www.politie.nl/klpd/internetonderzoek.

Thank you in advance for your cooperation.

Yours sincerely

<signature Ruud Bik>

R.G.C. Bik
Chief of Police, Netherlands Police Agency

CBS Privacy Guarantee
Your privacy is safeguarded in all our research. This is an obligation that the CBS has that is provided for in a special law. To safeguard your information, the CBS has taken a number of measures. For instance, there is a strict obligation of confidentiality for all members of staff, which is subject to prosecution. Information about people is separated from their names and addresses as quickly possibly. The information is processed using well-protected computer systems that unauthorised persons cannot access. The law guarantees that your information is only used for statistical purposes. No organisations can demand access to the information that the CBS gathers. There is never any personal information that can be recognised as such in the statistical information that the CBS publishes.

Not only does the CBS gather information itself, it also gets files from other institutions. For instance, it gets information from personal records databases, the work placement branches of the Employee Insurance Agency (*UWV WERKbedrijven*), social services and the salary administrations of many companies. We automatically combine the information that you yourself give in this research with information that we get from other institutions. The CBS uses this combined information to put together statistics about the Netherlands and we work as economically as possible.

APPENDIX 6
CBS WEIGHTING FACTORS

STATISTICS NETHERLANDS

PIM Division PPM Sector

Summary: Cybercrime Research 2011 was carried out by the Open University. For this, the CBS drew an unstratified sample drawn from private individuals aged 15 years and older. The CBS agreed with the Open University that the CBS would carry out the weighting for this research. This weighting is described in this report. The national/regional police section of the Safety Monitor was used to set up the weighting model; the Safety Monitor is conducted by the CBS. Two attributes were combined because their cell count was too low. The University of Applied Sciences Leeuwarden (NHL) used the final weightings to analyse the response files.

Keywords: Cybercrime, linear weighting

WEIGHTING CYBERCRIME

Koen Staats and Martijn Tennekes

Project number:	209674-12
BPA number:	PPM-2012-01-10-KSTS-MTES
Date:	10 January 2012

6.1 INTRODUCTION

The Open University (OU) conducted Cybercrime Research 2011. The project comprised a survey among private individuals aged 15 years and older. The questionnaire was structured as follows (see Noordelijke Hogeschool Leeuwarden, 2011):

1. Internet use
2. Incidents on the internet:
   Fraud via online retail sites and webshops
   Advance fee fraud and identity fraud
   Incidences in the private sphere
3. Personal background characteristics

For this research, the CBS drew a sample of 21,810 people. The data was gathered in the months of April, May and June in the same way as the Safety Monitor 2010 at a local level, namely: first via the internet (CAWI), then if preferred using PAPI, followed by CATI. The CBS enriched the microdata with background characteristics. As agreed with the Open University, the CBS also did the weighting. It was agreed that the Safety Monitor 2010 weighting model would be used as a guideline for the Cybercrime Research. The Safety Monitor 2010 weighting is described in Buelens and Van den Brakel (2011b).

The weighting model is described in this report. The reduction and attribution of the background variables is described in Section 2. In Section 3 the inclusion probabilities are determined and in Section 4 the weighting for the Cybercrime Research is described. Finally in Section 5 some conclusions are drawn and recommendations given.

6.2 Combining and attributing background variables

Some background characteristics, including municipality codes, were already linked to the response rate in the microdata that was supplied. Because the police regions were not noted, we linked these using municipality codes. The categories for all variables are included in the appendix. The background variable 'origin' in the response file had eight categories, including the category 'unknown'. Because the Safety Monitor only has two categories, the categories 'Native Dutch' and 'Other western countries' were combined to 'Native Dutch and western native' and the categories 'Morocco', 'Turkey', 'Suriname', 'Neth. Antilles and Aruba' and 'Other non-western countries' were combined to 'Other'. If the origin was unknown, it was assigned to 'Native and western native'.

The age given in response was used for each respondent. If these were not filled in or deemed to be incorrect,[48] age was determined on the basis of the municipal personal records database (GBA) and the starting date of the interview.

For gender, the values given as a response were used and where they were missing the GBA values were used. If this value was also not known, gender was assigned randomly since both genders are more or less equally represented.

Missing municipality codes were assigned through the municipality code of a random respondent for which the municipality code was known. This means that large municipalities had a relatively large chance of being selected. Police region, province and region and level of urbanisation can be derived from the municipality code.

48 In some cases the age given as a response was higher than 98 years. These were deemed to be incorrect because they were not consistent with the GBA age.

The size of household mentioned was also used and, where these were missing, household size according to the GBA were used. If both were missing the average household size according to age category (from age 11) to which the respondent belonged were assigned. This equates to four-person households for 15 to 19 year olds, three-person households for 20 to 24 year olds and 30 to 54 year olds, and two-person households for other age groups (25 to 29 and 55 and above).

6.3 Inclusion probabilities

The sample was drawn from all private individuals aged 15 and above who were registered in the Netherlands. Overall this amounted to 13,458,516 people. The distributed sample amounted to 21,810 and the net response rate was 10,300. The response rate percentage was therefore 47%. Because the sample was drawn without stratifications, the inclusion probability for all respondents i was the same:

The weighting is same as$d_i = 1/\ \pi_i$ for respondent i.

$\pi_i =$	n	=	10.300
	N		13.458.516

6.4 Weighting

Generally the response rate is selective for one or more background variables. By weighting the response rate according to a number of background variables, this selectivity is corrected. If one or more of these background variables are linked to a specific target variable, the weighting may lead to variance reduction for this target variable.

6.4.1 *Linear weighting*

For linear weighting, the generalised regression estimator was applied (Särndal, Swensson & Wretman, 1992). What this means, briefly, is that inclusion probabilities are adjusted as little as possible, so that the sum of each weighted background variable is the same as the known population total. The resulting probabilities are also known as end probabilities. In formulas, the end probability of respondent i is: $w_i = d_i c_i$, where c_i is called the correction probability. By definition, correction probabilities have an average of 1, and ideally are not widely distributed around 1.

The weighting was carried out with Bascula software (Nieuwenbroek & Boonstra, 2002) and was managed in R (R Development Core Team, 2011).

6.4.2 Weighting model

We used the Safety Monitor 2010 weighting model as a basis for our weighting model, as described in Section 3.2 of Buelens and Van den Brakel (2011b). This weighting model is as follows:

household size5 (1)
police region25 x gender (2)
police region25 x age (3)
provincieplus16 x origin2 (4)
provincieplus16 x urbanisation level5 (5)
gender x age11 (6)

The response mode attribute was omitted because the response mode in the Cybercrime Research was not registered properly.

This weighting model can also be used for the Cybercrime Research if the minimum cell content for each attribute is not too small. As a general rule, a minimum of 10 is used for sampling. Table B6.1 shows cells containing the lowest number of respondents for each attribute. For instance there are relatively few respondents who are members of a household comprising five or more people. For the second attribute, women from Het Gooi [an area around the Dutch town of Hilversum], and women from the Vechtstreek [a region in the Dutch provinces of Utrecht and North Holland] occur the least frequently.

Table B6.1 Cells with the lowest content and with contents of less than 10, per weighting attribute (see the appendix for the cell number definitions)

Attribute	Cells	Cell content
(1)	5 (household comprises five people or more)	1.160
(2)	14 x 2 (Gooi and Vechtstreek, Female)	73
(3)	11 x 3 (Zaanstreek-Waterland, aged 25 to 29 years)	4
	14 x 2 (Gooi and Vechtstreek, aged 20 to 24 years)	6
	14 x 5, 19 x 3 en 25 x 3	8
(4)	29 x 2 (Zeeland, Non-western ethnic minorities)	3
	22 x 2 (Drenthe, ethnic minorities)	6
	21 x 2 (Friesland, Non-western ethnic minorities)	8
	20 x 2 (Groningen, Non-western ethnic minorities)	9
(5)	26 x 5 (Utrecht Province excluding the Municipality of Utrecht, non-urban)	10
(6)	1 x 3 (Man, 25-29 jaar)	249

In order to increase cell content, some cells were combined. As the table shows, there were two attributes, namely (3) and (4), that needed to be combined.

Attribute (3) comprises the variables police region25 and age11. There are two options: combine some age categories or combine police regions in line with, for instance, the 12 provinces. We opted to reduce age to 6 categories (see Appendix CBS weighting factors), because this option best covers the attribute. After this reduction, the cell for 25 to 34 year olds in Zaanstreek-Waterland had the lowest content (14 respondents).

For attribute (4), the obvious option was to reduce regional divisions to provinceplus16 because origin 2 only consisted of two categories. Reducing these to 12 provinces had no influence on the low cell content because the provinces with few inhabitants, which included Zeeland, were the same size as they were at provinceplus16 level. For this reason, we opted for another regional division that is standard for the CBS, namely division into region. The provinces of Groningen, Friesland and Drenthe were then combined into the Northern Region and accounted for 23 non-western ethnic minorities in the response rate. For the other regions, this number was obviously (much) higher.

The two reductions mentioned above resulted in the following weighting model for the Cybercrime Research:

household size5 (7)
police region25 x gender (8)
police region25 x age6 (9)
region4 x origin2 (10)
provincieplus16 x urbanisation level5 (11)
gender x age11 (12)

6.4.3 Results

Figure B6.1a gives a histogram for the correction probabilities as well as some statistics. The correction probability has a good – not too wide – distribution, clustered around 1.0. The lowest correction probability is positive, namely 0.0106, therefore it was not necessary to do finite probabilities.

We also looked at nine important target variables, namely: presence of malware (Q68), loss through malware (Q73), fraud through seller (product/service never supplied) (Q79), fraud through seller (product/service was fake or bad quality) (Q96), fraud through buyer (Q114), ID fraud (Q623), extortion and blackmail (Q658), stalking (Q216) and threat (Q696).

The estimates for these variables seem plausible. Moreover, the corresponding variances are small in comparison with estimates that were made with other weighting models.

We then investigated the extent to which the response rate was selective for the background variables in the weighting. Population groups that were under-represented are automatically assigned a higher weighting. Figure B6.2 gives a table plot for the response file (see Tennekes, De Jonge & Daas, 2011). For this, the respondents were sorted according to correction probability (the first column), and subsequently grouped in 100 groups of the same size.

Figure B6.1 Correction probabilities for the weighting model (7)-(12) with boundaries

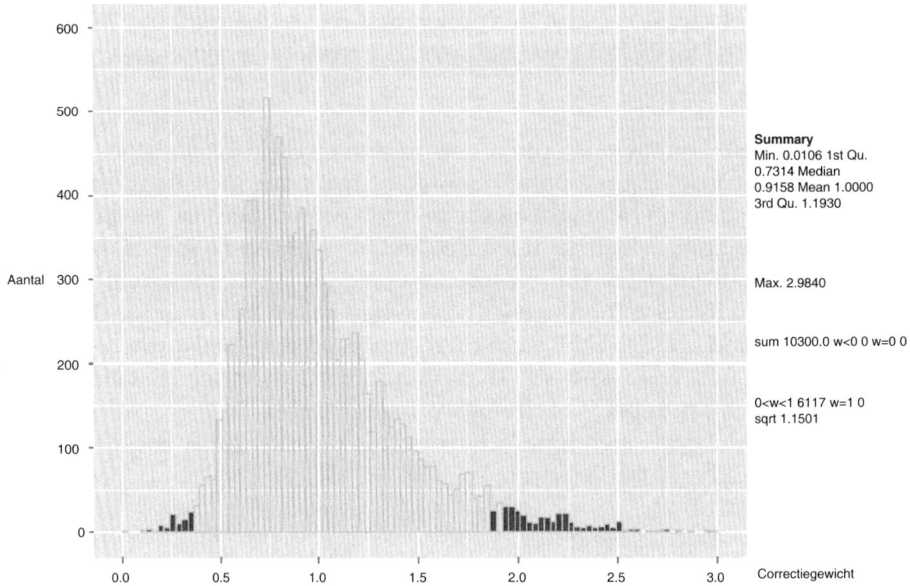

Figure B6.2 Table plot of the response file

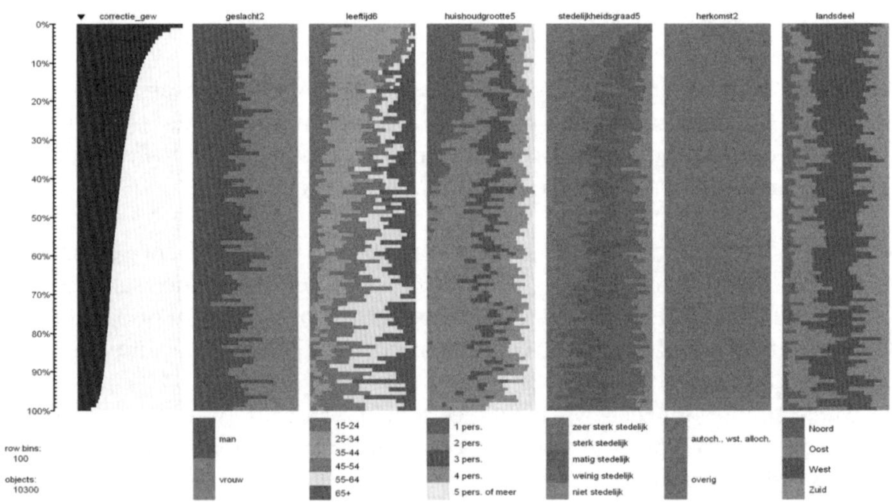

This table plot shows that:

- the response rate is not selective for gender (column 2);
- young people aged 15 to 34 years are under-represented (column 3);
- single-person households are under-represented and two-person households are over-represented (column 4);
- people in a highly urbanised areas are under-represented (column 5);
- non-western ethnic minorities including those from Suriname and the Dutch Antilles are very strongly under-represented (column 6);
- people from the west of the country (North and South Holland, Utrecht and Zeeland) are slightly are under-represented (column 7).

6.5 Conclusions and recommendations

We used the Safety Monitor 2010 weighting model as a guideline for the Cybercrime Research. Because some combinations, such as non-western ethnic minorities in Zeeland, occurred too infrequently in the response rate, we had to reduce the model to some degree.

Linear weighting resulted in a list of final probabilities that could be used to estimate target variables. The number of people that were swindled on the internet is an example of an interesting target variable.

For future research, it is advisable to keep track of the interviewing mode used per response (CAWI, PAPI or CATI) because measurement errors can be related to the various modes in a mixed-mode sample (see Buelens & Van den Brakel, 2011a).

References

Buelens, B.A.H. & J.A. van den Brakel (2011a). *Inference in surveys with sequential mixed-mode data collection* (CBS-discussion paper). Heerlen: Centraal Bureau voor de Statistiek.

Buelens, B.A.H. & J.A. van den Brakel (2011b). *Weging integrale veiligheidsmonitor 2010* (CBS-nota, BPA-nr DMK-2011-03-02-BBUS). Heerlen: Centraal Bureau voor de Statistiek.

Nieuwenbroek, N. & H.J. Boonstra (2002). *Bascula 4.0 Reference Manual*. Heerlen: Centraal Bureau voor de Statistiek.

Noordelijke Hogeschool Leeuwarden (2011). *Vragenlijst onderzoek naar (on)veiligheid in de digitale wereld* (digital publication). Leeuwarden: NHL Hogeschool.

R Development Core Team (2011). *R: A language and environment for statistical computing*. Wenen: R Foundation for Statistical Computing. www.R-project.org/.

Särndal, C.E., B. Swensson & J. Wretman (1992). *Model Assisted Survey Sampling*. New York: Springer Verlag.

Tennekes, M., E. de Jonge & P.J.H. Daas (2011). *Visual profiling of large statistical datasets* (CBS discussion paper, BPA-nr. DMK-2011-02-15-MTES). Heerlen/Den Haag: Centraal Bureau voor de Statistiek.

Appendix CBS weighting factors Variables

	household size5
1	Single-person households
2	Two-person households
3	Three-person households
4	Four-person households
5	Households comprising five people or more

	urbanisation level5
1	Extremely urbanised
2	Strongly urbanised
3	Moderately urbanised
4	Hardly urbanised
5	Not urbanised

	gender
1	Male
2	Female

	origin2
1	Native and western non-native
2	Other

	age6		age11
1	15 – 24	1	15 – 19
		2	20 – 24
2	25 – 34	3	25 – 29
		4	30 – 34
3	35 – 44	5	35 – 39
		6	40 – 44
4	45 – 54	7	45 – 49
		8	50 – 54
5	55 – 64	9	55 – 59
		10	60 – 64
6	65+	11	65+

region4		provinceplus 16		police region25	
		20	Groningen	1	Groningen
1	North	21	Friesland	2	Friesland
		22	Drenthe	3	Drenthe
		23	Overijssel	4	IJsselland
				5	Twente
2	East			6	North and East Gelderland
		25	Gelderland	7	Middle Gelderland
				8	South Gelderland
		24	Flevoland	25	Flevoland
		26	Province of Utrecht (excluding Municipality of Utrecht)	9	Utrecht
		16	Municipality of Utrecht		
				10	North Holland North
			North Holland	11	Zaanstreek-Waterland
		27	(excluding Amsterdam)	12	Kennemerland
				14	Gooi and Vechtstreek
3	West			13	Amsterdam-Amstelland
		13	Amsterdam		
		14	Rotterdam	17	Rotterdam-Rijnmond
		28	South Holland (excluding Rotterdam)	16	Middle Holland
			The Hague	18	South Holland South
				15	Haaglanden
		15	The Hague		
		29	Zeeland	19	Zeeland
				20	Middle and West Brabant
		30	North Brabant	21	Brabant North
4	South			22	South-East Brabant
		31	Limburg	23	North Limburg
				24	South Limburg

MILK MUSHROOMS OF NORTH AMERICA

A Field Identification Guide to the Genus *Lactarius*

ALAN E. BESSETTE

DAVID B. HARRIS

ARLEEN R. BESSETTE

Syracuse University Press

First Edition 2009
09 10 11 12 13 14   6 5 4 3 2 1

The paper used in this publication meets the minimum requirements of American National Standard for Information Sciences—Permanence of Paper for Printed Library Materials, ANSI Z39.48–1984.∞™

For a listing of books published and distributed by Syracuse University Press, visit our Web site at SyracuseUniversityPress.syr.edu.

ISBN 978-0-8156-3229-0

LIBRARY OF CONGRESS CATALOGING-IN-PUBLICATION DATA

Bessette, Alan.
Milk mushrooms of North America : a field identification guide to the genus Lactarius / Alan E. Bessette, David B. Harris, and Arleen R. Bessette. — 1st ed.
p. cm.
Includes bibliographical references and index.
ISBN 978-0-8156-3229-0 (hardcover : alk. paper)
1. Lactarius—North America—Identification—Handbooks, manuals, etc. 2. Mushrooms—North America—Identification—Handbooks, manuals, etc. I. Harris, David B. (David Bruce), 1951– II. Bessette, Arleen Rainis, 1951– III. Title.
QK629.R87B47 2009
579.5'9—dc22   2009014657

Front cover illustration: *Lactarius olympianus*
Back cover: *Lactarius fallax* var. *concolor*
Frontispiece, front flap: *Lactarius volemus* var. *volemus*
Back flap: *Lactarius fallax* var. *fallax*

Designed by Christopher Kuntze
Color separations by The Studio, Hartford, Vermont
Printed and bound in China by Everbest

It is with delight that we dedicate this book to WILLIAM C. ROODY.

Bill's contributions to the field of mycology are many and significant: a keen intellect, extensive knowledge, and uncanny perception. He has a rare talent for exquisitely capturing and preserving, through photography, the ephemeral beauty of all things mycological.

Bill brings a deep heart-rooted joy to the study of fungi. Anyone who has been fortunate enough to have taken one of his workshops or courses, or has spent time in the woods with him on forays, has experienced firsthand Bill's ability to teach and to foster a sense of discovery using his unique blend of humor, humility, and wisdom.

Generous in the sharing of his time and his knowledge, gentle in his touch upon this planet, witty with an offbeat and iconoclastic humor, Bill is part Puck, part mystic.

We are indebted to him in so many ways and are grateful for his being both our colleague and our friend.

Lactarius paradoxus

Simply because they are toadstools and hot,
they have been condemned without trial.
—Charles McIlvaine (1840–1909)

NOTICE Although this book includes information regarding the edibility of the mushrooms described, it is *not* intended to function as a manual for the identification and safe consumption of wild mushrooms. Readers interested in consuming wild fungi should consult other sources of information, including experienced mycologists and literary works, before eating any wild mushrooms. The authors and the publisher are not responsible for any undesirable outcomes that may occur for those who fail to read or heed this warning.

Contents

Lactarius luculentus var. *luculentus*

Preface

The milk mushrooms in the genus *Lactarius* are numerous and conspicuous elements of the summer and fall mycoflora. They are a distinctive group that even beginners can quickly learn to recognize at the generic level. However, it is more challenging to identify individual species. These handsome mushrooms are always represented in general mushroom guidebooks. The genus is a large one, with more than 250 species, varieties, and forms known from North America. Until now, the only reasonably thorough treatment of the genus has been in either technical monographs or articles in scientific journals. The illustrations in these esteemed works—on which we have relied heavily for taxonomic concepts—are not presented in color. Furthermore, the technical language and expertise required to use these materials effectively are significant barriers to the nonspecialist.

We hope that the current less-formal treatment will provide access for a broader audience and thus enhance the interest in this important and attractive group of mushrooms. Perhaps the amateur mycologist will benefit most from our field identification approach, but we believe that the accurate, high-quality color photos and species descriptions, which include microscopic detail, will serve as a useful reference to all who study the genus at whatever level of expertise. Some of the species appear here in color for the first time. The genus *Lactarius* tends to display more genetic diversity than most other genera, so we have frequently included multiple color images to demonstrate this variability.

Lactarius indigo var. *indigo*

Acknowledgments

Many people have assisted us with this work. We are grateful for their significant contributions. We thank Amy Heintz, Jessica Harris, and Donna Mitchell for their mycological notes, technical information, and assistance in collecting specimens. Seanna Annis, Harley Barnhart, Michael Beug, Robert Chapman, Dennis Desjardin, Vera Evenson, Dan Guravich, Marcia Guravich, Roy Halling, Richard Homola, Emily Johnson, David Lewis, Andy Methven, Hope Miller, Orson K. Miller, John Plischke III, Bill Roody, Kit Scates-Barnhart, Walt Sturgeon, Walt Sundberg, Harry Thiers, Steve Trudell, Nathan Wilson, and Michael Wood contributed slides that greatly enhance this book. We appreciate the efforts of Annie Barva, who copyedited the manuscript, and Christopher Kuntze, who designed the book. We are deeply indebted to Bill Roody, who read the manuscript, made many valuable suggestions for its improvement, and contributed immensely to several parts of the book, including the preface and introduction, especially the section on edibility. We are especially grateful to Alice Randel Pfeiffer and her staff at Syracuse University Press, who made this book possible.

MILK MUSHROOMS
OF
NORTH AMERICA

Lactarius deliciosus (Rovellons) for sale at the Boqueria Market in Barcelona, Spain.

Introduction to the Genus *Lactarius*

THE GENUS *LACTARIUS* DEFINED

Lactarius is a large genus, with more than two hundred species described from North America. They grow in forested areas throughout North America and fruit most commonly during summer and fall. Members of the genus *Lactarius* are small to large, mostly terrestrial, fleshy fruiting bodies with a cap, central stalk, and knife blade–like gills. They produce white, cream, yellow, or ochre spore deposits. No universal veil, partial veil, or ring is formed. The genus is easily recognized in the field because these mushrooms' gills, cap flesh, or stalk exudes a milk-like latex when cut. The latex may be clear and watery, white to cream, or variously colored immediately on exposure. The latex of some species slowly or rapidly changes color and may stain tissues. Latex production varies from scanty to copious depending on the species and on the mushroom's condition; dry specimens may not exude any latex.

Lactarius species have distinctly brittle flesh owing to the presence of inflated globose cells called "sphaerocysts" that occur in clusters termed "rosettes." The rosettes are distributed among the filamentous hyphae composing most of the flesh tissue. Members of this genus are also characterized by the presence of lactifers, or spores with amyloid ornamentation, and the absence of clamp connections in all tissues. *Lactarius* species are classified in the family Russulaceae along with members of the genus *Russula*. Although the two genera share many common features, the genus *Russula* is easily separated from *Lactarius* because its species do not produce a milk-like latex.

IDENTIFICATION FEATURES

Macroscopic features of importance in the identification of *Lactarius* species include size and shape of the fruiting body; characteristics of the cap, stalk, and gills; a description of the flesh and latex; odor; taste; spore deposit; habitat; and macrochemical tests. The cap, stalk, and gill color of many species in this genus is distinctive and an important character in the identification process. Other surface characters such as texture, the presence of an umbo, a bearded margin, zonation, and a scrobiculate stalk are also important identification features.

Some authors consider the number of tiers of lamellulae present to be a useful character for species identification. We have not included information about lamellulae in this work because the descriptions of many published species do not mention this feature, so it is difficult to make comparisons using this character. The color of the latex immediately on exposure to air and any subsequent change in color over time should be noted. It is also important to note whether the latex dries a specific color and whether tissues are stained by the latex.

Odor and taste are two very important features to determine when attempting to identify species of *Lactarius.* Although many species lack a distinctive odor, some have very distinctive odors that are very helpful in the identification process. Some of the peculiar odors detected in some species include that of fruit, spice, maple sugar or burnt sugar, fenugreek, fetid decay, hyacinth, coconut, anise, sperm, fish, and spoiled crab. The taste of both the latex and the flesh should be determined as valuable identification characters.

The taste of the flesh or latex of some species may be mild or slightly acrid to extremely acrid, bitter, or some combination of these possibilities.

Spore deposit color is often a valuable character for the identification of some mushroom genera and species. This character may not be as valuable for the identification of certain species and varieties of *Lactarius.* Although the spore deposit color for some *Lactarius* species and varieties is dark yellow or ochre, most are white to cream. Some white deposits become cream-colored as they air-dry. Thin deposits may be white, whereas thick deposits may be cream or yellow. In most instances, the original authors of *Lactarius* species and varieties with a white to cream spore deposit did not state the relative thickness of the spore deposit, an unfortunate fact that influences the reliability of this identification characteristic.

For additional information about macroscopic characters for the identification of *Lactarius,* see Methven's article "Contributions to a Study of the North American Species of *Lactarius*" (1993). Although many species of *Lactarius* may be identified using only macroscopic features, some require microscopic examination before species identification can be determined.

Important microscopic information includes descriptions of the spores, of the cystidia when appropriate, and of the cap cuticle. Most species of *Lactarius* have spores that occur within the range of 5–12 × 5–10 µm. Spore-size measurements should not include the height of the ornamentation and are most accurately determined from spores obtained in a spore deposit produced by a mature specimen. The height of the ornamentation and the shape of the spores should also be determined. Variation in spore ornamentation, from isolated warts and spines to distinct lines and ridges and complete reticulation, is shown in the scanning electron photomicrographs given here.

Cystidia are often of little value for the identification process; however, they are sometimes prominent and distinctive, and therefore should be noted when present. Two types may be observed: smaller filamentous elements commonly called "pseudocystidia" and prominent large cystidia called "macrocystidia."

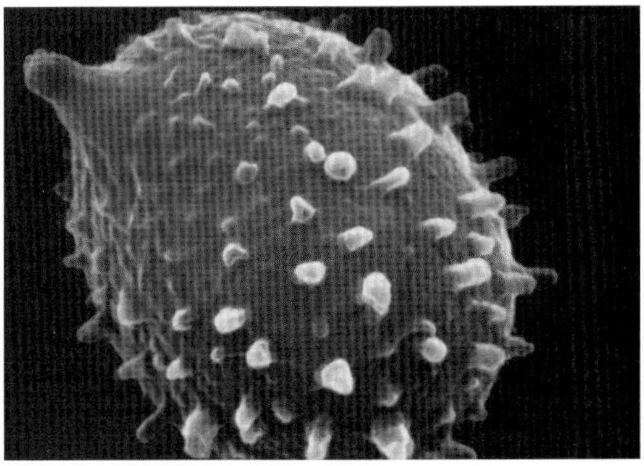

Lactarius deceptivus scanning electron photomicrograph of a spore showing isolated warts and spines.

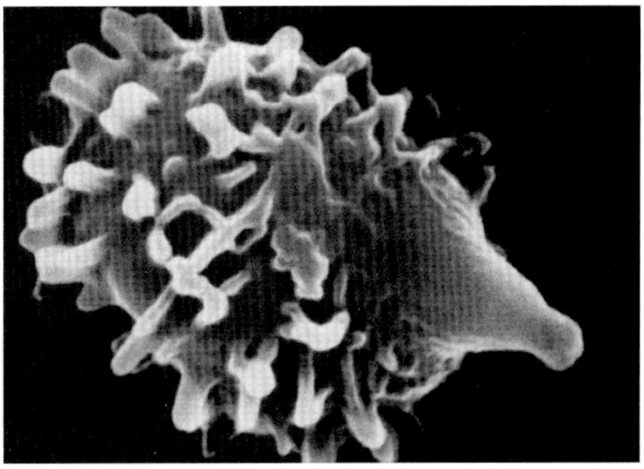

Lactarius camphoratus scanning electron photomicrograph of a spore showing isolated warts and spines, some of which connect to form nodulose ridges.

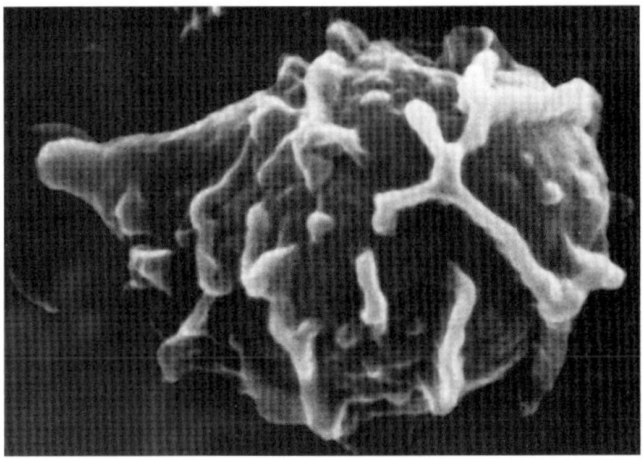

Lactarius resimus var. *resimus* scanning electron photomicrograph of a spore showing warts and ridges with a weakly developed partial reticulum.

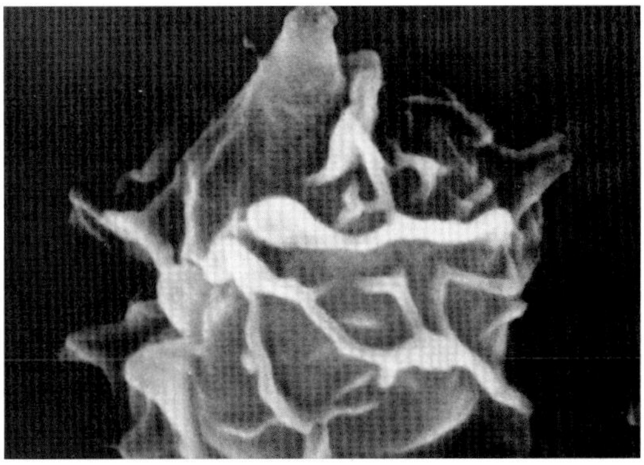

Lactarius uvidus var. *montanus* scanning electron photomicrograph of a spore showing isolated warts, widely spaced bands and ridges with free ends, and a broken to partial reticulum.

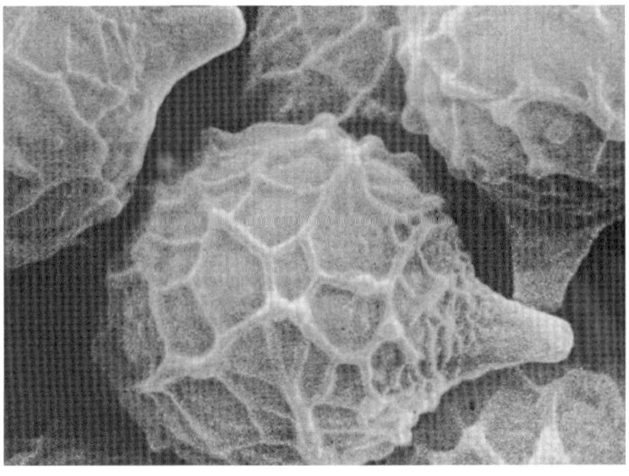

Lactarius gerardii var. *gerardii* scanning electron photomicrograph of spores showing a complete reticulum.

Several types of cap cuticles may be observed and are important in the identification of certain species. Some of the more commonly encountered types of cuticles include cutis, ixocutis, trichoderm, and ixotrichoderm.

ECOLOGY

The genus *Lactarius* is distributed worldwide. In North America, some species are common and widely distributed, whereas others are uncommon or rare and have a restricted distribution. The habitats in which they occur have a characteristic vascular plant flora because *Lactarius* species form ectomycorrhizae with members of the Betulaceae, Fagaceae, Pinaceae, and some Salicaceae. Several authors have documented the ectomycorrhizal relationship between *Lactarius* species and their host trees and shrubs (Giltrap 1982; Homola and Czapowskyj 1981; O. Miller 1983; Trappe 1962). According to Heilmann-Clausen and colleagues (1998), all species of *Lactarius* are known or assumed to be ectomycorrhizal. Some species fruit in either conifer or hardwood forests, whereas others occur in only one type of forest or in mixed woodlands where their host is present. In general, forested areas with more extensive habitat diversity tend to have greater *Lactarius* biodiversity. Some species associate with only a single host, but others associate with two or more hosts. *Lactarius manzanitae* grows on the ground exclusively associated with manzanita; *Lactarius controversus* associates with either poplar or willow; and *Lactarius indigo* grows in either conifer or hardwood forests.

Several published studies describe the distribution of *Lactarius* species in various habitats of North America. Bills (1986a, 1986b) has studied the distribution of *Lactarius* in the high-elevation forests of the southern Appalachians. Several investigators have conducted mycological studies of Alaska and the Alaskan arctic tundra (Kobayasi et al. 1967; Laursen and Ammirati 1982; Miller, Laursen, and Murray 1973; Wells and Kempton 1975). Hesler and A. H. Smith (1979) as well as Korhonen (1984) are among the many mycologists who have studied *Lactarius* species that are characteristic of sphagnum bogs. Other principle investigators who have contributed much information about the distribution of *Lactarius* in North America include Burlingham (1908), Coker (1918), Methven (1997), Murrill (1938), Peck (1907), and Singer (1975).

EDIBILITY OF *LACTARIUS* SPECIES

As a group, the milk mushrooms are not widely consumed in North America. Many are considered to be inedible because they have acrid-tasting flesh, and a few are known to be poisonous. However, there are some very good edible milk mushrooms that are easily recognized and often fruit in abundance. They are a resource that many Americans have yet to discover.

In some parts of the world, species of *Lactarius* are among the most highly prized of all edible wild mushrooms. For instance, in the Spanish and French Pyrenees, *Lactarius deliciosus* and *Lactarius sanguifluus* are consumed in great quantities.

During the fall of the year in Catalonia and in the Basque regions of Spain, these species are commonly sold in the markets and along roadsides at prices equal to or higher than some better-known edible mushrooms such as chanterelles (*Cantharellus* species) and ceps *(Boletus edulis)*. In the Catalan province of Bergueda, a four-day mushroom festival is held every October in which the gathering and cooking of rovellons *(Lactarius deliciosus)* are the principal attractions. During the fall mushroom season, many restaurants and tapas bars in northern Spain offer specialty dishes featuring rovellons.

In Scandinavia, especially Finland, and in the Slavic countries of eastern Europe, milk mushrooms are also very popular edibles, including some species that have acrid flesh. Milk mushrooms with acrid flesh are soaked in salt brine or parboiled to remove the peppery taste.

On the U.S. west coast, the Candy Cap, *Lactarius rubidus*, is much appreciated as a flavoring agent. Its sweet, brown sugar–like odor intensifies on drying, so this mushroom is often used in desert recipes. In the eastern United States, *Lactarius volemus* is the best-known and most popular edible milk mushroom. In the mountains of West Virginia, it is known as a "bradley" or "leatherback." The curious name *bradley* is probably a corruption of *bratling*, the German name for this species, which means "mushroom for roasting." Its flesh is sweet and has a mysterious smoky-fishy flavor that many people relish. *Lactarius volemus* is one of the few mushrooms with a strong enough flavor and texture to withstand prolonged cooking and heavy seasoning. This quality can be used to advantage in such dishes as baked beans and casseroles. They are also delicious simply grilled or roasted with a little oil over a campfire. Closely related species such as *Lactarius hygrophoroides*, *Lactarius luteolus*, and *Lactarius corrugis* have a milder flavor, but are also very good.

Other easily recognized milk mushrooms worth experimenting with include *Lactarius indigo*, *Lactarius paradoxus*, *Lactarius chelidonium*, *Lactarius thyinos*, *Lactarius pseudodeliciosus*, and *Lactarius subpurpureus*. These relatively mild-tasting species make good fillers to add to other more flavorful species. Although the edibility of many milk mushrooms that occur in North America is still unknown, they are generally regarded as safe if the flesh is mild tasting. Some acrid-tasting species such as *Lactarius deceptivus* become mild after cooking. However, anyone who wishes to experiment with species that are not clearly established edibles should do so with caution. Our advice is to stick to those mushrooms with a proven track record.

One cannot discuss edible milk mushrooms without mentioning the Lobster Mushroom *(Hypomyces lactifluorum)*. This parasitic fungus (see description and color illustration, p. 275) infects several milk mushrooms, including *Lactarius deceptivus*, *Lactarius piperatus*, *Lactarius subvellereus* var. *distans*, and *Russula brevipes*. It forms a brilliant orange crust over the host mushroom's entire fruiting body. When the host is an acrid-tasting species, the flesh amazingly becomes mild and pleasant after being parasitized. Once the host is infected, it can no longer produce spores, and it becomes impossible to identify accurately. It seems to go against all common sense when consuming edible wild mushrooms to eat any that cannot be identified with certainty, but the Lobster Mushroom is far and wide regarded as a safe edible. However, one should proceed with caution and probably not consume large quantities.

Aside from species that are known or suspected to be toxic, such as *Lactarius torminosus, Lactarius pubescens, Lactarius vinaceorufescens,* and *Lactarius chrysorrheus,* among others, some milk mushrooms' edibility may be subjective. Whether it is worth the trouble to parboil acrid-tasting species or soak them in salt brine in order to render them edible is a matter of individual taste and motivation. Even with the more popular species of milk mushrooms, opinions may vary as to their culinary value because of the characteristic grainy texture of their flesh. To some, the grainy flesh gives these mushrooms a "meaty" quality that lends itself well to grilling or broiling, especially after first marinating the caps in olive oil and balsamic vinegar for a couple of hours.

NOTES ON THE DESCRIPTIONS OF SPECIES AND VARIETIES

All descriptions are based on those of the original authors. In many instances, Lexemuel Hesler and Alexander Smith have modified or added to the original descriptions, as shown in their monograph *North American Species of Lactarius* (1979). Additional information as modified by Andrew S. Methven in *The Agaricales (Gilled Fungi) of California 10. Russulaceae 2.* Lactarius (1997) is also included in this book. Other sources of information are listed in the references section.

SCIENTIFIC NAME: A Latin scientific name is provided for each species and variety. The name used may not be the same one commonly found in other field guides, but instead may reflect a recent taxonomic change.

Immediately following the scientific name is an unabbreviated author citation for the convenience of mycologists who may find this information useful. In some instances, the author citation is simple; for example, *Lactarius californiensis* Hesler and A. H. Smith was described and named by Lexemuel R. Hesler and Alexander H. Smith. Sometimes, however, the original author's name is enclosed in parentheses and followed by the names of those who later reclassified the fungus; for example, *Lactarius fragilis* (Burlingham) Hesler and A. H. Smith was originally described by Burlingham as *Lactaria camphorata* subsp. *fragilis,* and later reclassified by Hesler and A. H. Smith.

SOURCE OF ORIGINAL PUBLICATION: Here we provide the name of the book or journal in which the original description of the species or variety was given, along with the volume number when appropriate, the year of publication, and page numbers.

SYNONYMS: All previously used or newly proposed noteworthy scientific names for each species or variety are presented here.

COMMON NAME: One or more common names are provided if previously published or reported. No new common names have been coined for this book.

CAP: Information about the size and shape of the cap as well as about the margin, surface texture, and color is provided here.

GILLS: Attachment, width, spacing, color, bruising reactions, and the presence or absence of forking are noted.

STALK: Information about the length, thickness, shape, texture, color, and staining reactions is provided here. Whether the stalk is solid or hollow is also often described.

FLESH: The thickness, texture, color, and staining reaction when cut are described in this section. Some species and varieties of *Lactarius* have a distinctive odor, and this information is noted. The flesh of some species has a distinctive taste and is indicated when known. *If you choose to taste the tissues of a mushroom, be advised that some mushrooms taste hot and peppery and may irritate, burn, or numb your mouth if chewed for an extended period.* Note also that there is no significant risk in properly tasting mushrooms *unless you swallow the tissue!* To taste mushrooms safely, place a small piece in your mouth, chew it for only a few seconds, and spit it out. If the taste is mild (not bitter or peppery), wait a minute and then chew a second small piece for fifteen to thirty seconds and again spit it out—some mushrooms' bitter or acrid tastes are subtle.

LATEX: The volume and color on exposure as well as any color change are noted here. In addition, the time required for color change, tissue staining reactions, and taste are also provided.

SPORE DEPOSIT: Spore deposit color is sometimes a valuable character for the identification of *Lactarius* species and varieties. The spore deposit color for some *Lactarius* species and varieties is dark yellow or ochre, but most are white to cream. Spore deposit color should be determined from thick deposits whenever possible. The spore deposit color determined by the author of each species or variety is presented in this section.

MACROSCOPIC TESTS: This section includes the color reactions obtained when various chemicals such as KOH, NH_4OH, and $FeSO_4$ are applied to the cap surface, flesh, gills, or latex.

MICROSCOPIC CHARACTERS: Information about spore size, shape, surface features, and the color of the spores and spore ornamentations in KOH and Melzer's is presented here. Additional information in this section includes a description of the cap cuticle and the presence of certain types of cystidia (when appropriate for identification or separation from other similar species or varieties).

OCCURRENCE: The habit of mushroom growth (solitary, scattered, in groups or clusters), substrate, habitat, fruiting period, known distribution, and frequency are described here. The fruiting period is stated as a month-to-month range and describes the time during which the mushroom is likely to occur. On occasion, mushrooms will appear outside of their expected fruiting period owing to unusual weather conditions. Frequency is estimated for all of North America. Species or varieties listed as "occasional" may be locally abundant in some areas or rare to absent in others.

EDIBILITY: Species known to be edible are listed as "edible." Any species described as "poisonous" or "edibility unknown" *should not be eaten!*

COMMENTS: This section includes descriptions of similar species or varieties and other useful or interesting information about the species described.

FIELD CHARACTERISTICS OF *LACTARIUS* SPECIES

The genus *Lactarius* is particularly well suited for field identifications, yet one cannot hope to identify every species based solely on macroscopic field characters. A large number of milk mushrooms essentially share the same general stature and differ only in color, subtle morphological features of the fruiting body, and ecology. Because most *Lactarius* species are medium-size mushrooms, size is of limited value except for those species that are either exceptionally large or exceptionally small. Cap color and surface features are of primary importance, as are the color and mutability of the latex that exudes from cut or broken tissue. The taste of the latex or flesh is also a valuable field character.

Most, if not all, milk mushrooms form ectomycorrhizal relationships with trees and shrubs where the fungal mycelium becomes integrated with the plant's root system, facilitating a mutually beneficial exchange of nutrients. These fungus-tree associations can be generalized or at times quite specific. Either way, the ecological situation in which *Lactarius* species occur is always important and should be noted. The field keys provided here utilize both morphology and ecology. The identification process begins with observations of fresh specimens at the time of collection. Whenever possible, collect several mushrooms in all stages of development. Specimens should be fresh, not old and dried. The individual who collects the specimens should take appropriate field notes at the time of collection. These observations will greatly assist the identification process. Important information to record includes the habitat and tree associate if known; substrate; color of the latex immediately on exposure and color change within five minutes after exposure; odor; and taste of the flesh and latex. In addition, it is often helpful to note the color of the dried latex and any tissue staining reaction. Be aware that although several species' latex color itself may remain unchanged, the latex may stain tissues a different color.

Latex taste determinations should be performed using young or mature specimens, but not old or dried material. The latex of some species may taste mild at first and then slowly bitter or acrid. Also, the latex of some species may taste bitter, astringent, disagreeable, metallic, or musky initially and then slowly acrid. Any change or sequence of changes in the taste of the latex should be noted. If latex is unobtainable, we suggest that you first attempt to identify the unknown milk mushroom using the key set of characters that indicate a watery, whey-like, white, or creamy white latex. Choices in the key regarding the taste of the latex will usually be correctly selected by tasting the flesh because the flesh of most species tastes exactly like the latex.

When checking for viscidity on dry specimens, moisten your finger with saliva and gently rub it in a small circle on a mushroom cap or stalk. Then slowly pull your finger away and observe whether a sticky substance is present, which indicates that the specimen is viscid when moist. Reposition your finger on the moistened area and slowly pull it away, repeating this process several times before determining whether the specimen is viscid.

Whenever possible, obtain a spore deposit from one or more mature specimens. Determination of the spore deposit color may be helpful for the identification of some species of *Lactarius.* It is also valuable as a source for spore measurements.

INFORMATION ABOUT THE FIELD KEYS TO *LACTARIUS* SPECIES

To begin the process of specimen identification, go to the Regional Key to *Lactarius* Species and Their Relatives. The field keys are divided into two sets covering eastern and western North America, with the Rocky Mountains forming a natural geographical and biological dividing line. The eastern region includes everywhere east of the Rockies, and the western region includes the Rocky Mountains and farther west. This boundary is convenient and practical because many *Lactarius* species are either eastern or western in distribution. Furthermore, this division reduces the number of species one must consider in the keys.

After selecting either the field key for eastern species or the field key for western species, always start the identification process at the beginning of the group key for that region and determine which specific field key group (A, B, C, or D) should be used. As an alternative, always begin using Field Key Group A. It will automatically transfer you to group B, C, or D if appropriate. The dichotomous keys provide the user with *two choices only* at each level, although two or more species may be included under each key choice. Whenever two or more species are listed under a single key choice, additional information is provided to help identify the species. Further information can be found in the species descriptions that follow the keys. If a character is variable or ambiguous, the keys accommodate both possible interpretations. Carefully read each pair of choices and select the one that most accurately describes your specimen. If neither choice appears to be correct, either you have made a mistake in the keying process, or the specimen you are attempting to identify is atypical, undescribed, or not included in this book.

Very similar species sometimes cannot be cleanly separated based on field features only. In these instances, the key culminates with a cluster of taxa rather than with a single entity. Individual species within a cluster are further defined with commentary that may provide a clue to the most likely candidate or may refer to microscopic features or macrochemical tests. However, at this stage it may be more judicious to refer directly to the illustrations provided and to detailed descriptions of species within the cluster. A picture is indeed often worth a thousand words.

When using the keys, do not confuse latex color changes and tissue staining reactions. Latex color change, as indicated in the keys, means that there is a difference in color between when the latex is observed immediately on exposure and when the latex is observed a few seconds or several minutes later or by the time the latex is dried. Tissue staining reactions include any observed tissue stains caused by interaction with the latex, by bruising of the tissue, or as a result of aging. Although the latex of some species changes color and stains tissues, the latex of other species remains unchanged and stains tissues a color different from the latex itself.

The odor of some species may be faint and thus easily missed. Therefore, we have included these species in more than one location in the keys to assure proper identification should this character be missed.

In addition to the other information provided, some key choices contain the phrases "reported only from" or "reported from," indicating a known distribution from one or only a few locations. Because the genus *Lactarius* is so poorly understood in North America, and because distribution records are so incomplete, it is usually wise not to eliminate a species solely on the basis of its distribution within a region.

We have tried to make these keys as user friendly as possible. With practice and increased familiarity with the diagnostic features for *Lactarius,* the nonspecialist will be able to identify confidently and quickly the majority of milk mushrooms he or she encounters.

Regional Key to *Lactarius* Species and Their Relatives

1a Fruiting body collected east of the Rocky Mountains → 2
1b Fruiting body collected in the Rocky Mountains or farther west → 4
  2a Fruiting body hypogeous to subhypogeous, subglobose to turban-shaped, lacking a stalk → *Zelleromyces* (p. 269)
  2b Fruiting body epigeous, *not* subglobose to turban-shaped → 3
3a Fruiting body hard and fibrous-tough to woody, growing on the ground at the base of hardwood trees, with a white to creamy white pore surface, lacking gills → *Bondarzewia berkeleyi* (p. 270)
3b Fruiting body fleshy with a distinct cap, central stalk, and gills, growing on the ground or decaying wood → **Key to Eastern *Lactarius* Species** (p. 12)
  4a Fruiting body hypogeous to subhypogeous, subglobose to turban-shaped, lacking a stalk → *Zelleromyces* (p. 269)
  4b Fruiting body surface distinctly ridged and pitted, lacking a stalk → 5
5a Fruiting body gasteroid, globose; surface distinctly ridged and pitted; lacking a stalk and gills or lacking irregularly oriented branching gill-like plates; hypogeous or subhypogeous under needle duff of conifers → *Lactarius rubriviridis* (p. 271)
5b Fruiting body surface smooth to somewhat wrinkled but *not* distinctly ridged or pitted, stalk present → 6
  6a Fruiting body hard and fibrous-tough to woody, growing on the ground at the base of hardwood trees, with a white to creamy white pore surface, lacking gills → *Bondarzewia berkeleyi* (p. 270)
  6b Fruiting body fleshy to firm but not hard and woody → 7
7a Fruiting body hypogeous, subhypogeous, or epigeous, with a distinct cap and stalk, and with irregularly oriented, branching gill-like plates that are crossveined and pitted; in young specimens, the gill-like plates covered with a peridium that may or may not become exposed at maturity → *Arcangeliella* species (p. 271)
7b Fruiting body fleshy with a distinct cap, central stalk, and gills, growing on the ground or decaying wood → **Key to Western *Lactarius* Species** (p. 40)

Keys to Eastern *Lactarius* Species

1a Color of latex immediately on exposure pale lemon yellow, yellow to dingy yellow, yellowish orange, orange, reddish orange, pale pinkish brown, dingy brownish, yellow-brown, dark vinaceous brown, wine red to dark vinaceous red, or dark blue → **Eastern Field Key Group A** (p. 13)

1b Color of latex immediately on exposure watery, whey-like, white to creamy white, or pinkish buff → 2

2a Latex color changing to pale yellow, greenish yellow, yellow, sulfur yellow, yellow-ochre, pale cinnamon, brownish, grayish, or olive-gray within *five* minutes → **Eastern Field Key Group A** (p. 13)

2b Latex color unchanging within *five* minutes (*note:* the latex of some species may intensify or change color after five minutes, may stain tissues or dry a color different from the freshly exposed latex) → 3

3a Taste of the latex or flesh disagreeable, astringent, bitter, or slightly to extremely acrid within *two* minutes → 4

3b Taste of the latex or flesh mild within *two* minutes → **Eastern Field Key Group B** (p. 20)

4a Odor of crushed flesh distinctive, variously described as fruity, spicy, fragrant, aromatic, similar to maple sugar, coconut, anise, geraniums, apples, raw pumpkin, ripe crushed blackberries, or lemon extract; or as disinfectant-like, spermatic, pungent, strong, alkaline, or peculiar to disagreeable → **Eastern Field Key Group A** (p. 13)

4b Odor of crushed flesh not distinctive → 5

5a Cap some shade of white, buff, yellow, orange, ochraceous to brownish ochre, tan, pale yellowish cinnamon, or pale pinkish cinnamon to pale rosy cinnamon → **Eastern Field Key Group C** (p. 26)

5b Cap some shade of red, brown, lilac, or gray → 6

6a Specimen margin distinctly bearded; or stalk distinctly scrobiculate; or latex slowly changing color or staining tissues or drying a different color → **Eastern Field Key Group C** (p. 26)

6b Specimen having a combination of all of the following features: margin *not* distinctly bearded; stalk *not* distinctly scrobiculate; latex unchanging, *not* staining tissues or drying a different color → **Eastern Field Key Group D** (p. 36)

EASTERN FIELD KEY GROUP A

1a Color of latex immediately on exposure pale lemon yellow, yellow to dingy yellow, yellowish orange, orange, reddish orange, pale pinkish brown, dingy brownish, yellow-brown, dark vinaceous brown, wine red to dark vinaceous red, or dark blue → 2

1b Color of latex immediately on exposure watery, whey-like, white to creamy white, or pinkish buff → 14

2a Latex dark blue

Lactarius indigo var. *indigo* (p. 191), cap 2–6" (5.0–15.5 cm) wide; latex scant; on the ground in conifer or hardwoods; eastern Canada south to Florida, west to Michigan and Texas, also reported from California

Lactarius indigo var. *diminutivus* (p. 191), cap 1⅛–2" (3–5 cm) wide; latex copious; on the ground among grasses and weeds, usually in pine woods; along the Gulf Coast from Florida to Texas

2b Latex pale lemon yellow, yellow to dingy yellow, yellowish orange, orange, reddish orange, pale pinkish brown, dingy brownish, yellow-brown, dark vinaceous brown, or wine red to dark vinaceous red → 3

3a Latex pale pinkish brown to dingy brownish, yellow-brown, dark vinaceous brown, or wine red to dark vinaceous red → 4

3b Latex pale lemon yellow, yellow to dingy yellow, yellowish orange, orange, or reddish orange → 6

4a Latex dark vinaceous brown or wine red to dark vinaceous red

Lactarius paradoxus (p. 216), cap zoned with bands of grayish blue, grayish purple, green and blue, staining green when bruised; odor not distinctive

Lactarius subpurpureus (p. 246), cap reddish pink to vinaceous pink, zoned with paler pink, sometimes more spotted than zonate, sometimes spotted with emerald green; odor not distinctive

4b Latex pale pinkish brown to dingy brownish or yellow-brown → 5

5a Cap dingy azure blue with dingy orange-brown areas or zones, fading to muddy orange-brown to dull reddish brown; odor of crushed flesh resembling the Yellow Morel; flesh taste slowly becoming slightly acrid → *Lactarius chelidonium* var. *chelidonioides* (p. 159)

5b Cap smoky yellowish brown; odor of crushed flesh not distinctive; flesh taste mild → *Lactarius petersenii* (p. 219)

6a Latex yellowish orange, orange, or reddish orange → 7

6b Latex pale lemon yellow or yellow to dingy yellow → 13

7a Cap with green to grayish green, bluish green, or dark green spots or stains at some stage in development → 8

7b Cap lacking green spots or stains in all stages → 11

8a Cap of young specimens grayish green over an orange, yellow, or brownish yellow ground color; flesh orange, not staining on exposure → *Lactarius deliciosus* var. *olivaceosordidus* (p. 169)

8b Cap of young specimens white to cream-colored or orange overall → 9

9a Cap of young specimens orange overall, fading to pale whitish orange on the disc and developing green spots in age → *Lactarius deterrimus* (p. 170)

9b Cap of young specimens covered with a white layer or cream-colored → 10

10a Cap of young specimens covered with a white layer; flesh taste slightly acrid in young specimens then becoming mild in older mushrooms; associated with pine;

Tennessee south to Florida, west to Texas → *Lactarius salmoneus* var. *curtisii* (p. 237)

10b Cap of young specimens cream-colored, becoming bluish green in part or wholly with age; flesh distinctly acrid; associated with hardwoods, especially red oak; reported only from Florida → *Lactarius pseudodeliciosus* var. *paradoxiformis* (p. 225)

11a Cap salmon orange to ochraceous orange or peach when young or mature; exposed flesh slowly staining coral to wine red or brownish vinaceous, especially in the stalk base; on the ground or among sphagnum mosses, associated with balsam fir or cedar; eastern Canada and the northeastern United States, west to Minnesota → *Lactarius salmonicolor* (p. 237)

11b Cap of young specimens covered with a white layer; exposed flesh staining darker orange or grayish green; associated with oak and pine; South Carolina to Florida, west to Texas → 12

12a Cap becoming orange nearly overall as the white layer disappears with age, staining orange when bruised; stalk usually *not* scrobiculate; spore deposit creamy white; South Carolina to Florida, west to Texas → *Lactarius salmoneus* var. *salmoneus* (p. 237)

12b Cap becoming yellowish with age, central portion pale pinkish buff to ochraceous buff, *not* staining when bruised; stalk somewhat scrobiculate; spore deposit ochraceous; reported only from Florida → *Lactarius pseudodeliciosus* var. *pseudodeliciosus* (p. 225)

13a Latex pale lemon yellow or dingy yellow to yellow-brown, unchanging; flesh taste slightly acrid, sometimes slowly

Lactarius chelidonium var. *chelidonioides* (p. 159), latex dingy yellow to yellow-brown; cap margin of young specimens *not* bearded or pubescent; odor of crushed flesh resembling the Yellow Morel

Lactarius scrobiculatus var. *pubescens* (p. 240), latex pale lemon yellow; cap margin of young specimens typically bearded or at least pubescent; odor not distinctive

13b Latex yellow, unchanging, or changing to dingy brownish yellow or dingy yellowish brown; flesh taste mild; odor not distinctive

Lactarius chelidonium var. *chelidonium* (p. 160), cap 2–3" (5–8 cm) wide, glabrous, disc depressed, grayish green to grayish yellow or yellow-brown; latex changing to dingy brownish yellow to dingy yellowish brown; associated with pines; throughout eastern North America

Lactarius xanthydrorheus (p. 267), cap ⅜–1" (9–25 mm) wide, conspicuously rugose-venose over the disc, papillate, dingy yellowish olive to brownish; associated with oaks; Florida west along the Gulf Coastal Plain to Texas

14a Latex color changing to pale yellow, greenish yellow, yellow, sulfur yellow, yellow-ochre, pale cinnamon, brownish, grayish, or olive-gray within *five* minutes → 15

14b Latex color unchanging within *five* minutes (*note:* the latex of some species may intensify or change color after five minutes, may stain tissues or dry a different color) → 36

15a Taste of the latex or flesh mild within *two* minutes → 16

15b Taste of the latex or flesh disagreeable, astringent, bitter, or slightly to extremely acrid within *two* minutes → 18

16a Odor of crushed flesh of mature specimens distinctly fishy; latex stains flesh and gills tawny brown → *Lactarius volemus* var. *volemus* (p. 265)

16b Odor of crushed flesh of mature specimens not distinctive → 17

17a Cap small, up to 1¼" (3.2 cm) wide

Lactarius xanthydrorheus (p. 267), cap dingy yellowish olive or more brownish, especially on the disc, papillate, conspicuously rugose-venose over the disc; usually associated with oak; Florida along the Gulf Coastal Plain to Texas

Lactarius occidentalis (p. 211), cap olive-brown to smoky brown, gradually becoming tawny to cinnamon or dark vinaceous brown, sometimes with a small umbo, translucent-striate at maturity, often wrinkled or pitted near the margin; associated with alder; reported from Maine

17b Cap medium, up to 4" (10 cm) wide; pinkish brown to pale grayish brown, lacking a papilla, glabrous; latex taste mild; on soil in woods; reported only from New York → *Lactarius maculosus* (p. 203)

18a Odor of crushed flesh described as "strong" or resembling ripe crushed blackberries or faintly to distinctly fragrant → 19

18b Odor not distinctive → 21

19a Odor of crushed flesh described as "strong;" cap slimy-viscid, glabrous, faintly zonate, pale orange-yellow with yellowish salmon tints over the disc; reported from North Carolina and Tennessee → *Lactarius delicatus* (p. 167)

19b Odor of crushed flesh resembling ripe crushed blackberries, or faintly to distinctly fragrant → 20

20a Odor of crushed flesh resembling ripe crushed blackberries; cap white; latex white, changing and staining tissues yellow; latex taste acrid; reported only from North Carolina → *Lactarius neuhoffii* var. *fragrans* (p. 210)

20b Odor of crushed flesh faintly to distinctly fragrant

Lactarius scrobiculatus var. *canadensis* (p. 239), cap whitish to olive-buff when young, soon becoming yellow; odor of crushed flesh faintly fragrant; latex white, changing to sulfur yellow, taste not distinctive or slightly acrid; stalk scrobiculate; widely distributed in northern and mountainous areas of North America

Lactarius hysginus var. *subroseus* (p. 189), cap vinaceous brown; odor of crushed flesh distinctly fragrant; taste acrid-soapy; latex white, changing to yellow or staining tissues yellow; stalk scrobiculate; widely distributed in New England

21a Cap white to milky white, whitish, white with yellowish or grayish tints, or pale buff → 22

21b Cap pinkish buff, cinnamon buff, pinkish cinnamon, vinaceous pink, or some shade of yellow, orange, brown, or lilac → 26

22a Cap margin distinctly pubescent to bearded (*note:* check young specimens if available) → 23

22b Cap margin *not* distinctly pubescent to bearded → 24

23a Stalk distinctly scrobiculate

Lactarius scrobiculatus var. *canadensis* (p. 239), cap dull yellow or sometimes whitish when young, viscid but soon dry; spores 7–9 × 5.5–7.0 µm

Lactarius scrobiculatus var. *pubescens* (p. 240), cap distinctly yellow when young, becoming cinnamon buff over the center with orange-yellow along the margin, moist to subviscid; spores 6.0–7.5 × 4.5–6.0 µm

23b Stalk indistinctly scrobiculate or lacking scrobiculations

Lactarius resimus var. *resimus* (p. 232), spores 6–8 × 5–6 µm

Lactarius resimus var. *regalis* (p. 232), spores 7–10 × 6–8 µm

24a Gill spacing subdistant to distant; cap surface velvety to tomentose; flesh stains orange with the application of KOH → *Lactarius subvellereus* var. *subdistans* (p. 250)

24b Gill spacing close; cap surface glabrous → 25

25a Cap whitish when young, soon becoming brownish orange then brownish red; latex white on exposure, soon changing to sulfur yellow, taste bitter to faintly acrid → *Lactarius colorascens* (p. 164)

25b Cap pale buff or dull white, sometimes with a faint lilac gray tinge; latex white, soon changing to pale yellow or yellow; taste acrid

Lactarius vinaceosporus (p. 264), stalk scrobiculate; cap pale buff, distinctly zonate; spore deposit pale grayish pink

Lactarius neuhoffii var. *neuhoffii* (p. 210), stalk *not* scrobiculate; cap dull white, sometimes with a faint lilac-gray tinge, azonate; spore deposit white

26a Cap pinkish buff, cinnamon buff, pinkish cinnamon to orange-cinnamon, brownish orange, vinaceous pink, ochraceous buff to pale yellow, tan, bright orange to saffron yellow or apricot orange → 27

26b Cap orange-brown to orange-red, dull brick red to brownish red, yellow-brown to dark brown, pinkish lilac to lilac-brown or lilac-gray → 35

27a Cap margin distinctly pubescent to bearded (*note:* check young specimens if available)

Lactarius pubescens var. *betulae* (p. 228), cap pale cinnamon pink with a darker cinnamon disc; margin coarsely bearded when young; stalk *not* scrobiculate, colored like the cap but slightly more pinkish; latex taste instantly very sharply acrid; associated with beech

Lactarius scrobiculatus var. *pubescens* (p. 240), cap distinctly yellow when young, becoming cinnamon buff over the center with orange-yellow along the margin, bearded when young; stalk usually somewhat scrobiculate, white; latex taste slightly acrid; associated with pines

27b Cap margin *not* distinctly pubescent to bearded → 28

28a Cap faintly to distinctly zonate → 29

28b Cap azonate → 32

29a Cap zonate with whitish and pink to vinaceous zones or sometimes more or less evenly vinaceous pink; latex taste astringent and disagreeable but not acrid; reported only from Massachusetts → *Lactarius incarnatozonatus* (p. 190)

29b Cap darker-colored; latex taste acrid or bitter → 30

30a Cap bright orange to saffron yellow, fading to paler yellow-orange or yellowish tan with age → *Lactarius croceus* (p. 166)

30b Cap whitish to pale yellowish cinnamon or pale pinkish cinnamon → 31

31a Cap whitish to pale yellowish cinnamon with darker spots when young; gills do not discolor or spot vinaceous or brown with age; associated with hardwoods, especially oak → *Lactarius chrysorrheus* (p. 160).

31b Cap pale pinkish cinnamon with pinkish buff at the margin when young; gills discolor or spot vinaceous or brownish with age; associated with pines → *Lactarius vinaceorufescens* (p. 263)

32a Cap bright orange to saffron yellow, coppery orange to cinnamon orange, or brownish orange to apricot orange

Lactarius thejogalus (p. 255), cap ¾–3⅛" (2–8 cm) wide, brownish orange to apricot orange or cinnamon orange; stalk usually with a conspicuous white strigose base; latex taste slowly becoming slightly acrid; typically associated with birch or beech; widely distributed in northern North America, south to North Carolina

Lactarius croceus (p. 166), cap 2–4" (5–10 cm) wide, bright orange to saffron yellow, fading to paler yellow-orange or yellowish tan with age; stalk base lacking conspicuous white strigosity; latex taste bitter to acrid; associated with hardwoods, especially oak; eastern Canada south to Georgia, west to Texas

Lactarius duplicatus (p. 172), cap ⅝–2⅛" (1.5–5.5 cm) wide, bright orange or coppery orange to cinnamon orange; stalk base with whitish mycelial hairs; latex taste bitter then acrid; found in mixed woods or among sphagnum mosses; Alaska, Ontario, and Nova Scotia

32b Cap whitish, pale ochraceous buff to cinnamon buff, pale yellowish, pale yellowish cinnamon, or pale tan to pinkish tan, sometimes with an orange-yellow margin → 33

33a Gills staining violaceous to brownish lilac when bruised; latex taste quickly very acrid; cap light ochraceous buff to pale yellow; reported only from North Carolina → *Lactarius pseudoaspideus* (p. 223)

33b Gills *not* staining violaceous to brownish lilac when bruised → 34

34a Cap small, ¾–1" (2.0–2.5 cm) wide, dry, velvety-tomentose, pale tan to pinkish tan or yellowish, becoming darker yellow on the disc; reported only from Texas → *Lactarius subvernalis* var. *subvernalis* (p. 252)

34b Cap medium, 1⅛–4" (3–10 cm) wide

Lactarius chrysorrheus (p. 160), cap whitish to pale yellowish cinnamon, fading to nearly whitish overall with age; flesh soon yellow when cut; stalk *not* scrobiculate; usually with oak; widely distributed in North America

Lactarius albolutescens (p. 143), cap yellowish to pale tan or pale dull pink, sometimes with a darker reddish disc; flesh not staining when cut; stalk *not* scrobiculate; under mixed pines and hardwoods; reported only from Texas

Lactarius scrobiculatus var. *pubescens* (p. 240), cap distinctly yellow when young, becoming cinnamon buff over the center with orange-yellow along the margin; flesh staining yellowish when cut; stalk usually scrobiculate; associated with pines; eastern Canada and the northeastern United States, west to Michigan

35a Gills soon staining dull lilac when bruised; cap sticky to slimy, pale pinkish lilac to lilac-brown → *Lactarius uvidus* var. *uvidus* (p. 261)

35b Gills *not* staining dull lilac when bruised (*note:* gills may stain brown quickly or slowly or not at all); cap dark yellowish brown to dark brown or gray-brown, often fading with age

Lactarius vietus (p. 262), cap azonate, dark brown to gray-brown when young, fading to pinkish brown or lilac-gray; gills soon staining gray to olive-gray or grayish brown when bruised; latex white on exposure, changing to olive-gray; flesh whitish, slowly staining grayish with the application of $FeSO_4$; widely distributed in North America

Lactarius frustratus (p. 176), cap zonate, dark yellowish brown with paler zones at first, becoming azonate with age; gills slowly staining pale yellow-brown when bruised; latex white to watery on exposure, soon changing to yellowish; flesh pale vinaceous, slowly staining pale yellow-brown when cut; eastern Canada, Michigan, and Florida

Lactarius subtomentosus (p. 249), cap azonate, dark yellowish brown, densely and minutely velvety under a hand lens; gills not staining when bruised; latex white on exposure, turning yellowish; reported only from North Carolina

Lactarius peckii var. *lactolutescens* (p. 218), cap dull brick red to brownish red, orange-brown to orange-red, or dull reddish orange, faintly to distinctly zonate with darker bay red to orange-red zones; gills staining rusty brown to reddish brown when bruised; latex white on exposure, quickly changing to ivory yellow, drying pale yellowish green; flesh not staining when cut; reported from Tennessee and Florida

36a Taste of the latex or flesh disagreeable, astringent, bitter, or slightly to extremely acrid within *two* minutes → 37

36b Taste of the latex or flesh mild within *two* minutes → **Eastern Field Key Group B** (p. 20)

37a Odor of crushed flesh distinctive, variously described as fruity, spicy, fragrant, aromatic, similar to maple sugar, coconut, anise, geraniums, apples, raw pumpkin, ripe crushed blackberries, or lemon extract; or as disinfectant-like, spermatic, pungent, strong, alkaline, or peculiar to disagreeable → 38

37b Odor of the crushed flesh not distinctive → **Eastern Field Key Group C** (p. 26)

38a Odor of crushed flesh resembling coconut or anise

Lactarius glyciosmus (p. 183), cap pale vinaceous gray to pale lilac-gray or whitish; flesh taste slowly and slightly acrid

Lactarius hibbardae var. *hibbardae* (p. 186), cap dark pinkish brown to dark pinkish gray, becoming paler pinkish brown to pinkish gray; flesh taste distinctly acrid; latex *not* drying grayish green

Lactarius hibbardae var. *glaucescens* (p. 186), cap brown to brownish gray, becoming paler and browner with age; flesh taste slowly acrid; latex drying pale grayish green

38b Odor of crushed flesh variously described, but *not* as resembling coconut or anise → 39

39a Cap pinkish cinnamon, vinaceous to dull vinaceous red, olive-brown, red-brown to reddish brown, purplish brown, grayish purple to brownish purple, pale gray to gray, or purplish gray → 40

39b Cap white, whitish, buff to pinkish buff, creamy white, pale yellow to orange-yellow, ochraceous, tan, or brownish pink → 42

40a Cap zonate

Lactarius quietus var. *incanus* (p. 230), latex taste mild then slowly weakly acrid; odor of crushed flesh sweet, fragrant, often resembling burnt sugar; gills close; cap dark purplish brown or purplish gray when young, becoming dark red-brown

Lactarius pyrogalus (p. 230), latex taste rapidly extremely acrid; odor of crushed flesh resembling apples with a resinous component; gills subdistant to distant; cap pinkish gray to light gray or grayish olive-brown

40b Cap azonate → 41

41a Latex taste slightly acrid to acrid

Lactarius highlandensis (p. 187), cap dull reddish brown, sometimes strongly umbonate, becoming areolate; associated with pines; reported only from North Carolina

Lactarius purpureoechinatus (p. 229), cap dull grayish purple, becoming vinaceous or dull brownish purple, sometimes with a slight blackish umbo, with conspicuous dark scales; associated with oaks; New England south to Florida

Lactarius fusco-olivaceus var. *graveolens* (p. 179), cap olive-brown, lacking an umbo; odor of crushed flesh alkaline; associated with pines; reported only from Tennessee

41b Latex disagreeable or bitter but *not* acrid

Lactarius camphoratus (p. 156), odor of crushed flesh fragrant like maple sugar or burnt sugar; cap dark red-brown, fading to pale vinaceous pink; stalk base typically with stiff hairs

Lactarius pungens (p. 229), odor of crushed flesh pungent; cap gray, tinged with cinnamon; stalk base lacking stiff hairs

42a Cap margin distinctly pubescent to bearded

Lactarius repraesentaneus (p. 231), cap pale yellow to orange-yellow; latex staining all tissue dull lilac to purple; odor of crushed flesh faintly fragrant

Lactarius pubescens var. *pubescens* (p. 228), cap white to cream; latex *not* staining tissues; odor of crushed flesh faintly geranium-like

42b Cap margin *not* distinctly pubescent to bearded (*note:* some species may have a tomentose or scurfy margin) → 43

43a Cap distinctly zonate

Lactarius psammicola f. *glaber* (p. 222), latex tastes strongly burning acrid, slowly stains tissues pinkish cinnamon; cap with light buff to pale tan and dull orange zones; odor of crushed flesh slightly fragrant

Lactarius carolinensis (p. 158), latex tastes acrid, slowly stains gills and stalk yellow; cap tan with dull yellowish brown zones; odor of crushed flesh faintly alkaline

Lactarius lanuginosus (p. 193), latex tastes astringent to slightly acrid, does not stain tissues; cap whitish to yellowish; odor of crushed flesh described as "strong"

43b Cap azonate or obscurely zonate → 44

44a Stalk distinctly scrobiculate

Lactarius pseudodelicatus (p. 224), odor of crushed flesh distinctly like lemon extract or disinfectant; cap pale yellow, becoming brownish to pale orange-brown with age; associated with aspen; reported from Michigan and Florida

Lactarius floridanus (p. 175), odor of crushed flesh described as aromatic; cap color variable, brownish pink to brownish orange, or buff with an ochraceous to dingy light yellow center; found in mixed oak and pine woods; reported only from Florida.

44b Stalk lacking scrobiculations or sometimes obscurely scrobiculate → 45

45a Cap white to whitish or pale grayish vinaceous, sometimes developing orange, ochraceous, or brownish ochre tinges with age → 46

45b Cap colored differently from 45a (*note:* some caps may be buff or ivory to pale yellow) → 47

46a Cap margin of young specimens distinctly inrolled and cottony or fibrillose

Lactarius deceptivus (p. 167), cap large to very large, 3–10" (7.5–25.5 cm) wide, whitish, soon developing yellowish to brownish stains, becoming coarsely scaly and darkening to dull brownish ochre with age; latex taste strongly acrid; odor of crushed flesh pungent

Lactarius vinaceopallidus (p. 263), cap medium, 2–2¾" (5–7 cm) wide, whitish to pale grayish vinaceous, *not* becoming coarsely scaly and dull brownish ochre with age; latex taste mild at first, then slowly becoming slightly acrid; odor of crushed flesh described as peculiar and disagreeable

46b Cap margin of young specimens *not* distinctly inrolled and cottony or fibrillose

Lactarius zonarius var. *riparius* (p. 268), cap dull white at first, slowly flushed buff, becoming stained dingy ochraceous with age, azonate when young, becoming obscurely zonate with age; odor of crushed flesh faintly fragrant; gills white, soon creamy yellow, then bright ochre-yellow at maturity

Lactarius neuhoffii var. *fragrans* (p. 210), cap white, *not* becoming stained dingy ochraceous with age, azonate; odor of crushed flesh resembling ripe crushed blackberries; gills white, *not* changing to bright ochre-yellow at maturity

47a Cap surface tomentose to appressed-tomentose or matted-tomentose, sometimes with agglutinated fibers, or papillate-rugulose, often becoming scaly when dry or with age

Lactarius floridanus (p. 175), cap color variable, brownish pink to brownish orange or buff with an ochraceous to dingy light yellow center, tomentose with long agglutinated fibers, viscid, becoming deeply depressed with age; odor of crushed flesh aromatic and persisting when dried; reported only from Florida

Lactarius agglutinatus (p. 142), cap cinnamon buff or ochraceous buff, darker when young, somewhat appressed-tomentose and papillate-rugulose, more or less scaly when dry, slimy when fresh, becoming dry, depressed, and funnel-shaped with age; odor of crushed flesh like raw pumpkin; reported from North Carolina and eastern Canada

Lactarius mordax (p. 205), cap pale yellow to tan when young, becoming ivory to cream with light brown spots when older, somewhat matted-tomentose when young, glabrous at maturity, becoming rimose to areolate-scaly with age, dry, sometimes deeply depressed and funnel-shaped when older; odor of crushed flesh spermatic; reported only from Texas

47b Cap surface glabrous

Lactarius alnicola var. *pungens* (p. 145), cap subviscid but soon dry, dull ochraceous to ochraceous tan with an ochraceous tawny disc; odor of crushed flesh pungent and described as distinct and peculiar; growing in mixed woods; reported only from Michigan

Lactarius pseudoaffinis (p. 223), cap viscid, dull pale yellow; odor of crushed flesh faintly fragrant; associated with hemlock; reported from North Carolina and Texas

Lactarius mordax (p. 205), cap pale yellow to tan when young, becoming ivory to cream with light brown spots with age, somewhat matted-tomentose when young, glabrous at maturity, becoming rimose to areolate-scaly with age, dry, sometimes deeply depressed and funnel-shaped when older; odor of crushed flesh spermatic; associated with pines; reported only from Texas

EASTERN FIELD KEY GROUP B

1a Odor of crushed flesh distinctive, variously described as fragrant, sweet, like maple sugar or burnt sugar, aromatic, like chicory or fenugreek, alkaline, spermatic, fishy, like spoiled crab, or fetid (*note:* check mature specimens if available; the odor of some young specimens may be faint or absent) → 2

1b Odor of crushed flesh *not* distinctive → 10

2a Odor of crushed flesh distinctly fishy or resembling spoiled crab or fetid (*note:* the odor of some young specimens may be faint or absent) → 3

2b Odor of crushed flesh *not* distinctly fishy or resembling spoiled crab or fetid (*note:* odor of crushed flesh may be spermatic, strongly alkaline, fragrant, sweet like maple sugar or burnt sugar, or aromatic) → 5

3a Cap whitish to buff, becoming brownish with age, dry, slightly velvety; gills staining yellow-brown to brown; latex watery white to white on exposure, sticky; flesh stains bluish olive with the application of $FeSO_4$; typically associated with oak; widely distributed in eastern North America → *Lactarius luteolus* (p. 201)

3b Cap dull honey yellow, yellow, orange-yellow, brown, or reddish brown to vinaceous brown → 4

4a Gills distant, very pale yellow to pinkish buff, slowly staining pinkish to lavender then pinkish gray to pale pinkish brown when bruised; cap dull orange to pale orange-brown, conspicuously more or less radially wrinkled to corrugated at maturity; odor of crushed flesh slightly to moderately fishy; spores 7–9 × 6.0–7.5 µm → *Lactarius hygrophoroides* var. *lavendulaceus* (p. 188)

4b Gills close, staining tawny brown to darker brown when bruised, *not* staining pinkish to lavender at any time

Lactarius volemus var. *volemus* (p. 265), cap dark orange-brown to cinnamon brown at the center, paler orange-brown toward the margin, glabrous or finely wrinkled at maturity; stalk pale orange-brown to dull orange; latex white on exposure, becoming creamy white then brownish or grayish; spores 7.5–10.0 × 7.5–9.0 µm; widely distributed in eastern North America

Lactarius volemus var. *flavus* (p. 264), cap yellow to orange-yellow, glabrous or becoming finely wrinkled with age; stalk pale yellow; latex white, unchanging; spores 6.5–9.0 × 6–8 µm; South Carolina to Florida, west to Texas

Lactarius corrugis (p. 166), cap reddish brown to vinaceous brown, paler and sometimes orange-brown on the margin, distinctly wrinkled to finely corrugated; stalk pale grayish cinnamon to pale pinkish cinnamon; latex white, unchanging; spores 9–12 × 8.5–12.0 µm; widely distributed in eastern North America

5a Odor of crushed flesh spermatic or strongly alkaline

Lactarius hygrophoroides var. *odoratus* (p. 188), odor of crushed flesh strongly alkaline; cap apricot buff to cinnamon buff; spores 7.0–9.5 × 5.5–7.5 µm; associated with conifers; reported from North Carolina and Texas

Lactarius allochrous (p. 144), odor of crushed flesh spermatic; cap dull date brown to olive-brown overall or pale grayish brown on the disc; spores 10–14 × 8.5–12.0 µm; associated with oak; reported only from Florida

5b Odor of crushed flesh faintly to distinctly fragrant, sweet like maple sugar or burnt sugar, or aromatic → 6

6a Cap surface with distinct erect fascicles of dark scales overall or especially along the margin, dull grayish purple, becoming vinaceous or dull brownish purple; typically associated with oak; New England and New York south to Florida → *Lactarius purpureoechinatus* (p. 229)

6b Cap surface lacking distinct erect fascicles of dark scales → 7

7a Cap surface becoming distinctly rimulose-areolate at maturity

Lactarius areolatus (p. 148), associated with oak; cap pecan brown to dark vinaceous red when young, becoming paler pecan brown to orangish brown or pale vinaceous red with age

Lactarius rimosellus (p. 232), associated with pines; cap dull ferruginous to rusty brown at first, soon becoming dull vinaceous pink to pinkish cinnamon, fading to pale vinaceous cinnamon with age

7b Cap surface *not* becoming distinctly rimulose-areolate at maturity → 8

8a Cap margin distinctly crenate to deeply scalloped

Lactarius fragilis var. *fragilis* (p. 175), cap golden brown to dull yellowish brown or reddish brown; gills close to subdistant; odor of crushed flesh resembling maple sugar; latex copious, watery on exposure; spores 6.0–7.5 × 6.0–7.5 µm

Lactarius atro-olivaceus (p. 151), cap dark olive-buff with buffy brown tints on the disc; gills distant; odor of crushed flesh slightly aromatic; latex white on exposure; spores 7–9 × 6.0–7.5 µm

8b Cap margin *not* distinctly crenate or scalloped → 9

9a Stalk distinctly scrobiculate; cap appressed-pubescent to distinctly pubescent, white to pale pinkish buff, slowly discoloring to dingy brownish, zonate along the margin; gills crowded; odor of crushed flesh faintly fragrant; spores 5.0–7.5 × 4–6 µm; associated with oak; reported only from Michigan → *Lactarius pinckneyensis* (p. 219)

9b Stalk *not* distinctly scrobiculate

Lactarius helvus (p. 184), odor of crushed flesh sweet, fragrant, like maple sugar or burnt sugar, or sometimes like chicory or fenugreek; cap orange-brown to light grayish brown to pale cinnamon brown, zoned with thin bands of dark grayish brown or water spots; latex watery on exposure; spores 6–9 × 5.5–7.5 µm; found among sphagnum mosses in bogs and among wet conifer or in mixed woods

Lactarius mutabilis (p. 209), odor of crushed flesh faintly aromatic, resembling maple sugar, stronger when dried; cap purplish brown to yellowish brown with purplish brown interzonal areas if zonate; latex white or somewhat watery on exposure; spores 7–10 × 6.0–7.5 µm; on the ground in conifer and mixed woods

Lactarius subisabellinus (p. 243), odor of crushed flesh somewhat fragrant at first; cap pale pinkish buff overall or slightly darker over the disc, azonate; latex copious, white on exposure; spores 7.0–9.5 × 6–9 µm; on the ground in mixed woods or hardwoods, especially with oak

10a Cap margin distinctly coarsely tomentose or bearded (*note:* check young specimens if available) → 11

10b Cap margin *not* distinctly coarsely tomentose or bearded (*note:* cap surface or margin may be velvety or pubescent) → 12

11a Latex staining tissues lilac to purple; cap margin distinctly bearded

Lactarius repraesentaneus (p. 231), cap light yellow to orange-yellow; latex staining all tissues dull lilac to purple; stalk scrobiculate; associated with spruce

Lactarius dispersus (p. 171), cap zonate with pale dingy tan and pale buff zones; latex staining tissues dull lilac, taste not stated in original description (*note:* flesh tastes mild or bitterish); stalk scrobiculate; spores 7.5–10.0 × 6.0–7.5 µm; found in mixed oak and pine woods

Lactarius speciosus (p. 241), cap pale cinnamon or orange-brown zoned with bands of pinkish tan and cinnamon brown; latex staining tissues dull lilac, taste slightly bitter or acrid; stalk scrobiculate; spores 10.0–13.5 × 9–11 µm; found in hardwoods and mixed woods

11b Latex staining tissues pink then light smoky brown; cap margin coarsely tomentose; cap whitish with creamy or honey-colored zones; stalk with a few cream-colored scrobiculations; reported from North Carolina → *Lactarius subtorminosus* (p. 249)

12a Cap distinctly zonate, sometimes only along the margin → 13

12b Cap azonate or obscurely zonate → 15

13a Stalk distinctly scrobiculate; cap appressed-pubescent to distinctly pubescent toward the margin, glabrous on the disc, white to pale pinkish buff, slowly discoloring to dingy brownish; latex staining the gills brownish; spores 5.0–7.5 × 4–6 µm; associated with oak; reported only from Michigan → *Lactarius pinckneyensis* (p. 219)

13b Stalk *not* distinctly scrobiculate → 14

14a Latex staining the gills dull purplish; narrow zones of the cap pale reddish brown to chestnut; broad zones of the cap dull olive-yellow with a reddish yellow tint;

spores 8.0–9.5 × 6.0–7.5 µm; reported only from Florida → *Lactarius praezonatus* (p. 221)

14b Latex *not* staining the gills

Lactarius bryophilus (p. 154), cap reddish, becoming subochraceous when older, with one or two narrow orange zones near the margin; gills close, *not* forked; latex scant, watery or rarely white; spores 7.5–10.5 × 6.5–7.5 µm; scattered among mosses in swamps; reported only from Massachusetts

Lactarius parvulus (p. 217), cap whitish with a pale pinkish cinnamon tint; gills crowded, forked; latex white on exposure; spores 4.5–7.0 × 4.0–5.5 µm; on soil in hammocks; reported only from Florida

15a Cap surface covered with flattened to erect scales (*note:* scales may be tiny)

Lactarius griseus (p. 184), cap small, ⅝–2" (1.5–5.0 cm) wide, covered with fibers and tiny scales, dark purple-brown to purple-gray when young, fading or drying brownish gray to dull gray over a dull yellowish ground color; on decaying wood or among sphagnum mosses in bogs or wet woodlands.

Lactarius purpureoechinatus (p. 229), cap medium, 1⅛–3⅛" (3–8 cm) wide, covered with erect fascicles of dark scales overall or especially toward the margin, dull grayish purple, becoming vinaceous or dull brownish purple; typically associated with oak

15b Cap surface *not* covered with scales → 16

16a Cap lilac-brown when young, fading to lilac-tan or pale lilac-gray and finally pale tan or pinkish buff at the center, slimy or sticky when fresh; gills becoming flushed dull brownish orange with age, slowly staining brown when bruised; typically associated with oak; widely distributed in eastern North America → *Lactarius argillaceifolius* var. *argillaceifolius* (p. 148)

16b Specimen lacking the combination of characters given in 16a → 17

17a Cap dingy pinkish gray with ochraceous tones, with orangey olive to dingy yellow-brown spots and often developing a dingy gray cast overall with age, slimy to viscid; gills soon staining lilac when bruised; stalk typically scrobiculate; flesh soon staining bright lilac when exposed; associated with hardwoods; widely distributed in eastern North America → *Lactarius subpalustris* (p. 245)

17b Specimen lacking the combination of characters given in 17a → 18

18a Cap reddish, becoming subochraceus when older, sometimes with one or two obscure narrow orange zones near the margin, viscid to glutinous; gills close, not staining when bruised; latex scant, watery or rarely white; scattered among mosses in swamps; reported only from Massachusetts → *Lactarius bryophilus* (p. 154)

18b Specimen lacking the combination of characters given in 18a → 19

19a Cap dull yellow-buff, pale pinkish buff to cinnamon buff, pale yellow, or pale vinaceous cinnamon → 20

19b Cap darker, some shade of ochraceous, orange, red, pinkish brown to reddish brown, brown to blackish brown, or dark fuscous gray → 21

20a Gills staining greenish when bruised; cap pale vinaceous cinnamon, often fading to pale yellow; spores 7–10 × 5.5–7.5 µm; in hardwoods; reported only from Mississippi → *Lactarius similis* (p. 240)

20b Gills *not* staining greenish (*note:* gills may not stain when bruised or may stain ochraceous salmon to light ochraceous buff)

Lactarius eburneus (p. 173), gills staining ochraceous salmon to light ochraceous buff, close to subdistant; cap dull yellow-buff to cinnamon buff; stalk white, slowly staining ochraceous tawny to ochraceous brown when bruised; spores 6.5–7.5 × 6.5–7.5 µm; under hardwoods; North Carolina and Texas

Lactarius subisabellinus (p. 243), gills *not* staining when bruised, close to crowded; cap pale pinkish buff or slightly darker, especially over the disc; stalk not staining when bruised; spores 7.0–9.5 × 6–9 µm; in mixed woods or hardwoods, usually associated with oak; Tennessee and North Carolina south to Florida, west to Mississippi

21a Cap with ochraceous to orange tones, buffy ochraceous to ochraceous orange, pinkish orange, bright orange, apricot orange, brownish orange, orange-brown to rusty orange-brown, bright golden orange-brown → 22

21b Cap lacking ochraceous to orange tones; cap pinkish cinnamon to reddish cinnamon, pinkish brown, brick red, reddish brown, yellowish brown, olive-brown, grayish brown, chocolate brown to dark brown, purplish brown, blackish brown, or dark fuscous gray → 26

22a Gill edges distinctly darker than the faces at maturity; gill faces pale vinaceous pink with vinaceous red edges; gills staining or discoloring to dull vinaceous red overall with age; cap surface glabrous at first, becoming radiately rugulose-tuberculate with age, dull brownish orange, with marginal areas soon fading to apricot buff or paler and usually retaining darker spots; stalk vinaceous orange, becoming deep vinaceous red or vinaceous brown with age; in mixed hardwoods, usually associated with beech → *Lactarius badiopallescens* (p. 153)

22b Gill edges colored like the faces at maturity → 23

23a Latex slowly staining gills vinaceous pink to dull vinaceous red, vinaceous cinnamon, or lilac-brown when bruised

Lactarius pervelutinus (p. 218), stalk cream color, base lacking cinnamon orange hairs; latex slowly staining gills vinaceous pink then lilac-brown; cap velvety, sometimes with a hoary sheen, rusty brown to brownish orange, becoming ochraceous toward the margin; spores 6.0–7.5 × 5–6 µm, prominences up to 0.2 µm high; reported only from Michigan

Lactarius subserifluus (p. 247), stalk cinnamon orange on the upper portion, dark rusty brown below, base with cinnamon orange hairs; latex slowly staining gills vinaceous cinnamon; cap glabrous, orange-brown; spores 6.0–7.5 × 6–7 µm, prominences up to 1.5 µm high; Michigan, Tennessee, and Florida

23b Latex *not* staining gills when bruised → 24

24a Gills close to crowded

Lactarius splendens (p. 241), cap bright orange to bright pinkish orange, viscid, glabrous, shiny; margin *not* translucent-striate; stalk orange-buff with a paler apex, lubricous, shiny; among sphagnum mosses under conifers

Lactarius subvelutinus (p. 251), cap ochraceous orange to bright golden orange-brown, dry, minutely velvety, and sometimes wrinkled; margin *not* translucent-striate; stalk colored like the cap or paler, dry, slightly velutinous; on the ground in woods and open places

Lactarius neotabidus (p. 209), cap rusty to cinnamon red or apricot orange, fading to orange-buff, moist, smooth to wrinkled, becoming scurfy; margin translucent-striate; stalk dark rusty red on the lower portion, apricot buff near the apex, dry, glabrous, base with radiating reddish tan hairs; among sphagnum mosses in bogs

24b Gills distant to very distant → 25

25a Cap buffy ochraceous with white flesh showing in the cracks, rugose-areolate toward the margin; gills very distant; stalk cracked on the lower portion like the cap margin; spores 4.5–7.5 × 4–5 µm; reported only from North Carolina → *Lactarius lentus* (p. 194)

25b Cap darker dull orange, orange-brown to rusty orange-brown, or cinnamon orange; margin smooth or rugose, but *not* areolate

Lactarius hygrophoroides var. *hygrophoroides* (p. 188), cap margin smooth or sometimes slightly wrinkled

Lactarius hygrophoroides var. *rugatus* (p. 188), cap margin conspicuously concentrically wrinkled

26a Gills staining when bruised, sometimes slowly → 27

26b Gills *not* staining when bruised → 34

27a Gill edges conspicuously darker than the faces, dark brown; cap blackish brown to yellowish brown, dry, velvety; latex white, staining gills pinkish and drying vinaceous brown; growing among sphagnum mosses in bogs → *Lactarius lignyotus* var. *canadensis* (p. 196)

27b Gill edges colored like the faces → 28

28a Cap small, 5⁄8–1 5⁄8" (1.0–3.5 cm) wide, olive-brown to smoky brown, gradually becoming tawny to cinnamon or dark vinaceous brown, translucent-striate at maturity, often wrinkled or pitted, especially near the margin; associated with alder; reported from Maine → *Lactarius occidentalis* (p. 211)

28b Cap medium to large, 1 1⁄2–5 7⁄8" (4–15 cm) wide → 29

29a Cap surface lubricous to viscid or slimy → 30

29b Cap surface dry → 31

30a Cap dark fuscous gray to dark brown; latex staining gills grayish cinnamon buff; spore deposit pinkish buff; gills close; spores 7.5–9.0 × 6.0–7.5 µm → *Lactarius mucidus* var. *fuscogriseus* (p. 206)

30b Cap pinkish cinnamon to reddish cinnamon or pecan brown; latex staining gills darker vinaceous cinnamon; spore deposit white; gills crowded; spores 7–8 × 5–6 µm → *Lactarius sublacustris* (p. 243)

31a Gills slowly staining brown when bruised; cap yellowish brown or darker on the disc, with a small umbo, dry, radiately wrinkled over the disc; spores 8–11 × 7–10 µm; associated with beech; reported from Michigan and Tennessee → *Lactarius gerardii* var. *fagicola* (p. 179)

31b Gills staining pinkish to reddish or pale reddish cinnamon, sometimes slowly → 32

32a Gills crowded; cap olive-brown to pale olive-brown; latex staining gills pale reddish cinnamon; reported only from Michigan; spores 6.5–8.5 × 6.0–7.5 µm → *Lactarius fumosus* var. *fumosoides* (p. 177)

32b Gills close to subdistant or distant → 33

33a Cap blackish brown to very dark yellowish brown, fading with age to dingy yellow-brown, velvety, often wrinkled; widely distributed in eastern North America

Lactarius lignyotus var. *lignyotus* (p. 196), spore deposit bright ochre; spores 9–11 × 9–10 µm, nearly globose, prominences up to 1.5 µm high

Lactarius gerardii var. *subrubescens* (p. 181), spore deposit white; spores 7–10 × 6.5–8.0 µm, broadly ellipsoid to globose, prominences up to 0.6 µm high

33b Cap paler, buff-brown to olive-brown, glabrous and dull; gills distant; associated with beech; spores 7–9 × 7–9 µm; reported from North Carolina and Tennessee → *Lactarius ruginosus* (p. 236)

34a Gill edges darker than the faces

Lactarius lignyotellus (p. 195), gills whitish to pale cream with dark dull brown edges; cap brown to blackish brown, dry, velvety, radiately rugulose; spores 9.5–12.0 × 9.5–11.0 µm; in spruce woods; North Carolina and West Virginia

Lactarius texensis (p. 254), gills dark to pale tan with dark brown edges; cap dark brown to blackish brown, dry, velvety-tomentose, uneven to distinctly rugulose; spores 7.0–9.5 × 7–9 µm; under hardwoods in a predominantly pine forest; reported only from Texas

34b Gill edges colored like the faces → 35

35a Cap surface viscid → 36

35b Cap surface moist or dry, *not* viscid → 37

36a Cap very small, ⅝–1" (1.5–2.5 cm) wide; growing among sphagnum mosses; cap dingy brown, margin striatulate; stalk with white stiff hairs at the base; reported only from New York; spores 7.5–9.0 × 6.0–7.5 µm → *Lactarius paludinellus* (p. 216)

36b Cap medium to large, 1⅛–4" (3–10 cm) wide; growing on soil in woods

Lactarius maculosus (p. 203), spores 9–12 × 7.5–11.0 µm; cap pinkish brown to pale grayish brown, sometimes spotted; reported from New York

Lactarius tephropeplis (p. 254), spores 7–8 × 6–7 µm; cap grayish brown to purplish brown, appearing frosted; reported from New Hampshire

37a Gills distant; cap velvety, dark dingy yellow-brown; stalk colored like the cap with a whitish base, somewhat velvety; latex watery white on exposure; spores 9–12 × 6.5–9.0 µm; reported only from Michigan → *Lactarius pseudogerardii* (p. 226)

37b Gills close → 38

38a Associated with alder in mountainous areas; cap dark reddish brown, soon fading to onion skin pink or light pinkish cinnamon, glabrous or finely scaly, especially on the disc; gills crossveined, often forked; white mycelium often on stalk base; spores 7.5–9.0 × 6.0–7.5 µm; reported from Michigan → *Lactarius alpinus* var. *mitis* (p. 146)

38b Associated with conifer or hardwoods, but not with alder

Lactarius hepaticus (p. 185), found under conifers, especially hemlock; widely distributed in eastern North America; cap dark rusty red to brick red, dark reddish brown, or chestnut brown, margin sometimes crenulate; spores 7.5–9.0 × 6–7 µm, ellipsoid, prominences up to 0.5 µm high

Lactarius muscicola (p. 208), found under hardwoods; reported only from Tennessee; cap dark reddish brown to dark brown, somewhat velvety; spores 7.5–9.0 × 7.5–9.0 µm, globose to subglobose, prominences up to 1.5 µm high

EASTERN FIELD KEY GROUP C

1a Cap various shades of green, olive to dark grayish green, usually zoned with dark green spots arranged concentrically → *Lactarius atroviridis* (p. 152)

1b Cap some shade of white, buff, tan, yellow, orange, red, cinnamon, brown, lilac, or gray → 2

2a Cap white, whitish, or cream, sometimes developing darker tones as specimens mature → 3

2b Cap some shade of buff, tan, yellow, orange, red, cinnamon, brown, lilac, or gray → 12

3a Cap margin distinctly pubescent to bearded (*note:* check young specimens if available);

disc reddish orange to vinaceous; stalk apex tinged pink; associated with birch and other hardwoods → *Lactarius pubescens* var. *pubescens* (p. 228)

3b Cap margin *not* distinctly pubescent to bearded → 4

4a Cap distinctly zonate; zones pale yellow and white; cap whitish to cream overall or with a tawny disc; stalk scrobiculate; latex taste slowly acrid → *Lactarius maculatipes* (p. 202)

4b Cap azonate or obscurely zonate → 5

5a Gills pale pink to vinaceous brown or pinkish cinnamon at maturity

Lactarius controversus (p. 164), cap white to whitish; latex *not* staining tissues, taste slowly acrid; cap margin *not* inrolled and cottony when young; associated with willow or poplar; northern United States and Canada

Lactarius vinaceopallidus (p. 263), cap whitish to pale grayish vinaceous; latex slowly staining gills brownish, taste mild then slowly becoming slightly acrid; cap margin inrolled and cottony when young; associated with conifers; reported from Michigan and Quebec

5b Gills white, whitish, cream, buff, yellowish, pale ochre, or tan → 6

6a Stalk milk white, tinged pale blue and developing more intense blue tones after mushroom picked → *Lactarius caeruleitinctus* (p. 155)

6b Stalk *not* tinged blue and *not* developing more intense blue tones after mushroom picked → 7

7a Cap margin distinctly inrolled and cottony when young

Lactarius deceptivus (p. 167), cap large to very large, 3–10" (7.5–25.5 cm) wide, whitish, soon developing yellowish or brownish stains; spores 9–13 × 7–9 µm, prominences up to 1.5 µm high; stalk cuticle lacking a gelatinous layer; associated with hemlock or oak; widely distributed in eastern North America

Lactarius pseudodeceptivus (p. 224), cap large, 2⅜–6¾" (6–17 cm) wide, whitish, soon developing yellowish or brownish stains; spores 8–11 × 6–8 µm, prominences up to 0.4 µm high; stalk cuticle containing a gelatinous layer; associated with conifers; reported from eastern Canada and Michigan

Lactarius arcuatus (p. 147), cap medium, 2⅜" (6 cm) wide, white, *not* developing yellowish or brownish stains; spores 5.5–7.0 × 4.5–6.0 µm, prominences up to 0.2 µm high; associated with oak; reported only from Florida

7b Cap margin *not* distinctly inrolled and cottony when young → 8

8a Latex on cut gills drying pale bluish green; gills crowded → *Lactarius glaucescens* (p. 181)

8b Latex on cut gills *not* drying pale bluish green (*note:* latex may stain gills pinkish or tawny ochraceous or may dry red or yellow) → 9

9a Latex on cut gills staining or drying pinkish to red

Lactarius subvernalis var. *cokeri* (p. 252), latex staining gills and flesh pinkish to pinkish orange; stalk staining pinkish when bruised; found under hardwoods, especially oak

Lactarius subvernalis var. *albo-ochraceus* (p. 253), latex drying red and fading to yellowish, *not* staining cut gills; stalk staining dingy yellow where bruised; associated with pines

9b Latex on cut gills *not* staining or drying pinkish to red → 10

10a Cap surface dry, unpolished to velvety, felty or appressed-fibrillose to silky

Lactarius vellereus var. *virescens* (p. 261), gills dull white with a flush of green near the stalk; spores 7.5–10.0 × 7.5–9.0 µm, prominences up to 0.2 µm high; reported only from Michigan

Lactarius subvellereus var. *subvellereus* (p. 251), gills pinkish buff to pale yellow, lacking a greenish flush near the stalk; spores 7.5–9.0 × 5.5–7.0 µm, prominences up to 0.2 µm high; eastern Canada south to Alabama, west to Michigan and Kansas

Lactarius tomentosomarginatus (p. 256), gills white when young, becoming buff then dull brown when older, lacking a greenish flush near the stalk; spores 9–11 × 7.0–8.5 µm, prominences up to 0.7 µm high; New England south to Florida, west to Michigan and Texas

10b Cap surface dry or viscid, glabrous → 11

11a Gills white to creamy white at maturity, usually *not* staining when bruised; latex taste quickly and strongly acrid; cap 1⅛–6" (3.0–15.5 cm) wide; spores 4.5–7.0 × 5.0–5.5 µm, prominences up to 0.2 µm high; in conifer or hardwoods; widely distributed in eastern North America → *Lactarius piperatus* var. *piperatus* (p. 220)

11b Gills more richly colored at maturity

Lactarius luteocanus (p. 200), cap ¾–2" (2–5 cm) wide, dull white becoming pinkish buff; gills white but soon spotting pale cinnamon; latex taste acrid to burning acrid; spores 7.5–9.0 × 6.5–7.5 µm, prominences up to 0.5 µm high; found in hardwood forests; reported only from Michigan

Lactarius angustifolius (p. 147), cap 1⅜–2" (3.5–5.0 cm) wide, white when young or mature; gills tan to yellowish, staining dull yellow-buff; latex taste quickly and extremely acrid; spores 5.0–7.8 × 4.5–6.5 µm, prominences up to 0.1 µm high; found in hardwood forests; reported only from Texas

Lactarius westii (p. 266), cap 2–2¾" (5–7 cm) wide, white to pale pinkish brown; gills yellowish to dingy brownish yellow; latex taste acrid; spores 9–11 × 8–10 µm, prominences up to 1.5 µm high; associated with oak; reported only from Florida

Lactarius zonarius var. *riparius* (p. 268), cap 2–4" (5–10 cm) wide, dull white at first, slowly flushed very pale buff to yellowish and finally pinkish buff, stained dingy ochraceous; gills white, soon creamy yellow then bright ochre-yellow, staining tawny brown when bruised; latex slowly and distinctly acrid; spores 7–9 × 6.0–7.5 µm, prominences up to 1 µm high; found in hardwood forests; reported from Michigan and eastern Canada

12a Cap light buff, pinkish buff, yellowish buff to ochraceous buff, pale yellow to orange-yellow, orange to reddish orange, ochraceous to brownish ochre, pale tan to tan, pale yellowish cinnamon, or pale pinkish cinnamon to pale rosy cinnamon → 13

12b Cap some shade of red, brown, lilac, or gray → 31

13a Cap margin distinctly coarsely strigose to bearded (*note:* check young specimens if available) → 14

13b Cap margin *not* distinctly coarsely strigose to bearded → 15

14a Latex staining tissues pinkish lilac to dull lilac or purple, or slowly changing to pinkish lilac

Lactarius repraesentaneus (p. 231), cap light yellow to orange-yellow; latex staining all tissues dull lilac to purple; stalk scrobiculate; associated with spruce

Lactarius dispersus (p. 171), cap zonate with pale dingy tan and pale buff zones; latex staining tissues dull lilac, taste not stated in original description (*note:* flesh tastes mild or bitterish); stalk scrobiculate; spores 7.5–10.0 × 6.0–7.5 µm; found in mixed oak and pine woods

Lactarius speciosus (p. 241), cap pale cinnamon or orange-brown zoned with bands of pinkish tan and cinnamon brown; latex staining tissues dull lilac, taste slightly bitter or acrid; stalk scrobiculate; spores 10.0–13.5 × 9–11 µm; found in hardwoods and mixed woods

Lactarius psammicola f. *psammicola* (p. 222), cap ochraceous buff to ochraceous orange, becoming dingy yellow-brown with conspicuous light buff zones; latex sometimes staining pinkish lilac or drying pinkish lilac; often scrobiculate; spores 7.5–9.0 × 6.0–7.5 µm; associated with oak

14b Latex *not* staining tissues lilac or purple and *not* drying pinkish lilac

Lactarius psammicola f. *psammicola* (p. 222), cap 1½–5½" (4–14 cm) wide, ochraceous buff to ochraceous orange, becoming dingy yellow-brown with conspicuous light buff zones; often scrobiculate; spores 7.5–9.0 × 6.0–7.5 µm; associated with oak

Lactarius torminosus var. *torminosus* (p. 257), cap 1½–4¾" (4–12 cm) wide, with dull reddish orange to orange-brown concentric zones over a pale pinkish ground color; stalk *not* scrobiculate; latex white, unchanging and not staining gills; spores 7.5–10.0 × 6.0–7.5 µm; associated with birch

Lactarius torminosus var. *nordmanensis* (p. 257), nearly identical to *Lactarius torminosus* var. *torminosus* except that the latex slowly changes to pale yellow on the gills, or the gills become spotted pale yellow, and it has been found under a mixture of aspen, birch, and conifers including hemlock

Lactarius subpaludosus (p. 244), cap ¾–2" (2–5 cm) wide, light buff overall or ochraceous buff on the disc, becoming ochraceous brown with age; stalk *not* scrobiculate; spores 6–8 × 4.5–6.0 µm; associated with birch

15a Cap distinctly zonate → 16

15b Cap azonate or obscurely zonate → 18

16a Stalk scrobiculate

Lactarius psammicola f. *glaber* (p. 222), cap zonate with light buff to pale tan and dull orange zones; latex staining tissues weakly pinkish cinnamon; stalk whitish, dull, often with an obscure annular line near the apex; spores 7.5–9.0 × 6.5–7.5 µm, prominences up to 1 µm high; associated with oak; Michigan, eastern Canada south to Florida, west to Texas

Lactarius psammicola f. *psammicola* (p. 222), nearly identical to *Lactarius psammicola* f. *glaber*, but latex staining gills and flesh pinkish lilac or slowly changing to pinkish lilac

Lactarius carolinensis (p. 158), cap tan with dull yellowish brown zones; latex staining gills and stalk yellow; associated with oak; spores 7–9 × 6.0–7.5 µm, prominences up to 0.8 µm high; Georgia, North Carolina, Tennessee, and Virginia

Lactarius ausablensis (p. 152), cap watery orange with pale ochraceous zones, becoming azonate with a pale dull ochraceous orange disc and pale yellow-orange margin with age; latex *not* staining tissues; spores 6–8 × 5.5–6.5 µm, prominences up to 0.3 µm high; associated with conifers; reported only from Michigan

16b Stalk *not* scrobiculate → 17

17a Cap pale yellow or pinkish tan

Lactarius dunfordii (p. 172), cap pale yellow, often with water spots; gills pale cream-colored; flesh taste acrid; latex white on exposure; spore deposit pale yellow; associated with pine; reported only from Tennessee

Lactarius moschatus (p. 206), cap pinkish tan; gills dark pinkish tan; flesh taste musky; latex watery to watery white on exposure; spore deposit whitish; associated with pine; reported only from Texas

17b Cap ochraceous, ochraceous orange to rusty orange, dull orange-red, tawny or brownish orange

Lactarius proximellus (p. 221), cap tawny to brownish orange, with darker brownish orange to cinnamon zones; stalk pale yellow, becoming pale bluish green where bruised; latex scant, taste very acrid; associated with oak; New England south to Florida, west to Texas

Lactarius yazooensis (p. 267), cap ochraceous orange to rusty orange or dull orange-red, gradually becoming paler and more ochraceous; stalk whitish, *not* becoming pale bluish green where bruised; latex copious, taste exceedingly acrid; associated with oak; Florida west along the Gulf Coastal Plain to Texas

Lactarius peckii var. *glaucescens* (p. 218), cap dull reddish orange, orange-brown, orange-red, brick red, or brownish red; latex copious, taste burning acrid, white on exposure, drying pale bluish green; spores 6.0–8.5 × 5.5–7.5 µm; found in mixed woods, often with oak; Tennessee south to Florida, west to Mississippi

18a Latex unchanging, *not* staining tissues or drying a different color → 26

18b Latex changing color staining tissues or drying a different color → 19

19a Latex soon staining gills and flesh rosy salmon; cap margin conspicuously plicate → *Lactarius subplinthogalus* (p. 246)

19b Latex *not* staining gills and flesh rosy salmon (*note:* latex may stain tissues or dry some other color) → 20

20a Latex slowly changing to yellow

Lactarius thejogalus (p. 255), cap brownish orange to apricot orange or cinnamon orange, fading to orange-buff; latex slowly changing to yellow (much more slowly than the flesh, which usually stains yellow quickly), taste slowly becoming slightly acrid; stalk usually with a conspicuous white strigose base; associated with birch and beech

Lactarius imperceptus (p. 190), cap pale cinnamon to pinkish cinnamon or pale reddish brown, typically pitted and stained with darker pinkish cinnamon; latex slowly darkening to yellow, taste acrid only or bitter then acrid, sometimes slowly; stalk with a whitish tomentose base; usually associated with pine or oak

20b Latex *not* changing to yellow → 21

21a Latex slowly staining tissues or drying olive-gray, pale olive to olive, grayish blue or bluish green → 22

21b Latex slowly or rapidly staining tissues or drying pinkish lilac to lilac, violaceous, lavender, brownish lavender, brownish, or lilac-brown to vinaceous brown → 23

22a Cap orange; latex acrid, staining tissues grayish blue; stalk staining blue when cut; spores 8–11 × 7.5–9.0 µm; found in hardwoods; reported only from Maine → *Lactarius aroostookensis* (p. 150)

22b Cap pale pinkish cinnamon to pale pinkish buff, pale yellow, pale ochraceous to pale ochre

Lactarius furcatus (p. 178), latex slowly changing to bluish green, taste moderately acrid; cap pale ochraceous, tomentose; gills repeatedly forked; spores 3.5–5.5 × 3.5–4.0 µm, prominences up to 0.2 µm high; reported from North Carolina and Mississippi

Lactarius affinis var. *viridilactis* (p. 141), latex drying pale olive to olive, taste very acrid; cap pale yellow to pale ochre or pale pinkish cinnamon; gills sometimes forked near the stalk; spores 8–10 × 6.5–8.0 µm, prominences up to 1 µm high; northern Great Lakes to New England and adjacent Canada

Lactarius midlandensis (p. 204), latex drying pale olive-gray, staining gills pale olive-gray, taste slowly becoming slightly acrid; cap pale pinkish cinnamon over the disc, fading to pale pinkish buff near the margin; gills sometimes forked near the stalk; spores 7.5–9.0 × 6–7 µm, prominences up to 0.5 µm high; reported from Michigan and eastern Canada

23a Cap brick red when young, slowly fading to a dull brownish orange and finally a dull pale pink; stalk base with vinaceous hairs; latex taste very slowly faintly acrid, staining tissues dingy vinaceous brown and drying yellowish on the gills of young specimens; eastern Canada south to Vermont, west to Michigan → *Lactarius carbonicola* (p. 157)

23b Cap colored differently from the choice in 23a → 24

24a Cap cinnamon buff with a rosy violaceous tint; flesh white, staining tawny brown when cut; latex staining flesh and gills brownish, taste bitter then acrid; described as growing on soil; reported only from South Carolina → *Lactarius argillaceifolius* var. *dissimilis* (p. 149)

24b Cap ivory to cream, pale olive-gray, light yellow, ochraceous buff to ochraceous orange, or tan, sometimes becoming dingy yellow-brown with age → 25

25a Latex tastes bitterish then slowly becomes slightly acrid, stains tissues lilac; cap light yellow; latex and gills staining purple-red with the application of $FeSO_4$; northeastern and central United States into Canada → *Lactarius aspideoides* (p. 150)

25b Latex soon distinctly acrid

Lactarius pseudoaspideus (p. 223), flesh staining violaceous when cut; latex taste quickly very acrid; cap light ochraceous buff to pale yellowish, glabrous; gills staining violaceous to brownish lilac; reported only from North Carolina

Lactarius echinatus (p. 173), flesh staining brownish lavender when cut; latex taste acrid and disagreeable; cap ivory yellow when young, sometimes becoming pale olive-gray, subtomentose to pruinose; gills staining dark brown to cinnamon; found under hardwoods; reported only from Texas

Lactarius mordax (p. 205), flesh staining lavender to pale brown when cut; latex taste very acrid; cap pale yellow to tan when young, becoming ivory to cream with light brown spots when older, tomentose; gills staining yellowish at first, then lavender and finally yellow-brown; associated with pines; reported only from Texas

Lactarius psammicola f. *psammicola* (p. 222), flesh staining pinkish lilac when cut, taste very acrid; cap ochraceous buff to ochraceous orange, becoming dingy yellow-brown with conspicuous light buff zones; gills slowly staining pinkish lilac; associated with oak; New England south to Florida, west to Texas, also reported from Michigan and Kansas

26a Stalk distinctly scrobiculate; cap slimy-viscid, glabrous, watery orange with pale ochraceous zones, becoming azonate with a pale dull ochraceous orange disc and a pale yellow margin when older; latex watery milk white; associated with conifers; reported only from Michigan → *Lactarius ausablensis* (p. 152)

26b Stalk *not* distinctly scrobiculate (*note:* may sometimes be slightly scrobiculate) → 27

27a Specimens collected under alder in alpine areas; cap small, ⅝–1½" (1.5–4.0 cm) wide, apricot orange to tawny yellow or ochraceous to yellowish; flesh white, staining pink with the application of $FeSO_4$; reported from New York → *Lactarius alpinus* var. *alpinus* (p. 146)

27b Specimens *not* collected in alpine areas → 28

28a Cap pinkish buff to pale pinkish cinnamon, lacking yellow to orange or ochraceous tones

Lactarius sumstinei (p. 253), cap pinkish buff to pale pinkish cinnamon, dry, glabrous or faintly radiately rugulose; gills distant; latex taste acrid; spores 8.5–11.0 × 9–11 µm, prominences up to 2 µm high; collected in grassy places in open woods; reported from Pennsylvania and Tennessee

Lactarius alachuanus var. *alachuanus* (p. 143), cap pale pinkish cinnamon to rosy cinnamon when young, becoming pinkish buff with age, moist to viscid when fresh but soon dry; gills close; latex white, usually abundant, taste moderately acrid; spores 7.5–9.0 × 6.0–7.5 µm, prominences up to 1.5 µm high; collected in mixed oak and pine woods; Tennessee and North Carolina south to Alabama and Florida

Lactarius alachuanus var. *amarissimus* (p. 143), a questionable variety nearly identical to *Lactarius alachuanus* var. *alachuanus,* with very bitter-tasting flesh that is not acrid and sparse, watery latex that is assumed *not* to taste acrid

28b Cap pale yellow, pale ochre-yellow, pale ochre, ochraceous tawny to reddish ochraceous, brownish orange to cinnamon orange or apricot orange → 29

29a Latex taste slowly becoming slightly acrid, usually slowly changing to yellow; flesh usually staining yellow quickly; stalk usually with a conspicuous white strigose base; cap brownish orange to apricot orange, fading to dull pale orange; typically associated with birch or beech → *Lactarius thejogalus* (p. 255)

29b Latex taste distinctly acrid, unchanging → 30

30a Cap ochraceous tawny to reddish ochraceous, viscid, margin indistinctly striate; gills subdistant, staining brown when bruised; stalk pale pinkish yellow; flesh or latex taste slowly becoming distinctly acrid; spores 5–6 × 5–6 µm; reported only from Florida → *Lactarius subtestaceus* (p. 248)

30b Cap paler, dull pale yellow, pale ochre-yellow or pale ochre; stalk white to buff; gills close to subdistant, *not* staining when bruised; flesh or latex taste acrid

Lactarius affinis var. *affinis* (p. 141), cap surface viscid to slimy when fresh; spore deposit white; spores 9–11 × 7–8 µm; under conifers or hardwoods; eastern Canada south to New York, west to Michigan

Lactarius pseudoaffinis (p. 223), cap surface viscid; spore deposit pale ochraceous yellow; spores 6.0–7.5 × 6.0–7.5 µm; associated with conifers, especially hemlock; reported from North Carolina and Texas

31a Cap margin distinctly bearded (*note:* check young specimens if available)

Lactarius dispersus (p. 171), cap conspicuously zonate with pale dingy tan and pale buff zones, the darker zones becoming darker brown with age or when dry; stalk scrobiculate; latex staining gills and flesh lilac to dull lilac; spores 7.5–10.0 × 6.0–7.5 µm; reported from West Virginia and North Carolina

Lactarius speciosus (p. 241), cap conspicuously zonate with bands of pinkish tan and cinnamon brown over a pale cinnamon or orange-brown ground color; stalk scrobiculate; latex staining gills and flesh lilac to dull lilac; spores 10.0–13.5 × 9–11 µm; eastern Canada south to Florida, west to Texas

31b Cap margin *not* distinctly bearded → 32

32a Stalk distinctly scrobiculate → 33

32b Stalk *not* distinctly scrobiculate (*note:* stalk may develop spotted or streaked stains with age or when bruised) → 34

33a Latex staining the gills lilac to dull lilac, dull brown to olive-brown, or olivaceous, taste bitter or acrid

Lactarius turpis (p. 259), latex staining the gills dull brown to olive-brown, taste very acrid; cap azonate, pale brownish yellow to dull ochre or olive-brown to brown with ochraceous tints, typically dark green to blackish on the disc; gills staining dull brown to olive-brown when bruised; associated with conifers, especially spruce and balsam fir; Canada and the northern United States, south to North Carolina

Lactarius maculatus (p. 203), latex staining the gills dull lilac, taste weakly to distinctly acrid; cap concentrically spotted and zonate especially toward the margin, grayish buff to dull grayish lilac, brownish lilac or brownish gray; gills staining dull lilac when bruised; found in hardwoods and mixed woods; eastern Canada south to Tennessee, west to Minnesota

Lactarius subpalustris (p. 245), latex staining the gills lilac, taste somewhat bitter; cap azonate to obscurely zonate, dingy pinkish gray with ochraceous tones, with orangey olive to dingy yellow-brown spots, often developing a grayish cast overall with age; gills staining lilac when bruised; found in hardwoods; Michigan, Tennessee, West Virginia, and Texas

Lactarius kauffmanii var. *kauffmanii* (p. 192), latex staining the gills olivaceous to grayish brown, taste acrid; cap azonate to obscurely zonate, blackish brown to grayish brown or vinaceous brown, becoming grayish to grayish vinaceous with age; gills staining olivaceous to grayish brown when bruised; found in conifer woods; Alaska south to Idaho and California

33b Latex *not* staining the gills; latex taste very acrid

Lactarius pseudoflexuosus (p. 225), cap faintly to distinctly zonate, pinkish gray to pale gray with gray-brown spots and streaks; stalk dry; gills crossveined; spores 6.5–9.0 × 6–7 µm; found in mixed woods; widely distributed in eastern North America

Lactarius pseudomaculatus (p. 226), cap faintly to distinctly zonate, purplish brown zones alternating with grayish bands; stalk dry; spores 6.0–7.5 × 5.5–6.5 µm; found in hardwoods; reported only from Tennessee

Lactarius depressus (p. 169), cap azonate, pale vinaceous to pale vinaceous brown when young, gradually becoming flushed cinnamon and finally more or less yellow-brown over the disc or with yellow-brown spots; stalk viscid but soon dry and shiny; spores 6.0–7.5 × 5.5–6.5 µm; found in mixed woods; reported from Michigan and Wisconsin

Lactarius hysginus var. *hysginus* (p. 189), cap somewhat zonate, dark reddish brown at the center, pinkish cinnamon on the margin; stalk slimy when fresh, becoming dry; spores 5.5–7.5 × 5.5–7.0 µm; associated with conifers; eastern Canada and the northeastern United States, west to Michigan, also reported from Texas

34a Latex slowly changing color, staining tissues or drying a different color (*note:* latex color change or staining reaction may be delayed up to one hour) → 35

34b Latex unchanging, *not* staining tissues or drying a different color → **Eastern Field Key Group D** (p. 36)

35a Gill edges dark brown, much darker than the faces; cap dark brown, velvety, dry; latex white on exposure, slowly changing to dark violet; growing among sphagnum mosses in bogs or wet woodlands → *Lactarius lignyotus* var. *marginatus* (p. 197)

35b Gill edges colored like the faces → 36

36a Latex staining tissues dull lilac or dark violet

Lactarius lignyotus var. *nigroviolascens* (p. 197), latex slowly changing to dark violet and staining tissues dark violet, taste pungent to slightly bitter but *not* acrid; cap dark brown, dry, velvety; spores 7–11 × 7–9 µm; growing in conifer bogs, swamps, or forests on humus or among sphagnum mosses; Maine, Michigan, New Hampshire, and New York

Lactarius uvidus var. *uvidus* (p. 261), latex white on exposure, soon changing to dingy cream, staining tissues dull lilac, taste mild at first, then bitter but *not* acrid; cap pale pinkish lilac to lilac-brown; spores 7.5–11.0 × 6.5–8.5 µm; macrocystidia present; growing in mixed woods; eastern Canada south to Tennessee, west to Wisconsin

Lactarius uvidus var. *acystidiosus* (p. 261), latex white, unchanging, staining tissues dull lilac; cap pale pinkish lilac to lilac-brown; spores 9–12 × 6.5–7.5 µm; lacking macrocystidia; growing in conifer woods; reported only from Nova Scotia

36b Latex *not* staining tissues dull lilac or dark violet (*note:* latex may change to, stain tissues, or dry a different color) → 37

37a Latex slowly changing to, staining tissues, or drying pinkish to vinaceous pink, reddish, red, or pale reddish cinnamon → 38

37b Latex slowly changing to, staining tissues, or drying some color other than the ones given in 37a → 39

38a Cap blackish brown to very dark yellowish brown, fading somewhat with age, dry, velvety

Lactarius lignyotus var. *lignyotus* (p. 196), cap margin sulcate to plicate; cap surface usually wrinkled; gills close to subdistant, white, slowly becoming pale ochraceous; latex taste slightly bitter, *not* acrid; spore deposit bright ochre; spores 9–11 × 9–10 µm

Lactarius gerardii var. *subrubescens* (p. 181), cap margin even or plicate; cap surface wrinkled; gills subdistant to distant, white but slowly becoming pale cream with age; latex taste slightly acrid, *not* bitter; spore deposit white; spores 7–10 × 6.5–8.0 µm

38b Cap much paler, pale dingy yellow-brown to whitish, dull brownish gray, or olive-brown to buff-brown, glabrous or becoming somewhat wrinkled with age

Lactarius fumosus var. *fumosus* (p. 178), cap dry, unpolished, usually becoming somewhat wrinkled with age, pale dingy yellow-brown to whitish overall, with a smoky tinge, sometimes with dull brown areas; gills crowded; latex taste acrid, sometimes slowly or faintly; spores 6–8 × 6–8 µm; widely distributed in eastern North America

Lactarius carminascens (p. 157), cap viscid, glabrous, dull brownish gray; gills close; latex taste bitter then acrid; spores 7.5–10.5 × 6.0–7.5 µm; reported only from Tennessee

Lactarius ruginosus (p. 236), cap dry, glabrous, olive-brown to buff-brown; gills distant; latex taste slowly acrid; spores 7–9 × 7–9 µm; reported from North Carolina and Tennessee

39a Latex slowly changing to yellow, staining tissues yellow, or drying yellowish → 40

39b Latex slowly changing to, staining tissues, or drying some shade of gray, olive, green, blue, or brown → 41

40a Cap pale cinnamon to pinkish cinnamon, pale reddish brown, or pinkish gray to light gray, grayish olive-brown, or pale yellowish brown

Lactarius imperceptus (p. 190), cap pale cinnamon to pinkish cinnamon or pale reddish brown, typically pitted and stained with darker pinkish cinnamon, usually with a small umbo at maturity; latex slowly darkening to yellow, sometimes staining flesh yellow, taste bitter then acrid, or acrid only, sometimes slowly; gills close; spores 8–11 × 7–8 µm; usually associated with pine or oak; widely distributed in eastern North America

Lactarius pyrogalus (p. 230), cap pinkish gray to light gray or grayish olive-brown to pale yellowish brown, sometimes with a slight purplish hue, zonate with gray-brown zones; latex drying yellowish, taste very acrid; spores 6.0–7.5 × 5–6 µm; in hardwoods or mixed woods; widely distributed in eastern North America

40b Cap much darker, dull yellowish brown or dark fuscous gray to dark brown

Lactarius mucidus var. *fuscogriseus* (p. 206), cap dark fuscous gray to dark brown, slimy-viscid; gills close; spores 7.5–9.0 × 6.0–7.5 µm; reported from Michigan and eastern Canada

Lactarius umbrinopapillatus (p. 260), cap dull yellowish brown, viscid, with an acute and small central papilla; gills subdistant; spores 7.5–9.0 × 6.0–7.5 µm; reported only from Maryland

41a Latex slowly changing to, staining tissues, or drying olive-buff to olive-gray, olivaceous to greenish olive, olive, greenish, or bluish green to grayish green, sometimes later staining tissues brown → 42

41b Latex slowly changing to, staining tissues, or drying pale yellow-brown to yellow-brown, olive-brown, grayish brown, dark vinaceous brown, or dark brown, at all times lacking greenish, grayish, bluish, or olive tones → 44

42a Cap distinctly zonate

Lactarius mackinawensis (p. 201), cap light violet-gray with cinnamon brown zones; stalk violaceous gray mottled with cinnamon buff; latex abundant, taste acrid, pinkish buff on exposure, drying olivaceous

Lactarius peckii var. *glaucescens* (p. 218), cap dull reddish orange, orange-brown, orange-red, brick red, or brownish red; stalk cinnamon buff, becoming pinkish cinnamon and finally walnut brown; latex copious, taste burning acrid, white on exposure, drying pale bluish green

Lactarius pyrogalus (p. 230), cap pinkish gray to light gray or grayish olive-brown to pale yellowish brown, sometimes with a slight purplish hue, zonate with gray-brown zones; stalk whitish with a slight tone of the cap color, base occasionally yellowish; latex white, taste rapidly becoming extremely acrid, drying bluish green to grayish green

42b Cap azonate or obscurely zonate → 43

43a Cap whitish, pale pinkish cinnamon, pinkish buff, pinkish gray, or light vinaceous gray, developing pale brick red to dull brick red tones with age

Lactarius allardii (p. 144), cap whitish when young, soon pale pinkish cinnamon to pinkish buff, often with grayish red tints, then becoming pale cinnamon to orange-brown and finally dull brick red; latex slowly staining gills dull green to olive then slowly dull brown, taste acrid; flesh rapidly stains vinaceous red with the application of $FeSO_4$

Lactarius trivialis (p. 258), cap pale pinkish gray to light vinaceous gray when young, developing cinnamon to pale brick red tones at maturity; latex *not* staining the gills, changing to orange-yellow with the application of KOH, taste slowly acrid

43b Cap darker-colored, olive-brown, grayish brown, dull vinaceous brown, or dark brown to blackish brown

Lactarius mucidus var. *mucidus* (p. 207), cap dark dingy chocolate brown on the disc, becoming pinkish buff toward the margin; latex drying bluish green to olive on the gills; stalk viscid; spores 7.5–10.0 × 6–8 µm, prominences up to 0.5 µm high

Lactarius mucidus var. *mucidioides* (p. 207), cap dark dull vinaceous brown; latex drying and staining gills pale grayish green; stalk viscid; spores 7.5–9.0 × 7–8 µm, prominences up to 0.6 µm high

Lactarius vietus (p. 262), cap dark brown to gray-brown when young, fading to pinkish brown or lilac-gray; latex changing to or drying olive-gray, staining gills gray to olive-gray or grayish brown; stalk dry or moist; spores 7.5–9.0 × 6.0–7.5 µm, prominences up to 0.4 µm high

Lactarius kauffmanii var. *kauffmanii* (p. 192), cap blackish brown to grayish brown, or vinaceous brown, becoming grayish to grayish vinaceous with age; latex slowly staining gills olivaceous to grayish brown; stalk slimy-viscid; spores 7–10 × 6.5–8.0 µm, prominences up to 1 µm tall

Lactarius olivaceobrunneus (p. 213), cap olive-brown to grayish brown with an ochraceous to buff disc; latex staining gills greenish; stalk viscid; spores 9.5–14.0 × 8.5–11.0 µm, prominences up to 2 µm high

44a Cap distinctly zonate, dark yellowish brown with paler zones, becoming azonate with age; gills and flesh slowly staining pale yellow-brown when cut; spores 7–9 × 6–7 µm, prominences up to 1.5 µm high; associated with hardwoods, especially oak → *Lactarius frustratus* (p. 176)

44b Cap azonate or obscurely zonate → 45

45a Cap with a small central papilla, margin often crenate-plicate, brick red when young, slowly fading to dull brownish orange and finally dull pale pink; stalk base with vinaceous hairs; flesh and gills staining dingy vinaceous brown; latex taste very slowly becoming faintly acrid; cap surface stains pale olive with the application of KOH; eastern Canada south to Vermont, west to Michigan → *Lactarius carbonicola* (p. 157)

45b Cap lacking a papilla → 46

46a Latex watery on exposure, staining gills dark vinaceous brown; flesh taste weakly acrid; cap dark vinaceous brown; associated with oak; spores 7–9 × 5.5–6.5 µm, prominences up to 0.7 µm high; reported from Michigan → *Lactarius nimkeae* (p. 210)

46b Latex white to creamy white on exposure

Lactarius argillaceifolius var. *argillaceifolius* (p. 148), cap lilac-brown when young, fading to lilac-tan or pale lilac-gray and finally to pale tan or pinkish buff at the center with age; gills broad, flushed dull brownish orange when older; latex creamy white on exposure, taste slowly becoming slightly acrid

Lactarius fumeacolor (p. 177), cap pale brownish gray to pale pinkish brown with buff tones over the center; gills narrow, white to buff; latex white on exposure, taste slowly acrid

EASTERN FIELD KEY GROUP D

1a Cap surface with conspicuous erect fascicles of dark scales overall or especially along the margin, dull grayish purple, becoming vinaceous or dull brownish purple; stalk colored like the cap or paler; latex slightly acrid → *Lactarius purpureoechinatus* (p. 229)

1b Cap surface lacking conspicuous erect scales → 2

2a Cap distinctly zonate → 3

2b Cap azonate or obscurely zonate → 5

3a Latex taste bitter then slowly acrid; cap cinnamon brown zoned with darker tones and white pruinose at first; gills pale pinkish; flesh dark pinkish cinnamon; in sandy humus under sweet gum; reported only from Florida → *Lactarius cognoscibilis* (p. 163)

3b Latex taste quickly acrid to extremely acrid → 4

4a Cap dull reddish orange, orange-brown, orange-red, or dark brownish red to dark bay red

Lactarius peckii var. *peckii* (p. 218), cap dull reddish orange, orange-brown, orange-red, or dull brick red to brownish red; gills close, soon tinged pinkish cinnamon and darkening at maturity, staining rusty brown to reddish brown when bruised; spore deposit white; associated with oak

Lactarius rufus var. *rufus* (p. 235), cap dark brownish red to dark bay red; gills crowded, whitish, becoming vinaceous buff to vinaceous tan with age, *not* staining when bruised; spore deposit cream to pale yellow; associated with pines

4b Cap paler, light gray, pinkish gray, lavender-gray to lilac-gray or light violet-gray, lacking orange or red tones

Lactarius pseudoflexuosus (p. 225), cap pinkish gray to pale gray with gray-brown spots and streaks; gills close to subdistant, crossveined; spores 6.5–9.0 × 6–7 µm

Lactarius circellatus var. *borealis* (p. 162), cap lilac-gray to lavender-gray; gills close, *not* crossveined; spores 7–9 × 5.0–6.5 µm

Lactarius mackinawensis (p. 201), cap light violet-gray with cinnamon brown zones or spots, fading and becoming azonate; gills close, *not* crossveined; spores 8–12 × 7.5–9.0 µm

5a Latex taste bitter or metallic but *not* acrid; cap small, ¾–1⅜" (2.0–3.5 cm) wide, distinctly rugose-venose, especially in the center, plicate-striate toward the margin, dark brown when young, becoming olive-brown to olive at maturity → *Lactarius louisii* (p. 198)

5b Latex taste acrid, sometimes slowly or slightly; acrid taste sometimes preceded by a bitter taste → 6

6a Cap 1⅛–3½" (3–9 cm) wide, usually with a small umbo, pale cinnamon to pinkish cinnamon or pale reddish brown, typically pitted and stained with darker pinkish cinnamon; latex taste acrid only or bitter then acrid, sometimes slowly; usually associated with pine or oak → *Lactarius imperceptus* (p. 190)

6b Cap lacking an umbo or, if umbonate, *not* with the combination of characters given in 6a → 7

7a Cap very small to small, ¼–1¼" (6–32 mm) wide

Lactarius minusculus (p. 205), cap glabrous, fulvous to cinnamon fulvous with a cream-colored, minutely scalloped margin; stalk lacking a white basal mycelium; among mosses or on decaying wood in moist woods; reported only from Vermont

Lactarius subgerardii (p. 242), cap finely wrinkled, dull gray-brown to pale smoky brown, blackish on the wrinkles; stalk often with a white basal mycelium; on soil or among mosses under hemlock; New Jersey, Tennessee, and West Virginia

7b Cap medium, greater than 1¼" (32 mm) wide → 8

8a Latex taste quickly becoming distinctly acrid → 9

8b Latex taste slowly or slightly acrid → 13

9a Cap light pinkish cinnamon with a distinct olive tint, viscid, glabrous, sometimes with a small umbo; spore deposit yellowish buff; spores 7.5–10.0 × 6.0–7.5 µm; associated with pine; reported only from Tennessee → *Lactarius subolivaceus* (p. 244)

9b Cap darker brown to red or some shade of gray to lavender-gray or lilac-drab → 10

10a Cap milk chocolate brown to medium brown or dark brownish red to dark bay red

Lactarius rufus var. *rufus* (p. 235), cap dark brownish red to dark bay red; latex copious in young specimens, taste intensely acrid; widely distributed in North America

Lactarius fusco-olivaceus var. *fusco-olivaceus* (p. 179), cap milk chocolate brown to medium brown; latex moderately acrid; reported only from Tennessee

10b Cap some shade of gray to lavender-gray or lilac-drab → 11

11a Gills crossveined; latex taste very acrid; cap pinkish gray to pale gray with gray-brown spots and streaks; stalk pale pinkish gray to gray, sometimes with a whitish bloom when young; found in conifer and hardwood forests; widely distributed in eastern North America → *Lactarius pseudoflexuosus* (p. 225)

11b Gills *not* crossveined; latex taste acrid → 12

12a Cap lilac-gray to lavender-gray; gills forked near the stalk; stalk pale lilac-gray; associated with conifers; reported from eastern Canada and Tennessee

12b Cap pale gray to gray or smoky gray, lacking lilac or lavender tones

Lactarius cinereus var. *cinereus* (p. 161), gills close; stalk dry; cap pale gray, sometimes darker gray on the disc, viscid; associated with hardwoods, especially beech; eastern Canada south to West Virginia

Lactarius glutinosus (p. 182), gills distant; stalk viscid; cap smoky gray, slimy-viscid when moist, becoming dry; found in mixed woods; reported only from Pennsylvania

13a Cap surface covered with fibers and tiny scales, dry, ⅝–2" (1.5–5.0 cm) wide, dark purple-brown to purple-gray when young, fading or drying brownish gray to dull gray over a dull yellowish ground color, depressed at the center with a small pointed umbo; growing on decaying wood or among sphagnum mosses in bogs or wet woodlands → *Lactarius griseus* (p. 184)

13b Cap surface *not* covered with fibers and tiny scales; *not* growing on decaying wood → 14

14a Cap surface conspicuously wrinkled, dry and velvety, brown to yellow-brown to tan, margin becoming crenate or wavy with age; gills subdistant to distant, crossveined; stalk dry, velvety, dark brown to yellow-brown → *Lactarius gerardii* var. *gerardii* (p. 180)

14b Cap surface *not* conspicuously wrinkled → 15

15a Cap olive-gray to olivaceous gray to olive-buff, becoming olive-buff with lilac tinges when older, viscid, soon dry and somewhat shiny; spore deposit pale yellow; typically associated with beech; eastern Canada west to Michigan, south to Texas → *Lactarius cinereus* var. *fagetorum* (p. 161)

15b Cap some shade of fulvous, brown, or red, lacking gray tones → 16

16a Associated with oak; reported only from Florida; cap dingy white at first, soon darkening to yellowish brown to dull fulvous; spores 9–11 × 7.8–8.5 µm → *Lactarius limacinus* (p. 198)

16b Associated with conifers

Lactarius oculatus (p. 212), cap dark reddish brown to orange-brown at the center, paler toward the margin, fading to pale orange-brown, but the small pointed umbo typically retaining a dark reddish brown color and resembling an eyespot; stalk often with a whitish basal mycelium; latex scant, watery to whey-like; growing among sphagnum mosses in bogs or on the ground among needles in conifer woods, especially with spruce and pine; eastern Canada south to Georgia, west to Wisconsin

Lactarius hepaticus (p. 185), cap dark rusty red to brick red, dark reddish brown to chestnut brown, often with a darker central spot; stalk lacking a whitish basal mycelium; latex white; growing on the ground in mossy areas under conifers, especially hemlock; widely distributed in eastern North America

Lactarius subumbrinus (p. 249), cap date brown; stalk lacking a whitish basal mycelium; latex sparse, white; growing in deep humus in a pine planting; reported only from North Carolina

Keys to Western *Lactarius* Species

1a Color of latex immediately on exposure orange, reddish orange, orange-red, dark red, dark blood red, purplish red, or dark blue → **Western Field Key Group A** (p. 40)

1b Color of latex immediately on exposure watery, whey-like, white to creamy white, or pinkish buff → 2

  2a Latex color changing to dingy cream, light yellow, yellow, sulfur yellow, or greenish gray within *five* minutes → **Western Field Key Group A** (p. 40)

  2b Latex color unchanging within *five* minutes (*note:* the latex of some species may intensify or change color after five minutes, may stain tissues or dry a different color) → 3

3a Taste of the latex or flesh mild within *two* minutes → **Western Field Key Group B** (p. 43)

3b Taste of the latex or flesh disagreeable, astringent, bitter, or slightly to extremely acrid within *two* minutes → 4

  4a Odor of crushed flesh distinctive, variously described as fruity or spicy, like maple sugar, coconut, or anise; fragrant or aromatic, like geranium, apple, raw pumpkin, ripe crushed blackberries, lemon extract; or disinfectant-like, spermatic, pungent, strong, alkaline, or peculiar to disagreeable → **Western Field Key Group A** (p. 40)

  4b Odor of crushed flesh *not* distinctive → 5

5a Cap some shade of white, buff, yellow, orange, ochraceous to brownish ochre, tan, pale yellowish cinnamon, or pale pinkish cinnamon to pale rosy cinnamon → **Western Field Key Group C** (p. 45)

5b Cap some shade of red, brown, lilac, or gray → 6

  6a Specimen margin distinctly bearded; or stalk distinctly scrobiculate; or latex slowly changing color, staining tissues or drying a different color → **Western Field Key Group C** (p. 45)

  6b Specimen having a combination of *all* of the following features: margin *not* distinctly bearded; stalk *not* distinctly scrobiculate; latex unchanging, *not* staining tissues or drying a different color → **Western Field Key Group D** (p. 50)

WESTERN FIELD KEY GROUP A

1a Color of latex immediately on exposure some shade of orange, red, or blue → 2

1b Color of latex immediately on exposure watery, whey-like, white to creamy white, or pinkish buff → 6

  2a Latex dark blue

  Lactarius indigo var. *indigo* (p. 191), cap 2–6" (5.0–15.5 cm) wide; latex scant; on the ground in conifer or hardwoods; eastern Canada south to Florida, west to Michigan and Texas, also reported from California

2b Latex some shade of orange or red → 3

3a Latex some shade of red → 4

3b Latex some shade of orange → 5

4a Cap azonate or slightly zoned on the margin, whitish to pale pinkish brown, becoming mottled with creamy to ochraceous orange or pinkish buff, often flushed green, olive, or olive-gray; gills staining green where injured; stalk *not* scrobiculate; latex scant, dark red; under pines; reported only from New Mexico → *Lactarius barrowsii* (p. 154)

4b Cap distinctly zonate with alternating bands of orange to brownish orange and paler zones between, developing greenish stains or flushes when older or bruised; stalk sometimes scrobiculate; latex scant, dark blood red to purplish red or paler and dingy orange-red; under conifers, especially Douglas fir and pines; Pacific Northwest south to California and New Mexico → *Lactarius rubrilacteus* (p. 234)

5a Flesh slowly staining dull dark red to vinaceous red or purplish when exposed

Lactarius deliciosus var. *areolatus* (p. 169), cap surface becoming areolate-scaly at maturity; gills close; widely distributed in western North America; spores 8.5–12.0 × 6.0–8.5 µm; macrocystidia absent on the gill faces

Lactarius deterrimus (p. 170), cap surface glabrous at maturity; gills subdistant; widely distributed in western North America; spores 8.0–11.5 × 6.5–9.0 µm; macrocystidia present on the gill faces

5b Flesh *not* staining when exposed

Lactarius deliciosus var. *olivaceosordidus* (p. 169), cap of young specimens grayish green over an orange, yellow, or brownish yellow ground color; macrocystidia present

Lactarius deliciosus var. *deliciosus* (p. 168), cap of young specimens grayish orange to brownish orange; macrocystidia absent

6a Latex color changing to light yellow, yellow, sulfur yellow, dingy cream, or greenish gray within *five* minutes → 7

6b Latex color unchanging within *five* minutes (*note:* the latex of some specimens may intensify or change color after five minutes, may stain tissues or dry a different color) → 15

7a Latex white on exposure, becoming greenish gray, taste extremely acrid; cap typically zonate, olive-brown to dark olive with alternating zones of green and dingy yellow-brown → *Lactarius olivaceoumbrinus* (p. 213)

7b Latex white to whey-like on exposure, becoming some shade of cream to yellow but *not* greenish gray, taste mild, acrid, or bitter → 8

8a Stalk distinctly scrobiculate

Lactarius scrobiculatus var. *canadensis* (p. 239), cap margin distinctly bearded to pubescent (*note:* check young specimens if available); cap typically yellow; spores 7–9 × 5.5–7.0 µm; associated with conifers; typically *not* semihypogeous

Lactarius scrobiculatus var. *montanus* (p. 239), cap margin fibrillose to tomentose when young, becoming glabrous at maturity; cap typically yellow; spores 8.0–9.5 × 5.5–7.0 µm; associated with conifers; often semihypogeous

Lactarius pubescens var. *betulae* (p. 228), cap margin coarsely bearded (*note:* check young specimens if available); cap dull vinaceous pink when young, fading to dull white to dingy pale yellowish with age; spores 6.5–8.0 × 5.5–6.5 µm; associated with birch

8b Stalk *not* distinctly scrobiculate → 9

9a Cap margin cottony-tomentose to distinctly bearded (*note:* check young specimens if available)

Lactarius resimus var. *resimus* (p. 232), flesh staining yellow when cut; cap 2⅜–6" (6–15 cm) wide, milky white overall with ochraceous zones, lacking pinkish tints; spores 6–8 × 5–6 µm

Lactarius resimus var. *regalis* (p. 232), identical to *Lactarius resimus* var. *resimus* except spores measure 7–10 × 6–8 µm

Lactarius pubescens var. *betulae* (p. 228), flesh *not* staining yellow when cut; cap dull vinaceous pink when young, fading to dull white to dingy pale yellowish with age; spores 6.5–8.0 × 5.5–6.5 µm

9b Cap margin *not* cottony-tomentose to distinctly bearded → 10

10a Gills and flesh staining dull lilac when bruised; latex taste mild at first, then bitter → *Lactarius uvidus* var. *uvidus* (p. 261)

10b Gills and flesh *not* staining dull lilac when bruised → 11

11a Cap very small, ⅜–1⅜" (1.0–3.5 cm) wide, translucent-striate at maturity, olive-brown to smoky brown; associated with alder or in mixed woods with cedar and alder → *Lactarius occidentalis* (p. 211)

11b Cap medium to large, ¾–4¾" (2–12 cm) wide, *not* translucent-striate at maturity, whitish to yellowish cinnamon, pale pinkish cinnamon to orangey cinnamon, bright orange to brownish orange, or reddish brown; *not* associated with alder or cedar → 12

12a Cap bright orange or coppery orange to orangey cinnamon, duller with age; stalk colored like the cap or paler, with a whitish basal mycelium; latex taste bitter then acrid; flesh staining vivid orange with the application of KOH; spores 7.5–10 × 6.0–7.5 µm; growing among sphagnum mosses; reported from Alaska → *Lactarius duplicatus* (p. 172)

12b Specimen lacking the combination of characters given in 12a → 13

13a Gills discoloring or spotting vinaceous or brownish with age; associated with pines → *Lactarius vinaceorufescens* (p. 263)

13b Gills *not* discoloring and *not* spotting vinaceous or brownish with age; associated with hardwoods, especially oak → 14

14a Cap whitish to pale yellowish cinnamon with darker spots when young, fading to nearly whitish overall when older; flesh and latex taste distinctly acrid, sometimes slowly → *Lactarius chrysorrheus* (p. 160)

14b Cap grayish orange to grayish red or brownish orange to reddish brown; flesh and latex taste slightly acrid or mild to slightly bitter or astringent, often with a bitter aftertaste → *Lactarius xanthogalactus* (p. 266)

15a Taste of the latex or flesh disagreeable, astringent, bitter, or slightly to extremely acrid within *two* minutes → 16

15b Taste of the latex or flesh mild within *two* minutes → **Western Field Key Group B** (p. 43)

16a Odor of crushed flesh distinctive, variously described either as sweetly fragrant, like coconut, anise, maple sugar or burnt sugar, geraniums, or as pungent, peculiar, disagreeable → 17

16b Odor of crushed flesh *not* distinctive → **Western Field Key Group C** (p. 45)

17a Odor of crushed flesh resembling coconut or anise

Lactarius glyciosmus (p. 183), cap pale vinaceous gray to pale lilac-gray or whitish; flesh taste slowly and slightly acrid

Lactarius hibbardae var. *hibbardae* (p. 186), cap dark pinkish brown to dark pinkish gray, becoming paler pinkish brown to pinkish gray; flesh taste distinctly acrid; latex *not* drying grayish green

17b Odor of crushed flesh variously described, but *not* as resembling coconut or anise → 18

18a Odor of crushed flesh sweetly fragrant or like maple sugar

Lactarius camphoratus (p. 156), odor of crushed flesh fragrant like maple sugar or burnt sugar; cap dark red-brown, fading to pale vinaceous pink; stalk base typically with stiff hairs

Lactarius gossypinus (p. 183), odor of crushed flesh sweetly fragrant; cap pale yellow to orange-yellow, indistinctly zonate with watery zones; margin inrolled and cottony when young

18b Odor variously described, but *not* sweetly fragrant or like maple sugar → 19

19a Stalk distinctly scrobiculate; cap pale olive-buff at first, soon becoming straw-colored then dingy dark ochraceous; margin incurved and coarsely strigose, the hairs becoming fuscous with age; odor of crushed flesh faintly pungent and disagreeable → *Lactarius payettensis* (p. 217)

19b Stalk *not* distinctly scrobiculate; cap white to cream, becoming reddish orange to vinaceous on the disc with age; margin inrolled and bearded with coarse white hairs when young; stalk apex often tinged pink, sometimes with a white basal mycelium; odor of crushed flesh faintly like geraniums → *Lactarius pubescens* var. *pubescens* (p. 228)

WESTERN FIELD KEY GROUP B

1a Odor of crushed flesh distinctive, variously described as fragrant, resinous, sweet like maple sugar or burnt sugar, or fishy → 2

1b Odor of crushed flesh *not* distinctive → 4

2a Odor of crushed flesh distinctly fishy; cap dark orange-brown to cinnamon brown at the center, paler orange-brown toward the margin → *Lactarius volemus* var. *volemus* (p. 265)

2b Odor of crushed flesh resinous to fragrant or sweet like maple sugar or burnt sugar → 3

3a Odor of crushed flesh sweet like maple sugar or burnt sugar; cap orange-brown to pale cinnamon brown, zoned with dark grayish brown; latex watery on exposure, *not* staining tissues; associated with sphagnum mosses in bogs or in wet conifer or mixed woods; reported only from western Canada → *Lactarius helvus* (p. 184)

3b Odor of crushed flesh resinous to fragrant; cap medium lilac-brown on buttons, becoming paler with ochraceous tinges over the disc; latex viscous, white on exposure, staining tissues lilac; associated with conifers, sometimes in open grassy areas; reported only from Alaska → *Lactarius cordovaensis* (p. 165)

4a Cap margin distinctly coarsely tomentose or bearded (*note:* check young specimens if available) → 5

4b Cap margin *not* distinctly coarsely tomentose or bearded (*note:* cap surface or margin may be velvety or pubescent) → 7

5a Latex staining gills pink then light smoky brown; cap whitish with creamy or honey-colored zones; spores 5.5–7.0 × 5.5–6.5 µm; reported only from western Canada → *Lactarius subtorminosus* (p. 249)

5b Latex staining gills dull lilac to purple → 6

6a Cap light yellow to orange-yellow; associated with spruce → *Lactarius repraesentaneus* (p. 231)

6b Cap pale grayish lilac with darker violaceous brown spots or zones, with lilac tints that fade to pinkish gray or pinkish buff; associated with alder in swampy areas or mixed woods → *Lactarius cascadensis* (p. 158)

7a Species reported only from Alaska; associated with birch or alder; cap light pinkish tan to pinkish brown, slimy-viscid; stalk creamy white, viscid, staining orange where handled or lavender from the latex → *Lactarius pallescens* var. *palmerensis* (p. 215)

7b Species *not* with the combination of characters given in 7a → 8

8a Cap milk white, whitish to olive-buff, pale pink to pale grayish pink, or pale brownish gray → 9

8b Cap more richly colored, some shade of orange, cinnamon, brown, or dark gray → 11

9a Latex staining flesh lilac; cap surface slimy-viscid, milk white, becoming pale grayish pink to pale pink and more grayish with age; spores 9.0–10.5 × 7–9 µm; among mosses in conifer or mixed woods → *Lactarius pallescens* var. *pallescens* (p. 214)

9b Latex staining flesh red or, with age, pinkish brown, or *not* staining flesh → 10

10a Latex staining flesh red or, with age, pinkish brown; cap surface dry, whitish then olive-buff with darker and lighter areas; spores 7.5–9.0 × 7.5–9.0 µm; associated with Ponderosa pine → *Lactarius pallidiolivaceus* (p. 215)

10b Latex *not* staining flesh; cap moist, becoming dry and finely cracked and scaly, pale brownish gray fading to pale pinkish gray; spores 7–9 × 5.5–6.0 µm; associated with alder → *Lactarius lepidotus* (p. 194)

11a Species collected in the Tundra growing among sedges and grasses; reported only from Alaska; cap brick red to orange-brown and glossy when young, becoming brownish orange with age → *Lactarius lanceolatus* (p. 193)

11b Species *not* with the combination of characters given in 11a → 12

12a Cap grayish orange to brownish orange, glabrous, striate, viscid; odor resembling coconut when specimen dried; found in coastal mixed conifer and hardwood forests; reported only from California → *Lactarius cocoseolens* (p. 162)

12b Cap darker-colored, brick red, some shade of brown to blackish, or purple → 13

13a Latex staining tissues dull lilac; cap pale to dark grayish purple or dark purplish brown, fading to vinaceous cinnamon with age; flesh staining reddish brown when exposed, taste strongly resinous; associated with conifers; widely distributed in the West → *Lactarius uvidus* var. *montanus* (p. 260)

13b Latex *not* staining tissues dull lilac → 14

14a Gill edges distinctly darker than the faces at maturity; cap surface dry, velvety, dark sooty brown to blackish; associated with conifers; reported from Alaska south to California → *Lactarius fallax* var. *fallax* (p. 174)

14b Gill edges colored like the faces at maturity → 15

15a Cap surface velvety, dry, dark yellowish brown to blackish brown

Lactarius lignyotus var. *lignyotus* (p. 196), flesh staining rosy pink to dull reddish when cut; gills close to subdistant; spore deposit bright ochre

Lactarius fallax var. *concolor* (p. 174), flesh staining vinaceous when cut; gills close to crowded; spore deposit pale yellow

15b Cap surface *not* velvety (*note:* cap surface may be moist, dry, or viscid, glabrous to minutely scurfy, wrinkled or pitted) → 16

16a Cap up to 2" (5 cm) wide at maturity → 17
16b Cap greater than 2" (5 cm) wide at maturity → 19
17a Cap striate to translucent-striate at maturity
Lactarius occidentalis (p. 211), cap often wrinkled or pitted near the margin, moist or dry, olive-brown to smoky brown; gills slowly staining pinkish tan to pinkish brown when bruised; flesh buff or tinged cinnamon; associated with alder or cedar; reported from California, Oregon, and Washington
Lactarius riparius (p. 233), cap glabrous, subviscid to viscid, brownish orange to brown or reddish brown; gills *not* staining when bruised; flesh pale orange; found in mountainous conifer forests in association with firs, alder, and willow; reported from California
17b Cap *not* translucent-striate at maturity → 18
18a Latex white on exposure, staining gills dark red-brown; cap surface slimy-viscid when moist, becoming somewhat shiny when dry, reddish brown to orange-brown; associated with conifers, especially spruce → *Lactarius atrobadius* (p. 151)
18b Latex whey-like to watery on exposure, *not* staining tissues; cap surface dry, sometimes rimose or scaly, cinnamon to ochraceous tawny; associated with pines → *Lactarius thiersii* (p. 256)
19a Cap dark fuscous gray to dark brown with a somewhat paler margin, slimy; latex slowly becoming yellowish on drying; growing among sphagnum mosses; reported from Oregon and Idaho → *Lactarius mucidus* var. *fuscogriseus* (p. 206)
19b Cap dark orange-brown to yellowish rusty brown or dark reddish brown, moist or dry, but *not* slimy → 20
20a Species associated with alder; growing in mountainous areas; odor of crushed flesh *not* distinctive when dried; cap dark reddish brown, soon fading to pale vinaceous brown to light pinkish cinnamon; macrocystidia prominently projecting → *Lactarius alpinus* var. *mitis* (p. 146)
20b Species associated with oak and sometimes conifers along the Pacific Coast; odor resembling maple sugar when dried; cap dull, dark orange-brown over the disc to yellowish rusty brown at the margin; macrocystidia not observed → *Lactarius rubidus* (p. 234)

WESTERN FIELD KEY GROUP C

1a Cap various shades of green, olive to dark grayish green, usually zoned with dark green spots arranged concentrically → *Lactarius atroviridis* (p. 152)
1b Cap some shade of white, buff, tan, yellow, orange, red, cinnamon, brown, lilac, or gray → 2
2a Cap white, whitish or cream, sometimes developing darker tones as specimens mature → 3
2b Cap some shade of buff, tan, yellow, orange, red, cinnamon, brown, lilac, or gray → 7
3a Cap margin distinctly pubescent to bearded (*note:* check young specimens if available); disc reddish orange to vinaceous; stalk apex tinged pink; associated with birch and other hardwoods → *Lactarius pubescens* var. *pubescens* (p. 228)
3b Cap margin *not* distinctly pubescent to bearded → 4

4a Gills pale pink to vinaceous brown or pinkish cinnamon at maturity; cap white to whitish; latex *not* staining tissues, taste slowly acrid; cap margin *not* inrolled and cottony when young; associated with willow or poplar; reported from the northwestern United States and Canada, Alaska, Colorado, and New Mexico → *Lactarius controversus* (p. 164)

4b Gills white, whitish, cream, buff, yellowish, pale ochre, or tan → 5

5a Cap margin distinctly inrolled and cottony when young

Lactarius deceptivus (p. 167), cap large to very large, 3–10" (7.5–25.5 cm) wide, whitish, soon developing yellowish or brownish stains; spores 9–13 × 7–9 µm, prominences up to 1.5 µm high; stalk cuticle lacking a gelatinous layer; associated with hemlock or oak; reported from western Canada

Lactarius pseudodeceptivus (p. 224), cap large, 2⅜–6¾" (6–17 cm) wide, whitish, soon developing yellowish or brownish stains; spores 8–11 × 6–8 µm, prominences up to 0.4 µm high; stalk cuticle containing a gelatinous layer; associated with conifers; reported from Washington

5b Cap margin *not* distinctly inrolled and cottony when young → 6

6a Gills very crowded, white to creamy white at maturity, usually *not* staining when bruised; latex taste quickly and strongly acrid; spores 4.5–7.0 × 5.0–5.5 µm, prominences up to 0.2 µm high; in conifer or hardwoods; reported only from California → *Lactarius piperatus* var. *piperatus* (p. 220)

6b Gills crowded, creamy buff at maturity, staining brown when injured; latex taste burning acrid; spores 9.0–10.5 × 7.5–9.0 µm; scattered under mixed aspen and conifers; reported only from Colorado → *Lactarius alnicola* var. *pitkinensis* (p. 145)

7a Cap some shade of buff, tan, yellow, orange, or pale cinnamon → 8

7b Cap some shade of red, brown, lilac, or gray → 25

8a Latex staining tissues lilac, violet, or purple → 9

8b Latex *not* staining tissues lilac, violet, or purple (*note:* latex may change to, stain tissues, or dry a different color) → 11

9a Cap margin distinctly coarsely strigose to bearded (*note:* check young specimens if available); cap light yellow to orange-yellow; stalk scrobiculate; associated with spruce → *Lactarius repraesentaneus* (p. 231)

9b Cap margin *not* distinctly coarsely strigose to bearded → 10

10a Cap brownish orange to orange-gray or yellow-brown with a grayish red disc, viscid; latex staining tissues lilac to violet; cap surface staining yellow with the application of KOH; reported from California and Oregon → *Lactarius californiensis* (p. 156)

10b Cap light yellow, slimy-viscid, glabrous; latex and gills staining purple-red with the application of $FeSO_4$ → *Lactarius aspideoides* (p. 150)

11a Stalk base covered with white to vinaceous strigose hairs or white mycelium or tomentum → 12

11b Stalk base lacking white to vinaceous hairs, mycelium, or tomentum → 14

12a Cap with a papilla or umbo

Lactarius carbonicola (p. 157), stalk base covered with vinaceous hairs; cap margin often crenate-plicate; cap brick red when young, slowly fading to dull brownish orange and finally dull pale pink; latex staining tissues dingy vinaceous brown, taste very slowly faintly acrid; cap surface staining pale olive with the application of KOH

Lactarius thejogalus (p. 255), stalk base covered with conspicuous white strigose hairs; cap margin *not* crenate-plicate; cap brownish orange to apricot orange or orangey cinnamon, fading to pinkish cinnamon and finally orange-buff; latex *not* staining tissues, taste slowly becoming slightly acrid

12b Cap lacking a papilla or umbo → 13

13a Cap margin distinctly coarsely strigose to bearded (*note:* check young specimens if available); cap with dull reddish orange to orange-brown concentric zones over a pale pinkish ground color; spores 7.5–10.0 × 6.0–7.5 µm → *Lactarius torminosus* var. *torminosus* (p. 257)

13b Cap margin *not* distinctly coarsely strigose to bearded; cap azonate, light orange to grayish orange with a scalloped margin; spores 5.5–6.5 × 5.5–6.5 µm → *Lactarius desjardinii* (p. 170)

14a Cap margin distinctly coarsely strigose to bearded (*note:* check young specimens if available)

Lactarius torminosus var. *torminosus* (p. 257), cap with dull reddish orange to orange-brown concentric zones over a pale pinkish ground color, viscid over the disc, dry toward the margin; spores 7.5–10.0 × 6.0–7.5 µm

Lactarius payettensis (p. 217), cap pale olive-buff at first, soon becoming straw-colored then dingy dark ochraceous, azonate, glutinous; hairs becoming fuscous with age; spores 8–10 × 7–8 µm

14b Cap margin *not* distinctly coarsely strigose to bearded → 15

15a Cap margin incurved at first, with a heavy roll of soft felt that is pale pinkish buff or nearly so; cap with cinnamon buff zones on a pinkish buff ground color; stalk scrobiculate; latex instantly very strongly acrid; cespitose under cottonwood trees; reported only from Colorado → *Lactarius sanmiguelensis* (p. 238)

15b Species *not* with the combination of characters given in 15a → 16

16a Cap distinctly zonate, orange with zones of apricot orange and light orangish yellow, viscid; latex staining gills orange to orange-brown; found in mountainous conifer forests; reported from the Pacific Northwest and Colorado → *Lactarius olympianus* (p. 214)

16b Cap azonate or obscurely zonate → 17

17a Stalk scrobiculate; cap yellow-ochre, paler near the margin, viscid to slimy, azonate or somewhat zonate; latex scant, white on exposure, staining cut flesh yellow; growing under conifers; widely distributed in the western United States → *Lactarius alnicola* var. *alnicola* (p. 145)

17b Stalk *not* scrobiculate → 18

18a Cap pale yellow to pale ochre-yellow, pale ochre, or pale pinkish cinnamon → 19

18b Cap darker colored, ochraceous tawny, yellow-orange, orange, apricot orange, orange-red, brownish orange, rusty orange, or reddish cinnamon → 21

19a Specimen growing on the ground under alder in alpine areas; cap tawny yellow to ochraceous or yellowish, sometimes more orange, dry, appressed-tomentose to finely scaly; reported from Alaska, Idaho, Oregon, and Washington → *Lactarius alpinus* var. *alpinus* (p. 146)

19b Specimen *not* with the combination of characters given in 19a → 20

20a Gills staining brownish, whitish at first, becoming buff to pale yellow and darkening with age; cap pale yellow on the disc, pale pinkish cinnamon toward the margin; associated with oak; reported from Oregon and California → *Lactarius argillaceifolius* var. *megacarpus* (p. 149)

20b Gills *not* staining, white to cream and unchanging; cap pale ochre-yellow to pale ochre, or pale pinkish cinnamon; growing under conifers or hardwoods; reported from western Canada → *Lactarius affinis* var. *affinis* (p. 141)

21a Specimen growing on the ground under alder in alpine areas; cap apricot orange to tawny yellow or sometimes ochraceous to yellowish, dry, appressed-tomentose to finely scaly; reported from Alaska, Idaho, Oregon, and Washington → *Lactarius alpinus* var. *alpinus* (p. 146)

21b Specimen *not* with the combination of characters given in 21a → 22

22a Specimen associated with manzanita; growing in mixed coastal conifer and hardwood forests; cap orange to brownish orange or sometimes brown with a paler margin; latex taste strongly acrid; reported only from California → *Lactarius manzanitae* (p. 204)

22b Specimen *not* with the combination of characters given in 22a → 23

23a Latex slowly changing to yellow; cap orange-red at first, becoming brownish red to brownish orange or rusty orange, yellowish along the margin, translucent-striate when moist; growing on the ground under conifers, especially in coastal forests; reported from California, Oregon, and Washington → *Lactarius substriatus* (p. 247)

23b Latex *not* changing to yellow → 24

24a Latex taste mild then slowly becoming bitter, *not* acrid; cap brownish orange to light brown or reddish brown on the disc, with an orange margin; stalk light orange to grayish orange; gills crowded; associated with conifers and mountain alders; reported from California, Colorado, and Washington → *Lactarius luculentus* var. *laetus* (p. 199)

24b Latex taste acrid (*note:* latex may taste mild or bitter at first)

Lactarius luculentus var. *luculentus* (p. 200), cap ochraceous tawny when moist, becoming ochraceous buff to tawny or reddish cinnamon, sometimes with a small umbo; gills close; associated with Douglas fir; reported from Alaska, Oregon, and Colorado

Lactarius subflammeus (p. 242), cap orange-red when young, becoming orange to yellow-orange; margin with short translucent striations; gills close to subdistant; growing under conifers or in mixed conifer-hardwood forests; reported from Washington south to Idaho, California, and Colorado

25a Cap margin distinctly bearded (*note:* check young specimens if available); cap vinaceous cinnamon to light pinkish cinnamon, sometimes with rose pink or salmon orange tones; latex strongly acrid, white on exposure, slowly changing to pale yellow on the gills; reported from Idaho and California → *Lactarius torminosus* var. *nordmanensis* (p. 257)

25b Cap margin *not* distinctly bearded → 26

26a Stalk scrobiculate → 27

26b Stalk *not* scrobiculate → 31

27a Latex white, slowly turning greenish gray; taste extremely acrid; cap olive-brown to dark olive with alternating zones of green and dingy yellow-brown; flesh unchanging when cut, *not* staining; cap staining purplish red with the application of KOH; spores 7–10 × 6–9 µm; growing under conifers; reported from Idaho, Washington, Oregon, and California → *Lactarius olivaceoumbrinus* (p. 213)

27b Specimen *not* with the combination of characters given in 27a → 28

28a Latex slowly staining gills dull brown to olive-brown or olivaceous to grayish brown → 29

28b Latex *not* staining gills → 30

29a Cap blackish brown to grayish brown or vinaceous brown, becoming grayish to grayish vinaceous with age, slimy-viscid; latex slowly staining gills olivaceous to grayish brown, taste acrid; spores 7–10 × 6.5–8.0 µm; reported from Alaska south to California and Idaho → *Lactarius kauffmanii* var. *kauffmanii* (p. 192)

29b Cap pale brownish yellow to dull ochre or olive-brown to brown with ochraceous tints, typically darker brown or dark green to blackish on the disc; latex staining gills dull brown to olive-brown, taste very acrid; cap surface staining reddish purple with the application of KOH; spores 6.3–8.8 × 4.8–6.5 µm; reported from Alaska south to California → *Lactarius turpis* (p. 259)

30a Cap dark brown, developing dingy yellow-brown tones, lacking reddish or purplish tints; growing under Sitka spruce; reported only from Oregon → *Lactarius kauffmanii* var. *sitchensis* (p. 193)

30b Cap dark reddish brown at the center, pinkish brown on the margin, or vinaceous brown to purplish brown overall

Lactarius hysginus var. *hysginus* (p. 189), gills whitish to buff when young, becoming orange-yellow at maturity

Lactarius hysginus var. *americanus* (p. 189), gills pale yellow when young, becoming tan to dull cinnamon

31a Latex slowly changing color, staining tissues or drying a different color (*note:* latex color change or staining reaction may be delayed up to one hour) → 32

31b Latex unchanging, *not* staining tissues or drying a different color → **Western Field Key Group D** (p. 50)

32a Latex staining tissues reddish; cap dry, unpolished, usually somewhat wrinkled with age, pale dingy yellow-brown to whitish with a smoky tinge, sometimes with dull brown areas; gills crowded; latex taste acrid, sometimes slowly or faintly; spores 6–8 × 6–8 µm; reported from western Canada → *Lactarius fumosus* var. *fumosus* (p. 178)

32b Latex slowly changing to, staining tissues, or drying some other color → 33

33a Latex slowly changing to yellow, staining tissues yellow, or drying yellowish → 34

33b Latex slowly changing to, staining tissues, or drying olive-buff to olive-gray, olivaceous, gray, or olive-brown to brown → 35

34a Cap orange-red at first, becoming brownish red to brownish orange or rusty orange with pale yellow along the margin, translucent-striate when moist; latex slowly becoming straw yellow, taste bitterish then slowly acrid; gills staining grayish orange when bruised; growing on the ground under conifers, especially in coastal forests; reported from California, Oregon, and Washington → *Lactarius substriatus* (p. 247)

34b Specimen *not* with the combination of characters given in 34a; cap olive-brown, pale smoky gray, or gray to charcoal gray

Lactarius pseudomucidus (p. 227), cap pale smoky gray to charcoal gray; latex very slowly becoming yellowish as it dries on the gills, slowly staining gills yellowish to tan or brownish, taste acrid; spores 7–9 × 6–7 µm; found under conifers; reported from Alaska south to California and Idaho

Lactarius caespitosus (p. 155), cap gray to olive-brown; latex slowly staining flesh yellowish and gills dingy brown, taste slowly becoming strongly acrid; spores 9–12 × 7–9 µm; cespitose, scattered, or gregarious under conifers; widely distributed in western North America

35a Latex drying olive-buff to pale olive-gray, *not* staining tissues; cap pinkish gray to light vinaceous gray when young, developing cinnamon to pale brick red tones at maturity, often spotted with cinnamon or brownish tints; stalk typically with a white basal mycelium or a white strigose base; latex turning orange-yellow with the application of KOH → *Lactarius trivialis* (p. 258)

35b Latex *not* drying olive-buff to pale olive-gray (*note:* latex may change to, stain tissues, or dry a different color) → 36

36a Cap predominantly some shade of orange, often with a light brown or reddish brown disc and an orange margin; latex mild, slowly becoming bitter but *not* acrid → *Lactarius luculentus* var. *laetus* (p. 199)

36b Specimen *not* with the combination of characters given in 36a; latex typically acrid → 37

37a Cap small, up to 1¾" (4.5 cm) wide at maturity, moderately dark grayish brown, glutinous; latex staining gills grayish brown; growing under hemlock in coastal conifer forests; reported from Alaska and California → *Lactarius glutigriseus* (p. 182)

37b Cap medium to large, 2–7" (5–20 cm) wide at maturity → 38

38a Cap dark vinaceous brown to reddish brown when young, fading to pale grayish brown or pale lilac-gray with age, sticky but *not* slimy; gills staining dingy brown when bruised; latex changing to or drying olive-gray; flesh slowly staining grayish with the application of $FeSO_4$; widely distributed in western North America → *Lactarius vietus* (p. 262)

38b Cap darker blackish brown to grayish brown or dark brown with yellow-brown tones

Lactarius kauffmanii var. *kauffmanii* (p. 192), cap blackish brown to grayish brown or vinaceous brown, becoming grayish to grayish vinaceous with age; latex slowly staining gills olivaceous to grayish brown; spore deposit whitish; growing on the ground under conifers; reported from Alaska south to Idaho and California

Lactarius kauffmanii var. *sitchensis* (p. 193), cap dark brown, developing dingy yellow-brown tones; latex white, *not* staining tissues; spore deposit yellow; growing on the ground under Sitka spruce; reported only from Oregon

WESTERN FIELD KEY GROUP D

1a Cap soon dry and conspicuously wrinkled, hygrophanous, dark mahogany red to brick red, becoming onion skin pink from the margin toward the disc; latex taste slightly acrid; on the ground or on decaying conifer wood, especially spruce, in conifer or mixed forests; reported from California, Oregon, and Washington → *Lactarius subviscidus* (p. 253)

1b Cap *not* conspicuously wrinkled → 2

2a Cap orange-red when young, becoming orange to yellow-orange, slimy-viscid → *Lactarius subflammeus* (p. 242)

2b Cap colored differently from the choice in 2a, lilac-gray to lavender-gray, or some shade of brownish red to brown → 3

3a Cap lilac-gray to lavender-gray, zonate or azonate; growing under conifers; reported from the Pacific Northwest, Idaho, and Alaska → *Lactarius circellatus* var. *borealis* (p. 162)

3b Cap some shade of brownish red to brown → 4

4a Specimen associated with manzanita in coastal mixed forests; reported only from California; cap up to 2" (5 cm) wide, brown or orange to brownish orange; latex strongly acrid → *Lactarius manzanitae* (p. 204)

4b Specimen *not* associated with manzanita → 5

5a Cap very small, up to 1¼" (3.2 cm) wide at maturity, broadly translucent-striate, dull reddish brown to dark brown, usually with an olive tone; latex taste slightly acrid; associated with alder → *Lactarius obscuratus* var. *obscuratus* (p. 211)

5b Cap greater than 1¼" (3.2 cm) wide at maturity; *not* translucent-striate and *not* associated with alder → 6

6a Cap distinctly reddish brown; gills pale yellow when young, becoming tan to dull cinnamon with age, latex sharply acrid; associated with conifers, including redwood; reported only from California → *Lactarius hysginus* var. *americanus* (p. 189)

6b Cap distinctly dull red to brownish red or bay red → 7

7a Specimen collected under oak; cap brownish red fading to orange-brown with age, azonate; gills close to subdistant; flesh taste slightly acrid; latex taste acrid; spores 7–9 × 7–9 µm; reported only from California → *Lactarius rufulus* (p. 235)

7b Specimen collected under conifers, among sphagnum mosses, or on decaying conifer wood → 8

8a Specimen collected under conifers, especially pine and spruce, or among sphagnum mosses; cap dull red to dark brownish red or dark bay red, sometimes zoned with slightly darker bands; gills crowded; latex copious in young specimens; latex and flesh taste intensely acrid; spores 8.5–12.0 × 6–8 µm; widely distributed in western North America → *Lactarius rufus* var. *rufus* (p. 235)

8b Specimen collected on decaying conifer wood; cap bay red, azonate; gills close; latex scant, taste acrid; flesh taste quickly becoming intensely acrid; spores 7–9 × 5.5–6.5 µm; reported only from Idaho → *Lactarius rufus* var. *parvus* (p. 236)

COLOR PLATES

Lactarius affinis var. *affinis* (A)

Lactarius affinis var. *affinis* (B)

Lactarius affinis var. *viridilactis* (A)

Lactarius affinis var. *viridilactis* (B)

Lactarius agglutinatus (A)

Lactarius agglutinatus (B)

Lactarius alachuanus var. *alachuanus*

Lactarius allardii (A)

Lactarius allardii (B)

Lactarius alnicola var. *alnicola* (A)

Lactarius alnicola var. *alnicola* (B)

Lactarius alpinus var. *mitis*

Lactarius angustifolius (A)

Lactarius angustifolius (B)

Lactarius areolatus

Lactarius argillaceifolius var. *argillaceifolius* (A)

Lactarius argillaceifolius var. *argillaceifolius* (B)

Lactarius argillaceifolius var. *argillaceifolius* (C)

Lactarius argillaceifolius var. *megacarpus* (A)

Lactarius argillaceifolius var. *megacarpus* (B)

Lactarius aspideoides (A)

Lactarius aspideoides (B)

Lactarius atrobadius

Lactarius atroviridis

Lactarius badiopallescens

Lactarius barrowsii

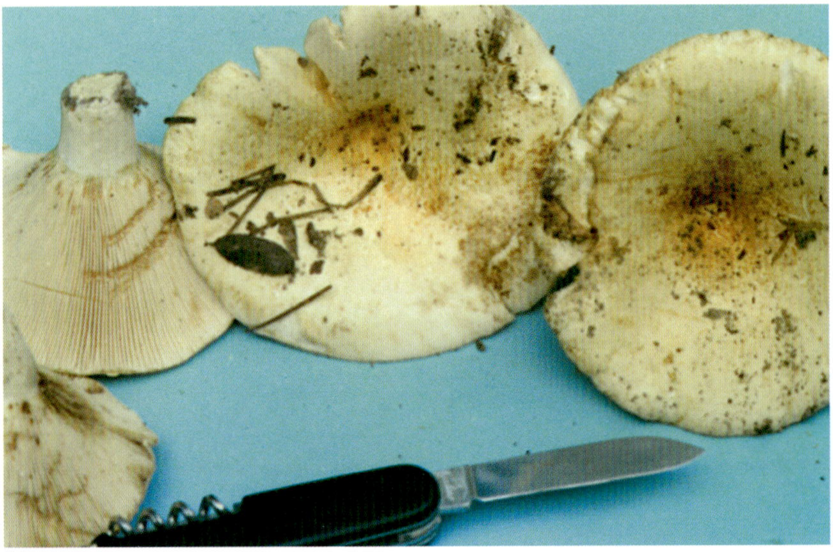

Lactarius caeruleitinctus

Lactarius caesptitosus

Lactarius camphoratus (A)

Lactarius camphoratus (B)

Lactarius carbonicola (A)

Lactarius carbonicola (B)

Lactarius chelidonium var. *chelidonioides* (A)

Lactarius chelidonium var. *chelidonioides* (B)

Lactarius chelidonium var. *chelidonium*

Lactarius chrysorrheus (A)

Lactarius chrysorrheus (B)

Lactarius cinereus var. *cinereus* (A)

Lactarius cinereus var. *cinereus* (B)

Lactarius cinereus var. *fagetorum* (A)

Lactarius cinereus var. *fagetorum* (B)

Lactarius circellatus var. *borealis*

Lactarius colorascens (A)

Lactarius colorascens (B)

Lactarius controversus

Lactarius corrugis (A)

Lactarius corrugis (B)

Lactarius croceus (A)

Lactarius croceus (B)

Lactarius croceus (C)

Lactarius deceptivus (A)

Lactarius deceptivus (B)

Lactarius deliciosus var. *deliciosus* (A)

Lactarius deliciosus var. *deliciosus* (B)

Lactarius deliciosus var. *olivaceosordidus*

Lactarius deterrimus (A)

Lactarius deterrimus (B)

Lactarius dispersus

Lactarius duplicatus

Lactarius eburneus

Lactarius fallax var. *concolor* (A)

Lactarius fallax var. *concolor* (B)

Lactarius fallax var. *fallax*

Lactarius floridanus (A)

Lactarius floridanus (B)

Lactarius fragilis var. *fragilis*

Lactarius frustratus

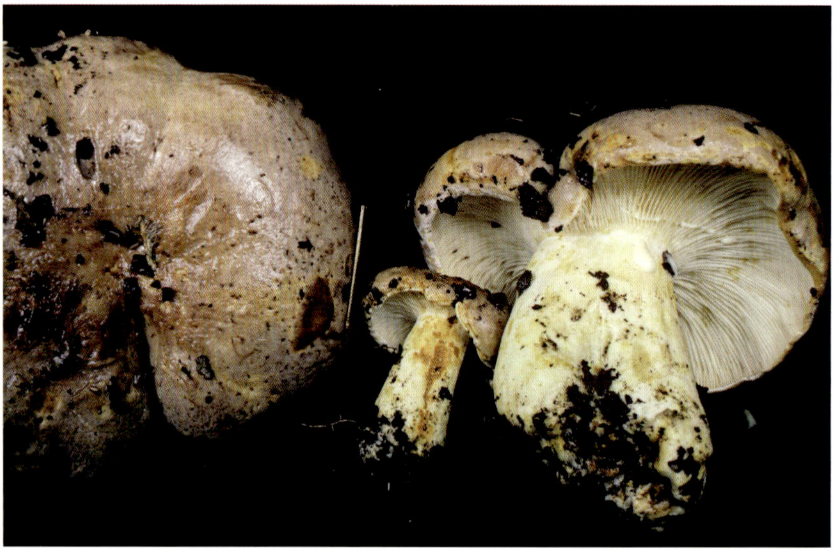

Lactarius fumeacolor

Lactarius fumosus var. *fumosoides*

Lactarius fumosus var. *fumosus*

Lactarius furcatus

Lactarius gerardii var. *fagicola*

Lactarius gerardii var. *gerardii* (A)

Lactarius gerardii var. *gerardii* (B)

Lactarius gerardii var. *gerardii* (C)

Lactarius gerardii var. *gerardii* (D)

Lactarius gerardii var. *subrubescens* (A)

Lactarius gerardii var. *subrubescens* (B)

Lactarius glaucescens

Lactarius glyciosmus

Lactarius gossypinus (A)

Lactarius hibbardae var. *glaucescens*

Lactarius hibbardae var. *hibbardae* (A)

Lactarius hibbardae var. *hibbardae* (B)

Lactarius hibbardae var. *hibbardae* (C)

Lactarius highlandensis (A)

Lactarius highlandensis (B)

Lactarius hygrophoroides var. *hygrophoroides* (A)

Lactarius hygrophoroides var. *hygrophoroides* (B)

Lactarius hygrophoroides var. *hygrophoroides* (C)

Lactarius hygrophoroides var. *rugatus* (A)

Lactarius hygrophoroides var. *rugatus* (B)

Lactarius hysginus var. *hysginus*

Lactarius imperceptus (A)

Lactarius imperceptus (B)

Lactarius imperceptus (C)

Lactarius indigo var. *diminutivus* (A)

Lactarius indigo var. *diminutivus* (B)

Lactarius indigo var. *indigo* (A)

Lactarius indigo var. *indigo* (B)

Lactarius indigo var. *indigo* (C)

Lactarius indigo var. *indigo* (D)

Lactarius kauffmanii var. *kauffmanii*

Lactarius lanceolatus

Lactarius lignyotellus

Lactarius lignyotus var. *canadensis*

Lactarius lignyotus var. *lignyotus*

Lactarius lignyotus var. *nigroviolascens*

Lactarius louisii (A)

Lactarius louisii (B)

Lactarius luculentus var. *laetus*

Lactarius luculentus var. *luculentus* (A)

Lactarius luculentus var. *luculentus* (B)

Lactarius luculentus var. *luculentus* (C)

Lactarius luteolus (A)

Lactarius luteolus (B)

Lactarius maculatipes (A)

Lactarius maculatipes (B)

Lactarius maculatipes (C)

Lactarius maculatus (A)

Lactarius maculatus (B)

Lactarius manzanitae (A)

Lactarius manzanitae (B)

Lactarius minisculus

Lactarius mucidus var. *fuscogriseus*

Lactarius mucidus var. *mucidioides*

Lactarius mucidus var. *mucidus*

Lactarius mutabilis

Lactarius neotabidus

Lactarius neuhoffii var. *neuhoffii*

Lactarius obscuratus var. *obscuratus*

Lactarius occidentalis

Lactarius oculatus

Lactarius olivaceoumbrinus

Lactarius olympianus (A)

Lactarius olympianus (B)

Lactarius pallescens var. *pallescens* (A)

Lactarius pallescens var. *pallescens* (B)

Lactarius pallescens var. *pallescens* (C)

Lactarius pallidiolivaceus

Lactarius paradoxus (A)

Lactarius paradoxus (B)

Lactarius payettensis

Lactarius peckii var. *peckii* (A)

Lactarius peckii var. *peckii* (B)

Lactarius peckii var. *peckii* (C)

Lactarius petersenii (A)

Lactarius petersenii (B)

Lactarius petersenii (C)

Lactarius piperatus var. *piperatus* (A)

Lactarius piperatus var. *piperatus* (B)

Lactarius proximellus (A)

Lactarius proximellus (B)

Lactarius psammicola f. *glaber* (A)

Lactarius psammicola f. *glaber* (B)

Lactarius psammicola f. *psammicola* (A)

Lactarius psammicola f. *psammicola* (B)

Lactarius pseudodeliciosus var. *pseudodeliciosus*

Lactarius pseudoflexuosus

Lactarius pseudomaculatus

Lactarius pseudomucidus (A)

Lactarius pseudomucidus (B)

Lactarius pseudomucidus (C)

Lactarius pubescens var. *betulae*

Lactarius pubescens var. *pubescens* (A)

Lactarius pubescens var. *pubescens* (B)

Lactarius purpureoechinatus

Lactarius pyrogalus (A)

Lactarius pyrogalus (B)

Lactarius quietus var. *incanus* (A)

Lactarius quietus var. *incanus* (B)

Lactarius quietus var. *incanus* (C)

Lactarius repraesentaneus (A)

Lactarius repraesentaneus (B)

Lactarius resimus var. *resimus*

Lactarius rimosellus

Lactarius rubidus (A)

Lactarius rubidus (B)

Lactarius rubrilacteus

Lactarius rufulus

Lactarius rufus var. *rufus* (A)

Lactarius rufus var. *rufus* (B)

Lactarius ruginosus

Lactarius salmoneus var. *salmoneus*

Lactarius salmonicolor (A)

Lactarius salmonicolor (B)

Lactarius salmonicolor (C)

Lactarius scrobiculatus var. *canadensis* (A)

Lactarius scrobiculatus var. *canadensis* (B)

Lactarius scrobiculatus var. *canadensis* (C)

Lactarius scrobiculatus var. *pubescens*

Lactarius speciosus

Lactarius splendens

Lactarius subflammeus

Lactarius subgerardii

Lactarius subpalustris

Lactarius subplinthogalus (A)

Lactarius subplinthogalus (B)

Lactarius subplinthogalus (C)

Lactarius subplinthogalus (D)

Lactarius subpurpureus (A)

Lactarius subpurpureus (B)

Lactarius subpurpureus (C)

Lactarius substriatus

Lactarius subvellereus var. *subdistans*

Lactarius subvellereus var. *subvellereus*

Lactarius subvernalis var. *cokeri* (A)

Lactarius subvernalis var. *cokeri* (B)

Lactarius subvernalis var. *cokeri* (C)

Lactarius subviscidus

Lactarius sumstinei (A)

Lactarius sumstinei (B)

Lactarius thejogalus (A)

Lactarius thejogalus (B)

Lactarius tomentosomarginatus (A)

Lactarius tomentosomarginatus (B)

Lactarius torminosus var. *nordmanensis*

Lactarius torminosus var. *torminosus* (A)

Lactarius torminosus var. *torminosus* (B)

Lactarius trivialis

Lactarius turpis (A)

Lactarius turpis (B)

Lactarius uvidus var. *montanus* (A)

Lactarius uvidus var. *montanus* (B)

Lactarius uvidus var. *montanus* (C)

Lactarius uvidus var. *uvidus* (A)

Lactarius uvidus var. *uvidus* (B)

Lactarius vietus

Lactarius vinaceopallidus

Lactarius vinaceorufescens (A)

Lactarius vinaceorufescens (B)

Lactarius vinaceosporus

Lactarius volemus var. *flavus*

Lactarius volemus var. *volemus* (A)

Lactarius volemus var. *volemus* (B)

Lactarius volemus var. *volemus* (C)

Lactarius xanthogalactus

Lactarius xanthydrorheus

Lactarius yazooensis

Lactarius zonarius var. *riparius*

Zelleromyces cinnabarinus (A)

Zelleromyces cinnabarinus (B)

Bondarzewia berkeleyi

Lactarius rubriviridis (A)

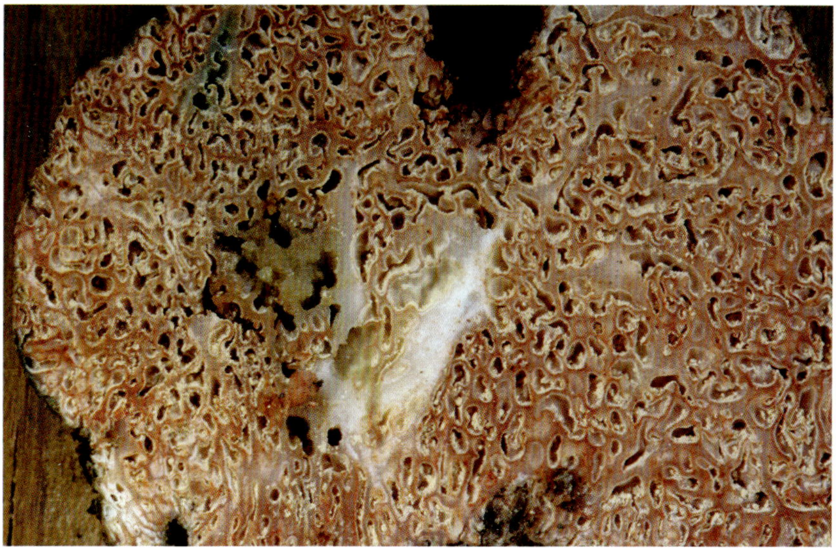

Lactarius rubriviridis (B)

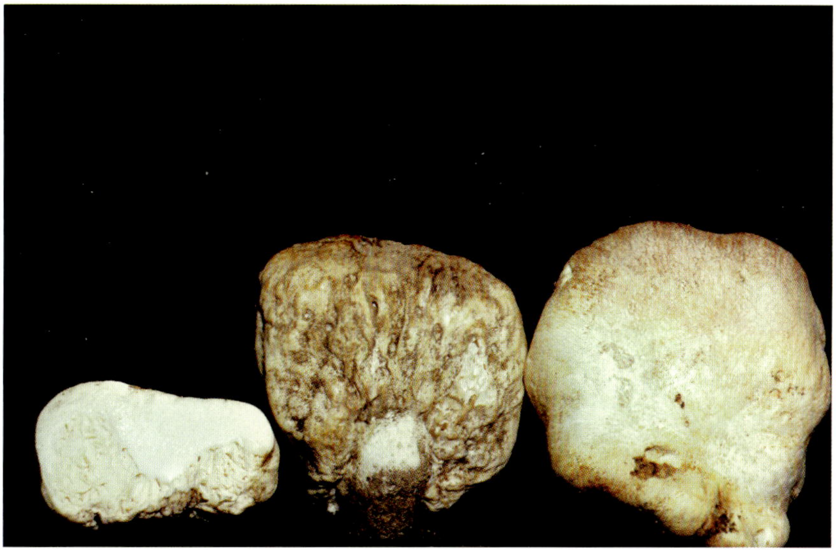

Arcangeliella crassa

Arcangeliella desjardinii (A)

Arcangeliella desjardinii (B)

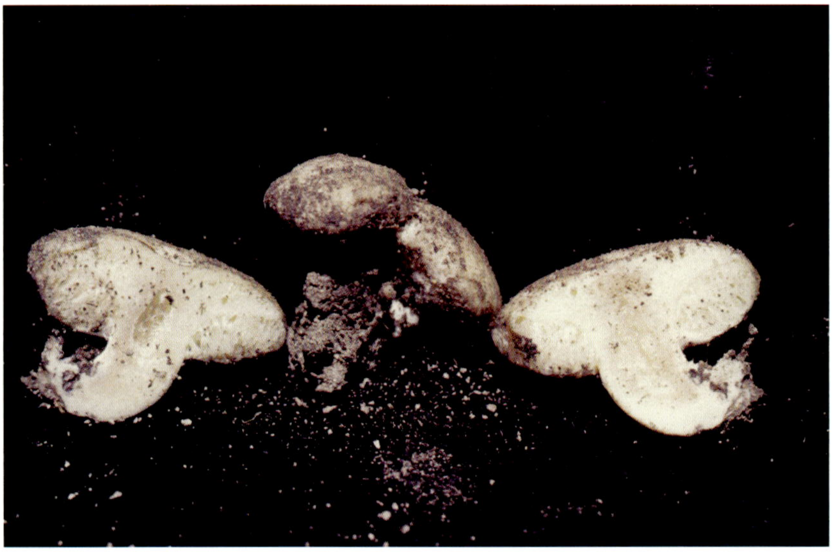

Arcangeliella parva

Hypomyces lactifluorum

Asterophora lycoperdoides

Species and Varieties: Descriptions

Lactarius affinis var. **affinis** Peck Illus. p. 54

Ann. Rep. N.Y. State Cab. 23 (1872), 116
Lactarius platyphyllus Peck, *Lactarius subinsulsus* Peck
Sticky Milk Cap

CAP: 2–4⅜" (5–11 cm) wide, convex, becoming broadly convex then shallowly depressed at the center with age; surface sticky to slimy when fresh, glabrous, pale ochre-yellow to pale ochre or pale pinkish cinnamon, lighter toward the margin.

GILLS: attached to slightly decurrent, close, broad, sometimes forked near the stalk, white to cream.

STALK: 1⅛–3⅛" (3–8 cm) long, ½–¾" (1.2–2.0 cm) thick, nearly equal, becoming hollow with age, glabrous, sticky when fresh, white or sometimes brownish.

FLESH: white; odor not distinctive; taste acrid.

LATEX: white on exposure, unchanging, not staining tissues; taste acrid.

SPORE DEPOSIT: white.

MICROSCOPIC CHARACTERS: spores 9–11 × 7–8 µm, elliptic, ornamented with warts and ridges that sometimes form a partial reticulum, prominences up to 1 µm high, hyaline, amyloid; cap cuticle a loose ixotrichoderm to an ixocutis

OCCURRENCE: scattered or in groups on the ground in conifer or hardwoods; July–October; eastern Canada south to New York, west to Michigan, also reported from western Canada; occasional.

EDIBILITY: unknown.

COMMENTS: *Lactarius affinis* var. *viridilactis* is very similar, but it has a yellowish spore deposit, gills that slowly stain greenish when bruised, and white latex that dries pale olive to olive. Other similar species include *Lactarius depressus, Lactarius midlandensis,* and *Lactarius pseudoaffinis.*

Lactarius affinis var. **viridilactis** (Kauffman) Hesler and A. H. Smith Illus. p. 54, 55

North American Species of Lactarius (1979), 421–422
Lactarius trivialis var. *viridilactis* Kauffman

CAP: 2–6" (5.0–15.5 cm) wide, convex with a depressed disc, becoming broadly funnel-shaped with age; margin inrolled at first, expanding and becoming uplifted and sometimes lobed; surface glabrous and sticky to slimy when young and moist, becoming shiny when dry, azonate, pale yellow to pale ochre or pale pinkish cinnamon.

GILLS: attached to slightly decurrent, broad, close to subdistant, pinkish cinnamon, becoming powdery with age, bruising greenish.

STALK: 1½–4¾" (4–12 cm) long, ⅜–1⅛" (1–3 cm) thick, nearly equal or enlarged toward the base, hollow, viscid when young, sometimes scrobiculate, pale pinkish cinnamon, occasionally with rusty brown stains at the base.

FLESH: firm and hard, whitish, turning dull cinnamon with age; odor not distinctive; taste acrid.

LATEX: white on exposure, unchanging, drying as pale olive to olive droplets; taste very acrid.

SPORE DEPOSIT: yellowish.

MICROSCOPIC CHARACTERS: spores 8–10 × 6.5–8.0 µm, broadly ellipsoid to ellipsoid, ornamented with isolated warts and ridges that form a partial reticulum, prominences up to 1 µm high, hyaline, amyloid; cap cuticle an ixolattice to an ixocutis

OCCURRENCE: scattered or in groups on the ground in mixed woods and pastures, July–October; northern Great Lakes to New England and adjacent Canada.

EDIBILITY: unknown.

COMMENTS: *Lactarius trivialis* differs in the color of its cap, especially when young. *Lactarius pallidus* W. Saunders and W. G. Smith (edibility unknown), a European species, lacks the acrid taste and staining reactions. *Lactarius midlandensis,* described from Michigan, is similar but has coarsely reticulated spores, and the taste of its latex is only slightly acrid.

Lactarius agglutinatus Burlingham

Illus. p. 55

Mem. Torrey Bot. Club 14 (1908), 42
Lactaria agglutinata Burlingham

CAP: 2⅜–4" (6–10 cm) wide, convex, becoming broadly depressed and funnel-shaped; margin inrolled and scurfy when young, becoming uplifted with age; surface slimy when fresh, becoming dry, faintly zoned when young, becoming azonate with age, somewhat appressed-tomentose and papillate-rugulose, more or less scaly when dry, cinnamon buff or ochraceous buff, darker when young.

GILLS: subdecurrent, narrow, close, sometimes forked near the stalk, buff to pale cream.

STALK: ¾–1½" (2–4 cm) long, ⅜–⅝" (1.0–1.5 cm) thick, nearly equal or tapered downward, glabrous, dry to slightly viscid, spongy then hollow, colored like the cap.

FLESH: thin, whitish; odor like raw pumpkin.

LATEX: white, unchanging when exposed, not staining tissues; taste acrid.

SPORE DEPOSIT: creamy white.

MICROSCOPIC CHARACTERS: spores 7.5–9.0 × 6.0–7.5 µm, broadly ellipsoid, ornamented with warts and ridges that form a partial reticulum, prominences up to 1.2 µm high, hyaline, amyloid; cap cuticle an ixocutis

OCCURRENCE: on soil in hardwoods and mixed woods; August; reported from Pink Beds, Pisgah National Forest, North Carolina, and from eastern Canada; distribution limits and frequency yet to be determined.

EDIBILITY: unknown.

COMMENTS: The original description by Burlingham, also restated in *North American Species of Lactarius* by Hesler and A. H. Smith (1979), gives the cap color as cinnamon buff or ochraceous buff and excludes any reference to orange. It is highly unlikely that Burlingham would have missed or neglected to mention the bright orange cap color shown and described in Weber and Smith's *A Field Guide to Southern Mushrooms* (1985) Based on Burlingham's description, Weber and A. H. Smith's concept of *Lactarius agglutinatus* is incorrect. The color illustration and description in *Mushrooms of Northeastern North America* (Bessette, Bessette, and Fischer 1997) was based on that of Weber and A. H. Smith and is thus also incorrect. *Lactarius lanuginosus* is similar, but it lacks the distinctive acute umbo on its cap.

Lactarius alachuanus var. **alachuanus** Murrill Illus. p. 56

Mycologia 30 (1938), 360
Lactaria alachuana Murrill

CAP: 2–3" (5.0–7.5 cm) wide, convex to nearly plane, often shallowly depressed and sometimes with a slight umbo; margin entire; surface azonate, glabrous, moist to viscid when fresh, pale pinkish cinnamon to pale yellowish cinnamon when young, becoming pinkish buff with age.

GILLS: narrowly attached to slightly decurrent, moderately broad, close, sometimes forking, pinkish buff, slowly darkening when bruised.

STALK: 1–2¾" (2.5–7.0 cm) long, ⅜–⅝" (10–16 mm) thick, nearly equal or tapered downward, often curved at the base, dry, solid, pinkish buff, with a white canescence, pinkish cinnamon when rubbed.

FLESH: moderately thick, firm, whitish; odor not distinctive or sometimes aromatic; taste slightly bitter then moderately acrid.

LATEX: white on exposure, unchanging, not staining the gills; taste slowly and moderately acrid.

SPORE DEPOSIT: white to creamy white.

MICROSCOPIC CHARACTERS: spores 7.5–9.0 × 6.0–7.5 µm, broadly ellipsoid, ornamented with warts and ridges that sometimes form a partial reticulum, prominences up to 1.5 µm high, hyaline, amyloid; cap cuticle an ixolattice.

OCCURRENCE: scattered or in groups on sandy soil and rotting wood in mixed oak and pine woods; October–February; Tennessee and North Carolina south to Alabama and Florida; infrequent to common.

EDIBILITY: unknown.

COMMENTS: Large fruitings are very common in central Florida following rainy periods. Considerable variation in cap color may be observed depending on moisture content. *Lactarius alachuanus* var. *amarissimus* (Murr.) Hesler and A. H. Smith (edibility unknown), a questionable variety that also has a pale pinkish cinnamon to pale yellowish cinnamon cap, very bitter flesh that is not acrid, and sparse watery latex that is assumed not to taste acrid, and it grows on the ground under laurel oaks in Florida.

Lactarius albolutescens Thiers Not Illustrated

Mycologia 49 (1957), 711

CAP: 1⅜–2⅜" (3.5–6.0 cm) wide, convex, becoming nearly plane and shallowly depressed; margin decurved when young, entire; surface dry, glabrous, azonate, yellowish to pale tan or pale dull pinkish, sometimes with a darker reddish disc.

GILLS: subdecurrent, narrow, close, pale grayish pink to pale lavender, not staining when bruised.

STALK: ¾–1" (1.8–2.5 cm) long, 5/16–⅜" (8–10 mm) thick, nearly equal or slightly tapered downward, dry, solid, glabrous, ochraceous buff.

FLESH: thick, pale buff, not staining on exposure; odor not distinctive; taste mild to weakly acrid.

LATEX: white on exposure, soon changing to greenish yellow; taste slowly acrid.

SPORE DEPOSIT: not obtained.

MICROSCOPIC CHARACTERS: spores 7.5–9.5 µm, ellipsoid to subglobose, ornamented with low lines and isolated warts that form a partial reticulum, prominences up to 1 µm high, hyaline, amyloid; cap cuticle an ixocutis.

OCCURRENCE: scattered or in groups in humus under mixed pines and hardwoods; December; reported from the Sam Houston National Forest, Texas; distribution limits and frequency yet to be determined.

EDIBILITY: unknown.

COMMENTS: *Lactarius controversus* is similar, but its latex does not change color shortly after exposure. *Lactarius vinaceosporus* is also similar but has yellowish gills.

Lactarius allardii Coker

Illus. p. 56

J. Elisha Mitchell Sci. Soc. 34 (1918), 12

CAP: 2⅜–6" (6.0–15.5 cm) wide, convex, becoming broadly convex with a depressed center; margin incurved and remaining so well into maturity; surface dry, somewhat velvety to nearly glabrous, azonate, whitish when very young or when covered by fallen leaves, soon pale pinkish cinnamon to pinkish buff, often with grayish red tints, then becoming pale cinnamon to orange-brown and finally dull brick red with age, typically streaked and spotted white, especially on the margin.

GILLS: attached to decurrent, close to subdistant at first, becoming nearly distant at maturity, white to ivory yellow.

STALK: ¾–2" (2–5 cm) long, ⅜–1⅛" (1–3 cm) thick, tapered downward to nearly equal, hollow, dry, glabrous, colored like the cap or paler.

FLESH: firm, compact, white, slowly staining pinkish then olivaceous when exposed; odor not distinctive or becoming pungent with age; taste acrid.

LATEX: white on exposure, slowly becoming greenish olive then brownish, staining gills dull green to olive then slowly dull brown; taste acrid.

SPORE DEPOSIT: white to creamy white.

MACROCHEMICAL TESTS: flesh rapidly staining vinaceous red with the application of $FeSO_4$.

MICROSCOPIC CHARACTERS: spores 8–11 × 5–8 µm, ellipsoid to subglobose, ornamented with warts and ridges that do not form a reticulum, prominences up to 0.2 µm high, hyaline, amyloid; cap cuticle a mass of interwoven hyphae with a few inflated cells, bearing a turf of erect fascicles of hyphoid, colorless, or ochraceous pileocystidia.

OCCURRENCE: scattered or in groups on the ground in hardwoods and mixed woods; New England south to Florida, west to Michigan and Texas; occasional.

EDIBILITY: unknown.

COMMENTS: *Lactarius similis*, reported only from Mississippi, is very similar but has a smaller, pale vinaceous cinnamon cap that often fades to pale yellow and mild-tasting latex.

Lactarius allochrous Singer

Not Illustrated

Sydowia 2 (1948), 41

CAP: 2–4½" (5.0–11.5 cm) wide, convex, becoming broadly convex to nearly plane with a depressed center or sometimes umbilicate; margin even; surface dry, azonate, subtomentose when young, becoming nearly glabrous except for minute reticulation on the disc, dull date brown to olive-brown overall or pale grayish brown on the disc.

GILLS: attached to decurrent, sometimes crossveined, moderately broad, distant, whitish to creamy white.

STALK: ¾–2" (2–5 cm) long, ½–1" (1.2–2.5 cm) thick, nearly equal or tapered downward, solid, becoming hollow with age, nearly glabrous down to a tomentose base, white overall or olive-brown to pale pinkish brown in the midportion.

FLESH: white, unchanging or staining brown when exposed; odor spermatic; taste mild.

LATEX: abundant, white on exposure, unchanging or slowly becoming brown, staining injured areas brown; taste mild.

SPORE DEPOSIT: not stated in the original description.

MACROCHEMICAL TESTS: flesh stains green or red and green mixed or grayish pink with the application of $FeSO_4$ and slowly yellow with KOH.

MICROSCOPIC CHARACTERS: spores 10–14 × 8.5–12.0 µm, ellipsoid to subglobose, ornamented with warts and ridges, prominences up to 0.8 µm high, hyaline, amyloid; cap cuticle a trichoderm.

OCCURRENCE: on the ground under hardwoods, especially oak; July–November; reported only from Florida, distribution and frequency yet to be determined.

EDIBILITY: unknown.

COMMENTS: *Lactarius hygrophoroides, Lactarius lentus,* and *Lactarius pervelutinus* are similar species but lack the date brown to olive-brown cap colors and have smaller spores.

Lactarius alnicola var. **alnicola** A. H. Smith Illus. p. 57

Brittonia 12 (1960), 319

CAP: 3⅛–8" (8–20 cm) wide, convex, becoming depressed to funnel-shaped with age; margin inrolled at first, then expanding and becoming uplifted; surface viscid to slimy, with matted fibrils beneath the gluten near the margin, azonate or somewhat zonate, yellow-ochre, paler near the margin.

GILLS: decurrent, narrow, crowded, forked near the stalk, whitish then becoming pale ochraceous buff.

STALK: 1⅛–2⅜" (3–6 cm) long, ¾–1⅛" (2–3 cm) thick, nearly equal or tapered downward, dry, solid then becoming hollow with age, hard, scrobiculate, whitish to ochraceous tan.

FLESH: thick, hard, whitish, slowly staining pale yellow; odor not distinctive; taste instantly acrid.

LATEX: scant, white on exposure, unchanging or very slowly changing to yellow, staining cut flesh yellow; taste acrid.

SPORE DEPOSIT: white to yellowish.

MICROSCOPIC CHARACTERS: spores 7.5–10.0 × 6.0–8.5 µm, ellipsoid, ornamented with warts and narrow bands that form a partial reticulum, prominences up to 1 µm high, hyaline, amyloid; cap cuticle an ixocutis.

OCCURRENCE: gregarious on the ground under alders and conifers; July–October; western United States; fairly common.

EDIBILITY: unknown.

COMMENTS: This species was originally found under alders with conifers nearby; researchers subsequently discovered that the species has a relationship with conifers, not with alders, as its name implies. *Lactarius alnicola* var. *pitkinensis* Hesler and A. H. Smith (edibility unknown), reported only from Ashcroft, Colorado, is very similar, but it has a white to cream-colored cap and white, unchanging latex. *Lactarius alnicola* var. *pungens* Hesler and A. H. Smith (edibility unknown), reported only from Michigan, is similar but has a subviscid and soon dry, dull ochraceous to ochraceous tan cap with an ochraceous tawny disc and whitish flesh with a pungent odor that is described as distinct and peculiar.

Lactarius alpinus var. **alpinus** Peck Not Illustrated

Ann. Rep. N.Y. State Mus. 27 (1875), 96–97

CAP: ⅝–1½" (1.5–4.0 cm) wide, convex, becoming broadly convex to nearly plane, slightly depressed to umbilicate, with a tiny papilla; margin inrolled at first, becoming decurved; surface dry, appressed-tomentose to finely scaly, azonate, apricot orange to tawny yellow or ochraceous to yellowish.

GILLS: attached, narrow, close, yellowish ochraceous to apricot orange.

STALK: ¾–1¼" (1.8–3.2 cm) long, ⅛–¼" (3–5 mm) thick, nearly equal, dry, solid to stuffed, pruinose, whitish with tints of orange to yellow-orange.

FLESH: thin, white; odor not distinctive; taste slowly becoming slightly acrid.

LATEX: scant, watery to milky white on exposure, unchanging; taste acrid.

SPORE DEPOSIT: white.

MACROCHEMICAL TESTS: cap or stalk flesh staining pink with the application of $FeSO_4$.

MICROSCOPIC CHARACTERS: spores 7.0–9.5 × 6–8 µm, broadly ellipsoid, ornamented with warts and ridges that form a partial to complete reticulum, prominences up to 0.5 µm high, hyaline, amyloid; cap cuticle not clearly defined, consisting of tangled hyphae often in tufts.

OCCURRENCE: solitary, scattered, or in groups on the ground under alder in alpine areas; July–September; reported from Alaska, Idaho, New York, Oregon, and Washington, fairly common.

EDIBILITY: unknown.

COMMENTS: *Lactarius alpinus* var. *mitis,* reported from the Pacific Northwest, the Great Lakes region, and northeastern North America, is similar, but it has a dark reddish brown cap that soon fades to pale vinaceous brown to light pinkish cinnamon, mild-tasting flesh and latex, paler gills, and a cap surface that may stain green with the application of $FeSO_4$.

Lactarius alpinus var. **mitis** Hesler and A. H. Smith Illus. p. 57

North American Species of Lactarius (1979), 497–499

CAP: ¾–3" (2.0–7.5 cm) wide, nearly plane with an inrolled margin, sometimes convex, occasionally papillate, becoming broadly depressed with an arched margin, sometimes becoming broadly vase-shaped with age, opaque, surface with fine cracks over the disc, becoming minutely squamulose, appearing smooth when moist, dark reddish brown, soon fading to pale vinaceous brown to light pinkish cinnamon.

GILLS: narrow, broadly adnate to short-decurrent, close, with forking, pallid to pale dull grayish vinaceous, becoming vinaceous to yellowish cinnamon with age.

STALK: 1¼–2" (3–5 cm) long, ⅜–⅝ (10–15 mm) thick at the apex, slightly enlarged downward, hollow to stuffed, fragile, unpolished to smooth, often with white mycelium at the base, colored like the gills

FLESH: thin, fragile, colored like the cap, odor not distinctive; taste mild.

LATEX: scant, white to whey-like, unchanging, taste mild.

SPORE DEPOSIT: white.

MICROSCOPIC CHARACTERS: spores 7.5–9.0 × 6.0–7.5 µm, broadly ellipsoid, with a distinct plage, ornamented with a broken to partial reticulum, numerous isolated warts, and short ridges, prominences up to 0.5 µm high, hyaline, amyloid; cap cuticle not clearly defined, consisting of tangled hyphae often in tufts.

OCCURRENCE: Scattered or in groups under alder in swampy or wet areas; late summer and fall; reported from the Pacific Northwest, the Great Lakes Region, and northeastern North America; fairly common.

EDIBILITY: unknown.

COMMENTS: *Lactarius alpinus* var. *alpinus* has a smaller apricot orange to tawny yellow or ochraceous to yellowish cap that is often slightly depressed to umbilicate and has a small papilla. Its gills are yellowish ochraceous to apricot orange.

Lactarius angustifolius Hesler and A. H. Smith Illus. p. 58

North American Species of Lactarius (1979), 190–191
Lactarius albus Thiers

CAP: 1⅜–2" (3.5–5.0 cm) wide, convex, becoming broadly convex to nearly plane with a broad depression; margin strongly incurved to inrolled at first, becoming decurved and finally plane at maturity; surface moist to dry, appearing glabrous but minutely velvety under a hand lens, azonate, white with pink, yellow, or brownish stains when dried.

GILLS: attached to subdecurrent, narrow, crowded, some forked midway or near the stalk, tan to yellowish, staining dull yellow-buff by the latex.

STALK: ¾–1½" (2–4 cm) long, ¼–½" (7–13 mm) thick, nearly equal or tapered downward, dry, stuffed, glabrous, white, staining yellow to olive-yellow when bruised.

FLESH: thick, compact, white, unchanging when cut; odor not distinctive; taste acrid.

LATEX: abundant, white on exposure, unchanging, staining the gills dull yellow-buff; taste quickly and extremely acrid.

SPORE DEPOSIT: not obtained.

MICROSCOPIC CHARACTERS: spores 5.0–7.8 × 4.5–6.5 µm, ellipsoid to subglobose, ornamented with warts and a few fine lines that sometimes form a partial reticulum, prominences up to 0.1 µm high, hyaline, amyloid; cap cuticle a trichoderm.

OCCURRENCE: gregarious to subcespitose on the ground under hardwoods; June; reported only from the Sam Houston National Forest, near Huntsville, Texas; distribution limits and frequency yet to be determined.

EDIBILITY: unknown.

COMMENTS: The white cap and stalk, pronounced staining of the gills to dull yellow-buff, small spores, and presence of a trichoderm are this species' distinctive features.

Lactarius arcuatus Murrill Not Illustrated

Mycologia 33 (1941), 440
Lactaria arcuata Murrill

CAP: 2⅜" (6 cm) wide, convex to depressed; margin distinctly inrolled and cottony when young; surface slightly viscid when moist, glabrous, azonate, white.

GILLS: attached or slightly decurrent, narrow, close, strongly arched, sometimes forked, white.

STALK: 1" (2.5 cm) long, ⅝" (1.5 cm) thick, nearly equal, dry, white, not staining when bruised.

FLESH: white, unchanging when exposed; odor not distinctive; taste bitter.

LATEX: white on exposure, unchanging; taste moderately acrid at once, eventually bitter.

SPORE DEPOSIT: white.

MICROSCOPIC CHARACTERS: spores 5.5–7.0 × 4.5–6.0 µm, subglobose to broadly ellipsoid, ornamented with a partial to complete reticulum and lacking isolated warts, prominences up to 0.2 µm high, hyaline, amyloid; cap cuticle an ixocutis.

OCCURRENCE: solitary on soil under laurel oak; June; reported only from Gainesville, Florida; distribution limits and frequency yet to be determined.

EDIBILITY: unknown.

COMMENTS: *Lactarius parvulus* is similar but has a white zonate cap with a pale reddish cinnamon tint and mild-tasting flesh. Also compare with *Lactarius deceptivus,* which has a much larger cap with white strongly acrid flesh and much larger spores.

Lactarius areolatus Hesler and A. H. Smith Illus. p. 58

North American Species of Lactarius (1979), 515–516

CAP: ¾–2¾" (2–7 cm) wide, convex, becoming nearly plane with a depressed center, sometimes with a low umbo; margin decurved; surface dry or moist, glabrous, becoming rimulose-areolate at maturity, pecan brown to dark vinaceous red when young, becoming paler pecan brown to orangish brown or pale vinaceous red with age, typically retaining the darker color over the central area.

GILLS: decurrent, narrow to moderately broad, close, yellowish when young, soon becoming spotted vinaceous and finally dark vinaceous to vinaceous brown overall.

STALK: ¾–3⅛" (2–8 cm) long, ⅛–⅝" (3–15 mm) thick, nearly equal overall, dry, becoming hollow with age, glabrous, colored like the cap or paler, often whitish toward the base.

FLESH: thin, brittle, colored like the cap or paler; odor fragrant, often sweet; taste mild or in rare instances faintly acrid or disagreeable.

LATEX: white to whey-like or watery on exposure, unchanging, not staining tissues; taste mild.

MICROSCOPIC CHARACTERS: spores 6.5–9.0 × 6–7 µm, subglobose to broadly ellipsoid, ornamented with warts and short bands that do not form a reticulum, prominences up to 1 µm high, hyaline, amyloid; cap cuticle a layer of versiform, inflated hyphal cells that form mounds.

OCCURRENCE: cespitose to scattered on the ground under oak; July–September; reported from Michigan, Mississippi, New York, and Ohio; distribution limits and frequency yet to be determined.

EDIBILITY: unknown.

COMMENTS: *Lactarius rimosellus* is very similar, but it has spores with isolated warts that are occasionally connected by fine lines or ridges, and it grows in conifer woods. Also compare with *Lactarius sublacustris.*

Lactarius argillaceifolius var. **argillaceifolius** Hesler and A. H. Smith Illus. p. 59

North American Species of Lactarius (1979), 366–369

CAP: 1⅝–7" (4–18 cm) wide, convex, becoming broadly convex with a depressed center; margin incurved, often remaining so into maturity; surface finely pubescent when young, becoming glabrous, slimy and sticky when wet, azonate, lilac-brown when young, fading to lilac-tan or pale lilac-gray and finally to pale tan or pinkish buff at the center.

GILLS: attached to slightly decurrent, broad, close, cream-colored when young, developing pinkish tints near the margin and finally flushed dull brownish orange with age, staining buff to olive-brown to dark brown when bruised.

STALK: 2⅜–3½" (6–9 cm) long, ⅝–1⅜" (1.5–3.5 cm) thick, nearly equal or tapering downward, slimy or dry, whitish, becoming spotted and stained brownish with age, but not scrobiculate.

FLESH: firm, white to buff; odor not distinctive; taste mild or slowly becoming slightly acrid.

LATEX: creamy white on exposure, staining the gills grayish brown to dark brown or olive-brown; taste mild or slowly becoming slightly acrid.

SPORE DEPOSIT: pinkish buff.

MICROSCOPIC CHARACTERS: spores 7–11 × 7–8 µm, subglobose to elliptic, ornamented with warts and ridges that sometimes form a partial reticulum, prominences up to 1 µm high, hyaline, amyloid; cap cuticle an ixotrichoderm in young specimens, becoming an ixolattice in mature specimens.

OCCURRENCE: scattered or in groups on the ground under hardwoods, especially oak; July–October; eastern Canada south to Florida, west to Minnesota and Texas; occasional.

EDIBILITY: unknown.

COMMENTS: *Lactarius argillaceifolius* var. *dissimilis* Hesler and A. H. Smith (edibility unknown), reported from South Carolina, is nearly identical, but it has white latex that tastes bitter then acrid, and its cap cuticle is a thick ixotrichoderm that collapses to an ixolattice with numerous dextrinoid hyphal incrustations present. The Vulgar Milk Cap, *Lactarius argillaceifolius* var. *megacarpus* is also similar, but it has a larger cap, white and unchanging latex with an acrid taste, and a more reticulate pattern on the spores, and it grows on the ground under oak in California, Oregon, and Washington. Also compare with *Lactarius fumeacolor.*

Lactarius argillaceifolius var. **megacarpus** Hesler and A. H. Smith Illus. p. 60

North American Species of Lactarius (1979), 369–371

CAP: 5½–10½" (14–27 cm) wide, broadly depressed with a highly irregular undulating margin, viscid, glabrous, light buff to pale yellow at the disk, becoming drab hazel to lilac drab toward the margin, azonate, strongly incurved at the margin.

GILLS: adnate, close to subdistant, pale, becoming warm buff to pale yellow with a hazel cast, staining brownish, with many tiers of lamellulae.

STALK: 6¼–7¾" (16–20 cm) long, 1½–1¾" thick (40–50 mm) thick at the apex, slightly viscid, glabrous, white at the base, pale buff toward the apex, somewhat wrinkled, hollow to stuffed.

FLESH: up to 1⅛" (3 cm) thick, whitish to off-white; odor not distinctive; taste acrid.

LATEX: creamy white, unchanging, acrid.

SPORE DEPOSIT: pinkish buff.

MICROSCOPIC CHARACTERS: spores 7.5–10.5 × 6.5–8.0 µm, broadly ellipsoid with a distinct plage, ornamented with low fine lines and ridges with some isolated warts, sometimes forming a partial reticulum, prominences 0.3–0.5 µm high, hyaline, amyloid; cap cuticle a thick ixocutis of narrow hyphae.

OCCURRENCE: on ground under oaks; in Oregon and California; October–January; occasional.

EDIBILITY: unknown.

COMMENTS: This species is similar to *Lactarius argillaceifolius* var. *argillaceifolius,* but it has a larger cap, white and unchanging latex with an acrid taste, and a more reticulate pattern on the spores. Also compare with *Lactarius fumeacolor.*

Lactarius aroostookensis Hesler and A. H. Smith Not Illustrated

North American Species of Lactarius (1979), 231–232

CAP: 1¾–3" (4.5–7.5 cm) wide, broadly convex to nearly plane, depressed over the disc; margin incurved to decurved; cap surface viscid, glabrous except for a narrow canescent band along the margin, with several obscure concentric zones, orange.

GILLS: attached, narrow, close, forked, creamy to dingy ochraceous, staining grayish blue when bruised.

STALK: 1¾–2½" (4.5–6.5 cm) long, ⅜–¾" (1–2 cm) thick, nearly equal down to a narrowed base, viscid when wet, hollow, glabrous, white to dingy white, staining blue when cut.

FLESH: thin, tough, white, staining blue; odor not distinctive; taste acrid.

LATEX: white on exposure, unchanging, staining tissues grayish blue; taste acrid.

SPORE DEPOSIT: ochraceous.

MICROSCOPIC CHARACTERS: spores 8–11 × 7.5–9.0 µm, broadly ellipsoid, ornamented with granules and ridges that form a small to widely meshed partial reticulum, prominences up to 0.8 µm high, hyaline, amyloid; cap cuticle a thick ixocutis.

OCCURRENCE: solitary under hardwoods; August; reported only from Aroostook County, Maine; distribution limits and frequency yet to be determined.

EDIBILITY: unknown.

COMMENTS: *Lactarius aspideoides* is similar, but it has a pale yellow slimy-viscid cap and stalk, flesh that tastes bitterish at first then slowly becomes slightly acrid, and gills that stain lilac when bruised.

Lactarius aspideoides Burlingham Illus. p. 60, 61

Bull. Torrey Bot. Club 34 (1907), 87
Bright Yellow Milk Cap

CAP: 1⅛–3⅛" (3–8 cm) wide, convex with a depressed disc, becoming funnel-shaped; margin incurved to decurved and glabrous; surface slimy-viscid, glabrous, azonate, light yellow.

GILLS: subdecurrent, narrow, crowded, sometimes forked near the stalk, pale yellow, staining lilac where injured.

STALK: 1⅛–2⅜" (3–6 cm) long, ⅜–⅝" (1.0–1.5 cm) thick, nearly equal, slimy-viscid, stuffed to hollow, glabrous, pale yellow.

FLESH: thin, brittle, pale yellow, staining lilac on exposure; odor not distinctive; taste bitter then slowly becoming slightly acrid.

LATEX: white on exposure, unchanging, staining gills lilac; taste bitter then slowly becoming slightly acrid.

SPORE DEPOSIT: pale yellow.

MACROCHEMICAL TESTS: latex and gills staining purple-red with the application of $FeSO_4$; cap surface and flesh negative with the application of KOH or $FeSO_4$.

MICROSCOPIC CHARACTERS: spores 7–9 × 6.5–8.0 µm, broadly ellipsoid, ornamented with warts and branching ridges that sometimes form a partial reticulum, prominences up to 1.5 µm high, hyaline, amyloid; cap cuticle an ixolattice of narrow hyphae.

OCCURRENCE: scattered or in groups on the ground under conifers and hardwoods; July–October; northeastern and central United States into Canada, also reported from the Pacific Northwest; occasional to fairly common.

EDIBILITY: unknown.

COMMENTS: *Lactarius aspideus* (Fries) Fries (edibility unknown)—a European species that has been reported from North Carolina, Michigan, Colorado, and Washington—is very similar, but it has a straw yellow to pale cream cap, a somewhat greasy stalk, and flesh that tastes mild then bitter. *Lactarius aroostookensis* is also similar, but it has an orange zonate cap, acrid-tasting flesh, and gills that stain grayish blue, not lilac. *Lactarius pseudoaspideus* has flesh that tastes distinctly acrid and gills that stain violaceous to brownish lilac.

Lactarius atrobadius Hesler and A. H. Smith Illus. p. 61

North American Species of Lactarius (1979), 450–451

CAP: 1⅛–2" (3–5 cm) wide, convex to broadly convex, depressed over the disc; margin decurved; surface slimy-viscid when wet, glabrous, becoming somewhat shiny and dry, azonate, reddish brown to orange-brown.

GILLS: subdecurrent, narrow, close, becoming subdistant, light pinkish cinnamon to orangey cinnamon, bruising dark red-brown when cut.

STALK: 1⅛–2⅜" (3–6 cm) long, ¼–½" (6–12 mm) thick, nearly equal or slightly tapered downward near the base, slimy-viscid when wet, soon dry, hollow, glabrous, colored like the cap when young, soon becoming paler.

FLESH: very thin, dingy vinaceous, unchanging when cut; odor not distinctive; taste mild.

LATEX: white on exposure, unchanging, staining gills dark red-brown; taste mild.

SPORE DEPOSIT: whitish to creamy.

MACROCHEMICAL TESTS: stalk negative with the application of $FeSO_4$.

MICROSCOPIC CHARACTERS: spores 7–9 × 6–7 µm, ellipsoid to broadly ellipsoid, ornamented with warts and ridges that form a partial reticulum, prominences up to 0.5 µm high, hyaline, amyloid; cap cuticle a modified ixotrichoderm.

OCCURRENCE: scattered or in groups on the ground under conifers, especially spruce; August–December; reported from California, Oregon, and Colorado; distribution limits and frequency yet to be determined.

EDIBILITY: unknown.

COMMENTS: *Lactarius hepaticus*, which occurs in eastern North America west to the Rocky Mountain states, is similar, but it has a moist to dry cap, flesh that slowly tastes acrid, and gills that do not stain brown. *Lactarius rufus* var. *rufus* is also similar, but it has a reddish brown cap, acrid-tasting flesh, and its gills do not stain brown.

Lactarius atro-olivaceus Hesler and A. H. Smith Not Illustrated

North American Species of Lactarius (1979), 125–126

CAP: 2¾" (7 cm) wide, broadly convex with a depressed center; margin crenate and finely wrinkled; surface dry, velvety, dark olive-buff, disc with buffy brown tints.

GILLS: subdecurrent, distant, not forked, white, staining brownish lavender when bruised.

STALK: 2¾" (7 cm) long, ⅝" (1.6 cm) thick, dry, spongy to hollow, velvety, dark olive-buff.

FLESH: white; odor slightly aromatic; taste mild.

LATEX: white on exposure, slowly changing to brownish lavender as it dries, staining tissues brownish lavender; taste mild.

SPORE DEPOSIT: white.

MICROSCOPIC CHARACTERS: spores 7–9 × 6.0–7.5 µm, broadly ellipsoid to subglobose, ornamented with isolated warts and wide ridges that form a partial to complete reticulum, prominences up to 0.5 µm high, hyaline, amyloid; cap cuticle a zone of inflated cells, with a dry turf of short subcylindric to slightly tapered pileocystidia.

OCCURRENCE: solitary on the ground in mixed woods; August; reported only from Cades Cove, Tennessee; distribution limits and frequency yet to be determined.

EDIBILITY: unknown.

COMMENTS: The dark olive-buff and velvety cap, white spore deposit, slightly aromatic odor, and white, mild-tasting latex that changes to brownish lavender are this species' distinctive features. *Lactarius lignyotus* var. *lignyotus* is similar, but it has a bright ochre spore deposit and larger, more globose spores.

Lactarius atroviridis Peck Illus. p. 61

Ann. Rep. N.Y. State Mus. 42 (1889), 23
Lactarius sordidus var. *hirsutus* Peck

CAP: 2⅜–5⅝" (6–15 cm) wide; broadly convex, becoming plane with a depressed center; margin incurved when young, remaining so into maturity; surface dry, scurfy to minutely scaly, pitted, various shades of green ranging from olive to dark grayish green, usually zoned with dark green spots arranged concentrically.

GILLS: attached to slightly decurrent, close, cream to pinkish white, occasionally forked near the stalk, staining greenish gray to brownish; edges typically olive-brown to greenish.

STALK: ¾–3⅛" (2–8 cm) long, ⅜–1⅛" (1–3 cm) thick, nearly equal, hollow, dry, colored and streaked like the cap, scrobiculate.

FLESH: whitish to pinkish brown, not staining; odor not distinctive; taste acrid.

LATEX: white on exposure, very slowly turning greenish, staining gills dark grayish green to greenish brown; taste acrid.

SPORE DEPOSIT: cream to buff.

MICROSCOPIC CHARACTERS: spores 7–10 × 6–9 µm, subglobose to elliptic, ornamented with warts and ridges that form a partial reticulum, prominences up to 0.5 µm high, hyaline, amyloid; cap cuticle composed of thin-walled, somewhat appressed hyphae often arranged in fascicles.

OCCURRENCE: solitary to scattered on the ground under conifers or hardwoods; July–November; eastern Canada south to Florida, west to Michigan and Texas, also reported from California; occasional.

EDIBILITY: unknown.

COMMENTS: *Lactarius olivaceoumbrinus*—reported from California, Idaho, Oregon, and Washington—is very similar but has larger spores. *Lactarius turpis* (Weinmann) (edibility unknown) is also similar, but it has an olive-brown or darker brown cap, sometimes with a dull honey yellow margin, and it lacks the dark green coloration.

Lactarius ausablensis Hesler and A. H. Smith Not Illustrated

North American Species of Lactarius (1979), 311–312

CAP: 2¾–3½" (7–9 cm) wide, convex, becoming broadly funnel-shaped at maturity; surface slimy-viscid, glabrous, zonate; zones watery orange with pale ochraceous zones between, becoming azonate with a pale dull ochraceous orange disc and a pale yellow-orange margin when older.

GILLS: decurrent, narrow, close, dull orange-buff, slowly staining dingy ochraceous when bruised.

Lactarius caeruleitinctus Murrill Illus. p. 62

J. Elisha Mitchell Sci. Soc. 55 (1939), 368
Lactaria caeruleitincta Murrill

CAP: 3½" (9 cm) wide, deeply funnel-shaped; margin even; surface dry, glabrous, azonate, white to whitish.

GILLS: narrowly attached, narrow, close, with multiple forks below the middle, white, staining pale brownish where bruised.

STALK: 1½" (4 cm) long, ⅝" (1.7 cm) thick, tapered slightly downward, finely pubescent to nearly glabrous, milk white tinged pale blue and becoming more intensely blue after picking.

FLESH: soft, white, watery; odor nauseating while drying; taste slowly and distinctly acrid.

LATEX: copious, whitish on exposure, unchanging, staining tissues pale brownish.

SPORE DEPOSIT: not stated in the original description.

MICROSCOPIC CHARACTERS: spores 9.0–10.5 × 6.0–7.5 µm, broadly ellipsoid, ornamented with low warts and ridges and with fine lines that form an obscure to partial reticulum, prominences up to 0.5 µm high, hyaline, amyloid; cap cuticle an indefinite zone of somewhat radial to interwoven appressed hyphae often in fascicles.

OCCURRENCE: solitary on soil in mixed woods; November; reported only from Newman's Lake, Florida; distribution limits and frequency yet to be established.

EDIBILITY: unknown.

COMMENTS: *Lactarius deceptivus* is similar but has a distinct cottony inrolled margin and lacks the pale blue stains on its stalk. Also compare with *Lactarius arcuatus* and *Lactarius parvulus.*

Lactarius caespitosus Hesler and A. H. Smith Illus. p. 63

North American Species of Lactarius (1979), 349–351

CAP: 1¾–6" (4.5–15.5 cm) wide, convex to broadly convex, disc shallowly depressed; margin inrolled at first, becoming decurved, glabrous; surface viscid, glabrous, azonate, gray to olive-brown.

GILLS: attached to subdecurrent, narrow to broad, close, whitish to pinkish buff, slowly staining dingy brown when bruised.

STALK: 1⅛–2¾" (3–7 cm) long, ⅜–1⅛" (1–3 cm) thick, nearly equal or tapered downward, subviscid to viscid, glabrous, hollow, whitish to pale brown or pale brownish gray.

FLESH: thick, brittle, white, changing to yellow after several hours; odor not distinctive; taste slowly acrid.

LATEX: scant, white on exposure, unchanging, slowly staining flesh yellowish and gills dingy brown; taste slowly becoming strongly acrid.

SPORE DEPOSIT: pale buff.

MICROSCOPIC CHARACTERS: spores 9–12 × 7–9 µm, broadly ellipsoid, ornamented with ridges that form a partial reticulum, prominences up to 0.5 µm high, hyaline, amyloid; cap cuticle an ixotrichoderm with a layer of compact hyphae below it.

OCCURRENCE: cespitose, scattered, or gregarious on the ground under conifers; July–October; western North America; common.

EDIBILITY: unknown.

COMMENTS: *Lactarius kauffmanii* var. *kauffmanii* is similar but has smaller spores with more distinct, higher ornamentation.

Lactarius californiensis Hesler and A. H. Smith Not Illustrated

North American Species of Lactarius (1979), 331–333

CAP: 1¾–4¾" (4.5–12.0 cm) wide, broadly convex to nearly plane, shallowly depressed over the disc; margin incurved to decurved, glabrous; surface viscid, glabrous, azonate, brownish orange to orange-gray or yellow-brown, with a grayish red disc.

GILLS: attached to subdecurrent, broad, close to subdistant, thick, forked near the stalk, white to pale yellow or pale orange, slowly bruising lilac to violet where injured.

STALK: 1½–3⅛" (4–8 cm) long, ½–¾" (1.2–2.0 cm) thick, nearly equal to slightly enlarged at the base, moist or dry, solid, glabrous, not scrobiculate, pale pinkish buff to pale ivory, sometimes staining brownish orange when bruised.

FLESH: thick, firm, white to pale yellow, staining lilac to violet when cut; odor not distinctive; taste slowly acrid.

LATEX: copious, white to whey-like on exposure, unchanging, staining tissues lilac to violet; taste slowly becoming strongly acrid.

SPORE DEPOSIT: pale yellow.

MACROCHEMICAL TESTS: cap surface staining yellow with the application of KOH.

MICROSCOPIC CHARACTERS: spores 7–9 × 6.0–7.5 µm, ellipsoid, ornamented with isolated warts and fine lines that form a partial reticulum, prominences up to 0.5 µm high, hyaline, amyloid; cap cuticle a thick ixocutis expanding into an ixolattice.

OCCURRENCE: scattered to gregarious on the ground in mixed woods; November; California and Oregon; uncommon.

EDIBILITY: unknown.

COMMENTS: *Lactarius pallescens* var. *pallescens* is nearly identical macroscopically, but it has a viscid stalk and larger spores, and its cap cuticle is an ixotrichoderm. *Lactarius uvidus* var. *montanus* is very similar, but its cap surface stains green with the application of KOH, and it has larger spores. *Lactarius cascadensis* is similar, but it has cinnamon buff to cinnamon gills and mild-tasting flesh.

Lactarius camphoratus (Fries) Fries Illus. p. 63

Epicr. Syst. Mycol. (1838), 346

Aromatic Milky, Spicy Milk Cap

CAP: ⅝–2" (1.5–5.0 cm) wide, broadly conic to broadly convex and depressed, with or without a small, pointed umbo; margin incurved at first, becoming decurved and arched, glabrous; surface moist to dry, glabrous, dark red-brown fading to pale vinaceous pink with age.

GILLS: attached to slightly decurrent, narrow, close to crowded, pale pinkish cinnamon to dull vinaceous red, not bruising or staining from the latex.

STALK: ⅝–2⅜" (1.5–6.0 cm) long, ⅛–⅝" (3–15 mm) thick, nearly equal or enlarged at the apex or base, moist or dry, fragile, becoming hollow with age, base with stiff hairs, colored like the cap but paler near the apex.

FLESH: brittle, thin, pale vinaceous pink; odor fragrant, like maple sugar or burnt sugar; taste disagreeable to bitter, but not acrid.

LATEX: milk white on exposure, soon becoming whey-like, unchanging and not staining tissues; taste disagreeable to bitter, but not acrid.

SPORE DEPOSIT: white to yellowish.

MICROSCOPIC CHARACTERS: spores 7.0–8.5 × 6.0–7.5 µm, globose to broadly ellipsoid, ornamented with isolated spines and ridges that do not form a reticulum, prominences up to 1 µm high, hyaline, amyloid; cap cuticle a zone of inflated cells.

OCCURRENCE: scattered or in groups on the ground in conifer or mixed woods, often with hemlock or pine; August–October; northeastern United States and Canada, west to Michigan, south to North Carolina, also reported from western Canada; common.

EDIBILITY: unknown.

COMMENTS: The odor of this species intensifies when the specimens are dried. *Lactarius rubidus,* reported from the Pacific Coast, has a similar odor, but its gills are light yellow, and its spores are reticulate. *Lactarius rufulus* grows on the ground under oak in California and lacks the fragrant odor and small, pointed umbo.

Lactarius carbonicola A. H. Smith Illus. p. 64

Brittonia 12 (1960), 342

CAP: ⅜–1½" (1–4 cm) wide, nearly plane with a depressed center and a small central papilla; margin distinctly arched to spreading, often crenate-plicate; surface moist, subhygrophanous, azonate or with broad obscure zones while cap color fading, glabrous, uneven, brick red when young, slowly fading to a dull brownish orange and finally a dull pale pink.

GILLS: decurrent, moderately broad, close when young, becoming subdistant at maturity, pale yellowish at first, soon pinkish buff and finally becoming dull cinnamon with age, staining dingy vinaceous brown when young.

STALK: ¾–1½" (2–4 cm) long, ⅛–¼" (3–5 mm) thick, fragile, nearly equal, moist or dry, becoming hollow with age, colored like the cap, with vinaceous hairs at the base.

FLESH: vinaceous buff, staining dingy vinaceous brown; odor not distinctive; taste very slowly becoming faintly acrid.

LATEX: scant, milk white on exposure, becoming somewhat watery, staining tissues dingy vinaceous brown, drying yellowish on the gills of young specimens; taste very slowly becoming faintly acrid.

SPORE DEPOSIT: white to yellowish.

MACROCHEMICAL TESTS: cap surface staining pale olive with the application of KOH.

MICROSCOPIC CHARACTERS: spores 6.0–8.5 × 5.0–6.5 µm, broadly ellipsoid to subglobose, ornamented with coarse, crooked bands and branches as well as with isolated warts or ridges that do not form a reticulum, prominences up to 1 µm high, hyaline, amyloid; cap cuticle a thick layer of irregularly shaped cells, broadly inflated hyphal cells, narrow lactifers, and upright to decumbent hyphae.

OCCURRENCE: gregarious to subcespitose on the ground, often on dried-up woodland pools, August–October; eastern Canada south to Vermont, west to Michigan and Idaho; occasional.

EDIBILITY: unknown.

COMMENTS: *Lactarius thejogalus* is very similar, but its cap margin is not arched or crenate-plicate; its stalk has a conspicuous white strigose base; it has slightly larger spores; and it lacks the subcespitose habit.

Lactarius carminascens Hesler and A. H. Smith Not Illustrated

North American Species of Lactarius (1979), 334

CAP: 1⅛–1¾" (3.0–4.5 cm) wide, broadly convex, becoming nearly plane; margin incurved, becoming decurved and finally upturned; surface viscid, glabrous, azonate, dull brownish gray.

GILLS: attached to subdecurrent, narrow, close, not forked, whitish, becoming pale pinkish, staining pinkish when bruised.

STALK: 1⅛–2" (3–5 cm) long, 3⁄16–5⁄16" (4–7 mm) thick, nearly equal or slightly tapered downward, dry, glabrous, stuffed, colored like the cap but paler.

FLESH: whitish; odor not distinctive; taste acrid.

LATEX: watery to whey-like on exposure, unchanging, staining the gills pinkish; taste bitter then acrid.

SPORE DEPOSIT: yellowish buff.

MICROSCOPIC CHARACTERS: spores 7.5–10.5 × 6.0–7.5 µm, ellipsoid, ornamented with large warts and ridges that form a partial reticulum, prominences up to 1 µm high, hyaline, amyloid; cap cuticle a poorly delimited ixocutis tending toward an ixolattice.

OCCURRENCE: on the ground in mixed woods; August; reported only from Cades Cove, Tennessee; distribution and frequency limits yet to be determined.

EDIBILITY: unknown.

COMMENTS: A dull brownish gray and viscid cap, watery to whey-like latex that stains tissues pinkish, and a yellowish buff spore deposit are this species' distinctive characters.

Lactarius carolinensis Hesler — Not Illustrated

Brittonia 12 (1960), 331

CAP: 1½–5⅛" (4–13 cm) wide, convex, becoming nearly plane with a depressed center; margin incurved at first, becoming decurved and remaining so well into maturity; surface slimy to viscid, glabrous, distinctly zonate, tan with dull yellowish brown zones.

GILLS: attached, narrow, close to crowded, sometimes forked, whitish at first, becoming pale pinkish buff at maturity, staining yellow.

STALK: ⅝–1⅛" (1.5–3.0 cm) long, ⅜–¾" (1–2 cm) thick, nearly equal, viscid when fresh, becoming hollow with age, whitish, staining yellow, scrobiculate.

FLESH: thick, white; odor faintly alkaline; taste acrid.

LATEX: white on exposure, unchanging or slowly turning yellow, staining the gills and stalk yellow; taste acrid.

SPORE DEPOSIT: white.

MICROSCOPIC CHARACTERS: spores 7–9 × 6.0–7.5 µm, ellipsoid to subglobose, ornamented with warts, bands, and branches that form a partial reticulum, prominences up to 0.8 µm high, hyaline, amyloid; cap cuticle an ixocutis.

OCCURRENCE: on soil or grass in lawns or in woods under oak or mixed woods; July–September; reported from Georgia, North Carolina, Tennessee, and Virginia; occasional.

EDIBILITY: unknown.

COMMENTS: *Lactarius maculatipes* is similar but has a whitish to cream-colored cap and white flesh that lacks an alkaline odor. *Lactarius dunfordii* is similar, but it has a pale yellow cap, white latex that does not stain the gills or flesh, and white flesh that lacks an alkaline odor; it lacks spots on the stalk; and it grows on the ground under pine.

Lactarius cascadensis Hesler and A. H. Smith — Not Illustrated

North American Species of Lactarius (1979), 336–337

CAP: 4–7" (10–18 cm) wide, broadly convex, becoming shallowly funnel-shaped; margin inrolled at first and covered with dense, downy hairs; surface slightly viscid when wet, soon dry, azonate to subzonate or rarely distinctly zonate, pale grayish lilac with darker violaceous brown spots or zones, with lilac tints fading to pinkish gray or pinkish buff with age.

GILLS: attached to subdecurrent, broad, close, cinnamon buff to nearly cinnamon, staining dull purple when bruised.

STALK: 1½–2⅜" (4–6 cm) long, ⅜–1" (1.0–2.5 cm) thick, nearly equal or tapered downward, dry, solid then becoming hollow, glabrous, cinnamon buff with a lilac tinge at the apex.

FLESH: white to lilac-tinted near the cuticle, changing to pale tan with age; odor slightly disagreeable; taste mild.

LATEX: scant, whey-like on exposure, unchanging, staining tissues dull purple; taste mild.

SPORE DEPOSIT: yellowish.

MICROSCOPIC CHARACTERS: spores 8.0–10.5 × 6.5–8.0 µm, broadly ellipsoid, ornamented with isolated warts and short ridges that form a partial reticulum, prominences up to 0.8 µm high, hyaline, amyloid; cap cuticle an ixocutis.

OCCURRENCE: scattered or in groups on the ground under alder in a swampy area or in mixed woods; September–October; Idaho, Oregon, Washington, and western Canada; occasional.

EDIBILITY: unknown.

COMMENTS: *Lactarius californiensis* is similar but has pale yellow to pale orange gills, and its flesh tastes strongly acrid.

Lactarius chelidonium var. **chelidonioides** Hesler and A. H. Smith Illus. p. 64, 65

North American Species of Lactarius (1979), 84–85
Lactarius chelidonioides A. H. Smith

CAP: 1¼–3⅛" (3–8 cm) wide, broadly convex to nearly plane with a depressed disc, becoming shallowly funnel-shaped, viscid then dry, glabrous, often slightly zonate, dingy azure blue with dingy orange-brown areas or zones, the blue gradually fading and becoming muddy orange-brown to dull reddish brown, staining green or olive in older specimens, often with water spots.

GILLS: decurrent, narrow, crowded, dingy yellow to yellow-brown or olive-buff, staining green when bruised.

STALK: 1¼–2¼" (3–6 cm) long, ⅜–1" (1.0–2.5 cm) thick, nearly equal to enlarged downward, dry, becoming hollow with age, glabrous, colored like the cap but paler.

FLESH: azure blue toward the top, paler to yellowish toward the gills; odor like the Yellow Morel, *Morchella esculenta;* taste slowly becoming slightly acrid.

LATEX: scant, dingy yellow to yellow-brown on exposure, unchanging, staining gills green.

SPORE DEPOSIT: pale buff.

MICROSCOPIC CHARACTERS: spores 7–9 × 5.0–6.5 µm, ellipsoid, ornamented with isolated warts and a few heavy bands that form a partial reticulum, prominences up to 1.0 µm high, hyaline, amyloid; cap cuticle an ixocutis.

OCCURRENCE: solitary, scattered, or in groups on the ground in conifer woods, especially under pine; August–October; northeastern North America; infrequent.

EDIBILITY: unknown.

COMMENTS: *Lactarius chelidonium* var. *chelidonium* is very similar, but it has brighter yellow latex that turns dingy brownish yellow to dingy yellowish brown and mild-tasting flesh that lacks the odor of the Yellow Morel, *Morchella esculenta.*

Lactarius chelidonium var. **chelidonium** Peck Illus. p. 65

Ann. Rep. N.Y. State Mus. 24 (1872), 74
Celandine Lactarius

CAP: 2–3" (5–8 cm) wide, convex, becoming broadly convex to nearly plane, disc depressed, slightly viscid, glabrous, grayish green to grayish yellow or yellow-brown, with bluish green tints when older, sometimes with a few narrow zones on the margin.

GILLS: attached to slightly decurrent, narrow, close, forked and wavy near the stalk, grayish yellow.

STALK: 1–1½" (2.5–4.0 cm) long, ¼–¾" (7–20 mm) thick, nearly equal, dry, glabrous, becoming hollow with age, colored like the cap.

FLESH: yellow at first, becoming blue overall, staining green where bruised; taste mild.

LATEX: scant, yellow on exposure, changing to dingy brownish yellow to dingy yellowish brown, staining gills green; taste mild.

SPORE DEPOSIT: yellowish.

MICROSCOPIC CHARACTERS: spores 8–10 × 6–7 µm, ellipsoid, ornamented with warts and ridges that form a partial reticulum, prominences up to 0.5 µm high, hyaline, amyloid; cap cuticle an ixocutis.

OCCURRENCE: on sandy soil under pines; July–September; eastern North America.

EDIBILITY: edible.

COMMENTS: *Lactarius chelidonium* var. *chelidonioides*, reported from northeastern North America, is similar, but its flesh slowly becomes slightly acrid, is azure blue in the upper half of the cap and paler to dingy yellowish near the gills, and has the same odor as the Yellow Morel, *Morchella esculenta,* and its latex is scant dingy yellow to yellow-brown.

Lactarius chrysorrheus Fries Illus. p. 65, 66

Epicr. Syst. Mycol. (1838), 342
Lactarius brevis Peck
Gold Drop Milk Cap

CAP: 1⅛–3½" (3–9 cm) wide, convex then soon slightly depressed over the disc, becoming broadly funnel-shaped with age; margin incurved at first, becoming decurved; surface moist to lubricous or subviscid, soon dry and whitish canescent, glabrous, azonate or with watery spots more or less arranged in zones, subhygrophanous, whitish to pale yellowish cinnamon with darker spots when young, fading to nearly whitish overall when older.

GILLS: attached to short-decurrent, narrow, close, sometimes forked near the stalk, whitish to pale orange-buff or slightly darker, not discoloring or spotting vinaceous or brown.

STALK: 1⅛–3⅛" (3–8 cm) long, ⅜–¾" (1–2 cm) thick, nearly equal, moist or dry, glabrous, becoming hollow with age, whitish, sometimes flushed orange-buff when older, at times somewhat strigose at the base.

FLESH: thin, whitish, soon yellow when cut; odor not distinctive; taste distinctly acrid (slowly at times).

LATEX: copious, white on exposure, quickly changing to yellow, not staining tissues; taste acrid (slowly at times).

SPORE DEPOSIT: pale yellow.

MICROSCOPIC CHARACTERS: spores 6–9 × 5.5–6.5 µm, broadly ellipsoid, ornamented with warts and ridges that sometimes form a partial reticulum, prominences up to 0.5 µm high, hyaline, amyloid; cap cuticle a thin ixocutis.

OCCURRENCE: solitary, scattered, or in groups on the ground among hardwoods and mixed woods, especially oak; July–October; widely distributed in North America; fairly common.

EDIBILITY: unknown.

COMMENTS: *Lactarius vinaceorufescens* is similar, but it has a darker cap and stalk; it grows on the ground under pine; and its gills stain vinaceous to brown. *Lactarius moschatus* is also similar, but it has watery to watery white latex that does not change color and white to whitish flesh that tastes musky.

Lactarius cinereus var. **cinereus** Peck Illus. p. 66

Ann. Rep. N.Y. State Mus. 24 (1872), 73

CAP: 1–2¾" (2.5–7.0 cm) wide, convex, becoming nearly plane with a depressed center and typically umbilicate with age; margin incurved when young; surface viscid, glabrous, pale gray, sometimes darker gray on the disc, azonate or rarely faintly zoned.

GILLS: decurrent, close, white, not staining when bruised.

STALK: 1½–3" (4.0–7.5 cm) long, ⅛–⅜" (3–10 mm) thick, nearly equal or slightly enlarged downward, dry, becoming hollow with age, colored like the cap.

FLESH: white on exposure, unchanging; odor not distinctive; taste acrid.

LATEX: white on exposure, unchanging, not staining tissues; taste acrid.

SPORE DEPOSIT: white.

MICROSCOPIC CHARACTERS: spores 6.5–9.0 × 5.0–6.5 µm, ellipsoid to broadly ellipsoid, ornamented with warts and ridges that occasionally form a partial reticulum, prominences up to 0.8 µm, hyaline, amyloid; cap cuticle an ixolattice.

OCCURRENCE: solitary, scattered, or in groups on the ground usually under hardwoods, especially beech; July–October; eastern Canada south to West Virginia; distribution limits and frequency yet to be determined.

EDIBILITY: unknown.

COMMENTS: *Lactarius cinereus* var. *fagetorum* is similar, but it has an olive-gray to olive-buff cap when young that becomes olive-buff with a lilac tinge at maturity, white flesh and latex that taste mild at first then become slightly to distinctly acrid, a pinkish buff to pale pinkish gray stalk, and a pale yellow spore deposit, and it grows on the ground in hardwoods and mixed woods, usually with beech, from eastern Canada west to Michigan and south to Texas.

Lactarius cinereus var. **fagetorum** Hesler and A. H. Smith Illus. p. 67

North American Species of Lactarius (1979), 396–398

CAP: 1–2⅜" (3–6 cm) wide, plane with an incurved margin, becoming shallowly funnel-shaped, viscid to dry and shiny, gray to olivaceous gray to olive-buff with lilac tinges, azonate or rarely faintly zoned.

GILLS: decurrent, crowded, narrow, white to cream-colored, spotting brownish with age.

STALK: 1½–2¾" (4–7 cm) long, ⅜–⅝" (8–15 mm) thick, slightly viscid and shiny then dry, hollow, colored like the cap.

FLESH: white; odor slight; taste mild then becoming slightly acrid in young specimens.

LATEX: milk-like, unchanging, not staining tissues; taste peppery to very acrid.

SPORE DEPOSIT: pale yellow.

MICROSCOPIC CHARACTERS: spores 6.0–7.5 × 5–6 µm, ellipsoid, ornamented with warts and ridges that occasionally form a partial reticulum, prominences from 0.2 to 0.7 µm high, hyaline, amyloid; cap cuticle an ixotrichoderm.

OCCURRENCE: scattered to gregarious on the ground associated with beech; late summer and fall; Great Lakes region, eastward, and south to Texas; occasional.

EDIBILITY: unknown.

COMMENTS: *Lactarius cinereus* var. *cinereus* is similar, but it has a white spore deposit, and its cap lacks the olive-gray to olive-buff with lilac-tinged coloration at maturity.

Lactarius circellatus var. **borealis** Hesler and A. H. Smith Illus. p. 67

North American Species of Lactarius (1979), 378–379

CAP: 1½–6" (4–15 cm) wide, convex to nearly plane with a depressed disc, becoming broadly funnel-shaped at maturity; margin inrolled at first, becoming decurved; surface subviscid then dry, glabrous, zonate or azonate, lilac-gray to lavender-gray.

GILLS: attached to subdecurrent, narrow, close, forked near the stalk, pale pinkish buff to pinkish ochraceous, with faint lilac tints, not staining when bruised.

STALK: 1¼–3" (3–8 cm) long, ⅜–1½" (1–4 cm) thick, nearly equal to tapered downward, somewhat viscid when young, soon dry, hollow, glabrous, pale lilac-gray.

FLESH: thick, pale grayish near the cuticle, whitish elsewhere, not staining when cut; odor not distinctive; taste acrid to bitter or strongly acrid.

LATEX: copious, white to cream on exposure, unchanging, not staining tissues; taste acrid.

SPORE DEPOSIT: dull white to cream.

MICROSCOPIC CHARACTERS: spores 7–9 × 5.0–6.5 µm, broadly ellipsoid, ornamented with isolated warts and long and short bands that form a zebroid appearance, prominences up to 0.5 µm high, hyaline, amyloid; cap cuticle a thick ixocutis.

OCCURRENCE: gregarious to scattered on the ground under conifers; August–September; Pacific Northwest north to Alaska, also reported from Idaho, eastern Canada, and Tennessee; distribution limits and frequency yet to be determined.

EDIBILITY: unknown.

COMMENTS: *Lactarius circellatus* var. *circellatus* Fries is a European species that has not yet been reported from North America. *Lactarius pyrogalus,* a similar species that occurs in eastern North America, has subdistant to distant gills and a more zonate cap.

Lactarius cocoseolens Methven Not Illustrated

Mycologia 77 (1985), 472

CAP: 1⅛–2⅜" (3–6 cm) wide, convex to nearly plane, becoming shallowly depressed over the disc; margin incurved to decurved, glabrous, striate; surface viscid, glabrous, azonate, grayish orange to brownish orange.

GILLS: attached to subdecurrent, narrow to somewhat broad, subdistant, not forked, orange-white, not staining when cut.

STALK: ⅝–1⅛" (1.5–3.0 cm) long, 3⁄16–⅜" (5–10 mm) thick, nearly equal or tapered slightly toward the base, moist, hollow, glabrous, streaked, grayish orange, to brownish orange, not scrobiculate.

FLESH: thin, white, unchanging or slowly staining yellow when cut; odor like coconut when specimen dried; taste mild.

LATEX: copious, white to whey-like on exposure, unchanging; taste mild.

SPORE DEPOSIT: white to pale cream.

MICROSCOPIC CHARACTERS: spores 6.5–8.0 × 5.5–6.5 µm, broadly ellipsoid to ellipsoid, ornamented with a partial to complete reticulum, prominences up to 0.6 µm high, hyaline, amyloid; cap cuticle an ixotrichoderm over a layer of interwoven hyphae with scattered inflated cells.

OCCURRENCE: scattered to gregarious on the ground in coastal mixed conifer and hardwood forests; September–December; California; uncommon.

EDIBILITY: unknown.

COMMENTS: The azonate, viscid, grayish orange to brownish orange cap, mild-tasting flesh that has the odor of coconut when dried, and white, unchanging latex are this species' distinctive features. Both *Lactarius glyciosmus* and *Lactarius hibbardae* var. *hibbardae* have the odor of coconut, but their flesh tastes acrid.

Lactarius cognoscibilis Beardslee and Burlingham — Not Illustrated

Mycologia 32 (1940), 577
Lactaria cognoscibilis Beardslee and Burlingham

CAP: 1⅜–3⅜" (3.5–8.5 cm) wide, broadly convex, becoming nearly plane and sometimes slightly depressed with age, occasionally with a small sharp umbo; margin arched, becoming upturned with age; surface slightly viscid when wet, becoming dry, cinnamon brown zoned with darker tones, white-pruinose at first, dull, fading and becoming azonate.

GILLS: attached to slightly decurrent, narrow, close, sometimes forked near the stalk, intervenose next to the cap, pale pinkish.

STALK: 1⅛–1⅜" (3.0–3.5 cm) long, ¼–½" (7–12 mm) thick, nearly equal down to an abruptly narrowed base, dry, solid, colored like the cap but paler.

FLESH: dark pinkish cinnamon; odor not distinctive; taste acrid.

LATEX: abundant, white on exposure, unchanging, not staining tissues; taste bitter then slowly acrid, more quickly acrid in young specimens.

SPORE DEPOSIT: pale pinkish buff.

MICROSCOPIC CHARACTERS: spores 7.5–10.0 × 6–8 µm, ellipsoid, ornamented with warts and ridges that form a partial reticulum, prominences up to 1 µm high, hyaline, amyloid; cap cuticle a poorly defined ixolattice.

OCCURRENCE: in sandy humus under sweet gum; December; reported only from the Black Hammock, Oviedo, Florida; distribution limits and frequency yet to be determined.

EDIBILITY: unknown.

COMMENTS: *Lactarius mutabilis* is very similar but has mild-tasting latex. *Lactarius frustratus* is also very similar, but it has white latex that soon changes to yellow and a stalk that stains dark vinaceous brown from the base upward, and it is reported only from Michigan.

Lactarius coleopteris Coker — Not Illustrated

J. Elisha Mitchell Sci. Soc. 34 (1918), 24

CAP: up to 5½" (14 cm) wide, convex, with a depressed center at maturity; margin rounded, irregular; surface glutinous to viscid, minutely appressed-fibrillose to nearly glabrous, azonate except for a few faint zones near the margin, dark reddish orange.

GILLS: attached to slightly decurrent, narrow, moderately crowded, sometimes forked near the stalk, whitish at first, becoming creamy buff at maturity, staining dull reddish brown when bruised.

STALK: 1⅛–1½" (3–4 cm) long, ¾–1⅛" (2–3 cm) thick, tapered downward, becoming hollow with age, glabrous, whitish to straw-colored with buffy red streaks or spots, typically pinkish white at the extreme apex.

FLESH: thick, firm, brittle, white, slowly staining ochraceous to dull green when cut or bruised; odor strongly pungent, like some beetles, especially when crushed; taste not stated in the original description.

LATEX: sparse, white on exposure, unchanging; acrid.

SPORE DEPOSIT: buff-yellow.

MICROSCOPIC CHARACTERS: spores 6–8 × 5–6 µm, subglobose to ellipsoid or subovoid, ornamented with a partial to nearly complete reticulum, prominences up to 0.4 µm high, hyaline, amyloid; cap cuticle an ixotrichoderm.

OCCURRENCE: on soil in mixed woods; September; collected in North Carolina; distribution limits and frequency yet to be determined.

EDIBILITY: unknown.

COMMENTS: The dark reddish orange cap, reddish brown staining of the gills, and strong pungent odor are this species' distinctive features. Similar species include *Lactarius hysginus* var. *hysginus* and *Lactarius bryophilus.*

Lactarius colorascens Peck Illus. p. 68

Bull. N.Y. State Mus. 94 (1905), 33

CAP: 1–2" (2–5 cm) wide, convex, becoming nearly plane with a depressed center; margin incurved at first, becoming decurved, sometimes becoming wavy and finely striate with age; surface moist, glabrous, whitish or pallid when young, becoming brownish orange then brownish red when older.

GILLS: attached to slightly decurrent, narrow, close, whitish at first, becoming yellowish with age, not staining vinaceous or brown.

STALK: 1–1⅜" (2.5–3.5 cm) long, ⅛–¼" (3–5 mm) thick, nearly equal, dry, solid, whitish when young, becoming brownish red to dull brown when older.

FLESH: thin, whitish; odor not distinctive; taste bitter to faintly acrid.

LATEX: white on exposure, soon changing to sulfur yellow; taste bitter to faintly acrid.

SPORE DEPOSIT: whitish.

MICROSCOPIC CHARACTERS: spores 6.0–7.5 × 5–6 µm, broadly ellipsoid, ornamented with warts and ridges that form a partial reticulum, prominences up to 0.5 µm high, hyaline, amyloid; cap cuticle a poorly delimited cutis of loosely arranged hyphae, 3–5 µm wide.

OCCURRENCE: scattered or in groups on the ground or among sphagnum mosses in mixed woods, August–October; widely distributed in eastern North America; occasional.

EDIBILITY: unknown.

COMMENTS: *Lactarius vinaceorufescens* is very similar, but it has a pinkish cinnamon cap that is not whitish when young, gills that become spotted vinaceous to brown, acrid latex, and slightly larger spores.

Lactarius controversus (Fries) Fries Illus. p. 68

Epicr. Syst. Mycol. (1838), 335
Willow Milky

CAP: 1⅝–8" (4–20 cm) wide, convex, becoming depressed to funnel-shaped; margin inrolled at first, with tiny matted fibers; surface viscid at first but soon dry, covered with tiny matted fibrils, white to whitish, sometimes with stains varying in color from pinkish to lavender to brownish, usually with indistinct, narrow, darker zones near the margin.

GILLS: attached to subdecurrent, narrow, close to crowded, with some forking near the stalk, pale pink to pale vinaceous brown.

STALK: 1–3⅛" (2.5–8.0 cm) long, ⅝–2" (1.5–5.0 cm) thick, nearly equal or tapered toward base, tacky but soon dry, stuffed then hollow, white, sometimes spotted.

FLESH: firm, white; odor not distinctive; taste slowly but strongly acrid.

LATEX: white on exposure, unchanging, not staining tissues; taste slowly acrid.

SPORE DEPOSIT: cream to pale pinkish cinnamon.

MICROSCOPIC CHARACTERS: spores 6.0–7.5 × 4.5–5.0 µm, ellipsoid, ornamented with warts and ridges that form a partial reticulum, prominences up to 0.5 µm high, hyaline, amyloid; cap cuticle an ixocutis.

OCCURRENCE: on the ground under willow or poplar; July–October; widely distributed across the northern United States and Canada, also reported from Alaska, Colorado, and New Mexico; fairly common.

EDIBILITY: unknown.

COMMENTS: The pinkish gill, whitish cap with variable staining, small spores, and association with willow and poplar are this species' distinctive features. *Lactarius albolutescens* is similar, but its latex changes to greenish yellow.

Lactarius cordovaensis Hesler and A. H. Smith — Not Illustrated

North American Species of Lactarius (1979), 330–331

CAP: 2⅛–4¾" (5.5–12.0 cm) wide, convex, becoming broadly convex and shallowly depressed; margin inrolled at first, becoming decurved; surface subviscid to waxy, pruinose then glabrous, zonate toward the margin, medium lilac-brown on buttons, becoming paler and ochraceous-tinged over the disc at maturity.

GILLS: attached to subdecurrent, narrow, close to crowded, frequently forked, orange-tan when young, becoming paler, stained lavender by the latex.

STALK: 1½–3⅛" (4–8 cm) long, ⅝–1" (1.5–2.5 cm) thick, nearly equal or subclavate, dry, hollow, unpolished, sometimes obscurely pruinose, subscrobiculate, pale ochre, staining faintly lilac where bruised.

FLESH: pale ochraceous to dull yellow-brown, staining lilac when cut; odor resinous to fragrant; taste resinous, not acrid.

LATEX: viscous, white on exposure, unchanging, staining tissues lilac; taste mild.

SPORE DEPOSIT: not stated in the original description.

MICROSCOPIC CHARACTERS: spores 7.5–9.0 × 6.5–7.5 µm, broadly ellipsoid to subglobose, ornamented with isolated warts and short ridges that do not form a reticulum, prominences up to 0.5 µm high, hyaline, amyloid; cap cuticle a tangled ixocutis.

OCCURRENCE: scattered to gregarious on the ground in open grassy-mossy areas under conifers; September; Alaska; distribution limits and frequency yet to be determined.

EDIBILITY: unknown.

COMMENTS: The medium lilac-brown cap and orange-tan gills that become paler at maturity, mild-tasting flesh, and white latex that stains tissues lilac are this species' distinctive features.

Lactarius corrugis Peck Illus. p. 69

Ann. Rep. N.Y. State Mus. 32 (1880), 31
Lactarius volemus var. *subrugosus* Peck
Corrugated-cap Milky

CAP: 1½–7⅞" (4–20 cm) wide; convex, becoming broadly convex to nearly plane with a depressed center when older; surface velvety, dry, azonate, distinctly wrinkled to finely corrugated, reddish brown to vinaceous brown, paler and sometimes orange-brown on the margin, often with a whitish bloom, especially when young.

GILLS: attached, close, occasionally forked, pale cinnamon to pale golden brown, staining darker brown when bruised.

STALK: 2–4⅜" (5–11 cm) long, ⅝–1⅛" (1.5–3.0 cm) thick, equal, solid, dry, velvety, pale grayish cinnamon to pale pinkish cinnamon, sometimes with a whitish bloom.

FLESH: whitish, staining brown; odor slightly to strongly fishy in mature mushrooms, often not distinctive in young specimens; taste mild.

LATEX: copious, white on exposure, unchanging, staining gills and flesh tawny brown; taste mild.

SPORE DEPOSIT: white.

MICROSCOPIC CHARACTERS: spores 9–12 × 8.5–12.0 µm, subglobose, ornamented with warts and ridges that form a partial reticulum, prominences up to 0.8 µm high, hyaline, amyloid; cap cuticle a zone of compact cells that bear a turf of pileocystidia.

OCCURRENCE: solitary to scattered on the ground in hardwoods and mixed woods, usually with oak present; July–November; widely distributed in eastern North America; fairly common.

EDIBILITY: edible.

COMMENTS: *Lactarius volemus* var. *volemus* is similar but has a less-wrinkled, dark orange-brown to cinnamon brown cap that is paler orange-brown toward the margin and somewhat smaller spores.

Lactarius croceus Burlingham Illus. p. 69, 70

Mem. Torrey Bot. Club 14 (1908), 37
Lactaria crocea Burlingham

CAP: 2–4" (5–10 cm) wide, convex, becoming broadly convex to nearly plane with a depressed center when older; margin incurved and downy when young; surface glabrous, slimy when wet, shiny when dry, bright orange to saffron yellow initially, fading to paler yellow-orange or yellowish tan with age, azonate or sometimes distinctly zoned with darker orange bands.

GILLS: attached to slightly decurrent, broad, close to subdistant, creamy buff to pale yellow-tan, staining sulfur yellow where cut or bruised.

STALK: 1⅛–2⅜" (3–6 cm) long, ⅜–¾" (1–2 cm) thick, nearly equal, stuffed becoming hollow, glabrous, at times velvety at the base, colored like the cap or paler, sometimes spotted brownish.

FLESH: thick, whitish, staining sulfur yellow before the latex changes color; odor not distinctive; taste bitter to acrid.

LATEX: white on exposure, soon changing to sulfur yellow, staining gills and flesh sulfur yellow; taste bitter to acrid.

SPORE DEPOSIT: yellowish.

MICROSCOPIC CHARACTERS: spores 7.5–10.0 × 5.5–7.5 µm, elliptic, ornamented with warts and ridges that form a partial reticulum, prominences up to 0.6 µm high, hyaline, weakly amyloid; cap cuticle an ixocutis.

OCCURRENCE: solitary or scattered on the ground under hardwoods, especially oak; July–November; eastern Canada south to Georgia, west to Texas; occasional.

EDIBILITY: unknown.

COMMENTS: The orange cap and white latex that changes to sulfur yellow are this species' distinctive features. Compare with *Lactarius ausablensis*, which has a cap with watery orange zones and ochraceous zones in between them and white latex that does not change to sulfur yellow, and which grows on the ground under conifers in Michigan.

Lactarius deceptivus Peck Illus. p. 70, 71

Ann. Rep. N.Y. State Mus. 38 (1885), 125
Deceptive Milk Cap, Deceptive Milky

CAP: 3–10" (7.5–25.5 cm) wide, convex, becoming broadly funnel-shaped; margin distinctly inrolled and cottony when young; surface dry, glabrous when young, whitish, often with yellowish or brownish stains, becoming coarsely scaly and darkening to dull brownish ochre with age.

GILLS: attached, close to subdistant, white at first then cream to pale ochre.

STALK: 1½–4" (4–10 cm) long, up to 1⅛" (3 cm) thick, nearly equal or tapered downward, dry, scurfy to nearly glabrous, white, staining brown with age.

FLESH: thick, white; odor pungent or not distinctive; taste strongly acrid.

LATEX: white on exposure, unchanging, staining tissues brown; taste strongly acrid.

SPORE DEPOSIT: white to whitish.

MACROCHEMICAL TESTS: dull brownish ochre and coarse cap scales staining reddish cinnamon with the application of KOH; flesh staining reddish cinnamon with the application of $FeSO_4$ and negative with KOH.

MICROSCOPIC CHARACTERS: spores 9–13 × 7–9 µm, broadly ellipsoid, ornamented with warts and spines that do not form a reticulum, prominences up to 1.5 µm high, hyaline, amyloid; cap cuticle a layer of somewhat uplifted hyphae; stalk cuticle a layer of repent hyphae bearing thick-walled, filamentous caulocystidia and lacking a gelatinous layer.

OCCURRENCE: solitary, scattered, or in groups on the ground in conifer or hardwoods, often under oak or hemlock; June–November; widely distributed in eastern North America, also reported from western Canada; fairly common.

EDIBILITY: edible when thoroughly cooked.

COMMENTS: *Lactarius pseudodeceptivus* is very similar, but it has spore ornamentation that forms a reticulum, and its stalk cuticle is an ixocutis. *Lactarius caeruleitinctus* is similar, but it has a milk white stalk with blue tints that develops more intense blue coloration after picking, and it lacks a cottony, inrolled margin. Other similar species include *Lactarius arcuatus* and *Lactarius parvulus.*

Lactarius delicatus Burlingham Not Illustrated

Mem. Torrey Bot. Club 14 (1908), 40
Lactaria delicata Burlingham

CAP: 2⅜–4¾" (6–12 cm) wide, convex with a depressed disc, becoming funnel-shaped; margin inrolled and covered with coarse short hairs at first, becoming decurved;

surface slimy-viscid, glabrous, faintly zonate, pale orange-yellow with yellowish salmon tints over the disc.

GILLS: attached to subdecurrent, narrow, close, sometimes forked near the stalk, whitish becoming pale buff to pale orange-yellow.

STALK: ⅝–2" (1.5–5.0 cm) long, ⅝–⅞" (1.5–2.3 cm) thick, nearly equal or tapered downward, viscid, glabrous, stuffed to hollow, scrobiculate, colored like the cap.

FLESH: firm, white; odor reported as strong.

LATEX: scant, white on exposure, soon changing to sulfur yellow; taste acrid.

SPORE DEPOSIT: whitish with a yellowish salmon tint.

MICROSCOPIC CHARACTERS: spores 7.0–9.5 × 6–7 µm, broadly ellipsoid, ornamented with isolated warts and ridges that form a partial reticulum, prominences up to 0.5 µm high, hyaline, amyloid; cap cuticle a thick ixocutis.

OCCURRENCE: on the ground in deciduous woods; July–August; North Carolina and Tennessee; distribution limits and frequency yet to be determined.

EDIBILITY: unknown.

COMMENTS: *Lactarius pseudodelicatus* is very similar, but it has a creamy white spore deposit, white latex that is unchanging, and flesh with a distinct odor of lemon extract or disinfectant and a slightly acrid to acrid taste. A similar species, *Lactarius alnicola* var. *pungens* Hesler and A. H. Smith (edibility unknown), is also similar, but it has a subviscid to dry, dull ochraceous to ochraceous tan cap with an ochraceous tawny disc and white unchanging latex.

Lactarius deliciosus var. **deliciosus** (Fries) S. F. Gray Illus. p. 71

Nat. Arr. Brit. Pls. 1 (1821), 624
Delicious Milk Cap, Orange-latex Milky

CAP: 1½–4¾" (4–12 cm) wide, convex to nearly plane or uplifted, usually with a shallowly depressed disc; margin incurved at first then becoming decurved and remaining so well into maturity; surface viscid when fresh, glabrous, obscurely zonate or spotted, grayish orange to brownish orange, staining dull green.

GILLS: attached to subdecurrent, narrow, close, sometimes forked near the stalk, light orange, staining dull green to grayish green when injured.

STALK: 1⅛–2⅜" (3–6 cm) long, ⅜–¾" (2–3 cm) thick, nearly equal, dry, glabrous, light orange, staining dull green, scrobiculation present or absent.

FLESH: moderately thick, light orange, not staining; odor not distinctive; taste mild.

LATEX: orange on exposure, unchanging, not staining tissues; taste mild.

SPORE DEPOSIT: pale yellow.

MICROSCOPIC CHARACTERS: 7–9 × 5.5–6.5 µm, ellipsoid, ornamented with warts and ridges that form a partial reticulum, prominences up to 0.5 µm high, hyaline, amyloid; macrocystidia absent; cap cuticle an ixocutis.

OCCURRENCE: scattered or gregarious in duff in coastal or montane conifer-hardwood forests; August–March; reported from California and western Canada; distribution limits and frequency yet to be determined.

EDIBILITY: edible.

COMMENTS: *Lactarius deliciosus* var. *olivaceosordidus*—reported from the Pacific Northwest, California, and New York—has an obscurely zonate or spotted cap that is grayish green over an orange, golden yellow, or brownish yellow ground color, mild-tasting pale orange flesh that does not stain on exposure, light orange gills that stain dark green when bruised, scant orange latex on exposure that does not change, and aciculate to filamentous macrocystidia with a subapical constriction, and it grows on the ground under Sitka spruce. *Lactarius deliciosus* var. *areolatus* A. H. Smith (edibility unknown)—reported from Alaska, California, Colorado, Idaho, New Mexico, and Wyoming—has a brownish orange to grayish orange or orange cap that stains grayish green to dull green, scant orange latex on exposure that is unchanging and slowly stains the flesh and gills reddish brown, and no macrocystidia, and it grows on the ground under conifers. *Lactarius salmonicolor* typically lacks green stains and grows on the ground under fir or among sphagnum mosses in bogs or wet woodlands.

Lactarius deliciosus var. **olivaceosordidus** Hesler and A. H. Smith Illus. p. 72

North American Species of Lactarius (1979), 95–97

CAP: 1½–3⅛" (4–8 cm) wide, convex to nearly plane with an incurved margin, becoming depressed at the disk then funnel-shaped at maturity, somewhat viscid then becoming dry, obscurely zonate, dark grayish green with yellowish undertones when young, becoming carrot orange with olive-green tones; margin smooth and faintly translucent-striate.

GILLS: decurrent, narrow, close, carrot orange then dingy yellow.

STALK: 1¼–2¾" (3–7 cm) long, ⅛–½" (3–12 mm) thick, enlarging downward, dry, dull reddish orange with green overtones.

FLESH: thin, yellowish in the middle, orange near the gills, and olive near the cuticle; odor not distinctive; taste mild and slowly becoming slightly acrid.

LATEX: scant, muddy carrot color, unchanging; taste mild.

SPORE DEPOSIT: pale buff.

MICROSCOPIC CHARACTERS: spores 8.5–10.5 × 6.5–8.0 µm, subglobose to broadly ellipsoid, ornamented with heavy bands and crests forming a partial reticulum, prominences up to 0.5 µm high, hyaline, amyloid; cap cuticle an ixocutis expanding to an ixolattice.

EDIBILITY: edible.

OCCURRENCE: scattered or gregarious on duff associated with Sitka spruce; reported from the Pacific Northwest, California, and New York; distribution limits and frequency yet to be determined.

COMMENTS: The green stains and dark gray-green caps of young specimens are this species' distinguishing features. Compare with *Lactarius deterrimus.*

Lactarius depressus Hesler and A. H. Smith Not Illustrated

North American Species of Lactarius (1979), 343–345

CAP: 1½–3½" (4–9 cm) wide, nearly plane with a depressed disc; margin incurved at first, expanding with age, weakly pruinose when young but soon glabrous; surface slimy-viscid, glabrous, azonate, pale vinaceous to pale vinaceous brown in young stages, gradually becoming flushed cinnamon and finally more or less yellow-brown over the disc or with yellow-brown to ochraceous spots.

GILLS: attached, broad, close, whitish to pale pinkish cinnamon, bruising darker where injured.

STALK: 2⅜–4" (6–10 cm) long, ⅝–1" (1.5–2.5 cm) thick, nearly equal or enlarged downward, viscid, soon dry and shiny, firm, hollow, scrobiculate, pale lilac-gray, becoming flushed cinnamon or darker.

FLESH: thick, firm, whitish or tinged lilac-gray; odor not distinctive; taste burning acrid.

LATEX: white to cream on exposure, unchanging; taste burning acrid.

SPORE DEPOSIT: pale yellow.

MACROCHEMICAL TESTS: flesh slowly staining olivaceous with the application of $FeSO_4$ and negative with KOH; cap surface slowly staining yellow with the application of KOH.

MICROSCOPIC CHARACTERS: spores 6.0–7.5 × 5.5-6.5 µm, broadly ellipsoid to subglobose, ornamented with isolated warts and ridges that form a partial reticulum, prominences up to 0.5 µm high, hyaline, amyloid; cap cuticle an ixotrichoderm becoming a well-developed ixolattice.

OCCURRENCE: scattered to gregarious at the edge of swamps under aspen, pine, birch, and shrubs; August–October; Michigan and Wisconsin; uncommon.

EDIBILITY: unknown.

COMMENTS: Because of the cap color, this species may be confused with *Lactarius affinis* var. *affinis*, but it has larger spores.

Lactarius desjardinii Methven — Not Illustrated

Official publication pending

CAP: 2–2¾" (5–7 cm) wide, nearly plane to uplifted with a depressed disc; margin incurved to decurved, glabrous, scalloped; surface subviscid to viscid, glabrous, azonate, light orange to grayish orange.

GILLS: attached to subdecurrent, narrowly broad, forked near the stalk, pale orange, not staining when bruised.

STALK: 1–1½" (2.5–4.0 cm) long, ⅜–⅝" (1.0–1.5 cm) thick, nearly equal or tapered downward, moist or dry, stuffed or hollow, glabrous, not scrobiculate, pale orange, with a white tomentum at the base.

FLESH: thick, white, unchanging; odor not distinctive; taste slightly acrid.

LATEX: white on exposure, unchanging, not staining tissues; taste acrid.

SPORE DEPOSIT: white to pale yellow.

MICROSCOPIC CHARACTERS: spores 5.5–6.5 × 5.5–6.5 µm, globose to subglobose, ornamented with a partial to complete reticulum, prominences up to 0.5 µm high, hyaline, amyloid; cap cuticle a thick ixocutis.

OCCURRENCE: scattered to gregarious on the ground in coastal mixed conifer and hardwood forests; October–December; California, uncommon.

EDIBILITY: unknown.

COMMENTS: *Lactarius subflammeus* is similar, but it has a brownish red to reddish brown cap, a brownish orange to light brown stalk, white latex that tastes slightly acrid, and larger ellipsoid spores. *Lactarius luculentus* var. *laetus* is also similar, but it has a brownish orange to light brown or reddish brown disc with an orange margin, a light orange to grayish orange stalk, mild-tasting latex, and larger spores.

Lactarius deterrimus Gröger — Illus. p. 72

Westfäl. Pilzbriefe. 7 (1968), 10

Lactarius deliciosus var. *piceus* Smotlacha

CAP: 1⅛–4¾" (3–12 cm) wide; convex, becoming broadly convex to nearly plane when older, with a depressed center, often broadly funnel-shaped; margin incurved at first, becoming decurved well into maturity; surface glabrous, obscurely zonate or azonate, sometimes spotted, light orange with a grayish orange disc, fading with age to pale whitish orange at the center, typically developing green spots.

GILLS: attached to slightly decurrent, moderately broad, subdistant, not forked, light orange, slowly staining reddish brown then dull green.

STALK: ¾–2" (2–5 cm) long, ¼–⅝" (6–16 mm) thick, equal or tapered toward the base, dry, glabrous, stuffed, becoming hollow with age, light orange, slowly staining green to grayish green where bruised, typically not scrobiculate.

FLESH: whitish to pale yellowish orange, slowly staining grayish red to reddish brown on exposure; odor not distinctive; taste mild.

LATEX: orange on exposure, unchanging, slowly staining cut surfaces grayish red to reddish brown; taste mild.

SPORE DEPOSIT: pale yellow.

MICROSCOPIC CHARACTERS: spores 8.0–11.5 × 6.5–9.0 µm, broadly ellipsoid to ellipsoid, ornamented with warts and ridges that form a partial reticulum, prominences up to 0.5 µm high, hyaline, amyloid; macrocystidia present on the gill faces, filamentous to fusoid, in dense clusters; cap cuticle an ixocutis.

OCCURRENCE: solitary, scattered, or in groups on the ground under conifers, especially spruce; July–October; widely distributed in North America; fairly common.

EDIBILITY: edible.

COMMENTS: *Lactarius deliciosus* var. *areolatus* A. H. Smith (edibility unknown) is very similar but lacks macrocystidia. *Lactarius deliciosus* var. *deliciosus* is similar, but it has orange latex that does not stain tissues, and it lacks macrocystidia. *Lactarius salmonicolor* typically lacks green stains and grows on the ground under fir.

Lactarius dispersus Hesler and A. H. Smith Illus. p. 73

North American Species of Lactarius (1979), 225–226

CAP: 1½–4" (4–10 cm) wide, convex with a depressed disc, expanding and becoming broadly funnel-shaped; margin edge bearded at first; surface subviscid, with a thin layer of inconspicuous fibrils, conspicuously zonate, zones pale dingy tan and pale buff, the darker zones becoming darker brown with age or when dry.

GILLS: decurrent, moderately broad, close to subdistant, dull white to pinkish buff, bruising dingy lilac then dull brown.

STALK: 1½–2⅜" (4–6 cm) long, ⅜–⅝" (1.0–1.7 cm) thick, nearly equal, dry, solid or hollow, unpolished, scrobiculate, dingy yellow-orange to pale dingy tan, or buff.

FLESH: pale white to buff, staining lilac from the latex; odor not distinctive; taste mild or bitterish.

LATEX: dingy white on exposure, unchanging, staining tissues dull lilac; taste not determined.

SPORE DEPOSIT: yellowish.

MICROSCOPIC CHARACTERS: spores 7.5–10.0 × 6.0–7.5 µm, broadly ellipsoid; ornamented with small warts and unconnected ridges that do not form a reticulum, prominences up to 1.5 µm high, hyaline, amyloid; cap cuticle a fibrillose ixocutis.

OCCURRENCE: solitary or scattered on the ground in mixed oak and pine woods; August–October; West Virginia and North Carolina; distribution limits and frequency yet to be determined.

EDIBILITY: unknown.

COMMENTS: *Lactarius speciosus* is very similar, but it has a white spore deposit and larger, more reticulate spores.

Lactarius dunfordii Hesler and A. H. Smith Not Illustrated

North American Species of Lactarius (1979), 263–264

CAP: 2⅜–4¾" (6–12 cm) wide, broadly convex, becoming nearly plane with a depressed center; margin incurved at first, becoming expanded and uplifted; surface glabrous, viscid, zonate, pale yellow, often with watery spots.

GILLS: attached to subdecurrent, medium broad, close, sometimes forked at the base, pale cream color, not staining when bruised.

STALK: 1⅛–2" (3–5 cm) long, ⅝–1" (1.4–2.5 cm) thick, nearly equal, white, not spotted.

FLESH: firm, white, not staining when exposed; odor not distinctive; taste acrid.

LATEX: white on exposure, unchanging, not staining tissues; taste acrid.

SPORE DEPOSIT: pale yellow.

MICROSCOPIC CHARACTERS: spores 7–9 × 6.0–7.5 µm, subglobose to broadly ellipsoid, ornamented with isolated warts and ridges that do not form a reticulum, prominences up to 1.5 µm high, hyaline, amyloid; cap cuticle an ixocutis.

OCCURRENCE: in groups on lawns under pine; October; reported from the residence of Dean Dunford, Knoxville, Tennessee; distribution and frequency limits yet to be established.

EDIBILITY: unknown.

COMMENTS: *Lactarius maculatipes* is very similar, but it has white latex that stains gills and flesh yellowish and a scrobiculate stalk, and it grows on the ground under oak. *Lactarius carolinensis* is similar but has a tan cap with darker yellowish brown zones, white flesh with a faintly alkaline odor, and a white spore deposit.

Lactarius duplicatus A. H. Smith Illus. p. 73

Brittonia 12 (1960), 329

CAP: ⅝–2⅛" (1.5–5.5 cm) wide, convex to nearly plane, disc shallowly depressed, with or without a slight umbo; margin inrolled, glabrous, becoming finely wrinkled with age; surface viscid, glabrous, azonate, bright orange or coppery orange to orangey cinnamon, becoming duller with age.

GILLS: attached to decurrent, narrow, close, sometimes forked, pinkish cinnamon to orange-pink, staining yellow from the latex.

STALK: 1⅛–2" (3–5 cm) long, 3⁄16–5⁄16" (5–8 mm) thick, nearly equal or enlarged downward, dry, fragile, pruinose to unpolished, colored like the cap or paler; base with whitish mycelial hairs.

FLESH: thin, brittle, pale white to buff; odor not distinctive; taste bitterish then acrid.

LATEX: white to whey-like on exposure, slowly changing to bright yellow; taste bitterish then acrid.

SPORE DEPOSIT: white.

MACROCHEMICAL TESTS: flesh staining vivid orange with the application of KOH and negative for $FeSO_4$.

MICROSCOPIC CHARACTERS: spores 7.5–10.0 × 6.0–7.5 µm, broadly ellipsoid to ellipsoid, ornamented with isolated warts and ridges that form a partial reticulum, prominences up to 0.7 µm high, hyaline, amyloid; cap cuticle an ixotrichoderm.

OCCURRENCE: scattered on the ground in mixed woods or among sphagnum mosses; August–October; Alaska, Ontario, and Nova Scotia; occasional.

EDIBILITY: unknown.

COMMENTS: *Lactarius substriatus*—reported from California, Oregon, and Washington—is very similar, but it has a translucent-striate margin when moist, darker cap colors especially when young, and a cream-colored spore deposit. *Lactarius minusculus,* reported only from New England, is also very similar, but it is a much smaller species with white, unchanging latex.

Lactarius eburneus Thiers Illus. p. 73

Mycologia 49 (1957), 715

CAP: 1¾–2½" (4.5–6.5 cm) wide, nearly plane, disc shallowly depressed, becoming shallowly funnel-shaped; margin incurved, becoming decurved to plane; surface dry, with minute hairs that can be seen with a hand lens, azonate, dull yellow-buff to cinnamon buff.

GILLS: attached to subdecurrent, moderately broad, close to subdistant, rarely forked, light buff, staining ochraceous salmon to light ochraceous buff, light buff when bruised.

STALK: 1⅛–1¾" (3.0–4.5 cm) long, ⁵⁄₁₆–⅝" (8–15 mm) thick, nearly equal, dry, stuffed, white, staining ochraceous tawny to ochraceous brown.

FLESH: thick, white, unchanging when cut; odor not distinctive; taste mild.

LATEX: scant, white on exposure, unchanging, staining the gills reddish and the stalk brown; taste mild.

SPORE DEPOSIT: not obtained.

MICROSCOPIC CHARACTERS: spores 6.5–7.5 µm, globose to subglobose; ornamented with a few heavy bands that sometimes form a partial reticulum, prominences up to 2.3 µm high, hyaline, amyloid; cap cuticle a single layer of small, variously shaped hyphal cells.

OCCURRENCE: scattered on the ground under hardwoods; June–September; North Carolina and Texas; distribution limits and frequency yet to be determined.

EDIBILITY: unknown.

COMMENTS: *Lactarius fumosus* var. *fumosus* is similar, but it has a pinkish buff spore deposit, mild-tasting white flesh that slowly becomes faintly acrid and slowly stains reddish salmon when cut, and spores with a partial to nearly complete reticulum.

Lactarius echinatus Thiers Not Illustrated

Mycologia 49 (1957), 716

CAP: 1⅜–3" (3.5–7.5 cm) wide, obtusely convex, becoming nearly plane, disc shallowly depressed; margin inrolled to incurved, becoming decurved to plane; surface dry, subtomentose to pruinose, azonate, ivory yellow when young, sometimes becoming pale olive-gray.

GILLS: attached, narrow, close to subdistant, forked near the stalk, yellowish to pale tan, bruising dark brown to cinnamon.

STALK: ¾–1" (2.0–2.5 cm) long, ½–⅝" (1.4–1.7 cm) thick, nearly equal or tapered downward, dry, stuffed, unpolished to pruinose, white or colored like the cap.

FLESH: thick, compact, white, changing to brownish lavender when cut; odor not distinctive; taste acrid.

LATEX: copious, white on exposure, sometimes slowly changing to brownish lavender; taste acrid and disagreeable.

SPORE DEPOSIT: not obtained.

MICROSCOPIC CHARACTERS: spores 6.5–8.0 × 5–6 µm, ellipsoid; ornamented with small warts and very thin lines that do not form a reticulum, prominences up to 0.4 µm high, hyaline, amyloid; cap cuticle a zone of inflated compressed cells with a turf of subcylindric to clavate pileocystidia.

OCCURRENCE: scattered on soil under hardwoods in a mixed pine-hardwood forest; June; Sam Houston National Forest, Texas; distribution limits and frequency yet to be determined.

EDIBILITY: unknown.

COMMENTS: The dry, tomentose, ivory yellow cap; the white flesh that changes to brownish lavender when cut; and the acrid-tasting latex are this species' distinctive features.

Lactarius fallax var. **concolor** A. H. Smith and Hesler Illus. p. 74

Brittonia 14 (1962), 406
Lactarius lignyotus var. *americanus* A. H. Smith and Hesler
Brittonia 14 (1962), 395

CAP: 1–3⅛" (2.5–8.0 cm) wide, convex with a small conic umbo when young, becoming broadly convex with or without the umbo; surface dry, glabrous, velvety to rugose under a hand lens, dark brown to blackish brown; margin inrolled, becoming wavy, somewhat ribbed.

GILLS: short-decurrent, close to crowded, multiple forks near the stalk, whitish at first, yellowing with age, edges colored like the cap.

STALK: 1⅛–1½" (3–4 cm) long, ¼–⅜" (6–10 mm) thick, equal or narrowing to the base, solid, velvety, colored like the cap but paler at the base.

FLESH: somewhat thick, firm, brittle, white, staining pale vinaceous; odor not distinctive; taste mild or faintly acrid.

LATEX: copious, white, unchanging; taste mild or faintly acrid.

SPORE DEPOSIT: pale yellow.

MICROSCOPIC CHARACTERS: spores 9–12 × 8.5–11.0 µm, globose, ornamented with a partial to broken reticulum, prominences from 0.8 to 2 µm high, hyaline, amyloid; cap cuticle a modified trichoderm.

OCCURRENCE: scattered to gregarious on the ground in northern alpine areas under conifers, especially fir; August–October; Alaska south to California; fairly common.

EDIBILITY: unknown.

COMMENTS: *Lactarius fallax* var. *fallax* is nearly identical but has gill edges that are colored like the cap.

Lactarius fallax var. **fallax** A. H. Smith and Hesler Illus. p. 74

Brittonia 14 (1962), 405
Lactarius picinus var. *maritimus* A. H. Smith and Hesler

CAP: 1⅛–3½" (3–9 cm) wide, convex to nearly plane with a small umbo, expanding to plane or becoming shallowly depressed, with or without an umbo; margin even or scalloped; surface dry and velvety, finely wrinkled over the disc, azonate, dark sooty brown to blackish.

GILLS: attached to subdecurrent, narrow, crowded, not forked, white at first, becoming creamy buff with age, edges brown like the cap, slowly staining vinaceous when bruised.

STALK: 1–2⅜" (2.5–6.0 cm) long, 5⁄16–⅝" (8–15 mm) thick, nearly equal, dry, solid, unpolished or velvety, paler brown than the cap.

FLESH: thin, brittle, whitish, staining pale vinaceous; odor not distinctive; taste mild or faintly acrid.

LATEX: copious, white on exposure, unchanging, slowly staining flesh and gills vinaceous.

SPORE DEPOSIT: yellowish.

MICROSCOPIC CHARACTERS: spores 7.5–10.0 × 7.0–9.5 µm, globose, ornamented with warts and ridges that form a partial reticulum, prominences up to 2 µm high, hyaline, amyloid; cap cuticle a trichoderm.

OCCURRENCE: scattered to gregarious on the ground or on very rotten conifer logs in alpine areas under conifers; August–October; Alaska south to California; fairly common.

EDIBILITY: unknown.

COMMENTS: *Lactarius fallax* var. *concolor* reported from Alaska south to Idaho and California, is nearly identical but has close to crowded gills that are not colored like the cap.

Lactarius floridanus Beardslee and Burlingham Illus. p. 75

Mycologia 32 (1940), 575
Lactaria floridana Beardslee and Burlingham

CAP: up to 4¾" (12 cm) wide, umbilicate with an arched, incurved margin at first, becoming deeply depressed with age; surface viscid, azonate to faintly zoned, tomentose with long agglutinated fibers, but not extending as a beard along the margin, color variable, brownish pink to brownish orange or buff with an ochraceous to dingy light yellow center.

GILLS: attached to subdecurrent, moderately broad, close, sometimes forked, whitish at first, becoming honey yellow at maturity.

STALK: ¾–1½" (2–4 cm) long, ½–⅞" (1.4–2.3 cm) thick, nearly equal, dry, firm, solid, pruinose at the apex, sometimes scrobiculate, pinkish buff to pale cinnamon buff, developing yellowish tints with age.

FLESH: firm, thick, white to pale yellowish pink; odor aromatic and persisting when dried; taste acrid.

LATEX: scant, white on exposure, unchanging; taste acrid.

SPORE DEPOSIT: not stated in the original description.

MICROSCOPIC CHARACTERS: spores 7.5–9.0 × 5–6 µm, ellipsoid to nearly oblong, ornamented with warts and ridges that form a partial reticulum, prominences up to 0.2 µm high, hyaline, amyloid; cap cuticle a layer of loosely spaced decumbent fascicles of thin-walled hyphae.

OCCURRENCE: in sandy soil under mixed live oak and pine; December–January; reported only from Florida; distribution limits and frequency yet to be determined.

EDIBILITY: unknown.

COMMENTS: The variable cap colors, agglutinated fibers, aromatic persisting odor, and narrow spores characterize this species.

Lactarius fragilis var. **fragilis** (Burlingham) Hesler and A. H. Smith Illus. p. 75

North American Species of Lactarius (1979), 503–504
Lactaria camphorata subsp. *fragilis* Burlingham

CAP: 1–1⅜" (2.5–3.5 cm) wide, convex to nearly plane, disc depressed and sometimes wrinkled, with or without an umbo; margin deeply scalloped; surface dry, glabrous or pruinose, azonate, golden brown to dull yellowish brown or reddish brown.

GILLS: subdecurrent, broad, close to subdistant, cinnamon buff to yellowish.

STALK: ¾–2" (2–5 cm) long, 3/16–¼" (4–6 mm) thick, stuffed or hollow, reddish brown.

FLESH: thin; odor like maple sugar; taste mild.

LATEX: copious, watery on exposure, unchanging, not staining tissues; taste mild.

SPORE DEPOSIT: pale yellow.

MICROSCOPIC CHARACTERS: spores 6.0–7.5 × 6.0–7.5 µm, globose to subglobose; ornamented with warts and ridges that form a partial to complete reticulum, prominences up to 1 µm high, hyaline, amyloid; cap cuticle composed of inflated cells three to five layers deep.

OCCURRENCE: on the ground in hardwoods or mixed woods, usually with oak present; July–October; North Carolina and Tennessee; distribution limits and frequency yet to be determined.

EDIBILITY: unknown.

COMMENTS: *Lactarius rubidus* is similar, but it has a dull, dark orange-brown disk with a yellowish rusty brown margin and a maple sugar odor when dried, and it grows on the ground under oak along the Pacific Coast.

Lactarius frustratus Hesler and A. H. Smith Illus. p. 76

North American Species of Lactarius (1979), 479–481

CAP: 1⅛–3⅛" (3–8 cm) wide, broadly convex, becoming depressed and finally shallowly funnel-shaped; margin incurved at first, becoming decurved, striate if moist; surface moist to subviscid or dry, glabrous, dark yellowish brown with paler zones at first, becoming azonate with age, paler toward the margin.

GILLS: decurrent, narrow to moderately broad, crowded, spotting cinnamon buff and finally darker, gradually flushed vinaceous buff overall, slowly staining pale yellow-brown when cut.

STALK: 1½–2¾" (4–7 cm) long, 5/16–½" (8–13 mm) thick, nearly equal, fragile, dry, becoming hollow with age, turning dark vinaceous brown from the base upward.

FLESH: pale vinaceous, slowly staining pale yellow-brown when cut; odor not distinctive; taste slowly becoming burning acrid or mild in old specimens.

LATEX: white to watery on exposure, soon changing to yellowish or unchanging; taste burning acrid or mild in old specimens.

SPORE DEPOSIT: yellowish.

MICROSCOPIC CHARACTERS: spores 7–9 × 6–7 µm, subglobose to broadly ellipsoid, ornamented with warts and ridges that sometimes form a partial reticulum, prominences up to 1.5 µm high, hyaline, amyloid; cap cuticle an ixolattice.

OCCURRENCE: scattered to gregarious under hardwoods, especially oak, at the edges of pools or wet places; July–October; reported from eastern Canada, Michigan, and Florida; distribution limits and frequency yet to be determined.

EDIBILITY: unknown.

COMMENTS: *Lactarius mutabilis* is very similar but has mild-tasting white to watery latex that does not change to yellowish. *Lactarius cognoscibilis* is also very similar, but it has white latex that does not change to yellowish, its stalk does not become dark vinaceous brown from the base upward, and it is reported only from Florida.

Lactarius fumeacolor Burlingham Illus. p. 76

Mycologia 37 (1945), 57
Lactaria fumeacolor Burlingham

CAP: up to 4¾" (12 cm) wide, convex, becoming centrally depressed and finally funnel-shaped; surface very viscid, glabrous except white-pruinose along the margin, azonate to faintly zoned, pale brownish gray to pale pinkish brown with buff tones over the center.

GILLS: subdecurrent, narrow, close, white to buff, staining yellow-brown, dark brown where injured.

STALK: 2–3⅛" (5–8 cm) long, ⅝–1" (1.5–2.5 cm) thick, nearly equal overall, slightly viscid, whitish to buff.

FLESH: white, staining yellow-brown to dark brown; odor not distinctive; taste not stated in the original description.

LATEX: white on exposure, slowly staining injured areas yellow-brown then dark brown; taste slowly acrid.

SPORE DEPOSIT: creamy yellow.

MICROSCOPIC CHARACTERS: spores 8.5–11.0 × 7–8 µm, ellipsoid, ornamented with short ridges and warts that do not form a reticulum, prominences up to 1.3 µm high, hyaline, amyloid; cap cuticle an ixolattice.

OCCURRENCE: on soil under live oak or mockernut; April–August; along the East Coast from New Hampshire south to Florida; uncommon.

EDIBILITY: unknown.

COMMENTS: *Lactarius argillaceifolius* var. *argillaceifolius* is very similar, but it has broad gills that flush dull brownish orange at maturity, spores that often have a partial reticulum, and cream-colored latex that tastes slightly acrid.

Lactarius fumosus var. **fumosoides** (Smith & Hesler) Hesler and A. H. Smith Illus. p. 76

North American Species of Lactarius (1979), 148–150

CAP: 1⅛–4" (3–10cm) wide, broadly convex with an inrolled margin, becoming shallowly depressed to funnel-shaped with age; margin irregular to scalloped or lobed; surface dry, unpolished to faintly velvety, azonate, olive-brown to deep olive-buff, smoky brown to pale dingy yellow brown, pallid toward the margin and rarely pallid overall.

GILLS: decurrent, narrow, crowded, thin, with many tiers of lamellulae, whitish, becoming pale pinkish buff to yellowish, staining pale reddish, cinnamon when bruised.

STALK: 1½–4" (4–10 cm) long, ⅜–¾" (10–20 mm) thick, nearly equal, sometimes abruptly narrowed at the base, stuffed to hollow, fragile, dry, unpolished, colored like the cap or paler, whitish toward the base, staining reddish when bruised.

FLESH: white, staining pale reddish cinnamon; odor very unpleasant when fresh; taste mild.

LATEX: scant, white, unchanging.

SPORE DEPOSIT: not reported.

MICROSCOPIC CHARACTERS: spores 6.5–8.5 × 9–11 µm, broadly ellipsoid to subglobose, ornamented with warts and ridges that form a broken obscure reticulum, prominences up to 1.0 µm high, hyaline, amyloid; cap cuticle a modified trichoderm with a distinct layer of inflated cells.

OCCURRENCE: scattered or in groups on the ground under aspen, birch, and pine; July–August; reported from Tennessee and Michigan; occasional.

EDIBILITY: unknown.

COMMENTS: *Lactarius fumosus* var. *fumosus,* widely distributed in eastern North America, is very similar but has attached to subdecurrent gills, a nondistinctive odor, and variable taste—from acrid to slowly acrid or very slowly faintly acrid.

Lactarius fumosus var. **fumosus** Peck Illus. p. 77

Ann. Rep. N.Y. State Mus. 24 (1872), 74
Lactarius eburneus var. *ervinii* Hesler and A. H. Smith
Lactarius fuliginellus A. H. Smith and Hesler
Lactarius fuliginosus var. *fumosus* (Peck) Saccardo
Lactarius fumosus var. *subalutaceus* A. H. Smith and Hesler
Lactarius fumosibrunneus A. H. Smith and Hesler
Smoky Milk Cap

CAP: 1⅛–4" (3–10 cm) wide, broadly convex to nearly plane, sometimes shallowly depressed; margin irregular, often wavy, lobed, or ribbed; surface dry, unpolished, azonate, usually becoming somewhat wrinkled with age, pale dingy yellow-brown to whitish overall, with a smoky tinge, sometimes with tawny olive, pinkish buff, or dull brown areas.

GILLS: attached to subdecurrent, narrow, crowded, whitish, becoming dingy yellow-buff, staining reddish when bruised.

STALK: 1½–4¼" (4–11 cm) long, ¼–⅝" (6–15 mm) thick, nearly equal, dry, dull, stuffed, colored like the cap, whitish toward the base, staining reddish, but more slowly than the gills.

FLESH: pale white, staining reddish salmon when cut; odor not distinctive; taste variable: quickly acrid then mild or mild then slowly acrid or very slowly faintly acrid.

LATEX: white on exposure, unchanging, staining tissues reddish.

SPORE DEPOSIT: pinkish buff.

MICROSCOPIC CHARACTERS: spores 6–8 × 6–8 µm, globose to subglobose, ornamented with ridges that form a partial reticulum, prominences up to 1.5 µm high, hyaline, amyloid; cap cuticle a palisade of cylindric to clavate cells.

OCCURRENCE: solitary, scattered, or in groups on the ground in woods; July–October; widely distributed in eastern North America, also reported from western Canada; occasional.

EDIBILITY: unknown.

COMMENTS: *Lactarius fumosus* var. *fumosoides* (A. H. Smith and Hesler) Hesler and A. H. Smith (edibility unknown), reported from Michigan and eastern Canada, is very similar, but it has decurrent gills, white flesh with an unpleasant odor and mild taste, and a more distinct layer of inflated cells in its cap cuticle. *Lactarius muscicola* has darker colors, and its gills do not stain reddish where bruised. We have placed *Lactarius eburneus* var. *ervinii* and *Lactarius fuliginellus* in synonymy with *Lactarius fumosus* var. *fumosus* because of the absence of significant differentiating characteristics.

Lactarius furcatus Coker Illus. p. 77

J. Elisha Mitchell Sci. Soc. 34 (1918), 18

CAP: 2⅜–4" (6–10 cm) wide, convex to broadly convex, becoming funnel-shaped at maturity; margin incurved at first, becoming plane and narrowly revolute; surface somewhat viscid, tomentose, azonate, pale ochraceous.

GILLS: decurrent, narrow, crowded, repeatedly forked, ochraceous with a salmon tint.
STALK: ¾–1⅛" (2–3 cm) long, about ½" (13 mm) thick, solid, firm, tough, surface viscid, light yellowish with small ochraceous spots.
FLESH: thin, white, with dull ochraceous zones; odor not distinctive; taste acrid.
LATEX: white on exposure, slowly changing to bluish green; taste moderately acrid.
SPORE DEPOSIT: pinkish ochraceous.
MICROSCOPIC CHARACTERS: spores 3.5–5.5 × 3.5–4.0 µm, ellipsoid to subglobose, ornamented with a few bands and occasional fine lines, prominences only up to 0.2 µm high, hyaline, amyloid; cap cuticle an ixocutis, bearing some nongelatinous hyphae on the surface.
OCCURRENCE: on soil; June; reported from North Carolina and Mississippi; distribution limits and frequency yet to be determined.
EDIBILITY: unknown.
COMMENTS: *Lactarius lanuginosus* is similar, but its gills are not repeatedly forked, and its latex is white and unchanging.

Lactarius fusco-olivaceus var. **fusco-olivaceus** Hesler and A. H. Smith

Not Illustrated

North American Species of Lactarius (1979), 392–393

CAP: 1½–2⅜" (4–6 cm) wide, convex, becoming nearly plane with a slightly depressed center; margin incurved at first, expanding at maturity, developing short striations with age; surface viscid, glabrous, azonate, milk chocolate brown to medium brown.
GILLS: attached to slightly subdecurrent, close to crowded, medium broad, tapered in both directions, white at first, becoming pale pinkish cinnamon, not staining when bruised.
STALK: 2–2¾" (5–7 cm) long, ⅜–½" (9–12 mm) thick, nearly equal down to a pointed base, dry, becoming hollow with age, glabrous, dingy brownish to pale cinnamon.
FLESH: thick on the disc, thinner on the margin; odor not distinctive.
LATEX: white on exposure, unchanging and not staining the gills or flesh; taste acrid.
SPORE DEPOSIT: white.
MICROSCOPIC CHARACTERS: spores 7.5–10.0 × 6.0–7.5 µm, broadly ellipsoid with a distinct plage, ornamented with a partial reticulum and isolated warts, prominences up to 1.2 µm high, hyaline, amyloid; cap cuticle an ixolattice of thin-walled, septate, branched hyphae that measure 3–6 µm wide.
OCCURRENCE: scattered on the ground in pine woods; October; reported from Cades Cove, Tennessee; distribution limits and frequency yet to be determined.
EDIBILITY: unknown.
COMMENTS: *Lactarius fusco-olivaceus* var. *graveolens* Hesler and A. H. Smith (edibility unknown) is nearly identical and has acrid-tasting latex, and its flesh has an alkaline odor when fresh. Similar species include *Lactarius imperceptus* and *Lactarius vietus.*

Lactarius gerardii var. **fagicola** Hesler and A. H. Smith

Illus. p. 77

North American Species of Lactarius (1979), 112–113
Lactarius fagicola A. H. Smith and Hesler, *Brittonia* 14 (1962), 381.

CAP: 1½–2⅛" (4.0–5.5 cm) wide, shallowly depressed over the disk with a small umbo; surface dry, velvety, azonate, brown, paler and grayer toward the margin, wrinkled over the center to uneven at the margin.
GILLS: distant, broad, decurrent, white, sometimes staining brownish.

STALK: 1½–2" (4.5 cm) long, ⅜" (10 mm) thick, equal, dry, unpolished or velvety, colored like the cap.
FLESH: brittle, thin, white, staining brownish; odor slightly fragrant; taste mild.
LATEX: scant, white, unchanging; taste mild or slowly becoming slightly acrid.
SPORE DEPOSIT: white.
MACROCHEMICAL TESTS: flesh staining dull brownish with the application of $FeSO_4$.
MICROSCOPIC CHARACTERS: spores 8–11 × 7–10 µm, subglobose to broadly ellipsoid, ornamented with a partial to complete reticulum, prominences up to 0.5 µm high, hyaline, weakly amyloid; cap cuticle composed of two to three layers of cells that bear a turf of flask-shaped pileocystidia or filamentous outgrowths.
OCCURRENCE: scattered or in groups on the ground under hardwoods, especially beech; July–October; reported from Michigan and Tennessee; occasional.
EDIBILITY: unknown.
COMMENTS: *Lactarius gerardii* var. *gerardii* is similar, but its flesh and gills do not stain brownish.

Lactarius gerardii var. **gerardii** Peck

Illus. p. 78, 79

Bull. Buffalo Soc. Nat. Sci. 1 (1873), 57
Gerard's Milky

CAP: 1¼–5⅛" (3–13 cm) wide; convex, becoming broadly convex to plane, wrinkled, with a depressed center when older, with or without an umbo; margin becoming uplifted and crenate or wavy with age; surface dry, slightly sticky when wet, velvety when dry, azonate, brown to yellow-brown to tan.
GILLS: attached to decurrent, broad, subdistant to distant, crossveined, whitish to cream.
STALK: 1⅜–3⅛" (3.5–8.0 cm) long, ⅜–¾" (8–20 mm) thick, nearly equal or enlarged downward, usually with an abruptly tapered base, stuffed when young, becoming hollow with age, dry, velvety, dark brown to yellow-brown, paler and often plicate at the apex.
FLESH: firm, thin, white, not staining; odor not distinctive; taste mild then slightly acrid.
LATEX: white on exposure, unchanging, not staining; taste mild then slightly acrid.
SPORE DEPOSIT: white.
MACROCHEMICAL TESTS: flesh staining yellow with the application of KOH.
MICROSCOPIC CHARACTERS: spores 7–10 × 7.5–9.0 µm, globose to subglobose or broadly ellipsoid, ornamented with warts and ridges that form a reticulum, prominences up to 0.8 µm high, hyaline, amyloid; cap cuticle composed of two to four layers of cells that bear a turf of cylindric, clavate, or flask-shaped pileocystidia.
OCCURRENCE: scattered or in groups on the ground under hardwoods or conifers; July–October; eastern Canada south to North Carolina, west to Michigan; occasional.
EDIBILITY: edible.
COMMENTS: *Lactarius gerardii* var. *fagicola* (A. H. Smith and Hesler) Hesler and A. H. Smith (edibility unknown), reported from Michigan and Tennessee, is very similar, but its flesh and gills slowly stain brownish when injured, it has mild-tasting flesh and latex, and it grows on the ground under beech. *Lactarius gerardii* var. *subrubescens*—reported from Maine to Florida, Tennessee, and Michigan—is also very similar, but its flesh stains vinaceous pink when exposed, it has a white spore deposit, and it grows on the ground in conifer or mixed conifer and hardwood forests. *Lactarius subgerardii* is also similar, but it has a paler gray-brown to smoky brown cap, a paler stalk, and closer, whitish gills that become creamy yellow at maturity. *Lactarius sumstinei* has a paler pinkish cinnamon cap, pinkish buff gills, and somewhat larger spores.

Lactarius gerardii var. **subrubescens** Hesler and A. H. Smith Illus. p. 79

North American Species of Lactarius (1979), 114–115
Lactarius subrubescens A. H. Smith and Hesler, *Brittonia* 14 (1962), 381.
Lactarius simulissimus A. H. Smith and Hesler, *Brittonia* 14 (1962), 381.

CAP: 1⅛–4⅝" (3–12 cm) wide, broadly convex, becoming funnel-shaped or plane, with or without an umbo; surface velvety, rivulose, rugose, azonate, brown to yellow-brown to tan; margin even to plicate.

GILLS: broadly adnate, becoming decurrent with age, broad, subdistant to distant, one to two tiers of lamellulae present, becoming white to pale cream with age, pinkish where cut.

STALK: 1½–3⅛" (4–8 cm) long, ⅛–1" (4–25 mm) thick, equal or constricted at the ends, stuffed when young, becoming hollow with age, dry, velvety, colored like the cap or paler, often plicate at the apex.

FLESH: firm, thin, white, staining vinaceous pink; odor not distinctive; taste mild to slightly acrid.

LATEX: white, unchanging, staining flesh and gills pink; taste mild to slightly acrid.

SPORE DEPOSIT: white.

MICROSCOPIC CHARACTERS: spores 7–10 × 6.5–8.0 µm, broadly ellipsoid to globose, ornamented with a complete reticulum, prominences up to 0.6 µm high and 0.2–0.5 µm wide, hyaline, amyloid; cap cuticle composed of three to five layers of cells that bear a turf of cylindric, clavate, or flask-shaped pileocystidia.

OCCURRENCE: scattered or in groups on the ground under hardwood or conifers; July–October; eastern Canada, south to North Carolina, west to Michigan; occasional.

EDIBILITY: unknown.

COMMENTS: See the comments under *Lactarius gerardii* var. *gerardii.*

Lactarius glaucescens Crossland Illus. p. 80

Naturalist 1900 (1900), 5–10
Lactarius piperatus var. *glaucescens* (Crossland) Hesler and A. H. Smith

CAP: 1½–4¾" (4–12 cm) wide, convex, becoming nearly plane with a depressed center; margin inrolled to incurved at first, becoming decurved; surface dry, dull to somewhat shiny, glabrous, sometimes rimose-areolate in dry weather, white to pale cream when young, becoming dingy yellow-brown with age, especially over the center.

GILLS: subdecurrent to decurrent, broad, crowded, often forked, whitish to dull cream, very slowly staining brown when bruised.

STALK: 1⅛–3½" (3–9 cm) long, ⅜–1⅛" (1–3 cm) thick, tapered downward or sometimes nearly equal, dry, solid, glabrous, white to pale cream.

FLESH: thick, hard, pale cream, unchanging or very slowly staining pale bluish green when cut; odor not distinctive or faintly pungent; taste acrid.

LATEX: white to whitish on exposure, not staining tissues, drying pale bluish green; taste very acrid.

SPORE DEPOSIT: white to yellowish.

MACROCHEMICAL TESTS: latex staining yellow to orange with the application of KOH.

MICROSCOPIC CHARACTERS: spores 6.5–9.0 × 5–7 µm, broadly ellipsoid, ornamented with warts and fine lines that do not form a reticulum, prominences up to 0.2 µm high, hyaline, amyloid; cap cuticle a zone of irregular cells that give rise at the surface to a loose turf of narrow hyphae.

OCCURRENCE: solitary, scattered, or in groups on the ground under hardwoods, especially oak; July–December; eastern Canada south to Florida, west to Michigan and Texas; occasional to fairly common.

EDIBILITY: poisonous, as reported by Florida mycologist Robert S. Williams.

COMMENTS: *Lactarius piperatus* var. *piperatus* is very similar, but it has white latex that does not change to bluish green when dry.

Lactarius glutigriseus Wells and Kempton Not Illustrated

Beihefte zur Nova Hedwigia 51 (1975), 349

CAP: ¾–1¾" (2.0–4.5 cm) wide, convex, expanding and sometimes slightly depressed, with or without a small umbo; margin inrolled at first, becoming decurved at maturity; surface glutinous, glabrous, azonate or sometimes appearing to have a zone around the disc, moderately dark grayish brown.

GILLS: attached, narrow, close, frequently forked, white, unchanging or staining grayish brown by the latex.

STALK: 1⅛–1½" (3–4 cm) long, 3⁄16–¼" (4–6 mm) thick, enlarged downward, tacky to subviscid, glabrous, hollow, brittle, whitish near the apex and base, and colored like the cap in the middle portion.

FLESH: thin, brittle, pale white to pale brownish gray; odor not distinctive; taste slowly and slightly acrid.

LATEX: abundant, white on exposure, unchanging, staining gills grayish brown; taste strongly acrid or sometimes bitter.

SPORE DEPOSIT: white.

MACROCHEMICAL TESTS: cap surface and flesh negative with the application of KOH, NH_4OH, or $FeSO_4$; cap and stalk flesh staining dark vinaceous with the application of phenol.

MICROSCOPIC CHARACTERS: spores 7.5–9.5 × 6.0–7.5 µm, broadly ellipsoid, ornamented with isolated warts and ridges that form a partial to complete reticulum, prominences up to 1 µm high, hyaline, amyloid; cap cuticle an ixolattice to an ixotrichoderm.

OCCURRENCE: gregarious on the ground in coastal conifer forests under hemlock; August–October; reported from Alaska and California; uncommon.

EDIBILITY: unknown.

COMMENTS: *Lactarius mucidus* var. *mucidus* is similar, but it has white latex that dries green or olive on the gills. *Lactarius pseudomucidus* is also similar, but its cap and stalk are charcoal gray and slimy. In *Agaricales (Gilled Fungi) of California, 10. Russulaceae 2.* Lactarius (1997), A. S. Methven describes this species' cap as brownish orange to grayish orange.

Lactarius glutinosus Sumstine Not Illustrated

Mycologia 33 (1941), 18

Lactaria glutinosa Sumstine

CAP: 1½–2⅜" (4–6 cm) wide, convex, becoming broadly convex with a depressed disc; margin sometimes sulcate; surface slimy-viscid when moist, becoming dry, glabrous, azonate, smoky gray.

GILLS: slightly decurrent, distant, white.

STALK: 1⅛–1½" (3–4 cm) long, ¼–⅝" (5–15 mm) thick, tapered downward, viscid, solid, glabrous, appearing striate at times, colored like the cap but paler.

FLESH: thin, white; taste acrid.

LATEX: white on exposure, unchanging, not staining tissues; taste acrid.

SPORE DEPOSIT: not obtained.

MICROSCOPIC CHARACTERS: spores 7.0–8.5 × 6–7 µm, ellipsoid to subglobose, ornamented with broad bands that form a partial to complete reticulum, prominences up to 0.5 µm high, hyaline, amyloid; cap cuticle cellular with a turf of colorless pileocystidia.

OCCURRENCE: on the ground in mixed woods; August; reported only from Pocono Manor, Pennsylvania; distribution limits and frequency yet to be determined.

EDIBILITY: unknown.

COMMENTS: *Lactarius mucidus* var. *mucidus* is similar, but it has a darker brown cap, and its latex dries bluish green to olive on the gills.

Lactarius glyciosmus (Fries) Fries Illus. p. 80

Epicr. Syst. Mycol. (1828), 348

CAP: ¾–3½" (2–8 cm) wide, convex, becoming plane then shallowly depressed to funnel-shaped; surface dry, coated with tiny matted fibers, pale vinaceous gray to pale lilac-gray or whitish.

GILLS: close, subdecurrent to decurrent, pinkish buff to pinkish cinnamon, typically crossveined.

STALK: ¾–3½" (2–9 cm) long, ⅛–⅜" (3–10 mm) thick, nearly equal, dry, glabrous or nearly so, whitish to pale vinaceous gray.

FLESH: pale buff; odor fragrant, like coconut; taste slowly and slightly acrid.

LATEX: white on exposure, unchanging, not staining gills or flesh; taste slowly and slightly acrid.

SPORE DEPOSIT: pale cream to pinkish buff.

MACROCHEMICAL TESTS: cap surface staining dull pale yellow with the application of KOH.

MICROSCOPIC CHARACTERS: spores 6–10 × 5–7 µm, ellipsoid to subglobose, ornamented with warts and ridges that sometimes form a partial reticulum, prominences up to 0.8 µm high, hyaline, amyloid; cap cuticle a layer of interwoven hyphae with some cells conspicuously enlarged, especially in older specimens.

OCCURRENCE: scattered or in groups on the ground or among mosses under birch and alder or in mixed woods; August–November; eastern Canada west to Alaska, northern United States; fairly common.

EDIBILITY: edible.

COMMENTS: *Lactarius hibbardae* var. *hibbardae* also has flesh with a fragrant, coconut-like odor, but it has a much darker cap, and its flesh is distinctly acrid. Also compare *Lactarius lepidotus,* which has a finely cracked and scaly cap and mild-tasting flesh that lacks a fragrant odor.

Lactarius gossypinus Hesler and A. H. Smith Illus. p. 80, 81

North American Species of Lactarius (1979), 291–292

CAP: 2⅜–4¾" (6–12 cm) wide, broadly convex with a depressed disc, becoming broadly funnel-shaped; margin inrolled and cottony at first; surface viscid, pale yellow to orange-yellow, indistinctly zonate with watery zones.

GILLS: decurrent, narrow, crowded, faintly cream-colored, becoming pink-tinged with age.

STALK: ¾–2" (2–5 cm) long, ⅜–1⅛" (1–3 cm) thick, dry, hollow, dull, white to brownish orange-yellow, scrobiculate when young, but spots soon disappearing.

FLESH: cottony; odor sweetly fragrant; taste bitter, not acrid.

LATEX: watery to whey-like on exposure, becoming slightly yellowish, staining tissues yellow.

SPORE DEPOSIT: white.

MICROSCOPIC CHARACTERS: spores 7.5–8.5 × 6.0–7.5 µm, broadly ellipsoid, ornamented with isolated warts and ridges that form a low partial reticulum, prominences up to 0.2 µm high, hyaline, amyloid; cap cuticle an ixocutis.

OCCURRENCE: on the ground under pine and fir; September; reported only from Grand Teton National Park, Wyoming; distribution limits and frequency yet to be determined.

EDIBILITY: unknown.

COMMENTS: *Lactarius scrobiculatus* varieties lack the pinkish tint on the gills and have an acrid, not bitter, taste.

Lactarius griseus Peck

Illus. p. 81

Ann. Rep. N.Y. State Cab. 23 (1872), 120
Lactarius glabripes A. H. Smith

CAP: ⅝–2" (1.5–5.0 cm) wide, convex, becoming broadly convex to nearly plane with a depressed center and a small pointed umbo, often becoming funnel-shaped with age; margin inrolled when young, becoming expanded to uplifted with age; surface dry, covered with fibers and tiny scales, azonate, dark purple-brown to purple-gray overall when young, fading or drying brownish gray to dull gray over a dull yellowish ground color when older, remaining darkest over the disc.

GILLS: decurrent, broad, close to subdistant, whitish, becoming pinkish or purplish buff with age, not staining when cut or bruised.

STALK: ¾–2½" (2.0–6.5 cm) long, ⅛–⅜" (3–10 mm) thick, equal or enlarged slightly downward, hollow, dry, colored like the gills at the apex, purplish below the apex when young, becoming pale rosy brown with age, base coated with coarse white hairs.

FLESH: white to yellow; odor not distinctive; taste mild or slowly acrid.

LATEX: white on exposure, drying yellowish, not staining flesh or gills; taste mild or slowly acrid, especially in young specimens.

SPORE DEPOSIT: yellowish.

MICROSCOPIC CHARACTERS: spores 7–10 × 6–8 µm, subglobose to broadly ellipsoid, ornamented with warts and ridges that do not form a reticulum, prominences up to 1 µm high, hyaline, amyloid; cap cuticle a layer of repent hyphae, the surface bearing numerous columns (scales) of erect septate hyphae with elongated cells, some with incrustations on their walls.

OCCURRENCE: in groups or clusters on decaying wood or among sphagnum mosses in bogs or wet woodlands; June–October; eastern Canada south to Tennessee and North Carolina, west to Michigan; occasional to fairly common.

EDIBILITY: unknown.

COMMENTS: The small size, depressed to funnel-shaped cap with tiny scales, and growth on wood or among sphagnum mosses are this species' distinctive characters.

Lactarius helvus (Fries : Fries) Fries

Illus. p. 81, 82

Epicr. Syst. Mycol. (1838), 347
Lactarius aquifluus Peck, *Lactarius helvus* var. *aquifluus* Peck
Burnt-sugar Milky, Waterdrop Milk Cap

CAP: 1⅛–5⅛" (3–15 cm) wide; broadly convex, becoming plane with a slightly depressed center when older, with or without an umbo; margin incurved when young, becoming expanded with age; surface dry, covered with tiny fibrils, orange-brown to light grayish brown to pale cinnamon brown, zoned with thin bands of dark grayish brown or water spots.

GILLS: attached to the stalk, slightly decurrent, narrow to broad, close, often forked near the stalk, creamy white becoming pale orange-tan to pale pinkish cinnamon.

STALK: 1⅝–3⅛" (4–8 cm) long, ⅜–¾" (1–2 cm) thick, nearly equal or enlarged at the base, stuffed then becoming hollow with age, dry, pruinose, colored like the cap, whitish at the base.

FLESH: pale whitish to tan, not staining when bruised; odor variously described as sweet, fragrant, like maple sugar or burnt sugar, also described as resembling chicory or fenugreek, especially when drying; taste mild.

LATEX: watery on exposure, unchanging, not staining; taste mild.

SPORE DEPOSIT: white to cream.

MICROSCOPIC CHARACTERS: spores 6–9 × 5.5–7.5 µm, elliptic, ornamented with warts and ridges that form a partial reticulum, prominences up to 0.4 µm high, hyaline, amyloid; cap cuticle a thick layer of loosely woven hyphae with some terminal cells arranged in fascicles.

OCCURRENCE: scattered and in groups or clusters on the ground in wet conifer and mixed woods and among sphagnum mosses in bogs; July–November; eastern Canada south to West Virginia, west to Minnesota and Wisconsin, also reported from Texas and western Canada; fairly common.

EDIBILITY: edible and quite good.

COMMENTS: Other species of *Lactarius* that also have a sweet, fragrant odor like maple or burnt sugar include *Lactarius camphoratus, Lactarius mutabilis, Lactarius quietus* var. *incanus,* and *Lactarius rubidus.* The fragrant odor is often enhanced by wrapping specimens in waxed paper for several minutes or by drying them.

Lactarius hepaticus Plowright

Illus. p. 82

Boudier, *Icon. Mycol.* 4 (1905), 28
Lactaria nitida Burlingham, *Lactarius nitidus* Burlingham

CAP: 1⅛–2¾" (3–7 cm) wide, convex to nearly plane with a depressed disc, sometimes with a small umbo; margin decurved, sometimes slightly crenulate; surface moist, glabrous, azonate, dark rusty red, brick red, dark reddish brown or chestnut brown, often with a darker central spot.

GILLS: decurrent, narrow to medium broad, close, sometimes forked, pale pinkish buff to dull vinaceous, not staining when bruised.

STALK: 1–2¾" (2.5–7.0 cm) long, ⅛–⅜" (4–10 mm) thick, nearly equal, dry, solid, glabrous, colored like the cap or paler, especially toward the apex.

FLESH: thin, fragile, cream to pale pinkish buff, unchanging when cut; odor not distinctive; taste slowly acrid or mild.

LATEX: white on exposure, unchanging or sometimes slowly changing to pale yellow, not staining tissues; taste slowly acrid or mild.

SPORE DEPOSIT: cream-colored.

MACROCHEMICAL TESTS: cap surface staining dull olive with the application of KOH.

MICROSCOPIC CHARACTERS: spores 7.5–9.0 × 6–7 µm, ellipsoid, ornamented with isolated warts and ridges that form a partial reticulum, prominences up to 0.5 µm high, hyaline, amyloid; cap cuticle a short ixotrichoderm.

OCCURRENCE: solitary, scattered, or in groups on the ground in damp mossy areas under conifers, especially hemlock; July–October; eastern North America west to the Rocky Mountains; fairly common.

EDIBILITY: unknown.

COMMENTS: The white latex exuded by North American specimens of *Lactarius hepaticus* typically does not change to pale yellow. Older specimens tend not to have the acrid taste that young specimens do, but even the immature specimens sometimes do not taste acrid. *Lactarius atrobadius*—reported from California, Oregon, and Colorado—is similar, but it has a slimy-viscid cap and stalk when wet and mild-tasting flesh, and its gills stain dark red-brown when bruised. *Lactarius subolivaceus,* reported only from Tennessee, has a viscid, light pinkish cinnamon cap with a distinct olive tint and grows on the ground under pines.

Lactarius hibbardae var. **glaucescens** Hesler and A. H. Smith Illus. p. 83

North American Species of Lactarius (1979), 402–404

CAP: ¾–2¾" (2–7 cm) wide, broadly convex to plane with an inrolled to decurved margin, becoming depressed with a horizontal margin, with or without an umbo, surface fibrillose to scurfy, dry, unpolished, azonate, light brown, drab, becoming browner with age.

GILLS: decurrent, close, narrow, forking near the stalk, pinkish buff to pale ochraceous buff, becoming a little darker ochraceous buff to cinnamon buff with age.

STALK: ⅜–2⅜" (1.2–6.0 cm)long, ⅛–7⁄16" (4–11 mm) thick, equal, solid, brittle, hoary, pale ochraceous buff.

FLESH: thin, brittle, pale ochraceous buff; odor fragrant, like anise; taste slowly acrid.

LATEX: white to whey-like, not staining, drying pale grayish green; taste slowly acrid.

SPORE DEPOSIT: pale cream.

MICROSCOPIC CHARACTERS: spores 6.5–8.0 × 5.5–6.5 µm, ellipsoid, ornamented with bands and free-ending branches forming a partial reticulum, prominences up to 0.4 µm high, hyaline, amyloid; cap cuticle composed of repent dry hyphae, sometimes with tufts of pileocystidia.

OCCURRENCE: on ground or among mosses in conifer woods; September–October; reported from Massachusetts, Michigan, and Vermont; occasional.

EDIBILITY: unknown.

COMMENTS: This species is distinguished by its latex, which dries grayish green and has an anise-like fragrant odor.

Lactarius hibbardae var. **hibbardae** Peck Illus. p. 83, 84

J. Mycol. 14 (1908), 2

CAP: ⅝–4" (1.5–10.0 cm) wide; convex, becoming broadly convex to plane with a depressed center, sometimes with an umbo; margin incurved, becoming expanded to uplifted and wavy with age; surface fibrillose to scurfy, dry, not sticky or slimy, dark pinkish brown to dark pinkish gray, becoming paler pinkish brown to pinkish gray with age, faintly zoned with slightly darker colors.

GILLS: attached to slightly decurrent, close to crowded, pale pinkish buff to cream, not staining or slowly staining very slightly brownish when cut or bruised.

STALK: ¾–4" (2–10 cm) long, ⅛–⅝" (4–15 mm) thick, nearly equal or tapered downward, hollow, pruinose, dry, becoming colored like the gills or like the cap with age, whitish at the base.

FLESH: whitish with tinges of pinkish gray or pinkish brown; odor fragrant, like anise or coconut; taste distinctly acrid.

LATEX: white on exposure in young specimens, becoming watery in mature fruiting bodies; taste acrid.

SPORE DEPOSIT: white to cream.

MACROCHEMICAL TESTS: cap surface staining yellowish to orange with the application of KOH and yellow with NH_4OH.

MICROSCOPIC CHARACTERS: spores 6.5–9.0 × 5.0–6.5 µm, elliptic, ornamented with warts and ridges that form a partial to distinct reticulum, prominences up to 0.4 µm high, hyaline, amyloid; cap cuticle a cutis composed of repent to somewhat erect hyphae with hyphal incrustations present.

OCCURRENCE: solitary to scattered on the ground under conifers or hardwoods or among sphagnum mosses; June–October; widely distributed from eastern Canada to Alaska and in the northern United States, south to West Virginia; fairly common.

EDIBILITY: unknown.

COMMENTS: *Lactarius hibbardae* var. *glaucescens* is very similar, but it has pale ochraceous buff flesh with a fragrant odor similar to anise and white or watery latex that tastes slowly acrid and dries pale grayish green, and it grows in conifer woods in Michigan and New England. *Lactarius glyciosmus* also has flesh with a fragrant, coconut-like odor, but it has a much paler grayish to whitish cap, and its flesh slowly tastes slightly acrid. *Lactarius pungens* is similar, but it has pale ochraceous buff gills, white latex that tastes bitter, and somewhat larger spores, and its cap cuticle is an ixolattice to an ixotrichoderm.

Lactarius highlandensis Hesler and A. H. Smith Illus. p. 84

North American Species of Lactarius (1979), 518–519

CAP: ¾–1½" (2–4 cm) wide, convex, becoming broadly convex, sometimes strongly umbonate; margin incurved and often crimped; surface minutely fibrillose to glabrous, dull reddish brown, fading and becoming areolate.

GILLS: decurrent, narrow, close, very short, whitish at first, becoming dull reddish brown at maturity.

STALK: 3⅛–5⅛" (8–13 cm) long, 3⁄16–⅜" (5–11 mm) thick, nearly equal, dry, glabrous, hollow, dull reddish brown or paler.

FLESH: odor aromatic; taste acrid.

LATEX: watery on exposure, unchanging, not staining tissues; taste acrid.

SPORE DEPOSIT: white.

MICROSCOPIC CHARACTERS: spores 7.0–9.5 × 6–8 µm, ellipsoid to subglobose, ornamented with isolated warts and occasional connecting line, prominences up to 1.0 µm high, hyaline, amyloid; cap cuticle a zone of cells, many of which are elongated vertically in young caps, cells separating in older specimens.

OCCURRENCE: on the ground in deep pine needles; August; reported only from Highlands, North Carolina; distribution limits and frequency yet to be determined.

EDIBILITY: unknown.

COMMENTS: *Lactarius rimosellus* is similar, but its latex is not acrid, and it is not as strongly umbonate.

Lactarius hygrophoroides var. **hygrophoroides** Berkeley and Curtis Illus. p. 85

Ann. Mag. Nat. Hist. (3rd ser.) 4 (1859), 293
Lactarius distans Peck
Hygrophorus Milky

CAP: 1⅛–4" (3–10 cm) wide, broadly convex, becoming nearly plane with a depressed center when older, sometimes broadly funnel-shaped; margin incurved, becoming uplifted with age; surface dry, glabrous to slightly velvety, sometimes becoming slightly wrinkled toward the margin with age, dull orange to orange-brown or dull orangey cinnamon.

GILLS: attached to slightly decurrent, broad, distant at maturity, crossveined, white to cream to yellowish buff.

STALK: 1⅛–2" (3–5 cm) long, ¼–⅝" (5–15 mm) thick, nearly equal, solid, dry, pale orange-brown to orange-yellow.

FLESH: white; odor not distinctive; taste mild.

LATEX: white on exposure, unchanging, not staining gills or flesh; taste mild.

SPORE DEPOSIT: white.

MICROSCOPIC CHARACTERS: spores 7.5–10.5 × 6.0–7.5 µm, elliptic, ornamented with warts and ridges, prominences up to 0.4 µm high, hyaline, amyloid; cap cuticle a zone of inflated, compressed cells forming a variable turf of pileocystidia with a subcylindric or tapered apex.

OCCURRENCE: solitary, scattered, or in groups on the ground under hardwoods; July–October; eastern Canada south to Florida, west to Michigan and Texas; occasional to fairly common.

EDIBILITY: edible.

COMMENTS: *Lactarius hygrophoroides* var. *odoratus* Hesler and A. H. Smith = *Lactarius cystidiosus* Thiers (edibility unknown) is similar, but it has white flesh with a strongly alkaline odor and white to pale cream gills that stain pinkish gray when bruised, grows on the ground under conifers, and has been reported from North Carolina and Texas. *Lactarius hygrophoroides* var. *rugatus* = *Lactarius rugatus* is also similar, but it has conspicuous concentric wrinkles near the cap margin and white flesh that stains vinaceous to dull red with the application of $FeSO_4$, it grows on the ground under hardwoods, especially oak, and it has been reported from eastern Canada south to Florida and west to Michigan and Texas. *Lactarius hygrophoroides* var. *lavendulaceus* Hesler and A. H. Smith (edibility unknown) is also similar, but it has whitish flesh that has a moderately strong fishy odor and slowly stains greenish gray with the application of $FeSO_4$ and very pale yellow to pinkish buff gills that slowly stain pinkish to lavender or pinkish gray to pale pinkish brown when bruised, and has been reported from Michigan, Tennessee, Florida, and Texas. Also compare with *Lactarius allochrous, Lactarius lentus,* and *Lactarius pervelutinus.*

Lactarius hygrophoroides var. **rugatus** Hesler and A. H. Smith Illus. p. 86

North American Species of Lactarius (1979), 175–176
Lactarius rugatus K. & R., *Bull. Soc. Mycol. France* 69 (1953), 362

CAP: 1¾–3⅛" (4.5–8.0 cm) wide, convex to plane, becoming cup-shaped with a depressed center; surface dull and velvety, with concentric wrinkles near the margin, dry, rusty orange-brown, darker toward the center, azonate; margin incurved and lobed.

GILLS: subdecurrent, distant, thick and rigid, with three to four tiers of lamellulae, narrow, cream-colored then pale golden color when older, not staining or only staining weakly brown when bruised.

STALK: 1⅜–2⅜" (3.5–6.0 cm) long, ½–⅝" (1.3–1.6 mm) thick, nearly equal, stuffed, tomentose, dry, orangey cream to vinaceous cinnamon.

FLESH: thick, rigid, odor not distinctive, taste mild.

LATEX: white to watery, abundant, not staining, taste mild.

SPORE DEPOSIT: white.

MACROCHEMICAL TESTS: flesh staining dull brownish red to rose color with the application of $FeSO_4$.

MICROSCOPIC CHARACTERS: spores 7.5–9.0 × 6.0–7.5 µm, ellipsoid, ornamented with a partial to broken reticulum with isolated warts and ridges, prominences up to 0.5 µm high, hyaline, amyloid; cap cuticle composed of five to seven layers of cells with a turf of pileocystidia at the upper surface.

OCCURRENCE: solitary or scattered on the ground under hardwoods; July–October; eastern Canada south to Florida, west to Michigan and Texas; occasional.

EDIBILITY: unknown.

COMMENTS: *Lactarius hygrophoroides* var. *hygrophoroides* is similar but does not have the concentric wrinkles near the margin and has white flesh that does not stain vinaceous to dull red with the application of $FeSO_4$.

Lactarius hysginus var. **hysginus** Fries Illus. p. 86

Epicr. Syst. Mycol. (1838), 337

CAP: 1⅛–3½" (3–9 cm) wide, convex, becoming broadly convex to plane with a depressed center, often broadly funnel-shaped; margin incurved when young, becoming expanded to uplifted with age; surface glabrous, sticky to slimy when fresh, shiny when dry, dark reddish brown at the center, pinkish cinnamon on the margin, fading with age.

GILLS: attached to slightly decurrent, narrow, close to crowded, whitish to buff when young, becoming orange-yellow at maturity, not staining when cut or bruised.

STALK: 1⅛–3⅛" (3–8 cm) long, ⅜–⅝" (1.0–1.5 cm) thick, equal, hollow, slimy when young, becoming dry, colored like the cap or paler, whitish at the apex, scrobiculate.

FLESH: whitish; odor not distinctive; taste acrid.

LATEX: white on exposure, unchanging, not staining flesh or gills; taste acrid.

SPORE DEPOSIT: yellowish.

MACROCHEMICAL TESTS: cap cuticle staining pinkish brown with the application of $FeSO_4$.

MICROSCOPIC CHARACTERS: spores 5.5–7.5 × 5.5–7.0 µm, globose to elliptic, with warts and ridges that form a partial reticulum, prominences up to 0.5 µm high, hyaline, amyloid; cap cuticle an ixotrichoderm.

OCCURRENCE: scattered or in groups on the ground under conifers; July–October; eastern Canada and the northeastern United States, west to Michigan, also reported from Idaho and Texas; occasional.

EDIBILITY: unknown.

COMMENTS: *Lactarius hysginus* var. *americanus* Hesler and A. H. Smith (edibility unknown) has pale yellow gills when young that become tan to dull cinnamon with age and has been collected under conifers, including redwood near Trinidad, California. *Lactarius hysginus* var. *subroseus* Hesler and A. H. Smith (edibility unknown) has white latex that changes to yellow or stains the gills or flesh yellow, and it grows in conifer or mixed woods in New England. Similar species include *Lactarius bryophilus, Lactarius coleopteris,* and *Lactarius manzanitae.*

Lactarius imperceptus Beardslee and Burlingham Illus. p. 87

Mycologia 32 (1940), 581
Lactaria impercepta Beardslee and Burlingham

CAP: 1⅛–3½" (3–9 cm) wide, broadly convex to nearly plane, usually slightly depressed on the disc with a small umbo at maturity, glabrous, azonate; surface dry to slightly sticky when wet, pale cinnamon to pinkish cinnamon or pale reddish brown, typically pitted and stained with darker pinkish cinnamon, margin sometimes becoming striate with age.

GILLS: attached to slightly decurrent, close, whitish to pinkish white, usually staining brownish, occasionally forked at the stalk.

STALK: 1⅛–3½" (3–9 cm) long, ¼–¾" (6–20 mm) thick, tapered downward or nearly equal overall, solid, dry to moist, pinkish white, darkening with age, glabrous, with a whitish tomentose base.

FLESH: whitish, sometimes staining yellow when exposed; odor not distinctive; taste acrid, sometimes slowly.

LATEX: white to creamy white on exposure, sometimes slowly darkening to yellow on exposure; taste bitter then acrid or acrid only, sometimes slowly.

SPORE DEPOSIT: white to pale cream.

MACROCHEMICAL TESTS: flesh staining pale olive with the application of $FeSO_4$.

MICROSCOPIC CHARACTERS: 8–11 × 7.0–8.5 µm, broadly ellipsoid, ornamented with heavy bands that do not form a complete reticulum, prominences up to 1.5 µm high, hyaline, amyloid; cap cuticle a short, tangled ixotrichoderm to ixolattice.

OCCURRENCE: solitary, scattered, or in groups on the ground or in the needle litter of conifers or hardwoods, especially pine or oak; July–November; widely distributed throughout eastern North America; occasional to fairly common.

EDIBILITY: unknown.

COMMENTS: The staining of the flesh and the color change of the latex are variable features, especially if the fruiting bodies are soaked following heavy rainfall. Similar species include *Lactarius fusco-olivaceus* var. *fusco-olivaceus, Lactarius fusco-olivaceus* var. *graveolens,* and *Lactarius subumbrinus.*

Lactarius incarnatozonatus Hesler and A. H. Smith Not Illustrated

North American Species of Lactarius (1979), 309–310

CAP: 2–3½" (5–9 cm) wide, nearly plane with a depressed center, becoming vase-shaped; margin pruinose and incurved at first but soon glabrous, becoming decurved; surface viscid then dry and appearing varnished, glabrous, zonate with whitish and pink to vinaceous zones, or sometimes more or less evenly vinaceous pink.

GILLS: decurrent, narrow, close, pale pinkish buff, becoming dingy brownish where bruised.

STALK: 1½–2⅜" long, ⅜–⅝" (1.0–1.5 cm) thick, narrowed toward the bottom, whitish canescent, with glabrous vinaceous spots, not discoloring appreciably with age.

FLESH: white, unchanging; odor not distinctive; taste astringent and disagreeable but not acrid.

LATEX: white on exposure, changing to yellow, not staining tissues; taste astringent and disagreeable but not acrid.

SPORE DEPOSIT: whitish to yellowish.

MACROCHEMICAL TESTS: flesh staining pinkish buff with the application of $FeSO_4$.

MICROSCOPIC CHARACTERS: spores 6.5–8.0 × 6–7 µm, ellipsoid, ornamented with warts and ridges that sometimes form a partial reticulum, prominences up to 0.8 µm high, hyaline, amyloid; cap cuticle a thick ixocutis.

OCCURRENCE: gregarious in a mixed conifer-hardwood forest; August; reported only from Amherst, Massachusetts; distribution limits and frequency yet to be determined.

EDIBILITY: unknown.

COMMENTS: *Lactarius subpurpureus* has a reddish pink to vinaceous pink zonate cap that becomes spotted with emerald green, whitish to pale pinkish flesh that tastes mild or slightly acrid, dark vinaceous red latex that tastes mild to faintly acrid, and larger spores that measure 8–11 × 6.5–8.0 µm.

Lactarius indigo var. **diminutivus** Hesler and A. H. Smith Illus. p. 88

North American Species of Lactarius (1979), 69–70

CAP: 1⅛–2" (3–5 cm) wide, convex to convex-depressed, becoming broadly funnel-shaped; surface viscid to slimy, glabrous, unpolished to velvety when dry, subzonate with zones appearing at maturity, dark blue when fresh, gray-blue with a silvery sheen when dry, becoming gray-green to olive-green with age, sometimes striate at the margin; margin inrolled at first.

GILLS: decurrent to long decurrent, broad, close, with several tiers of lamellulae, colored like the cap, becoming green with age, staining indigo when bruised, aging slowly to gray-green or olive.

STALK: ⅝–1" (1.5–2.5 cm) long, 3/16–7/16" (5–8 mm) thick, tapered downward, solid, becoming hollow with age, colored like the cap.

FLESH: white, quickly changing to dark blue, then to green after thirty minutes.

LATEX: copious, deep indigo blue, unchanging, staining tissues dark indigo; taste mild.

SPORE DEPOSIT: white.

MICROSCOPIC CHARACTERS: spores 7–9 × 6.0–7.5 µm, subglobose to broadly ellipsoid, ornamented with a broken to full reticulum of unconnected lines and warts, prominences up to 0.5 µm high, hyaline, amyloid; cap cuticle an ixocutis.

OCCURRENCE: scattered or in groups on the ground among grasses and weeds usually in pine woods; December and January; reported along the Gulf Coast from Florida to Texas; common.

EDIBILITY: unknown.

COMMENTS: *Lactarius indigo* var. *indigo*—reported from eastern Canada south to Florida and west to Michigan, Texas, and California—is similar, but its cap is a more robust 2–6" (5.0–15.5 cm) wide. It has a viscid, zonate to azonate cap that is dark blue, fading to grayish blue to grayish with a silvery luster, and a scant dark blue latex that slowly changes to dark green, and it grows on the ground under conifer or hardwoods. Also compare with *Lactarius paradoxus.*

Lactarius indigo var. **indigo** (Schweinitz) Fries Illus. p. 88, 89

Epicr. Syst. Mycol. (1838), 341

Indigo Milk Cap, Indigo Milky

CAP: 2–6" (5.0–15.5 cm) wide, convex to convex-depressed, becoming broadly funnel-shaped; margin inrolled at first; surface viscid, glabrous, zonate to nearly azonate, dark blue when fresh, fading to grayish blue to grayish with a silvery luster, often with dark green areas where bruised.

GILLS: attached to short-decurrent, broad, close, sometimes forked near the stalk, dark blue at first, becoming paler blue at maturity, developing yellowish tints with age, staining green when bruised.

STALK: ¾–3⅛" (2–8 cm) long, ⅜–1" (1.0–2.5 cm) thick, nearly equal or tapered downward, becoming hollow with age, viscid but soon dry, dark blue when young, paler blue when older, sometimes with a sheen, often scrobiculate.

FLESH: thick, firm, whitish, rapidly staining dark blue on exposure, then slowly becoming greenish; odor not distinctive; taste mild or rarely becoming slightly bitter then slightly acrid.

LATEX: scant, dark blue on exposure, slowly becoming dark green; taste mild.

SPORE DEPOSIT: creamy white.

MICROSCOPIC CHARACTERS: spores 7–9 × 5.5–7.5 µm, broadly ellipsoid to subglobose, ornamented with ridges that form a partial to complete reticulum, prominences up to 0.5 µm high, hyaline, amyloid; cap cuticle an ixocutis.

OCCURRENCE: solitary, scattered, or in groups on the ground among conifers or hardwoods; July–January; eastern Canada south to Florida, west to Michigan and Texas, also reported from California; fairly common in the southern part of its range, occasional northward.

EDIBILITY: edible.

COMMENTS: The name *indigo* refers to this mushroom's dark blue color. *Lactarius indigo* var. *diminutivus*, reported along the Gulf Coast from Florida to Texas, is similar but has a much smaller (1⅛–2" [3–5 cm] wide), viscid to slimy cap that is dark blue at first and soon becomes gray-blue then gray-green to olive-green with age, as well as copious, unchanging dark blue latex on exposure, and it grows on the ground, often among grasses and weeds, usually in pine woods. Also compare with *Lactarius paradoxus*.

Lactarius kauffmanii var. **kauffmanii** Hesler and A. H. Smith Illus. p. 90

North American Species of Lactarius (1979), 351–354

CAP: 2–7¾" (5–20 cm) wide, broadly convex, disc depressed; margin inrolled and minutely tomentose at first, becoming elevated with age; surface slimy-viscid, streaked under the slime, glabrous, azonate to obscurely zoned, blackish brown to grayish brown or vinaceous brown, becoming grayish to grayish vinaceous with age.

GILLS: attached to subdecurrent, narrow to broad, close, forked near the stalk, whitish to pale pinkish buff or pale ochraceous salmon, flushed pale pinkish cinnamon or having brown stains when older, staining olivaceous to grayish brown.

STALK: 2–4" (5–10 cm) long, ⅜–1⅛" (1–3 cm) thick, often thicker in the midportion, sometimes nearly equal or enlarged in either direction, slimy-viscid, distinctly to obscurely scrobiculate, varnished when dry, hollow, dingy whitish to pale vinaceous cinnamon or tan.

FLESH: thick, violaceous brown near the cuticle, pale pinkish brown near the gills; odor not distinctive; taste mild then acrid.

LATEX: white on exposure, unchanging, slowly staining gills olivaceous to grayish brown; taste acrid.

SPORE DEPOSIT: whitish.

MICROSCOPIC CHARACTERS: spores 7–10 × 6.5–8.0 µm, broadly ellipsoid, ornamented with a few isolated warts and elongated ridges that form a partial reticulum, prominences up to 1 µm high, hyaline, amyloid; cap cuticle an ixotrichoderm with a basal zone of narrow repent hyphae.

OCCURRENCE: on the ground in conifer woods; July–November; Alaska south to Idaho and California, east to Michigan and Wisconsin; common only in its western range.

EDIBILITY: unknown.

COMMENTS: The spore deposit color, latex color change, and staining reaction of injured tissues are all highly variable characters for this mushroom. *Lactarius kauffmanii* var. *sitchensis* Hesler and A. H. Smith (edibility unknown), reported only from Oregon, has a yellow spore deposit, white latex that does not stain tissues, and a dark brown cap that develops dingy yellow-brown tones, and it grows on the ground under Sitka spruce. *Lactarius caespitosus* is similar, but it has larger spores with a lower, less distinct, partial reticulum.

Lactarius lanceolatus O. K. Miller and Laursen

Illus. p. 90

Canad. J. Bot. 51 (1973), 43

CAP: 1–2⅛" (2.5–5.5 cm) wide, convex, becoming broadly convex to nearly plane with a slightly depressed center, sometimes with a small umbo; margin incurved at first and remaining so well into maturity, sometimes finely crenulate; surface slightly viscid or dry, glabrous, often becoming concentrically rimulose-areolate with age, brick red to orange-brown and glossy when young, becoming dull and brownish orange with age.

GILLS: attached to short-decurrent, moderately broad, close to subdistant, pinkish buff to tan at first, becoming light orange-brown at maturity.

STALK: 1–1½" (2.5–4.0 cm) long, ⅛–⅜" (3–10 mm) thick, nearly equal or enlarged slightly downward, dry, glabrous, hollow, light orange-brown.

FLESH: firm, white, not staining when cut; odor not distinctive; taste mild then slightly bitter.

LATEX: white or watery white on exposure, unchanging, not staining tissues; taste mild or slightly astringent to slightly bitter.

SPORE DEPOSIT: white.

MICROSCOPIC CHARACTERS: spores 7–11 × 5.5–8.0 µm, globose to subglobose, ornamented with warts and ridges that form a partial reticulum, prominences up to 1 µm high, hyaline, amyloid; macrocystidia numerous, fusiform; cap cuticle a trichoderm of interwoven refractive hyphae, 4–7 µm wide, with numerous pileocystidia.

OCCURRENCE: gregarious in tundra dominated by sedges and grasses; July–August; reported from Alaska; distribution limits and frequency yet to be determined.

EDIBILITY: unknown.

COMMENTS: The brick red to orange-brown cap colors, light orange-brown stalk, mild then slightly bitter flesh, large spores, and unusual habitat are this species' distinctive features.

Lactarius lanuginosus Burlingham

Not Illustrated

Mem. Torrey Bot. Club 14 (1908), 43
Lactaria lanuginosa Burlingham

CAP: 1⅝–4" (4–10 cm) wide, convex with a depressed disc, becoming broadly convex then funnel-shaped, with a small umbo; margin incurved at first, with a fine short tomentum, becoming decurved and glabrous at maturity; surface viscid, with a coarse white tomentum, zonate especially along the margin, whitish to yellowish.

GILLS: subdecurrent, narrow, close, sometimes forked, whitish to dingy yellowish or darker.

STALK: ¾–1½" (2–4 cm) long, ⅜–¾" (1.0–1.8 cm) thick, nearly equal or tapered downward, somewhat viscid or dry, stuffed or hollow, pubescent, white to dingy yellowish.

FLESH: white, unchanging when cut; odor described as strong.

LATEX: white on exposure, unchanging, not staining tissues; taste astringent to slightly acrid.

SPORE DEPOSIT: white.

MICROSCOPIC CHARACTERS: spores 5.5–7.5 × 4.5–5.5 µm, ellipsoid, ornamented with bands and lines that form a partial reticulum, prominences up to 0.5 µm, hyaline, amyloid; cap cuticle a thick ixocutis.

OCCURRENCE: on the ground under hardwood trees: August–September; reported only from North Carolina, distribution limits and frequency yet to be determined.

EDIBILITY: unknown.

COMMENTS: *Lactarius furcatus* is similar, but its latex changes to bluish green, and its gills are repeatedly forked. Another similar species, *Lactarius agglutinatus,* has a papillate-rugulose cap that is faintly zoned when young and azonate at maturity.

Lactarius lentus Coker — Not Illustrated

J. Elisha Mitchell Sci. Soc. 34 (1918), 56

CAP: 2⅛" (5.5 cm) wide, convex, becoming nearly plane with age; margin even; surface moist to dry, azonate, glabrous on the disc, rugose-areolate toward the margin, buffy ochraceous with white flesh showing in the cracks.

GILLS: narrowly attached, moderately broad, very distant, sometimes forked near the stalk, white, not staining when bruised.

STALK: 1⅛" (3 cm) long, ⅜" (1.1 cm) thick, tapered downward, solid, somewhat scurfy and cracked like the cap margin on the lower portion, whitish on the upper portion, buffy ochraceous toward the base.

FLESH: thin, firm, white, not staining when exposed; odor not distinctive; taste mild.

LATEX: white on exposure, unchanging, not staining tissues; taste mild.

SPORE DEPOSIT: white.

MICROSCOPIC CHARACTERS: spores 4.5–7.5 × 4–5 µm, elliptic to ovate, ornamented with small warts and faint ridges, prominences up to 0.3 µm high, hyaline, amyloid; cap cuticle an ixocutis.

OCCURRENCE: on soil in woods; June; reported from North Carolina; distribution limits and frequency yet to be established.

EDIBILITY: unknown.

COMMENTS: Coker based his description on a single specimen. *Lactarius pinckneyensis* is similar but has crowded gills. Other similar species include *Lactarius hygrophoroides, Lactarius allochrous,* and *Lactarius pervelutinus.*

Lactarius lepidotus Hesler and A. H. Smith — Not Illustrated

North American Species of Lactarius (1979), 408–409

CAP: ¾–1½" (2–4 cm) wide, convex, becoming nearly plane with a depressed center, sometimes with a tiny papilla in the depression; margin incurved at first, becoming uplifted and wavy at maturity; surface moist at first, becoming dry and finely cracked and scaly at maturity, azonate, pale brownish gray when young and moist, fading to pale pinkish gray with age.

GILLS: attached, narrow, close, pale grayish pink and darkening with age.

STALK: ¾–1⅛" (2–3 cm) long, ⅛–3⁄16" (2–4 mm) thick, nearly equal overall, fragile, glabrous or nearly so, pale grayish pink.

FLESH: colored like the cap, not staining on exposure; odor not distinctive; taste mild or slightly acrid.

LATEX: white on exposure, unchanging; taste mild or slightly acrid.

SPORE DEPOSIT: not stated in the original description.

MICROSCOPIC CHARACTERS: spores 7–9 × 5.5–6.0 µm, ellipsoid, ornamented with warts and ridges that sometimes form a partial reticulum, prominences up to 0.5 µm high, hyaline, amyloid; cap cuticle composed of repent hyphae that are sometimes inflated, the terminal elements cystidioid and often grouped to form squamules.

OCCURRENCE: on soil under alder; September; reported only from Mount Rainier National Park, Washington; distribution limits and frequency yet to be determined.

EDIBILITY: unknown.

COMMENTS: *Lactarius glyciosmus* is similar but has tiny matted fibers on its cap and slightly acrid flesh with a distinctly fragrant coconut odor.

Lactarius lignyotellus A. H. Smith and Hesler Illus. p. 90

Brittonia 14 (1962), 410

CAP: 1⅛–1½" (3–4 cm) wide, convex, becoming broadly convex with a depressed center or shallowly vase-shaped, often with a central conic papillate umbo; margin subplicate at maturity; surface dry, velvety, azonate, radiately rugulose, medium brown to blackish brown or dark brownish black.

GILLS: attached to short-decurrent, narrow, subdistant or distant, rarely forked, whitish when young, becoming pale cream when older, with dark dull brown edges.

STALK: 1½–2¾" (4–7 cm) long, 3⁄16–⅛" (4–9 mm) thick, nearly equal, dry, velvety, plicate at the apex, colored like the cap or paler.

FLESH: thin, white; odor not distinctive; taste mild.

LATEX: white on exposure, unchanging, not staining tissues; taste mild.

SPORE DEPOSIT: pale cream.

MICROSCOPIC CHARACTERS: spores 9.5–12.0 × 9.5–11.0 µm, globose, ornamented with rods and spines connected by fine lines that form an inconspicuous partial reticulum, prominences up to 2 µm high, hyaline, amyloid; cap cuticle a trichoderm.

OCCURRENCE: on soil in spruce woods; August; reported from Clingmans Dome, Great Smoky Mountains National Park, North Carolina, and from West Virginia; distribution limits and frequency yet to be determined.

EDIBILITY: unknown.

COMMENTS: *Lactarius texensis* is very similar, but it has darker gills and spore ornamentation that forms a more conspicuous partial reticulum, and its cap cuticle consists of a poorly formed hymeniform layer of clavate to odd-shaped cells. *Lactarius fallax* and *Lactarius lignyotus* varieties are also similar, but their latex stains injured tissues. *Lactarius gerardii* varieties have two to three layers of cells in their cap cuticles.

Lactarius lignyotus var. **canadensis** A. H. Smith and Hesler Illus. p. 91

Brittonia 14 (1962), 398
Lactarius lignyotus var. *parvulus* A. H. Smith and Hesler, *Brittonia* 14 (1962), 401
Lactarius lignyotus var. *insignis* A. H. Smith and Hesler, *Brittonia* 14 (1962), 399
Lactarius gracilentus A. H. Smith and Hesler, *Brittonia* 14 (1962), 412

CAP: 1⅛–3½" (3–9 cm) wide, convex becoming depressed with an arched margin and finally funnel-shaped, with a small pointed umbo when young and retaining the umbo into maturity; surface dry, velvety, often wrinkled around the center, azonate, blackish brown fading to dark or pale yellowish brown; margin sulcate to lobed at maturity.

GILLS: adnate to short decurrent, broad, subdistant, progressing to distant at maturity, white becoming pale ochraceous tan, edges dark brown at first and fading as the gills mature.

STALK: 2⅜–4¾" (6–12 cm) long, ¼–½" (6–12 mm) thick, nearly equal, solid, with distinct longitudinal ridges near the apex at times, dry, colored like the cap.

FLESH: white, staining pinkish where cut; no odor or very slight brown sugar odor; taste mild.

LATEX: white, staining broken surfaces pink, drying vinaceous brown; taste mild.

SPORE DEPOSIT: pinkish buff.

MACROCHEMICAL TESTS: flesh slowly staining pinkish with $FeSO_4$, no reaction in KOH.

MICROSCOPIC CHARACTERS: spores 9.5–12.0 × 9.0–10.5 µm, 7–9 µm excluding ornamentation, subglobose, ornamented with strongly amyloid bands forming a partial reticulum that is littered with fine lines, large warts, and spines, wall nonamyloid, prominences up to 2.4 µm high; cap cuticle a staggered layer of short chains of flask-shaped cells, with a basal layer of scattered inflated cells not arranged into a subcutis.

OCCURRENCE: scattered or in groups on sphagnum bogs with spruce; July–October; widely distributed in the northern United States and in Canada; fairly common.

EDIBILITY: unknown.

COMMENTS: *Lactarius lignyotus* var. *lignyotus*—reported from eastern North America, the Pacific Northwest, and California—is almost identical, but it has close to subdistant gills that are white with white edges and mild to slightly bitter-tasting white latex that is unchanging and stains the gills reddish, and it grows on the ground among mosses under conifers, in hardwoods with oak, or in bogs.

Lactarius lignyotus var. **lignyotus** Fries Illus. p. 91

Monogr. Hymen. Suec. 2 (1863), 177
Chocolate Milky

CAP: ¾–4" (2–10 cm) wide, convex with an incurved margin and a small pointed umbo when young, becoming nearly plane or with a depressed disc and retaining the umbo; surface velvety, dry, usually wrinkled, azonate, blackish brown, slowly fading to dingy yellow-brown with age; margin sulcate to plicate.

GILLS: attached to somewhat decurrent, close to subdistant, white, slowly becoming pale ochraceous.

STALK: 2–4½" (5–11 cm) long, ¼–½" (5–13 mm) thick, enlarged downward or nearly equal, solid, with distinct longitudinal ridges at the apex, dry, velvety, blackish brown to pale yellow-brown with a white base.

FLESH: white, staining rosy pink to dull reddish when cut; odor not distinctive; taste mild or slightly bitter, not acrid.

LATEX: copious, white on exposure, unchanging, staining gills reddish; taste mild to slightly bitter, not acrid.

SPORE DEPOSIT: bright ochre.

MICROSCOPIC CHARACTERS: spores 9–11 × 9–10 µm, nearly globose, ornamented with warts and ridges that form a partial reticulum, prominences up to 1.5 µm high, hyaline, amyloid; cap cuticle a trichoderm.

OCCURRENCE: scattered or in groups on the ground and among mosses under conifers, among hardwoods with oak, or in bogs; August–October; widely distributed in eastern North America, also reported from the Pacific Northwest and California; fairly common.

EDIBILITY: unknown.

COMMENTS: *Lactarius lignyotus* var. *canadensis,* reported from eastern Canada and New England west to Michigan, has subdistant gills that are white with dark brown edges at first but become distant and pale ochraceous tan with age, as well as mild-tasting, white, and unchanging latex that stains tissues reddish and dries vinaceous brown, and it grows on sphagnum mosses under spruce in bogs. *Lactarius lignyotus* var. *nigroviolascens*—reported from Maine, Michigan, New Hampshire, and New York—has white latex that slowly changes to dark violet on exposure, stains tissues dark violet, and tastes pungent but not acrid, and it grows in conifer bogs, swamps, or forests on humus or among sphagnum mosses. *Lactarius lignyotus* var. *marginatus* (A. H. Smith and Hesler) Hesler and A. H. Smith (edibility unknown), reported only from Maine and Michigan, is nearly identical to the *nigroviolascens* variety but has dark brown gill edges and white latex that changes to dark violet and stains tissues dark violet. Also compare with *Lactarius lignyotellus* and *Lactarius texensis.*

Lactarius lignyotus var. **nigroviolascens** Hesler and A. H. Smith Illus. p. 91

North American Species of Lactarius (1979), 131–134
Lactarius nigroviolascens Atk. in Burl., *Mycologia* 24 (1932), 461

CAP: 1⅛–3⅞" (3–10 cm) wide, broadly convex, depressed then expanding to plano-depressed or shallowly funnel-shaped, usually with an umbo; surface wrinkled, velvety, dry, azonate, blackish brown to dark yellow-brown, fading to pale dingy yellow-brown with age; margin even when young, becoming short striate or crenate with age.

GILLS: adnate and becoming short decurrent with age, distant to subdistant, white changing to ochraceous, then cinnamon buff with age, edges colored like the face.

STALK: 3½–3⅞" (3–10 cm) long, ⅛–⅝ (4–15 mm) thick, equal or nearly so, often with distant longitudinal ridges at the apex, dry, colored like the cap or paler, whitish at the base.

FLESH: white, staining dark violet; odor pungent; taste mild.

LATEX: scant to abundant, white, slowly changing to dark violet and staining tissues dark violet; taste pungent, not acrid.

SPORE DEPOSIT: warm buff to yellow.

MICROSCOPIC CHARACTERS: spores 7–11 × 7–9 µm, globose to subglobose, ornamented with warts and irregular coarse ridges and fines lines that form a partial to complete reticulum, prominences up to 3 µm high, hyaline, amyloid; cap cuticle composed of brown irregular flask-shaped cells, with paler pileocystidia forming a palisade-like turf.

OCCURRENCE: solitary or in groups on the ground or among sphagnum mosses in conifer swamps; August–October; reported from Maine, New Hampshire, New York, and Michigan; rare.

EDIBILITY: unknown.

COMMENTS: This species' defining characteristics are a white latex that slowly changes to dark violet on exposure, stains tissues dark violet, and tastes pungent but not acrid, as well as growth in conifer bogs, swamps, or forests on humus or among sphagnum mosses. *Lactarius lignyotus* var. *marginatus* (A. H. Smith and Hesler) Hesler and A. H. Smith (edibility unknown), reported only from Maine and Michigan, is nearly identical but has dark brown gill edges.

Lactarius limacinus Beardslee and Burlingham Not Illustrated

Mycologia 32 (1940), 579
Lactaria limacina Beardslee and Burlingham
Lactaria praeviscida Murrill

CAP: 3⅛–4¾" (8–12 cm) wide, convex with a depressed disc, becoming broadly funnel-shaped; margin with a tangled tomentum and projecting fibrils when young, soon glabrous; surface slimy-viscid, glabrous, dingy white at first, soon darkening to yellowish brown to dull fulvous, sometimes streaked rusty brown.

GILLS: subdecurrent, narrow, close to subdistant, whitish when young, becoming dull cinnamon at maturity.

STALK: ⅝–1¼" (1.5–3.0 cm) long, ⅜–¾" (1–2 cm) thick, slimy, rarely scrobiculate, whitish at first, becoming colored like the cap with age.

FLESH: whitish to buff or tinged the same color as the cap; odor not distinctive; taste astringent then slowly acrid.

LATEX: white on exposure, unchanging; taste slowly acrid.

SPORE DEPOSIT: cream.

MICROSCOPIC CHARACTERS: spores 9–11 × 7.0–8.5 µm, broadly ellipsoid, ornamented with isolated warts and short ridges that form a partial reticulum, prominences up to 1.5 µm high, hyaline, amyloid; cap cuticle a thick ixolattice.

OCCURRENCE: on ground under live oak; December; reported only from Florida; distribution limits and frequency yet to be determined.

EDIBILITY: unknown.

COMMENTS: The slimy-viscid, dingy white cap that soon darkens to yellowish brown or dull fulvous, slimy stalk, whitish flesh that tastes astringent then slowly acrid, and growth on the ground under oak are this species' distinctive features.

Lactarius louisii Homola Illus. p. 92

Mycotaxon 3 (3) (1976), 331–336

CAP: ¾–1⅜" (2.0–3.5 cm) wide, convex with a distinct umbo, becoming nearly plane, sometimes with a depressed center, usually retaining a conspicuous umbo; margin incurved then arched, becoming crenate and wavy with age; surface moist, subpruinose, distinctly rugose-venose especially in the center, plicate-striate toward the margin, azonate, dark brown when young, becoming olive-brown to olive at maturity, often slightly mottled with dingy yellow over the disc.

GILLS: attached to distinctly decurrent, moderately broad, subdistant to distant, cream to light yellow.

STALK: ⅝–1¼" (1.5–3.0 cm) long, ⅛–¼" (3–7 mm) thick, nearly equal down to a pointed base, often curved and twisted, dry, subpruinose, becoming hollow with age, apex honey yellow, becoming olive-brown then dark brown downward, often with a white basal mycelium.

FLESH: very brittle, thin, cream to light yellow, unchanging when cut, odor not distinctive; taste bitter or metallic but not acrid.

LATEX: scant, watery on exposure, unchanging, not staining tissues; taste not stated in the original description.

SPORE DEPOSIT: white.

MACROCHEMICAL TESTS: flesh negative with the application of KOH.

MICROSCOPIC CHARACTERS: spores 6–8 × 5.5–6.5 µm, subglobose to ellipsoid, ornamented with low warts, ridges, and fine lines that form a partial reticulum, prominences up to 0.5 µm high, hyaline, amyloid; cap cuticle a layer of inflated cells, often with clavate to fusoid apical cells that form a turf.

OCCURRENCE: scattered to gregarious on buried wood or among sphagnum in wet areas of deciduous woods that are predominantly oak and maple; August; reported from Pennsylvania; distribution and frequency yet to be determined.

EDIBILITY: unknown.

COMMENTS: This species was named by Richard Homola to honor his father, Louis Homola. *Lactarius xanthydrorheus,* reported from Florida west along the Gulf Coastal Plain to Texas, is similar, but it has watery latex that instantly changes to yellow on exposure and mild-tasting flesh.

Lactarius luculentus var. **laetus** Hesler and A. H. Smith Illus. p. 92

North American Species of Lactarius (1979), 456–457

CAP: 1⅛–2⅜" (3–6 cm) wide, broadly convex to plane, becoming broadly depressed with age, having a small umbo at times; surface smooth, slightly viscid when wet, soon dry, azonate, sometimes with water spots, brilliant orange, paler at the margin.

GILLS: crowded, narrow, with three to four tiers of lamellulae present, pale reddish clay color, sometimes slowly staining brownish.

STALK: 1⅝–2" (4–5 cm) long, 3⁄16–½" (5–7 mm) thick, equal or enlarged downward, hollow, firm, soon fragile, surface smooth, colored like the gills or cap.

FLESH: thin, firm, pallid to pale yellow; odor not distinctive; taste mild, slowly becoming bitter.

LATEX: white, copious, unchanging, slowly staining gills brownish; taste mild, slowly becoming bitter.

SPORE DEPOSIT: unknown.

MICROSCOPIC CHARACTERS: spores 8–10 × 7.0–8.5 µm, broadly ellipsoid, ornamented with a few prominent bands that have Y branching and with isolated warts and ridges that do not form a reticulum, prominences from 0.4 to 0.7 µm high, hyaline, amyloid; cap cuticle a well-developed to shortened, lax trichoderm showing slime.

OCCURRENCE: in groups on the ground under conifers and alders; September; reported from Washington south to California and Colorado; fairly common.

EDIBILITY: unknown.

COMMENTS: This species is more generally encountered than *Lactarius luculentus* var. *luculentus,* which is similar, but its flesh has a slightly bitter taste that slowly turns acrid, and it differs microscopically.

Lactarius luculentus var. **luculentus** Burlingham Illus. p. 93

Mycologia 28 (1936), 260
Lactaria luculenta Burlingham

CAP: 1–3" (2.5–7.5 cm) wide, broadly convex to nearly plane, depressed over the disc, sometimes with a small umbo; margin even; surface subviscid to viscid, glabrous, azonate, ochraceous tawny when moist, becoming ochraceous buff to tawny or reddish cinnamon.

GILLS: attached to decurrent, narrow, close, pale tawny, not staining when bruised.

STALK: ¾–2" (2–5 cm) long, ¼–⅝" (7–15 mm) thick, slightly viscid, hollow, colored like the cap.

FLESH: firm; odor not distinctive; taste of mature specimens slightly bitter then slowly acrid.

LATEX: white on exposure, unchanging; taste mild to somewhat astringent and stinging the tongue.

SPORE DEPOSIT: buff-colored.

MICROSCOPIC CHARACTERS: spores 7.5–9.0 × 6.0–7.5 µm, broadly ellipsoid, ornamented with isolated warts and ridges that form a partial reticulum, prominences up to 0.3 µm high, hyaline, amyloid; cap cuticle an ixotrichoderm collapsing to an ixolattice.

OCCURRENCE: on the ground under Douglas fir; September–November; reported from Alaska, Oregon, and Colorado; distribution limits and frequency yet to be determined.

EDIBILITY: unknown.

COMMENTS: *Lactarius subflammeus* is similar, but it has a brownish red to reddish brown cap, a brownish orange to light brown stalk, slightly acrid-tasting latex, and a white spore deposit. *Lactarius luculentus* var. *laetus*, reported from Washington south to California and Colorado, is also similar, but it has a brownish orange to light brown or reddish brown disc and an orange margin, a light orange to grayish orange stalk, and mild-tasting latex that slowly becomes bitter. Also compare with *Lactarius substriatus*, which has white latex that slowly changes to yellow, and *Lactarius desjardinii*, which has a white to pale yellow spore deposit and acrid-tasting latex.

Lactarius luteocanus Hesler and A. H. Smith Not Illustrated

North American Species of Lactarius (1979), 250–251

CAP: ¾–2" (2–5 cm) wide, convex, becoming broadly convex with a depressed center; margin incurved at first, becoming decurved, faintly pubescent at first; surface viscid when fresh, glabrous or nearly so, azonate to faintly zonate, dull white becoming more or less pinkish buff or in some areas cinnamon buff.

GILLS: subdecurrent, narrow, close, white but soon spotting pale cinnamon, becoming pinkish buff with tan spots when older.

STALK: ¾–2⅜" (2–6 cm) long, ¼–⅝" (6–14 mm) thick, nearly equal or tapered downward, fragile, dry, shiny, becoming hollow with age, white, becoming whitish to yellowish at maturity.

FLESH: firm, white; odor not distinctive; taste acrid to burning acrid.

LATEX: milk white on exposure, unchanging; taste acrid to burning acrid.

SPORE DEPOSIT: white.

MACROCHEMICAL TESTS: cap surface and gills staining yellow with the application of 30 percent KOH.

MICROSCOPIC CHARACTERS: spores 7.5–9.0 × 6.5–7.5 µm, broadly ellipsoid to subglobose, ornamented with warts and ridges that form a partial to nearly complete reticulum, prominences up to 0.5 µm high, hyaline, amyloid; macrocystidia numerous, conspicuously projecting; cap cuticle an ixocutis.

OCCURRENCE: gregarious on rich, wet humus along small streams in hardwood forests; September; reported only from the Highlands Recreation Area near Pontiac, Michigan; distribution limits and frequency yet to be determined.

EDIBILITY: unknown.

COMMENTS: *Lactarius zonarius* var. *riparius* is similar, but it has a pinkish buff spore deposit and lacks macrocystidia.

Lactarius luteolus Peck

Illus. p. 94

Bull. Torrey Bot. Club 23 (1896), 412
Lactaria praeseriflua Murrill
Lactarius foetidus Peck
Buff Fishy Milky

CAP: 1–3⅛" (2.5–8.0 cm) wide, convex to nearly plane, often shallowly depressed when older; surface dry, slightly velvety, azonate, whitish to buff with a white bloom, becoming brownish with age.

GILLS: attached to slightly decurrent, close, white then cream, staining yellow-brown to brown.

STALK: 1–2⅜" (2.5–6.0 cm) long, ¼–¾" (6–20 mm) thick, tapered downward or nearly equal, solid to stuffed, dry, slightly velvety, whitish to buff, staining brown.

FLESH: white, staining brown; odor not distinctive in young specimens, but soon becoming fishy or unpleasant and resembling spoiled crab; taste mild.

LATEX: copious, sticky, watery white to white on exposure, unchanging, staining gills brown; taste mild.

SPORE DEPOSIT: white to cream.

MACROCHEMICAL TESTS: flesh staining bluish olive with the application of $FeSO_4$ and slightly orange-buff with KOH.

MICROSCOPIC CHARACTERS: spores 7–9 × 5.5–7.0 µm, elliptic, ornamented with warts and ridges that sometimes form a partial reticulum, prominences up to 0.8 µm high, hyaline, amyloid; cap cuticle cellular, bearing a turf of filamentous to capitate pileocystidia.

OCCURRENCE: solitary, scattered, or in groups on the ground in hardwoods or mixed woods, usually with oak present; June–November; eastern Canada south to Florida, west to Michigan and Texas; fairly common.

EDIBILITY: edible.

COMMENTS: The slightly velvety whitish cap, copious sticky latex that stains tissues brown, the strong fishy to spoiled crab–like odor of mature specimens' flesh, and the small spores are this species' distinctive features.

Lactarius mackinawensis Hesler and A. H. Smith

Not Illustrated

North American Species of Lactarius (1979), 346–347

CAP: 1⅛–5⅞" (5–15 cm) wide, convex and shallowly depressed at first, becoming broadly funnel-shaped with age; margin incurved and minutely pubescent; surface slimy-viscid when wet but soon dry, glabrous, light violet-gray with cinnamon brown zones or spots, fading and becoming azonate; margin pinkish buff.

GILLS: decurrent, narrow, close, pinkish buff to yellowish, not staining, darker where bruised.

STALK: 1½–3⅛" (4–8 cm) long, ⅜–1" (1.0–2.5 cm) thick, nearly equal, viscid when wet but soon dry, stuffed or hollow, violaceous-gray mottled with cinnamon buff.

FLESH: hard, rigid, pale pinkish tan to whitish; odor not distinctive; taste acrid.

LATEX: abundant, pinkish buff on exposure, unchanging or sometimes drying olivaceous, not staining tissues or sometimes staining them slightly ochraceous; taste acrid.

SPORE DEPOSIT: pale yellow.

MICROSCOPIC CHARACTERS: spores 8–12 × 7.5–9.0 µm, broadly ellipsoid, ornamented with nodulose ridges and isolated warts that do not form a reticulum, prominences up to 1 µm high, hyaline, amyloid; cap cuticle an ixotrichoderm, becoming an ixolattice, finally with the appearance of an ixocutis (old caps).

OCCURRENCE: on the ground in mixed woods and edges of sphagnum bogs; July–September; Michigan and eastern Canada; distribution limits and frequency yet to be determined.

EDIBILITY: unknown.

COMMENTS: *Lactarius trivialis* has similar coloring, but it has white latex.

Lactarius maculatipes Burlingham Illus. p. 94, 95

Mycologia 35 (1942), 8

Lactaria maculatipes Burlingham

CAP: 2–3½" (5–9 cm) wide, broadly convex, becoming nearly plane with a depressed center, often becoming broadly funnel-shaped with age; margin incurved at first, becoming expanded and uplifted; surface glabrous, slimy and sticky when fresh, whitish to cream overall, becoming tawny on the disc when older, with pale yellow zones and spots that darken with age.

GILLS: decurrent, narrow, crowded, sometimes forked, whitish, becoming pinkish buff, staining yellowish to pale ochre when cut or bruised.

STALK: 1¼–3⅛" (3–8 cm) long, ⅜–1" (1.0–2.5 cm) thick, tapering downward, slimy, colored like the cap, spotted and streaked with darker tan, staining yellow when bruised or with age, scrobiculate.

FLESH: white, slowly staining yellowish on exposure; odor not distinctive; taste slowly acrid.

LATEX: white on exposure, unchanging, staining gills and flesh yellowish; taste slowly acrid.

SPORE DEPOSIT: pinkish buff to yellowish.

MICROSCOPIC CHARACTERS: spores 6.5–8.0 × 6.0–7.5 µm, subglobose to broadly ellipsoid, ornamented with warts and ridges that sometimes form a partial reticulum, prominences up to 1 µm high, hyaline, amyloid; cap cuticle a distinct thick ixocutis.

OCCURRENCE: scattered or in groups on the ground under oak, July–January; West Virginia, North Carolina, and Tennessee south to Florida, west to Texas, also reported from Michigan and Minnesota; fairly common in the southern part of its range.

EDIBILITY: unknown.

COMMENTS: *Lactarius dunfordii,* reported only from Tennessee, is very similar, but it has white latex that does not stain the gills and flesh, lacks spots on the stalk, and grows on the ground under pine. *Lactarius carolinensis* is similar but has a tan cap with darker yellowish brown zones, white flesh with a faintly alkaline odor, and a white spore deposit.

Lactarius maculatus Peck Illus. p. 95, 96

Ann. Rep. N.Y. State Mus. 41 (1888), 74
Lactarius uvidus var. *magnus* Peck

CAP: 3½–7" (9–18 cm) wide, convex when young, becoming centrally depressed then broadly funnel-shaped at maturity; surface glabrous, sticky when fresh, concentrically spotted and zonate, especially toward the margin, grayish buff to dull grayish lilac, brownish lilac, or brownish gray.

GILLS: attached to decurrent, narrow, close, sometimes forked, whitish to creamy white then becoming darker with age, staining dull lilac when bruised, sometimes forked.

STALK: 2–4¾" (5–12 cm) long, ¾–1½" (2–4 cm) thick, nearly equal, scrobiculate, colored like the cap or paler, glabrous but not sticky, becoming hollow with age.

FLESH: pale grayish, staining dull lilac on exposure; odor not distinctive; taste weakly to distinctly acrid.

LATEX: whitish to creamy white on exposure, unchanging, staining tissues dull lilac; taste weakly to distinctly acrid.

SPORE DEPOSIT: white.

MICROSCOPIC CHARACTERS: spores 9–12 × 7.0–10.5 µm, broadly ellipsoid, ornamented with isolated warts and ridges that do not form a reticulum, prominences up to 2 µm high, hyaline, amyloid; cap cuticle an ixocutis.

OCCURRENCE: solitary, scattered, or in groups on the ground around hardwoods and mixed woods; August–October; eastern Canada south to Tennessee, west to Minnesota; infrequent.

EDIBILITY: unknown.

COMMENTS: *Lactarius subpalustris* is similar, but its cap is not concentrically spotted and zonate, and its flesh and latex taste mild. *Lactarius uvidus* var. *uvidus* is also similar, but it typically has an azonate cap, and its flesh tastes mild then slowly bitter. *Lactarius maculosus* has a pinkish brown to pale grayish brown cap and mild-tasting white latex that becomes slightly yellow on exposure and does not stain tissues.

Lactarius maculosus Murrill Not Illustrated

Mycologia 8 (1916), 193
Lactaria maculosa Murrill

CAP: up to 4" (10 cm) wide, convex, becoming broadly convex to nearly plane with a depressed center; margin incurved at first, becoming decurved and remaining so well into maturity; surface somewhat viscid when fresh, glabrous, azonate, sometimes spotted, pinkish brown to pale grayish brown.

GILLS: attached, narrow, close to crowded, dull whitish to pale pinkish tan, not staining when bruised.

STALK: 2" (5 cm) long, ¾" (2 cm) thick, sharply tapered downward, dry, becoming hollow with age, glabrous, colored like the cap but paler, with more white intermixed; flesh white except at the base, where it is lilac-tinted.

FLESH: thick, white, not staining when exposed; odor not distinctive; taste mild.

LATEX: white on exposure, becoming slightly yellow, not staining tissues; taste mild.

SPORE DEPOSIT: not stated in the original description.

MICROSCOPIC CHARACTERS: spores 9–12 × 7.5–11.0 µm, subglobose to broadly ellipsoid, ornamented with ridges that sometimes form a partial reticulum, prominences up to 2.5 µm high, hyaline, amyloid; cap cuticle an ixolattice to ixocutis.

OCCURRENCE: on soil in woods; September; reported only from New York; distribution limits and frequency yet to be determined.

EDIBILITY: unknown.

COMMENTS: *Lactarius subpalustris* is similar, and its latex tastes mild, but the latex stains tissues lilac. *Lactarius maculatus* is also similar, but it has whitish, unchanging latex that stains tissues dull lilac and tastes weakly to distinctly acrid. *Lactarius uvidus* var. *uvidus* has white latex that becomes dingy pale cream on exposure and stains tissues dull lilac.

Lactarius manzanitae Methven

Illus. p. 96

Mycologia 77 (1985), 475–476

CAP: ¾–2" (2–5 cm) wide, convex to nearly plane; margin incurved at first, becoming decurved, minutely pubescent then glabrous; surface viscid, glabrous, azonate, orange to brownish orange or brown with a distinctly paler margin.

GILLS: attached to subdecurrent, narrow, close to subdistant, forked near the stalk, pale orange, not staining when bruised.

STALK: ⅝–1" (1.5–2.5 cm) long, 3⁄16–5⁄16" (4–8 mm) thick, nearly equal or tapered downward, dry to moist, glabrous, stuffed or hollow, streaked, light orange.

FLESH: thin, pale orange, not staining when cut; odor not distinctive; taste slowly acrid.

LATEX: white on exposure, unchanging; taste strongly acrid.

SPORE DEPOSIT: white.

MICROSCOPIC CHARACTERS: spores 6–7 × 5.5–6.5 µm, subglobose to broadly ellipsoid, ornamented with isolated warts and ridges that form a partial reticulum, prominences up to 0.6 µm high, hyaline, amyloid; cap cuticle an ixotrichoderm to an ixolattice with a thick layer of interwoven hyphae below.

OCCURRENCE: scattered to gregarious in duff and in coastal mixed conifer and hardwood forests in association with manzanita; November–December; California; uncommon.

EDIBILITY: unknown.

COMMENTS: *Lactarius hysginus* var. *americanus* Hesler and A. H. Smith (edibility unknown)is similar but is more robust and has a dark vinaceous-brown cap and pale yellow to dull cinnamon gills.

Lactarius midlandensis Hesler and A. H. Smith

Not Illustrated

North American Species of Lactarius (1979), 422–423

CAP: 2–4¾" (5–12 cm) wide, depressed at first, becoming deeply depressed to broadly funnel-shaped; margin arched and inrolled when young and remaining so well into maturity; surface viscid, glabrous, azonate or with a few faint zones near the disc, pale pinkish cinnamon over the disc, fading to pale pinkish buff near the margin.

GILLS: decurrent, narrow, moderately close, sometimes forked near the stalk, whitish at first, becoming dull yellowish, staining olive-gray when bruised.

STALK: 2⅜–3½" (6–9 cm) long, ⅜–1⅛" (1–3 cm) thick, nearly equal, sometimes with a pinched base, viscid when fresh, sometimes scrobiculate, colored like the gills.

FLESH: thick, firm, whitish to pale pinkish buff; odor not distinctive; taste slowly and slightly acrid.

LATEX: milk white on exposure, drying pale olive-gray, staining the gills pale olive-gray; taste slowly and slightly acrid.

SPORE DEPOSIT: pinkish buff.

MICROSCOPIC CHARACTERS: spores 7.5–9.0 × 6–7 µm, ellipsoid, ornamented with warts and ridges that form a partial to complete reticulum, prominences up to 0.5 µm high, hyaline, amyloid; cap cuticle an ixolattice.

OCCURRENCE: scattered on the ground under pine; September; reported from Michigan and eastern Canada; distribution limits and frequency yet to be determined.

EDIBILITY: unknown.

COMMENTS: Compare with *Lactarius affinis* var. *viridilactis,* a variety with which it probably should be place in synonymy. Also compare with *Lactarius pseudoaffinis.*

Lactarius minusculus Burlingham Illus. p. 97

Bull. Torrey Bot. Club 34 (1907), 88

CAP: ⅜–1⅛" (1–3 cm) wide, broadly convex, with a small umbo, becoming nearly plane and shallowly depressed; margin minutely scalloped, substriate, pruinose when young; surface viscid, glabrous, sometimes shining, azonate, fulvous to cinnamon fulvous with a cream-colored margin.

GILLS: attached to decurrent, broad, close, seldom forked, whitish, not staining.

STALK: 1" (2.5 cm) long, about ⅛" (3–4 mm) thick, nearly equal, dry, glabrous, becoming hollow with age, slightly paler than the cap.

FLESH: thin, fragile, white to pinkish cinnamon, not staining; taste acrid.

LATEX: white on exposure, unchanging, not staining tissues; taste acrid.

SPORE DEPOSIT: white.

MICROSCOPIC CHARACTERS: spores 7–8 × 6–7 µm, broadly ellipsoid to subglobose; ornamented with a few isolated warts and ridges that form a partial reticulum, prominences up to 0.5 µm high, hyaline, amyloid; cap cuticle a short lax ixotrichoderm to an ixolattice.

OCCURRENCE: among mosses or on decaying wood in moist woods; July; reported only from New England; distribution limits and frequency yet to be determined.

EDIBILITY: unknown.

COMMENTS: *Lactarius duplicatus* is similar, but it is a much larger species with white to whey-like latex that slowly changes to bright yellow.

Lactarius mordax Thiers Not Illustrated

Mycologia 49 (1957), 710

CAP: 2⅜–5" (6.0–12.5 cm) wide, convex to nearly plane and shallowly depressed, sometimes becoming deeply depressed and funnel-shaped; margin inrolled and appearing somewhat matted-tomentose when young, becoming decurved to nearly plane and glabrous at maturity; surface dry, dull, tomentose, becoming rimose to areolate-scaly with age, azonate, pale yellow to tan when young, becoming ivory to cream with light brown spots when older.

GILLS: subdecurrent, close to crowded, sometimes forked near the stalk and partway to the margin, white when young, becoming pale ochraceous buff to pale pinkish buff, staining yellowish at first, then lavender, and finally yellow-brown.

STALK: 1⅛–2⅜" (3–6 cm) long, ¾–1⅛" (2–3 cm) thick, nearly equal or tapered downward, base sometimes bulbous, dry, glabrous, stuffed or hollow, white when young, becoming ivory to tan with age, sometimes staining yellow when bruised.

FLESH: thick, white, staining lavender to pale brown; odor not distinctive or sometimes spermatic; taste acrid.

LATEX: abundant, white on exposure, unchanging, staining tissues lavender to pale brown; taste very acrid.

SPORE DEPOSIT: not obtained.

MICROSCOPIC CHARACTERS: spores 7.5–9.0 × 6–7 µm, ellipsoid, ornamented with isolated warts, crests, and bands that do not form a reticulum, prominences up to 0.5 µm high, hyaline, amyloid; cap cuticle a layer of appressed interwoven narrow hyphae with a loose tangle of similar hyphae above.

OCCURRENCE: gregarious in humus under pine in mixed woods; May; reported only from Navasota, Texas; distribution limits and frequency yet to be determined.

EDIBILITY: unknown.

COMMENTS: The dry pale yellow to cream-colored cap that becomes rimose to areolate-scaly with age, dry white to tan stalk, white flesh that stains lavender to pale brown, acrid white latex, and association with pine are in combination this species' distinctive features.

Lactarius moschatus Hesler and A. H. Smith — Not Illustrated

North American Species of Lactarius (1979), 461

CAP: 1⅛–1½" (3–4 cm) wide, broadly convex to plane with a slightly depressed center; margin even; surface somewhat viscid then soon dry, faintly zonate, pinkish tan.

GILLS: attached to subdecurrent, narrow, close, colored like the cap but darker, not staining when bruised.

STALK: ⅝–¾" (1.6–2.0 cm) long, ¼–5⁄16" (5–8 mm) thick, tapered slightly downward, dry, solid, whitish with a pinkish tint.

FLESH: white or whitish; odor not distinctive; taste musky.

LATEX: watery to watery white on exposure, unchanging, not staining the gills.

SPORE DEPOSIT: whitish.

MICROSCOPIC CHARACTERS: spores 6–8 × 5.5–6.5 µm, ellipsoid, ornamented with warts and ridges that form a partial reticulum, prominences up to 0.8 µm high, hyaline, amyloid; cap cuticle an ixocutis.

OCCURRENCE: on soil among humus in pine and mixed woods; November; reported only from Brazoria County, Texas; distribution limits and frequency yet to be determined.

EDIBILITY: unknown.

COMMENTS: *Lactarius chrysorrheus* is similar, but its latex quickly changes to yellow, and its flesh lacks the musky taste.

Lactarius mucidus var. **fuscogriseus** Hesler and A. H. Smith — Illus. p. 97

North American Species of Lactarius (1979), 361–362

CAP: 1½–3⅞" (4–10 cm) wide, broadly convex to nearly plane, becoming vase-shaped with age; surface slimy-viscid at first, appearing varnished when dry, azonate to subzonate, dark fuscous gray, becoming somewhat ash gray with age; margin incurved when young, paler than the disk.

GILLS: decurrent, close, narrow, pale vinaceous fawn, turning slightly darker with age, spotted grayish cinnamon buff from latex.

STALK: 1⅛–2⅜" (3–6 cm) long, ⅜–1" (10–25 mm) thick, hollow, viscid but soon dry, colored like the gills, with some spotting.

FLESH: pale vinaceous buff; odor not distinctive; taste mild to slightly acrid.

LATEX: white, slowly drying yellowish and spotting the gills grayish cinnamon buff; taste mild to slightly acrid.

SPORE DEPOSIT: pale pinkish buff to yellowish.

MICROSCOPIC CHARACTERS: spores 7.5–9.0 × 6.0–7.5 µm, ellipsoid, ornamented with a complete reticulum of irregular meshes and heavy ridges, prominences up to 0.8 µm high, hyaline, amyloid; cap cuticle an ixolattice.

OCCURRENCE: in groups in sphagnum moss; September; reported from Michigan, Oregon, Idaho, Ontario, and Quebec; occasional.

COMMENTS: The distinguishing characteristics of this species are that its latex dries yellowish and its margin color is paler than the disk. Also compare with *Lactarius kauffmanii* var. *kauffmanii.*

Lactarius mucidus var. **mucidioides** Hesler and A. H. Smith Illus. p. 97

North American Species of Lactarius (1979), 362–364

CAP: 1³⁄₁₆–3⁹⁄₁₆" (3–9 cm) wide, convex, becoming broadly convex to plane, disc uneven, with or without an umbo; surface viscid, smooth, azonate, dark dull vinaceous brown, becoming paler with age and cinnamon drab to vinaceous buff at the margin; margin incurved to inrolled when young, often lobed.

GILLS: adnate to short-decurrent, close, narrow, some forking near the stalk, pale pinkish buff becoming more yellowish, staining grayish green.

STALK: 2–3½" (5–9 cm) long, ⅜–¹¹⁄₁₆" (10–17 mm) thick, enlarged at the base or at times nearly equal, smooth, viscid, waxy, stuffed to hollow, colored like the gills.

FLESH: thin, firm, pale vinaceous buff; odor not distinctive; taste acrid.

LATEX: white, drying pale gray-green to olive-buff, staining gills grayish green; taste acrid.

SPORE DEPOSIT: cream color.

MICROSCOPIC CHARACTERS: spores 7.5–9.0 × 7–8 µm, broadly ellipsoid, ornamented with a partial to nearly complete reticulum with angular meshes and some branches with free ends, prominences up to 0.2–0.6 µm high, hyaline, amyloid; cap cuticle a layer of interwoven hyphae supporting branching hyphae arranged in an ixotrichoderm or an ixolattice.

OCCURRENCE: on ground under conifers; July–August; eastern North America; occasional.

EDIBILITY: unknown.

COMMENTS: *Lactarius mucidus* var. *mucidus,* reported throughout eastern North America, is similar, but it is dark, dingy chocolate brown on the disc with pale pinkish buff toward the margin, and it has a cream-colored spore deposit, acrid-tasting flesh, and white latex that dries bluish green to olive and stains tissues bluish green.

Lactarius mucidus var. **mucidus** Burlingham Illus. p. 98

Mem. Torrey Bot. Club 14 (1908), 56
Lactaria mucida Burlingham

CAP: 1⅛–3½" (3–9 cm) wide, convex, becoming broadly convex to nearly plane with a depressed disc, sometimes with a low acute umbo; margin decurved and remaining so well into maturity, becoming even or striate with age; surface viscid to glutinous, glabrous, azonate, dark dingy chocolate brown on the disc, becoming pinkish buff toward the margin.

GILLS: attached to subdecurrent, medium broad, close, sometimes forked, white to cream, staining bluish green from the dried latex.

STALK: 1½–3⅛" (4–8 cm) long, 5⁄16–⅜" (7–10 mm) thick, nearly equal, viscid, glabrous, solid or hollow, colored like the cap but paler.

FLESH: thick, firm, white; odor not distinctive; taste acrid.

LATEX: white, drying bluish green to olive on the gills; taste acrid.

SPORE DEPOSIT: white.

MICROSCOPIC CHARACTERS: spores 7.5–10.0 × 6–8 µm, ellipsoid, ornamented with isolated warts and ridges that form a partial reticulum, sometimes suggesting a zebra-like pattern, prominences up to 0.5 µm high, hyaline, amyloid; cap cuticle an ixotrichoderm.

OCCURRENCE: on the ground in conifer woods; June–November; eastern North America; occasional.

EDIBILITY: unknown.

COMMENTS: *Lactarius mucidus* var. *fuscogriseus* reported from Michigan, Oregon, Idaho, Ontario, and Quebec—is similar, but it has a slimy, dark fuscous gray to dark brown cap with a somewhat paler margin, mild to slightly acrid-tasting white latex that slowly becomes yellowish on drying, pale pinkish stalk and gills, and a pale pinkish buff spore deposit. *Lactarius mucidus* var. *mucidioides,* reported throughout eastern North America, is similar, but it has a dark, dull vinaceous brown cap that becomes paler with age, acrid-tasting flesh, white latex that stains tissues grayish green and dries pale grayish green on the gills, pale pinkish buff stalk and gills, and a cream-colored spore deposit. *Lactarius pseudomucidus* also has acrid, white, and unchanging latex, but its latex does not dry or stain the gills bluish green. *Lactarius glutinosus* also has white, unchanging latex but grayer coloration.

Lactarius muscicola Hesler and A. H. Smith Not Illustrated

North American Species of Lactarius (1979), 120–121

CAP: 1–1⅛" (2.5–3.0 cm) wide, convex with a depressed center; margin incurved at first, becoming decurved; surface dry, somewhat velvety, dark reddish brown to dark brown.

GILLS: attached to subdecurrent, somewhat broad, close, white when young, becoming yellowish, not staining when bruised.

STALK: 1¼–1⅝" (3–4 cm) long, 5⁄16–¼" (4–6 mm) thick, nearly equal, dry, solid, glabrous, colored like the cap but paler, especially at the base.

FLESH: whitish, unchanging; odor not distinctive; taste mild.

LATEX: white on exposure, unchanging, not staining tissues.

SPORE DEPOSIT: ochraceous buff.

MICROSCOPIC CHARACTERS: spores 7.5–9.0 × 7.5–9.0 µm, globose to subglobose, ornamented with ridges that form a partial reticulum, prominences up to 1.5 µm high, hyaline, amyloid; cap cuticle a modified trichoderm with lower cells that are somewhat inflated; stalk cuticle a turf of brown caulocystidia.

OCCURRENCE: in deep moss in deciduous woods; September; reported only from Cades Cove, Tennessee; distribution limits and frequency yet to be determined.

EDIBILITY: unknown.

COMMENTS: *Lactarius fumosus* is similar, but it has paler cap colors and whitish gills that stain reddish when bruised, and it lacks brown caulocystidia.

Lactarius mutabilis Peck Illus. p. 98

Ann. Rep. N.Y. State Mus. 43 (1890), 20

CAP: 1⅛–4" (3–10 cm) wide, rounded to convex at first, becoming nearly plane and often slightly depressed with age; margin incurved at first, becoming decurved and remaining so well into maturity; surface subviscid and zonate when wet, becoming azonate and dry, purplish brown to yellowish brown, with pinkish brown interzonal areas if zonate, often with a sheen over the disc.

GILLS: attached to subdecurrent, narrow, close, sometimes forked near the stalk, whitish, becoming tinged yellowish to pale pinkish brown, sometimes with dingy reddish stains.

STALK: 1⅛–3⅛" (3–8 cm) long, ¼–½" (6–14 mm) thick, nearly equal or enlarged downward, dry, glabrous, becoming hollow with age, colored like the cap or paler.

FLESH: thick, colored like the cap, not staining; odor faintly aromatic, resembling maple sugar, stronger when specimens are dried; taste mild.

LATEX: white or somewhat watery white on exposure, unchanging, not staining tissues or sometimes staining the gills pinkish or reddish; taste mild.

SPORE DEPOSIT: whitish to cream or dull creamy yellow.

MICROSCOPIC CHARACTERS: spores 7–10 × 6.0–7.5 µm, ellipsoid, ornamented with warts and ridges that form a partial reticulum, prominences up to 1.2 µm high, hyaline, amyloid; cap cuticle an ixocutis.

OCCURRENCE: on the ground in conifer and mixed woods; June–September; reported from New York south to Georgia, west to Michigan and Ohio; occasional.

EDIBILITY: unknown.

COMMENTS: *Lactarius quietus* var. *incanus* is very similar, but it has white to watery latex that tastes acrid and a pinkish buff spore deposit, and it grows on the ground under oak. *Lactarius cognoscibilis* is also very similar, but it has white latex that tastes bitter then slowly acrid. *Lactarius frustratus* is similar, but it has white to watery latex that soon changes to yellowish and tastes slowly acrid.

Lactarius neotabidus Redhead and A. H. Smith Illus. p. 98

Mycotaxon 17 (1983), 521–522

Lactarius canadensis A. H. Smith

CAP: ⅜–1¾" (1.0–4.5 cm) wide, convex to nearly plane with a depressed disc, becoming funnel-shaped, sometimes with a slight umbo; margin decurved to uplifted, translucent-striate; surface moist, smooth to wrinkled, becoming scurfy, azonate, rusty to cinnamon red or apricot orange, fading to orange-buff or paler.

GILLS: decurrent, narrow to somewhat broad, close, light to pinkish buff, sometimes spotting darker with age.

STALK: ¾–2 (2–5 cm) long, 1⁄16–3⁄16" (1.5–4.0 mm) thick, nearly equal, fragile, dry, glabrous, dark rusty red on the lower portion, gradually paler upward and apricot buff near the apex; base with radiating reddish tan hairs.

FLESH: thin, fragile; odor not distinctive; taste mild.

LATEX: white to watery white on exposure, unchanging, not staining the tissues; taste mild.

SPORE DEPOSIT: white.

MICROSCOPIC CHARACTERS: spores 7–10 × 6–8 µm, broadly ellipsoid, ornamented with isolated warts and widely spaced heavy bands that form a partial or complete reticulum, prominences up to 1 µm high, hyaline, amyloid; cap cuticle a distinct layer of intermingled clavate, vesiculose, cuneiform, and allantoid cells.

OCCURRENCE: gregarious among sphagnum mosses in bogs; August–October; reported from Michigan and Ontario; distribution limits and frequency yet to be determined.

COMMENTS: This species' rusty to cinnamon red or apricot orange cap with a translucent-striate margin, rusty red stalk with reddish tan hairs, white to watery and mild-tasting latex, and association with sphagnum mosses in bogs are its distinctive features. *Lactarius oculatus* is quite similar, but its cap lacks a translucent-striate margin, and its latex slowly tastes faintly acrid and then mild.

Lactarius neuhoffii var. **neuhoffii** Hesler and A. H. Smith Illus. p. 99

North American Species of Lactarius (1979), 179–181

CAP: 2⅜–4¾" (6–12 cm) wide, convex with a depressed disc, becoming shallowly funnel-shaped; margin inrolled at first, becoming decurved; surface dry, glabrous, dull white or with a faint lilac-gray tinge.

GILLS: decurrent, narrow, crowded to close, forked, white when young, staining ochraceous, soon becoming pinkish buff.

STALK: 1–1⅜" (2.5–3.5 cm) long, ⅝–1⅛" (1.5–3.0 cm) thick, nearly equal down to a pinched base, dry, solid, dull, white, staining dingy ochraceous to cinnamon buff where handled.

FLESH: white, slowly and slightly discoloring; odor not distinctive; taste extremely acrid.

LATEX: copious, white on exposure, soon changing to pale yellow, staining gills dingy ochraceous; taste extremely acrid.

SPORE DEPOSIT: white.

MACROCHEMICAL TESTS: cut surfaces staining vinaceous to vinaceous brown with the application of $FeSO_4$ and negative with KOH.

MICROSCOPIC CHARACTERS: spores 7.5–9.5 × 6.5–8.0 µm, broadly ellipsoid, ornamented with small warts and fine lines that form a partial reticulum, prominences up to 0.2 µm high, hyaline, amyloid; cap cuticle a poorly defined zone of interwoven hyphae and inflated cells.

OCCURRENCE: scattered or in groups on the ground under oak; July–September; widely distributed east of the Great Plains; occasional.

EDIBILITY: unknown.

COMMENTS: *Lactarius piperatus* var. *piperatus* is very similar, but it has narrower crowded gills and white latex that is unchanging or slowly dries yellow. *Lactarius neuhoffii* var. *fragrans* (Burlingham) Hesler and A. H. Smith (edibility unknown), reported only from North Carolina, has white flesh with the odor of ripe, crushed blackberries, a white cap that is minutely velvety when young, and white acrid latex that dries and stains yellow.

Lactarius nimkeae Hesler and A. H. Smith Not Illustrated

North American Species of Lactarius (1979), 524–525

CAP: about 2" (5 cm) wide, convex; margin pruinose at first, becoming glabrous; surface dry, glabrous, azonate, dark vinaceous brown.

GILLS: attached, narrow, close, grayish pink, staining dark vinaceous brown when bruised.

STALK: about 2" (5 cm) long, 5⁄16" (8 mm) thick, clavate, dry, dull, colored like the cap near the base, paler above the base.

FLESH: pale vinaceous tan; odor not distinctive; taste weakly acrid.
LATEX: watery on exposure, unchanging, staining gills dark vinaceous brown.
SPORE DEPOSIT: cream-colored.
MICROSCOPIC CHARACTERS: spores 7–9 × 5.5–6.5 µm, ellipsoid to subglobose, ornamented with isolated spines, prominences up to 0.7 µm high, hyaline, amyloid; cap cuticle a thick layer of tangled hyphae and inflated cells, with projecting, scattered, tubular hyphae.
OCCURRENCE: solitary in grassy oak woods; August; reported from Ann Arbor, Michigan; distribution limits and frequency yet to be determined.
COMMENTS: This species was named in honor of Mrs. Carol Nimke, who collected it.

Lactarius obscuratus var. **obscuratus** (Lasch) Fries Illus. p. 99

Epicr. Syst. Myc. (1838), 346

CAP: ¼–1¼" (6–32 mm) wide, convex to broadly convex, usually with a slight umbo, typically depressed at maturity; margin entire, even or finely scalloped; surface moist or dry, glabrous, smooth to very finely rugulose, broadly translucent-striate, azonate, dull reddish brown to dark brown, usually with an olive tone, especially on the disc when young, becoming orange-brown to cinnamon or paler toward the margin at maturity.
GILLS: attached to subdecurrent, medium broad, close to subdistant, pale yellowish cream at first, darkening when older, with paler edges.
STALK: ⅝–1⅛" (1.5–3.0 cm) long, ⅛–¼" (2–5 mm) thick, slightly enlarged downward or nearly equal overall, soon hollow, dry, pruinose, more or less colored like the cap or darker reddish brown.
FLESH: thin, pale reddish to pale reddish ochraceous, distinctly olive under the umbo and cuticle when moist; odor not distinctive; taste slightly acrid.
LATEX: scant to abundant, white on exposure, unchanging, not staining tissues; taste slightly acrid.
SPORE DEPOSIT: whitish.
MICROSCOPIC CHARACTERS: spores 6.0–8.5 × 5.0–6.5 µm, broadly ellipsoid to subglobose, ornamented with warts and ridges that form a partial reticulum, prominences up to 1 µm high, hyaline, amyloid; cap cuticle a palisade of short, clavate elements.
OCCURRENCE: scattered or in groups on the ground under alder; July–September; reported from the Pacific Northwest; distribution limits and frequency yet to be determined.
EDIBILITY: unknown.
COMMENTS: *Lactarius occidentalis*—reported from California, Oregon, Washington, and Maine—is similar, but it has an olive-brown to smoky brown cap that gradually becomes tawny to cinnamon or dark vinaceous brown, white to whey-like latex that sometimes changes to yellow, mild-tasting flesh, and larger spores that measure 8–10 × 6.5–8.0 µm.

Lactarius occidentalis A. H. Smith Illus. p. 99

Brittonia 12 (1960), 347

CAP: ⅜–1⅜" (1.0–3.5 cm) wide, convex, becoming broadly convex to nearly plane with a depressed disc, sometimes with a small umbo, becoming shallowly funnel-shaped with age; margin incurved at first, becoming decurved and finally uplifted with age; surface moist, opaque, becoming translucent-striate at maturity, often wrinkled or pitted, especially near the margin, azonate, olive-brown to smoky brown, gradually becoming tawny to cinnamon or dark vinaceous brown.

GILLS: attached to subdecurrent, narrow, close, light pinkish cinnamon, becoming reddish tan with age, slowly staining pinkish tan to pinkish brown when bruised.

STALK: 1⅛–2⅜" (3–6 cm) long, about ¼" (5–6 mm) thick, enlarged downward to nearly equal, solid, surface glabrous, unpolished, olive-brown at first, fading to pale olive-brown over time, with a paler apex.

FLESH: thin, fragile, buff or tinged cinnamon; odor not distinctive; taste mild.

LATEX: white to whey-like on exposure, usually soon changing to yellow.

SPORE DEPOSIT: white.

MICROSCOPIC CHARACTERS: spores 8–10 × 6.5–8.0 µm, ellipsoid, ornamented with warts and ridges that do not form a reticulum, prominences up to 0.6 µm high, hyaline, amyloid; cap cuticle a staggered layer of clavate to vesiculose cells.

OCCURRENCE: scattered, under alder or in mixed woods with cedar and alder; July–November; California, Oregon, and Washington, also reported from Maine; occasional.

EDIBILITY: unknown.

COMMENTS: The olive-brown to smoky brown cap, buff or cinnamon-tinged flesh that tastes mild, white to whey-like latex that sometimes changes to yellow, and association with alder are this species' distinctive features. *Lactarius obscuratus* var. *obscuratus*, reported only from the Pacific Northwest, is similar, but it has a dull reddish brown to dark brown cap with an olive tone that becomes orange-brown to cinnamon or paler at maturity, white latex that does not change to yellow, slightly acrid-tasting flesh, and smaller spores that measure 6–8.5 × 5.0–6.5 µm.

Lactarius oculatus (Peck) Burlingham Illus. p. 100

Bull. Torrey Bot. Club 34 (1907), 89
Lactarius subdulcis var. *oculatus* Peck
Eyespot Milky

CAP: ⅜–1¾" (1.0–4.5 cm) wide, broadly convex, becoming nearly plane when older, with a slightly depressed center and small pointed umbo; surface sticky when fresh, shiny when dry, azonate, dark reddish brown to orange-brown at the center, paler toward the margin, fading to pale orange-brown, but the umbo usually retaining the dark reddish brown color well into maturity and resembling an eyespot.

GILLS: attached to slightly decurrent, broad, close to subdistant, cream to pinkish buff, staining light pinkish brown to dull cinnamon with age.

STALK: ¾–1¾" (2.0–4.5 cm) long, ⅛–⅜" (3–10 mm) thick, nearly equal or enlarged slightly downward, hollow, glabrous, moist but not sticky, dull pinkish brown to pinkish orange, often with whitish mycelium at the base.

FLESH: thin, fragile, watery, pinkish brown; odor not distinctive; taste very slowly becoming faintly acrid, then fading.

LATEX: scant, watery to whey-like on exposure, unchanging; taste very slowly becoming faintly acrid, then fading.

SPORE DEPOSIT: pale yellow.

MICROSCOPIC CHARACTERS: spores 7.5–9.0 × 6–7 µm, elliptic, ornamented with warts and ridges that typically do not form a reticulum, prominences up to 0.6 µm high, hyaline, amyloid; cap cuticle a thick layer of hyphal segments mixed in an interwoven pattern.

OCCURRENCE: scattered or in groups in sphagnum mosses in bogs or growing on the ground among needles in conifer woods, especially with spruce and pine; July–October; eastern Canada south to Georgia, west to Wisconsin; fairly common.

EDIBILITY: edible.

COMMENTS: *Lactarius thejogalus* is similar, but it has dull white to pale vinaceous flesh that soon stains yellow on exposure, white latex that slowly turns yellow, and a conspicuous white strigose stalk base, and it grows on the ground in hardwoods or mixed forests, usually with birch present. *Lactarius umbrinopapillatus* is also similar, but it has a dull yellowish brown cap with a dingy tan marginal area and white latex that stains cut surfaces yellow in a few minutes, and it grows on the ground under pine. Also compare with *Lactarius neotabidus,* which has a conspicuously translucent-striate margin and white to watery white, mild-tasting latex.

Lactarius olivaceobrunneus Hesler — Not Illustrated

North American Species of Lactarius (1979), 345–346

CAP: 1⅛–2¾" (3–7 cm) wide, convex, becoming broadly convex to nearly plane with a slightly depressed disc; margin incurved to decurved; surface viscid, slightly fibrillose, azonate, olive-brown to grayish brown, ochraceous to buff over the disc.

GILLS: attached to decurrent, medium broad, close, whitish then creamy buff, stained greenish by the latex.

STALK: 1½–2½" (4.0–6.5 cm) long, ¼–⅜" (6–11 mm) thick, nearly equal, viscid, glabrous, hollow, brownish orange.

FLESH: thin, whitish; odor not distinctive; taste acrid.

LATEX: white on exposure, unchanging, staining gills greenish; taste acrid.

SPORE DEPOSIT: not obtained.

MICROSCOPIC CHARACTERS: spores 9.5–14.0 × 8.5–11.0 µm, ellipsoid to subglobose, ornamented with bands that form a partial to complete reticulum, with some free branches and fine lines, prominences up to 2 µm high, hyaline, amyloid; cap cuticle an ixocutis of slender, interwoven, gelatinous hyphae.

OCCURRENCE: on the ground in mixed conifer and hardwoods; July–August; reported from Tennessee, North Carolina, and South Carolina; distribution limits and frequency yet to be determined.

EDIBILITY: unknown.

COMMENTS: *Lactarius argillaceifolius* var. *argillaceifolius* is similar, but it has a lilac-brown to pale lilac-gray cap without olive tones, darker gills, and smaller spores.

Lactarius olivaceoumbrinus Hesler and A. H. Smith — Illus. p. 100

North American Species of Lactarius (1979), 219–221

CAP: 1½–4" (4–10 cm) wide, convex, becoming nearly plane with a slightly depressed center; margin inrolled and pubescent at first; surface glabrous and viscid, zonate to azonate when older, olive-brown to dark olive with alternating zones of green and dingy yellow-brown.

GILLS: decurrent, narrow, crowded, often forked near the stalk, whitish at first, becoming greenish then olive-gray.

STALK: ½–4" (1.5–10.0 cm) long, ¼–⅝" (7–15 mm) thick, enlarged toward the base, solid, becoming hollow with age, viscid then dry, glabrous, scrobiculate, olive-brown to dark olive.

FLESH: thick, firm, pale olivaceous, unchanging when cut; odor not distinctive; taste acrid.

LATEX: copious, white on exposure, rapidly or slowly turning greenish gray; taste extremely acrid.

SPORE DEPOSIT: light buff.

MACROCHEMICAL TESTS: cap surface staining purplish red with the application of KOH.

MICROSCOPIC CHARACTERS: spores 7–10 × 6–9 µm, ellipsoid to subglobose, ornamented with isolated warts, bands, and branches that form a partial reticulum, prominences up to 1.5 µm high, hyaline, amyloid; cap cuticle an ixocutis.

OCCURRENCE: solitary to gregarious on the ground under conifers; July–November; Idaho, Washington, Oregon, and California; occasional.

EDIBILITY: unknown.

COMMENTS: *Lactarius turpis* (Weinmann) Fries (edibility unknown) is very similar but has a viscid cap and stalk when fresh and smaller spores.

Lactarius olympianus Hesler and A. H. Smith Illus. p. 100, 101

North American Species of Lactarius (1979), 239–242

CAP: 2⅜–4¾" (6–12 cm) wide, convex with a depressed disc, becoming broadly funnel-shaped; margin decurved well into maturity then becoming uplifted, glabrous; surface viscid, glabrous, zonate, orange with zones of apricot orange and light orangish yellow.

GILLS: attached, narrow, close to subdistant, white to pale buff or dingy yellow, staining dingy orange to orange-brown when bruised.

STALK: 1½–2⅜" (4–6 cm) long, ⅜–1" (1.0–2.5 cm) thick, nearly equal to tapered downward, whitish with a white bloom at first, becoming dingy ochraceous at the base when handled.

FLESH: thin, fragile, white; odor not distinctive; taste acrid.

LATEX: white on exposure, unchanging, staining gills orange to orange-brown; taste acrid.

SPORE DEPOSIT: cinnamon buff.

MICROSCOPIC CHARACTERS: spores 8–11 × 7.5–9.0 µm, broadly ellipsoid, ornamented with warts and ridges that form a partial to complete reticulum, prominences up to 1.5 µm high, hyaline, amyloid; cap cuticle an ixocutis.

OCCURRENCE: scattered to gregarious in montane conifer forests; July–November; Pacific Northwest and Colorado; fairly common.

EDIBILITY: unknown.

COMMENTS: *Lactarius deliciosus, Lactarius deterrimus,* and *Lactarius salmonicolor* are similar, but they have orange, not white, latex on exposure.

Lactarius pallescens var. **pallescens** Hesler and A. H. Smith Illus. p. 101, 102

North American Species of Lactarius (1979), 323–326

CAP: 1⅛–4" (3–10 cm) wide, convex to nearly plane, depressed over the disc; margin incurved at first, becoming decurved, faintly downy; surface slimy-viscid, glabrous, azonate, milk white when young, slowly becoming pale grayish pink to pale pink and more grayish with age, sometimes developing ochraceous to pale rusty stains.

GILLS: attached to subdecurrent, moderately broad, close to subdistant, forked near the stalk, white to pale yellow or pale ochraceous, staining pale lilac to lilac when bruised, sometimes developing orange to grayish orange stains with age.

STALK: 1–3⅛" (2.5–8.0 cm) long, ⅜–¾" (1–2 cm) thick, nearly equal, slimy-viscid, solid or hollow, shiny when dry, white to pale yellow or pale orange, staining grayish orange.

FLESH: thick, white to grayish yellow, staining lilac; odor not distinctive; taste mild.

LATEX: copious, white on exposure, unchanging, staining tissues pale lilac to lilac; taste mild.

SPORE DEPOSIT: white to creamy.

MACROCHEMICAL TESTS: cap surface staining yellow with the application of KOH.

MICROSCOPIC CHARACTERS: spores 9.0–10.5 × 7–9 µm, ellipsoid, ornamented with isolated warts and short bands and ridges that form a partial reticulum, prominences up to 1 µm high, hyaline, amyloid; cap cuticle an ixotrichoderm when young, becoming an ixolattice with age.

OCCURRENCE: scattered to gregarious on soil or among mosses in conifer or mixed conifer and hardwoods; August–January; southwestern Canada south to California, also reported from Idaho; fairly common.

EDIBILITY: unknown.

COMMENTS: *Lactarius pallescens* var. *palmerensis* Hesler and A. H. Smith (edibility unknown), reported only from Alaska, is very similar, but it has a light pinkish tan to pinkish brown cap and a creamy white stalk that stains orange where handled or lavender from the latex, and it grows on the ground under alder and birch. *Lactarius californiensis* is nearly identical macroscopically, except its stalk is moist or dry, not viscid, its cap cuticle is a thick ixocutis, and it has smaller spores. Also compare with *Lactarius uvidus* var. *uvidus* and *Lactarius uvidus* var. *montanus.*

Lactarius pallidiolivaceus Hesler and A. H. Smith Illus. p. 102

North American Species of Lactarius (1979), 151–152
Lactarius fumosus var. *occidentalis* A. H. Smith and Hesler

CAP: 1½–2¾" (4–7 cm) wide, irregularly shaped, somewhat convex, often shallowly depressed, sometimes becoming deeply depressed; margin somewhat eroded and rimose; surface dry, dull, appearing glabrous but minutely velvety under a hand lens, whitish, then olive-buff with darker and lighter areas.

GILLS: attached, close, usually subdistant, thin, fragile, white when young, becoming yellow to ochraceous yellow, staining pale pinkish brown when bruised.

STALK: 1⅛–2" (3–5 cm) long, ⅜–¾" (1–2 cm) thick, tapered downward, dry, glabrous, solid, extremely hard, nonbrittle, white, staining pinkish brown when bruised.

FLESH: white changing to red when cut; odor not distinctive; taste mild.

LATEX: scant, white on exposure, staining flesh red or older specimens pinkish brown, staining gills and stalk pinkish brown; taste mild.

SPORE DEPOSIT: pale yellow.

MICROSCOPIC CHARACTERS: spores 7.5–9.0 × 7.5–9.0 µm, globose to subglobose, ornamented with a partial reticulum, prominences up to 1 µm high, hyaline, amyloid; cap cuticle poorly defined, of lax to upright subcylindric cells, arising from an indistinct zone of interwoven hyphae and inflated cells.

OCCURRENCE: gregarious on the ground under ponderosa pine; October–November; reported from California and Oregon; uncommon.

EDIBILITY: unknown.

COMMENTS: The name *pallidiolivaceus* refers to the cap's whitish to olive-buff colors.

Lactarius paludinellus Peck Not Illustrated

Ann. Rep. N.Y. State Mus. 38 (1885), 133

CAP: ⅝–1" (1.5–2.5 cm) wide, broadly convex to nearly plane, sometimes with a slightly depressed disc, usually with a small blackish umbo; margin striatulate; surface viscid, glabrous, dingy brown, paler with age.

GILLS: attached to subdecurrent, moderately close, cream-colored.

STALK: ¾–1⅜" (2.0–3.5 cm) long, ⅛–3⁄16" (3–4 mm) thick, nearly equal, dry, glabrous, stuffed or hollow, with white stiff hairs at the base, colored like the cap or paler.

FLESH: not stated in the original description.

LATEX: white on exposure, unchanging; taste mild.

SPORE DEPOSIT: not stated in the original description.

MICROSCOPIC CHARACTERS: spores 7.5–9.0 × 6.0–7.5 µm, broadly ellipsoid, ornamented with isolated warts and ridges that form a partial reticulum, prominences up to 0.5 µm high, hyaline, amyloid; cap cuticle a zone of inflated cells and tubular hyphae at the surface, appearing to be a weak ixolattice.

OCCURRENCE: among sphagnum mosses in shaded marshes; August; Sand Lake, New York; distribution limits and frequency yet to be determined.

EDIBILITY: unknown.

COMMENTS: The dingy brown, viscid cap with its small blackish umbo, white stiff hairs at the stalk base, mild-tasting white latex, and growth among sphagnum mosses are this species' distinctive features.

Lactarius paradoxus Beardslee and Burlingham Illus. p. 102, 103

Mycologia 32 (1940), 584

Lactaria paradoxa Beardslee and Burlingham

Silver-blue Milky

CAP: 2–3⅛" (5–8 cm) wide, broadly convex, becoming plane with a depressed center, often funnel-shaped when older; margin incurved at first, becoming expanded to uplifted; surface glabrous, slimy to sticky when wet, with a silvery sheen when young; zoned with bands of grayish blue, grayish purple, green and blue, staining green when bruised.

GILLS: attached to slightly decurrent, narrow to broad, close, occasionally forked near the stalk, pinkish orange, staining blue-green when bruised.

STALK: 1–1¼" (2–3 cm) long, ⅜–⅝" (1.0–1.5 cm) thick, nearly equal or tapered downward, hollow, dry, colored like the cap, staining green when bruised or with age.

FLESH: thick, whitish with greenish to bluish tints, slowly staining greenish when cut or bruised; odor not distinctive; taste mild or slightly acrid.

LATEX: scant, dark vinaceous brown on exposure, staining tissues green; taste mild or slightly acrid.

SPORE DEPOSIT: cream to yellow.

MICROSCOPIC CHARACTERS: spores 7–9 × 5.5–6.5 µm, broadly ellipsoid, ornamented with warts and ridges that form a partial reticulum, prominences up to 1 µm high, hyaline, amyloid; cap cuticle an ixocutis.

OCCURRENCE: solitary, scattered, or in groups on the ground or in grass under pine, oak, and palmetto palm; August–February; eastern Canada south to Florida, west to Michigan and Texas; occasional in its northern range, common along the Gulf Coastal Plain.

EDIBILITY: edible.

COMMENTS: *Lactarius chelidonium* var. *chelidonium* is similar, but it has a grayish green cap with blue and yellow tints, and yellow latex. *Lactarius chelidonium* var. *chelidonioides* is also similar, but it has a sordid azure blue cap with dingy orange-brown areas or zones that loses its blue color with age and becomes dull orange-brown to reddish brown, and its latex is scant dingy yellow to yellow-brown.

Lactarius parvulus Murrill — Not Illustrated

Bull. Torrey Bot. Club 67 (1940), 58
Lactaria parvula Murrill

CAP: ¾" (2 cm) wide, convex to slightly depressed; margin even; surface slightly viscid when moist, zonate, glabrous, whitish with a pale pinkish cinnamon tint.
GILLS: narrowly attached, narrow, crowded, forked, white, not staining when bruised.
STALK: 1⅛" (3 cm) long, ¼" (6 mm) thick, nearly equal, glabrous, white, not staining when bruised.
FLESH: white, unchanging when exposed; odor not distinctive; taste mild.
LATEX: white on exposure, unchanging, not staining tissues; taste mild.
SPORE DEPOSIT: not stated in the original description.
MICROSCOPIC CHARACTERS: spores 4.5–7.0 × 4.0–5.5 µm, ellipsoid, ornamented with warts and fine lines that form a reticulum, prominences up to 0.5 µm high, hyaline, amyloid; cap cuticle an ixocutis.
OCCURRENCE: solitary on soil in a hammock; July; reported only from Florida; distribution limits and frequency yet to be determined.
EDIBILITY: unknown.
COMMENTS: *Lactarius arcuatus* is similar, but it has a white, azonate cap that lacks a pale pinkish cinnamon tint, and its flesh tastes acrid then bitter.

Lactarius payettensis A. H. Smith — Illus. p. 103

Brittonia 12 (1960), 324

CAP: 3⅛–6¼" (8–16 cm) wide, broadly convex to nearly plane with a depressed disc, becoming broadly funnel-shaped; margin incurved and remaining so well into maturity, glutinous, coarsely strigose, the hairs becoming fuscous with age; surface viscid to glutinous, glabrous over the disc, azonate, pale olive-buff at first, soon becoming straw-colored then dingy dark ochraceous.
GILLS: decurrent, narrow, close to subdistant, cream-colored, becoming dingy ochraceous with age.
STALK: ¾–2" (2–5 cm) long, ¾–1½" (2–4 cm) thick, nearly equal with a pinched-off base, dry, dull, glabrous, hollow, hard, scrobiculate, staining dark yellow-brown with age or where handled.
FLESH: thick, firm, hard, pale white to dingy ochraceous over time; odor faintly pungent and disagreeable; taste instantly and strongly acrid.
LATEX: scant, white on exposure, unchanging, staining the gills and flesh dingy yellow to dark ochraceous; taste not stated in the original description.
SPORE DEPOSIT: pale cream-colored.
MICROSCOPIC CHARACTERS: spores 8–10 × 7–8 µm, ellipsoid, ornamented with isolated warts and a sparse network of lines that form a partial reticulum, prominences up to 0.5 µm high, hyaline, amyloid; cap cuticle a thick ixocutis.
OCCURRENCE: scattered on the ground under spruce and fir, with some alder and aspen

present; July–October; reported from Idaho and Colorado; distribution limits and frequency yet to be determined.

EDIBILITY: unknown.

COMMENTS: The viscid to glutinous olive-buff to dingy dark ochraceous cap with marginal hairs that become fuscous with age, strongly acrid flesh, white latex that stains the gills dingy ochraceous, and the scrobiculate stalk that stains yellow-brown when handled are this species' distinctive characters.

Lactarius peckii var. **peckii** Burlingham Illus. p. 103, 104

Mem. Torrey Bot. Club 14 (1908), 76
Lactaria peckii Burlingham
Peck's Milky

CAP: 2–6" (5.0–15.5 cm) wide, broadly convex with a depressed center; margin inrolled at first, becoming decurved and remaining so well into maturity, sometimes striate on young specimens; surface dry, velvety when young, then scurfy to nearly glabrous; color variable, typically dull brick red or brownish red but also orange-brown to orange-red or dull reddish orange, often paler toward the margin, usually distinctly zoned with darker bay red to orange-red bands, often fading with age.

GILLS: decurrent, close, narrow, pale cinnamon buff at first, soon tinged pinkish cinnamon and darkening with age, staining rusty brown to reddish brown.

STALK: ¾–2⅜" (2–6 cm) long, ⅜–1" (1.0–2.5 cm) thick, nearly equal, becoming hollow with age, covered with a whitish bloom when young, colored like the cap but usually paler, often spotted reddish brown or dull orange when older, but not scrobiculate.

FLESH: firm, pale vinaceous brown, not staining when cut; odor not distinctive; taste extremely acrid.

LATEX: copious, white on exposure, unchanging, not staining tissues; taste extremely acrid.

SPORE DEPOSIT: white.

MICROSCOPIC CHARACTERS: spores 6.0–7.5 µm, globose to subglobose, ornamented with warts and ridges that form a partial to complete reticulum, prominences up to 0.8 µm high, hyaline, amyloid; cap cuticle a layer of loosely tangled, interwoven, thin-walled, septate, hyaline hyphae.

OCCURRENCE: solitary, scattered, or in groups on the ground in oak woods; July–November; New England south to Florida, west to Texas; occasional to fairly common.

EDIBILITY: unknown.

COMMENTS: This species has gills that are among the darkest in the genus. *Lactarius peckii* var. *glaucescens* Hesler and A. H. Smith (edibility unknown), reported from Tennessee south to Florida and west to Mississippi, is nearly identical except that its latex dries pale bluish green. *Lactarius peckii* var. *lactolutescens* Hesler (edibility unknown), reported from Tennessee and Florida, is also nearly identical, but it has very acrid white latex that quickly changes to ivory yellow on exposure and dries pale yellowish green.

Lactarius pervelutinus Hesler and A. H. Smith Not Illustrated

North American Species of Lactarius (1979), 170–171

CAP: 1½–1¾" (4.0–4.5 cm) wide, convex-depressed; margin incurved; surface dry, velvety with a hoary sheen, rusty brown to brownish orange, becoming ochraceous toward the margin.

GILLS: broadly attached, narrow, subdistant, cream-colored, slowly staining vinaceous pink then lilac-brown.

STALK: 1⅛" (3 cm) long, ⅝" (1.8 cm) thick, nearly equal, dry, solid, cream-colored.

FLESH: firm, brittle, yellowish white; odor not distinctive; taste mild.

LATEX: milk white to creamy white on exposure, unchanging, slowly staining gills vinaceous pink then lilac-brown; taste mild.

SPORE DEPOSIT: creamy white.

MACROCHEMICAL TESTS: cap surface staining a weak olive-buff with the application of KOH.

MICROSCOPIC CHARACTERS: spores 6.0–7.5 × 5–6 µm, broadly ellipsoid, ornamented with a partial reticulum or with warts and ridges not connected, prominences less than 0.2 µm high; cap cuticle a thick basal cellular layer producing a dense turf of flexuous or straight elements that sometimes branch.

OCCURRENCE: scattered under hardwoods and deciduous shrubs; August; reported from Michigan; distribution limits and frequency yet to be determined.

EDIBILITY: unknown.

COMMENTS: Similar species include *Lactarius lentus, Lactarius allochrous,* and *Lactarius hygrophoroides* var. *hygrophoroides.*

Lactarius petersenii Hesler and A. H. Smith Illus. p. 104, 105

North American Species of Lactarius (1979), 106–107

CAP: 1⅛–1¾" (3.0–4.5 cm) wide, broadly convex with a center that is depressed to upturned and broadly depressed; margin decurved, becoming uplifted with age; surface dry, minutely velvety, with radiating fine wrinkles, smoky yellowish brown.

GILLS: attached to decurrent, medium broad, close, not forked, white to cream, staining brown where bruised.

STALK: 1¼–1½" (3–4 cm) long, ¼–⅜" (6–10 mm) thick, nearly equal, dry, hollow with age, minutely velvety, colored like the cap.

FLESH: white, unchanging when cut; odor not distinctive; taste mild.

LATEX: dingy brownish to pale pinkish brown on exposure, unchanging, staining gills brownish; taste mild.

SPORE DEPOSIT: white.

MICROSCOPIC CHARACTERS: spores 7.5–10.0 × 6–8 µm, ellipsoid to broadly ellipsoid, ornamented with warts and fine lines that form an obscure reticulum, prominences up to 0.3 µm high, hyaline, amyloid; cap cuticle composed of four to six layers of cells below a layer of brown pileocystidia.

OCCURRENCE: solitary or scattered on the ground under hemlock or in mixed woods with hemlock present; June–September; reported from Tennessee, Ohio, and West Virginia.

EDIBILITY: unknown.

COMMENTS: *Lactarius pseudogerardii* is very similar, but it has distant gills and watery white latex that slowly turns pale cinnamon and does not stain the gills.

Lactarius pinckneyensis Hesler and A. H. Smith Not Illustrated

North American Species of Lactarius (1979), 246–247

CAP: 2–4" (5–10 cm) wide, convex-depressed, becoming broadly funnel-shaped; margin incurved at first, becoming decurved and arched at maturity; surface slightly viscid but soon dry, appressed-pubescent to distinctly pubescent toward the margin, glabrous on the disc, zonate along the margin, white to pale pinkish buff, slowly discoloring to dingy brownish.

GILLS: attached, becoming decurrent with age, narrow, crowded, white then slowly becoming pinkish buff to pale yellowish, staining brownish when bruised.

STALK: ¾–1⅛" (2–3 cm) long, ⅜–½" (1.0–1.3 cm) thick, shape not stated in the original description, hollow at maturity, white, scrobiculate.

FLESH: odor faintly fragrant; taste mild.

LATEX: scant, white on exposure, unchanging, staining the gills brownish; taste mild.

SPORE DEPOSIT: not stated in the original description.

MICROSCOPIC CHARACTERS: spores 5.0–7.5 × 4–6 µm, ellipsoid, ornamented with warts and ridges that do not form a reticulum, prominences up to 0.5 µm high, hyaline, amyloid; cap cuticle an ixocutis.

OCCURRENCE: on soil under oak; July; reported only from Pinckney, Michigan; distribution limits and frequency yet to be determined.

EDIBILITY: unknown.

COMMENTS: Although the margin is somewhat pubescent at first, it is not bearded. *Lactarius groenlandicus* Terkelsen (edibility unknown), reported only from Greenland, is very similar, but it has a bearded margin and grows on the ground under willows.

Lactarius piperatus var. **piperatus** (Fries) S. F. Gray Illus. p. 105, 106

Nat. Arr. Brit. Pls. 1 (1821), 623
Lactarius piperatus var. *pargamenus* (Fries) Bataille
Peppery Milky, Peppery White Milk Cap

CAP: 1⅛–6" (3.0–15.5 cm) wide, convex, becoming plane to depressed and finally funnel-shaped; margin incurved at first, becoming decurved and remaining so well into maturity, sometimes uplifted with age; surface dry, azonate, glabrous or sometimes uneven to finely wrinkled, white when young, becoming creamy white with ochraceous to dingy tan stains when older.

GILLS: attached to decurrent, narrow, very crowded, often forked one or more times, white at first, becoming pale cream at maturity, usually not staining, but sometimes staining yellowish when bruised.

STALK: ¾–3⅛" (2–8 cm) long, ⅜–1" (1.0–2.5 cm) thick, nearly equal, dry, firm, solid, pruinose, white.

FLESH: white, unchanging when cut, not staining or sometimes slowly staining yellowish; odor not distinctive; taste quickly and strongly acrid.

LATEX: white on exposure, unchanging, not staining tissues or sometimes slowly staining the gills yellowish and drying yellow; taste quickly and strongly acrid.

SPORE DEPOSIT: white.

MICROSCOPIC CHARACTERS: spores 4.5–7.0 × 5.0–5.5 µm, ellipsoid, ornamented with fine lines and isolated particles that do not form a reticulum, prominences up 0.2 µm high, hyaline, amyloid; cap cuticle a zone of inflated cells.

OCCURRENCE: solitary, scattered, or in groups on the ground under conifers or hardwoods; July–September; widely distributed in eastern North America, also reported from California; fairly common.

EDIBILITY: edible.

COMMENTS: *Lactarius glaucescens* = *Lactarius piperatus* var. *glaucescens* (edible) is very similar, but it has white to whitish latex that does not change on exposure and dries pale bluish green. *Lactarius piperatus* var. *piperatus* is the type species for the genus.

Lactarius praezonatus Murrill Not Illustrated

Lloydia 6 (1943), 208
Lactaria praezonata Murrill

CAP: 1⅛–1½" (3–4 cm) wide, convex to broadly convex-depressed; margin even; surface viscid, finely roughened, distinctly multizonate, the narrow zones pale reddish brown to chestnut, the broad zones dull olive-yellow with a reddish yellow tint.

GILLS: attached, narrow, close, pale olive-yellow, drying white, staining dull purplish where bruised.

STALK: ¾–1⅛" (2–3 cm) long, about ¼" (5–6 mm) thick, nearly equal, dry, glabrous, pale reddish brown to chestnut.

FLESH: thin, dull olive-yellow with a reddish yellow tint; odor not distinctive; taste mild.

LATEX: white on exposure, unchanging, staining the gills dull purplish; taste mild.

SPORE DEPOSIT: not stated in the original description.

MICROSCOPIC CHARACTERS: spores 8.0–9.5 × 6.0–7.5 µm, ellipsoid, ornamented with warts and ridges that form a partial reticulum, prominences up to 1 µm high, hyaline, amyloid; cap cuticle a layer of hyaline, uninflated, thin-walled hyphae with ascending free hyphal tips (an ixolattice as seen in Melzer's).

OCCURRENCE: scattered on the ground; October; reported only from Gainesville, Florida; distribution limits and frequency yet to be determined.

EDIBILITY: unknown.

COMMENTS: *Lactarius maculatus* also has a conspicuously zoned cap, but its flesh has an acrid taste. *Lactarius uvidus* var. *uvidus* has mild-tasting latex that becomes bitter, a whitish stalk, and typically an azonate cap.

Lactarius proximellus Beardslee and Burlingham Illus. p. 106

Mycologia 32 (1940), 578
Lactaria proximella Beardslee and Burlingham

CAP: 1–2⅜" (2.5–6.0 cm) wide, broadly convex-umbilicate, then expanding to shallowly funnel-shaped; margin arched, at length uplifted and more or less fluted, sometimes striate; surface viscid when wet, whitish pruinose in the center, distinctly zonate, zones tawny to brownish orange, with darker brownish orange to cinnamon zones.

GILLS: attached to slightly decurrent, narrow to moderately broad, close, sometimes forked near the stalk, whitish at first, becoming pale brownish yellow.

STALK: ½–¾" (1.3–2.0 cm) long, 5⁄16–⅜" (8–10 mm) thick, nearly equal or enlarged slightly at the apex, pruinose when young, pale yellow, becoming pale bluish green where bruised.

FLESH: pale cream; odor not distinctive.

LATEX: scant, white on exposure, unchanging; taste very acrid.

SPORE DEPOSIT: very pale yellow.

MICROSCOPIC CHARACTERS: spores 7.5–9.0 × 6.0–7.5 µm, broadly ellipsoid, ornamented with warts and ridges that form a partial reticulum, prominences up to 0.5 µm high, hyaline, amyloid; cap cuticle an ixolattice collapsing to an ixocutis.

OCCURRENCE: on sandy soil under oaks; August–January; New England south to Florida, west to Texas, also reported from Michigan; occasional.

EDIBILITY: unknown.

COMMENTS: The stocky stature, tawny to brownish orange zonate cap, acrid latex, and growth under oaks are this species' distinctive features.

Lactarius psammicola f. **glaber** Hesler and A. H. Smith Illus. p. 107

North American Species of Lactarius (1979), 268–270

CAP: 2⅜–5⅞" (6–15 cm) wide, convex depressed with an arched margin, becoming broadly funnel-shaped; surface smooth, viscid, zonate with alternating zones of light buff and pale tan to darker dull orange; margin pubescent to naked.

GILLS: decurrent, narrow, close, some forked, pinkish buff to cinnamon buff, staining darker.

STALK: ¾–1⅞" (2–5 cm) long, ⅝–1⅜" (15–30 mm) thick, narrowing downward, dry, hard, stuffed to hollow, whitish and unpolished, scrobiculate, sometimes with an obscure annular line near the apex; veil absent.

FLESH: thick, whitish, sometimes with watery zones; odor slightly fragrant; taste very strongly burning acrid.

LATEX: milk white, drying dingy buff, slowly staining tissues pinkish cinnamon, staining white paper yellow; taste very acrid.

SPORE DEPOSIT: pinkish buff.

MICROSCOPIC CHARACTERS: spores 7.5–9.0 × 6.5–7.5 µm, broadly ellipsoid, ornamented with warts and ridges that do not form a reticulum, prominences from 0.5 to 1.0 µm high, hyaline, amyloid; cap cuticle an ixocutis.

OCCURRENCE: on ground in groups under oak, hickory, and witch hazel; July–October; reported from Michigan and eastern Canada south to Florida, west to Texas; occasional.

EDIBILITY: unknown.

COMMENTS: *Lactarius psammicola* f. *psammicola*—reported from New England south to Florida, west to Texas, and Michigan and Kansas—is very similar but has a glutinous, coarsely fibrillose cap that is ochraceous buff to ochraceous orange with conspicuous light buff zones and that becomes dingy yellow-brown with age. It also has dingy buff flesh that lacks the slightly fragrant odor.

Lactarius psammicola f. **psammicola** A. H. Smith Illus. p. 107, 108

Pap. Michigan Acad. Sci. 26 (1941), 62

CAP: 1½–5½" (4–14 cm) wide, convex to broadly convex and deeply depressed, expanding to broadly vase-shaped; margin inrolled at first, becoming decurved, coarsely strigose at first, becoming matted-fibrillose with age; surface glutinous, coarsely fibrillose, the fibrils agglutinated, ochraceous buff to ochraceous orange, becoming dingy yellow-brown with age, with conspicuous light buff zones, especially when young.

GILLS: decurrent, narrow, close, sometimes forked near the stalk, whitish to light buff at first, becoming darker and sordid ochraceous with age, sometimes staining pinkish lilac.

STALK: ⅜–1⅛" (1–3 cm) long, ⅜–¾" (1–2 cm) thick, tapered downward, dry, stuffed to hollow, whitish to grayish, often scrobiculate.

FLESH: thick, dingy buff, sometimes staining pinkish lilac; odor not distinctive; taste acrid.

LATEX: copious, white on exposure, slowly changing to pale dingy pinkish lilac, or not changing or staining this color; taste very acrid.

SPORE DEPOSIT: yellowish.

MACROCHEMICAL TESTS: flesh staining pale dull bluish gray with the application of $FeSO_4$.

MICROSCOPIC CHARACTERS: spores 7.5–9.0 × 6.0–7.5 µm, ellipsoid, ornamented with warts and ridges that sometimes form a partial reticulum, prominences up to 0.5 µm high, hyaline, amyloid; cap cuticle an ixocutis.

OCCURRENCE: on the ground in hardwoods or mixed woods, usually with oak present; July–January; New England south to Florida, west to Texas, also reported from Michigan and Kansas.

EDIBILITY: unknown.

COMMENTS: *Lactarius psammicola* f. *glaber*, reported from Michigan and eastern Canada south to Florida and west to Texas, is very similar, but it has a glabrous, viscid cap with light buff to pale tan and dull orange zones and whitish flesh with a slightly fragrant odor.

Lactarius pseudoaffinis Hesler and A. H. Smith — Not Illustrated

North American Species of Lactarius (1979), 437–438

CAP: 2⅜–3⅛" (6–8 cm) wide, convex, becoming nearly plane with a slightly depressed center; margin faintly short-striate; surface viscid, glabrous, azonate, dull pale yellow.

GILLS: narrowly attached, broad, close to nearly subdistant, white to ivory white, becoming pale yellow at maturity, not staining when bruised.

STALK: 1–1½" (2.5–4.0 cm) long, 5⁄16–½" (8–12 mm) thick, nearly equal overall, viscid when fresh, firm, becoming hollow with age, sometimes slightly scrobiculate, whitish to buff.

FLESH: firm, white, not staining when exposed; odor faintly fragrant; taste not stated in the original description.

LATEX: white on exposure, unchanging, not staining tissues; taste acrid.

SPORE DEPOSIT: pale ochraceous yellow.

MICROSCOPIC CHARACTERS: spores 6.0–7.5 × 6.0–7.5 µm, globose to subglobose, ornamented with warts and ridges that form a partial to complete reticulum, prominences up to 0.5 µm high, hyaline, amyloid; cap cuticle an ixotrichoderm to an ixolattice.

OCCURRENCE: on soil under hemlock; August; reported from North Carolina and Texas; distribution limits and frequency yet to be determined.

EDIBILITY: unknown.

COMMENTS: *Lactarius affinis* var. *affinis* is similar but has a white spore deposit and slightly larger spores. Also compare with *Lactarius midlandensis.*

Lactarius pseudoaspideus Hesler and A. H. Smith — Not Illustrated

North American Species of Lactarius (1979), 232–233

CAP: 1¼–4" (3–10 cm) wide, convex, depressed; margin incurved at first, becoming decurved, silky; surface slightly viscid, glabrous, azonate, light ochraceous buff to pale yellow.

GILLS: attached, medium broad, close to crowded, sometimes forked near the stalk, white to yellowish buff, staining violaceous to brownish lilac.

STALK: 1½–2½" (4.0–6.5 cm) long, ¼–¾" (6–20 mm) thick, nearly equal or enlarged downward, often curved at the base, slightly viscid, stuffed to hollow, glabrous, colored like the cap.

FLESH: thick, white, becoming violaceous when cut; odor not distinctive; taste quickly very acrid.

LATEX: copious, white on exposure, turning grayish, staining gills violaceous to lilac brown; taste quickly very acrid.

SPORE DEPOSIT: not obtained.

MICROSCOPIC CHARACTERS: spores 8–10 × 7.5–9.0 µm, ellipsoid to subglobose, ornamented with numerous bands, fine lines, and isolated warts, prominences up to 1.2 µm high, hyaline, amyloid; cap cuticle an ixocutis.

OCCURRENCE: on the ground; August; reported only from Bryson City, North Carolina; distribution limits and frequency yet to be determined.

EDIBILITY: unknown.

COMMENTS: *Lactarius aroostookensis* is similar, but it has an orange zonate cap, and its latex stains grayish blue, not violaceous to brownish lilac. *Lactarius aspideus* is also similar, but it has an azonate cap, and its latex stains tissues lilac.

Lactarius pseudodeceptivus Hesler and A. H. Smith — Not Illustrated

North American Species of Lactarius (1979), 242–244

CAP: 2⅜–6¾" (6–17 cm) wide, convex, becoming depressed and finally broadly funnel-shaped; margin distinctly inrolled and cottony when young; surface dry, becoming slimy in wet weather, matted-fibrillose to matted-tomentose, whitish at first, soon pinkish buff on the margin and finally dull cinnamon over the disc.

GILLS: attached then decurrent, narrow, close, with multiple forks near the stalk, creamy white when young, becoming brown with age, staining brownish by the latex.

STALK: 1½–2¾" (4–7 cm) long, ¾–1⅛" (2–3 cm) thick, nearly equal overall or tapered downward, dry, solid, firm, dull white.

FLESH: thick, hard, white, slowly staining brownish when exposed; odor not distinctive; taste distinctly acrid.

LATEX: copious, white on exposure, unchanging, taste acrid.

SPORE DEPOSIT: white.

MICROSCOPIC CHARACTERS: spores 8–11 × 6–8 µm, ellipsoid, ornamented with warts and ridges that form a reticulum, prominences up to 0.4 µm high, hyaline, amyloid; cap cuticle a layer of appressed narrow hyphae; stalk cuticle an ixocutis.

OCCURRENCE: scattered to gregarious on soil under conifers; July–October; reported from eastern Canada, Michigan, and Washington; occasional.

EDIBILITY: unknown.

COMMENTS: *Lactarius deceptivus* is very similar, but its stalk cuticle lacks a gelatinous layer, and its spore ornamentation does not form a reticulum.

Lactarius pseudodelicatus A. H. Smith — Not Illustrated

Brittonia 12 (1960), 310

CAP: 3⅛–5⅞" (8–15 cm) wide, broadly funnel-shaped; margin incurved, with a thin matted tomentum or agglutinated fibrils; surface viscid, glabrous, faintly zonate, pale yellow, becoming more brownish to pale orange-brown with age.

GILLS: subdecurrent, narrow, close, forked near the stalk, pale pinkish buff to pale orange-brown, becoming darker with age, staining dingy honey yellow or brownish when bruised.

STALK: ¾–1½" (2–4 cm) long, ⅜–¾" (1–2 cm) thick, nearly equal, dry, hollow, brittle, covered with large, glabrous, pale honey scrobiculations over a white ground color, becoming dingy ochraceous with age.

FLESH: thick, firm, fragile; odor distinctly of lemon extract or disinfectant; taste slightly acrid to acrid.

LATEX: white on exposure, unchanging, staining tissues dingy honey yellow or brownish where injured.

SPORE DEPOSIT: creamy white.

MICROSCOPIC CHARACTERS: spores 6.0–7.5 × 5.0–6.5 µm, ellipsoid, ornamented with crooked branched lines or ridges that form a partial reticulum, prominences up to 1 µm high, hyaline, amyloid; cap cuticle an ixocutis.

OCCURRENCE: gregarious on the ground under aspen; August; reported from Michigan and Florida; distribution limits and frequency yet to be determined.

EDIBILITY: unknown.

COMMENTS: *Lactarius delicatus* is very similar, but it has a whitish spore deposit with a yellowish salmon tint, flesh that is reported as having a strong odor, and white latex that becomes sulfur yellow and tastes acrid.

Lactarius pseudodeliciosus var. **pseudodeliciosus** Beardslee and Burlingham

Illus. p. 108

Mycologia 32 (1940), 582
Lactaria pseudodeliciosa Beardslee and Burlingham

CAP: 2⅜–3⅜" (6.0–8.5 cm) wide, broadly convex-umbilicate, expanding to funnel-shaped; margin incurved at first, becoming decurved, with agglutinated fibrils when young (use a hand lens); surface viscid when wet, azonate to faintly zonate, nearly white at first, becoming yellowish with age, central portion pale pinkish buff to ochraceous buff.

GILLS: attached to subdecurrent, honey yellow with orange tones, intervenose; gill spacing and width not stated in the original description.

STALK: ½–1" (1.2–2.5 cm) long, ⅜–¾" (1–2 cm) thick, solid, somewhat scrobiculate, white-tomentose on lower half.

FLESH: turning grayish green when cut; odor not distinctive.

LATEX: scant, ochraceous orange to apricot orange; taste slowly acrid.

SPORE DEPOSIT: ochraceous.

MICROSCOPIC CHARACTERS: spores 7–9 × 6.0–7.5 µm, ellipsoid, ornamented with broad and narrow bands that form a reticulum, prominences up to 0.5 µm high, hyaline, amyloid; cap cuticle an ixocutis.

OCCURRENCE: on soil under oak and pine; November–February; reported only from Florida; distribution limits and frequency yet to be determined.

EDIBILITY: unknown.

COMMENTS: *Lactarius pseudodeliciosus* var. *paradoxiformis* (Murrill) Hesler and A. H. Smith (edibility unknown), reported only from Florida, has a cream-colored cap that becomes partly or wholly bluish green, slightly fragrant flesh that has a distinctly acrid taste, and ochraceous gills and stalk that become spotted bluish green with age or when bruised, and it grows on the ground under hardwoods, especially red oak.

Lactarius pseudoflexuosus Hesler and A. H. Smith

Illus. p. 108

North American Species of Lactarius (1979), 383–384

CAP: 1½–4" (4–10 cm) wide, convex, becoming nearly plane with a depressed center when older; margin inrolled with a very inconspicuous grayish tomentum (use a hand lens) on young specimens, becoming glabrous at maturity; surface sticky when wet, soon moist to dry, glabrous at maturity, pinkish gray to pale gray with gray-brown spots and streaks, faintly to distinctly zoned.

GILLS: attached, close to subdistant, crossveined, pale pinkish buff when young, becoming pale pinkish cinnamon at maturity, sometimes forking.

STALK: 1⅛–2" (3–5 cm) long, ⅜–1⅛" (1–3 cm) thick, nearly equal or tapered downward, uneven and often scrobiculate, dry, becoming hollow with age, pale pinkish gray to gray, sometimes with a whitish bloom when young.

FLESH: thick, brittle, whitish; odor not distinctive; taste very acrid.

LATEX: dull creamy buff on exposure, unchanging; taste very acrid.

SPORE DEPOSIT: pale pinkish buff.

MICROSCOPIC CHARACTERS: spores 6.5–9.0 × 6–7 µm, broadly elliptic to subglobose, ornamented with warts and ridges that form a partial reticulum, prominences up to 0.8 µm high, hyaline, amyloid; cap cuticle a poorly delimited ixocutis of narrow, repent hyphae.

OCCURRENCE: solitary, scattered, or in groups on the ground in mixed conifer and hardwood forests; July–October; widely distributed in eastern North America; uncommon.

EDIBILITY: unknown.

COMMENTS: *Lactarius pseudomaculatus* is very similar, but it has a white spore deposit, milk white latex on exposure, and a cap margin with an appressed brownish tomentum.

Lactarius pseudogerardii Hesler and A. H. Smith Not Illustrated

North American Species of Lactarius (1979), 123–125

CAP: 1⅛–2¾" (3–7 cm) wide, broadly convex, becoming depressed on the disc to shallowly funnel-shaped; margin incurved at first, becoming nearly plane at maturity; surface dry, velvety, azonate, dark dingy yellow-brown.

GILLS: decurrent, distant, moderately broad, pinkish buff to pale tan.

STALK: 1⅛–2" (3–5 cm) long, ¼–⅜" (5–10 mm) thick, nearly equal, dry, somewhat velvety, colored like the cap, with a whitish base.

FLESH: whitish, unchanging when cut; odor not distinctive; taste mild.

LATEX: watery white on exposure, slowly turning pale cinnamon, not staining tissues; taste mild.

SPORE DEPOSIT: white.

MICROSCOPIC CHARACTERS: spores 9–12 × 6.5–9.0 µm, broadly ellipsoid, ornamented with minute warts connected by obscure fine lines that sometimes form an obscure reticulum, prominences up to 0.2 µm high, hyaline, amyloid; cap cuticle a turf of short and cylindric to tapered pileocystidia.

OCCURRENCE: scattered or in groups on the ground in woods; August; reported only from Edgewood, Michigan; distribution limits and frequency yet to be determined.

EDIBILITY: unknown.

COMMENTS: *Lactarius petersenii* is very similar, but it has close gills and dingy brownish to pale pinkish brown latex on exposure that stains gills brownish.

Lactarius pseudomaculatus Hesler and A. H. Smith Illus. p. 109

North American Species of Lactarius (1979), 381–382

CAP: 4–6" (10.0–15.5 cm) wide, broadly convex, becoming nearly plane with a slightly depressed disc; margin inrolled and long remaining so, covered by a conspicuous layer of appressed brownish tomentum that gradually becomes grayish, appearing cottony-tomentose under a hand lens, at maturity or with age appearing somewhat appressed-fibrillose; surface viscid when young and fresh, becoming dry to the touch with age, faintly but distinctly zoned with purplish brown zones alternating with grayish bands.

GILLS: subdecurrent, narrow, close, often forked, pinkish buff at first, becoming cinnamon or darker with age, sometimes spotted darker brown.

STALK: 1⅛–2⅜" (3–6 cm) long, ¾–1⅛" (2–3 cm) thick, nearly equal, dry, becoming hollow with age, pinkish buff, becoming pale tan at maturity, scrobiculate.

FLESH: white, slowly becoming very pale buff with age; odor not distinctive; taste very acrid.

LATEX: copious, milk white on exposure, unchanging, not staining tissues; taste extremely acrid.

SPORE DEPOSIT: pure white.

MICROSCOPIC CHARACTERS: spores 6.0–7.5 × 5.5–6.5 µm, broadly ellipsoid to subglobose, ornamented with warts and ridges that form a partial reticulum, prominences up to 0.8 µm high, hyaline, amyloid; cap cuticle a poorly delimited ixocutis of narrow, somewhat appressed hyphae.

OCCURRENCE: gregarious on soil under hardwoods; August; reported only from Tennessee; distribution limits and frequency yet to be determined.

EDIBILITY: unknown.

COMMENTS: *Lactarius pseudoflexuosus* is very similar, but it has a pale yellow spore deposit and dull creamy buff latex on exposure, and the cap margin of young specimens has a very inconspicuous grayish tomentum.

Lactarius pseudomucidus Hesler and A. H. Smith Illus. p. 109, 110

North American Species of Lactarius (1979), 356–357

CAP: 1⅛–4¾" (3–12 cm) wide, convex to nearly plane, with a shallowly depressed disc, becoming broadly funnel-shaped; margin inrolled at first, becoming decurved, wavy, or scalloped and often minutely furrowed with age; surface slimy, glabrous, azonate, charcoal gray to pale smoky gray.

GILLS: attached to subdecurrent, narrow to somewhat broad, close to subdistant, white with a grayish tinge, slowly staining yellowish to tan or brownish when bruised.

STALK: 1⅛–4¼" (3–11 cm) long, 3⁄16–⅝" (5–15 mm) thick, enlarged downward, very slimy, hollow, fragile, smoky gray to dingy brown.

FLESH: thin, grayish; odor not distinctive; taste slowly acrid or bitterish then acrid.

LATEX: thin, white on exposure, very slowly changing to yellowish as dried on the gills, slowly staining gills yellowish to tan or brownish; taste acrid.

SPORE DEPOSIT: white.

MICROSCOPIC CHARACTERS: spores 7–9 × 6–7 µm, broadly ellipsoid, ornamented with heavy bands that form a complete reticulum, prominences up to 1.2 µm high, hyaline, amyloid; cap cuticle a basal layer of interwoven hyphae with an ixotrichoderm above.

OCCURRENCE: solitary to gregarious on the ground under conifers; August–November; Alaska south to California and Idaho; common.

EDIBILITY: unknown.

COMMENTS: *Lactarius mucidus* var. *mucidus* is very similar but has a browner cap, a less slimy stalk, and latex that dries bluish green. *Lactarius glutigriseus* is almost identical macroscopically, but it has larger spores that are less strongly ornamented.

Lactarius pubescens var. **betulae** (A. H. Smith) Hesler and A. H. Smith Illus. p. 110

North American Species of Lactarius (1979), 282–285
Lactarius betulae A. H. Smith, *Brittonia* 12 (1960), 309

CAP: 1⅛–3⅛" (3–8 cm) wide, convex-depressed with an incurved margin, becoming shallowly depressed with an arched margin and then somewhat funnel-shaped; surface slightly viscid to dry, covered with densely matted wooly hairs, pale pinkish cinnamon to darker cinnamon at the center; margin coarsely bearded.
GILLS: decurrent, somewhat close, narrow, pinkish or pallid with pinkish reflections, staining yellow.
STALK: 1⅛–3⅛" (3–8 cm) long, ⅜–¾" (10–18 mm) thick, equal, unpolished to slightly hairy to powdery when older, dry, solid then hollow, slightly more pinkish than the cap.
FLESH: thick, fragile, whitish to pinkish; odor not distinctive; taste slowly and slightly acrid.
LATEX: scant, white, soon turning yellow, staining tissues yellow; taste slowly becoming slightly acrid.
SPORE DEPOSIT: white to cream color.
MICROSCOPIC CHARACTERS: spores 6.5–8.0 × 5.5–6.5 µm, ellipsoid, ornamented with strongly amyloid ridges and branches forming a broken reticulum with isolated warts, prominences from 0.4 to 0.8 µm high, hyaline, amyloid; cap cuticle scarcely differentiated from the context with thin-walled radial hyphae in masses.
OCCURRENCE: in groups or scattered on the ground under birch; August–September; widely distributed in North America; fairly common.
EDIBILITY: unknown.
COMMENTS: *Lactarius pubescens* var. *pubescens* is similar, but its flesh has a faint odor of geraniums or is sometimes pungent, and its latex is white and unchanging.

Lactarius pubescens var. **pubescens** Fries Illus. p. 110, 111

Epicr. Syst. Mycol. (1838), 335
Lactarius villosus Clements
Downy Milk Cap

CAP: 1–4¾" (2.5–12.0 cm) wide, obtuse to convex, becoming broadly convex with a depressed center; margin inrolled and bearded with coarse white hairs when young; surface dry and fibrillose except for the disc, which is sticky and glabrous when fresh, azonate, white to cream, becoming reddish orange to vinaceous on the disc with age.
GILLS: attached to slightly decurrent, crowded, seldom forked, whitish to pale yellow with pinkish tinges, slowly staining brownish ochraceous when bruised.
STALK: ¾–2½" (2.0–6.5 cm) long, ¼–½" (6–13 mm) thick, nearly equal or tapered downward, silky, becoming hollow with age, whitish when young, becoming ochraceous from the base up when older, apex usually tinged pinkish, often with a white basal mycelium.
FLESH: firm, white; odor faintly like geraniums or sometimes pungent; taste acrid.
LATEX: white on exposure, unchanging, not staining tissues; taste acrid.
SPORE DEPOSIT: cream with a pinkish tint.
MICROSCOPIC CHARACTERS: spores 6.0–8.5 × 5.0–6.5 µm, elliptic, ornamented with warts and ridges that sometimes form a partial reticulum, prominences up to 1.5 µm high, hyaline, amyloid; cap cuticle a layer of thin-walled hyphae.
OCCURRENCE: scattered or in groups on the ground in wet areas under birch and other

hardwoods; August–October; reported from eastern North America, the Pacific Northwest, Arizona, California, Colorado, Idaho, and western Canada; occasional.

EDIBILITY: unknown.

COMMENTS: We have placed *Lactarius villosus* in synonymy with *Lactarius pubescens* var. *pubescens* because of a lack of significant differentiating characteristics. *Lactarius pubescens* var. *betulae,* widely distributed in North America, has a dull vinaceous pink cap when young that fades to dull white or dingy pale yellow with age, whitish flesh that lacks a distinctive odor, scant and slowly acrid white latex that on exposure soon turns yellow, and a white to cream spore deposit. Compare with *Lactarius torminosus* var. *torminosus,* which has a darker-colored cap and larger spores. Also compare with *Lactarius subpaludosus,* which has acrid-tasting white latex that slowly changes to creamy yellow, and *Lactarius subtorminosus,* which has mild-tasting latex.

Lactarius pungens Hesler and A. H. Smith Not Illustrated

North American Species of Lactarius (1979), 389–390

CAP: 1–1⅜" (2.5–3.5 cm) wide, convex, becoming broadly convex to nearly plane, sometimes obscurely umbonate; margin even; surface viscid, glabrous, azonate, gray tinged with cinnamon.

GILLS: attached, narrow, close, not forked, pale ochraceous buff, unchanging where bruised.

STALK: 1–2⅛" (2.5–5.5 cm) long, about 3⁄16" (4–5 mm) thick, nearly equal or enlarged downward, glabrous, solid, not scrobiculate, light ochraceous buff.

FLESH: whitish, unchanging when cut; odor pungent; taste bitter.

LATEX: white on exposure, unchanging, not staining tissues; taste bitter.

SPORE DEPOSIT: ivory yellow.

MICROSCOPIC CHARACTERS: spores 7.0–10.5 × 6.0–8.5 µm, broadly ellipsoid, ornamented with coarse warts and ridges that form a partial reticulum, prominences up to 1 µm high, hyaline, amyloid; cap cuticle an ixolattice to an ixotrichoderm.

OCCURRENCE: on soil in mixed woods; August; reported only from Cades Cove, Great Smoky Mountains National Park, Tennessee; distribution and frequency yet to be determined.

EDIBILITY: unknown.

COMMENTS: *Lactarius hibbardae* var. *hibbardae* is similar, but it has pinkish buff to cream gills, white to watery latex that tastes acrid, and somewhat smaller spores, and its cap cuticle is a cutis.

Lactarius purpureoechinatus Hesler and A. H. Smith Illus. p. 111

North American Species of Lactarius (1979), 399–400

CAP: 1⅛–3⅛" (3–8 cm) wide, convex, soon depressed, sometimes with a slight blackish umbo; margin incurved and tomentose at first, becoming decurved and finally arched and more or less upturned; surface dry, fibrillose, the fibrils forming erect fascicles of dark scales overall or especially along the margin, sometimes with one or two watery zones toward the margin, dull grayish purple, becoming vinaceous or dull brownish purple.

GILLS: attached to subdecurrent, moderately broad, subdistant to distant, whitish at first, soon becoming vinaceous buff to dull grayish red.

STALK: 1⅛–2⅜" (3–6 cm) long, ¼–⅝" (5–15 mm) thick, nearly equal, dry, glabrous, hollow, colored like the cap or paler.

FLESH: pale vinaceous to dingy vinaceous or whitish with tints of the cap surface color; odor fragrant or not distinctive.

LATEX: white or whey-like on exposure, unchanging, not staining tissues; taste mild or slightly acrid.

SPORE DEPOSIT: pale yellow.

MICROSCOPIC CHARACTERS: spores 6.5–8.0 × 5.5–6.5 µm, broadly ellipsoid, ornamented with bands arranged in a zebroid manner, prominences up to 1.2 µm high, hyaline, amyloid; cap cuticle composed of repent hyphae with fascicles of erect hyphae (the scales).

OCCURRENCE: scattered or in groups on the ground under hardwoods and mixed woods, usually with oak present; June–October; New England and New York south to Florida; occasional.

EDIBILITY: unknown.

COMMENTS: The conspicuous pointed scales, the color of the cap and stalk, and the whitish gills that turn vinaceous buff to dull grayish red are distinctive.

Lactarius pyrogalus (Fries) Fries Illus. p. 111, 112

Epicr. Syst. Mycol. (1838), 339

CAP: 1¼–5⅛" (4–13 cm) wide, convex, becoming nearly plane and depressed; margin inrolled at first, becoming decurved; surface lubricous to slightly viscid, glabrous, pinkish gray to light gray or grayish olive-brown to pale yellowish brown, sometimes with a slight purplish hue, zonate with gray-brown zones.

GILLS: attached to decurrent, moderately broad, subdistant to distant, pale yellowish when young, becoming ochre-yellow with a slight vinaceous tone at maturity.

STALK: 1⅛–2¾" (3–7 cm) long, ¼–½" (5–12 mm) thick, nearly equal down to a somewhat smaller base, dry or sometimes lubricous to viscid, whitish with a slight tone of the cap color, base occasionally yellowish.

FLESH: white or sometimes tinged the same color as the cap, very slowly becoming pale creamy yellow when cut; odor like apple with a resinous component or not distinctive; taste very acrid.

LATEX: white to creamy white on exposure, unchanging, not staining tissues, drying yellowish on injured tissues; taste rapidly becoming extremely acrid.

SPORE DEPOSIT: not stated in the original description.

MICROSCOPIC CHARACTERS: spores 6.0–7.5 × 5–6 µm, broadly ellipsoid, ornamented with unbranched ridges that form a zebroid pattern but not a reticulum, prominences up to 1 µm high, hyaline, amyloid; cap cuticle a poorly delimited ixolattice becoming an ixocutis.

OCCURRENCE: solitary, scattered, or in groups on the ground in hardwood or mixed-woods forests; July–October; widely distributed in eastern North America; occasional.

EDIBILITY: unknown.

COMMENTS: The pinkish gray zonate cap, distant yellowish gills, and very acrid-tasting flesh and latex are this species' distinctive features. A variant of this species in which the latex dries grayish green is sometimes encountered.

Lactarius quietus var. **incanus** Hesler and A. H. Smith Illus. p. 112, 113

North American Species of Lactarius (1979), 478–479

CAP: 1¼–4⅜" (3–11 cm) wide, broadly convex, becoming plane with a depressed center at maturity; margin incurved at first, becoming expanded to uplifted, opaque when young, becoming slightly translucent-striate with age; surface coated with a layer of tiny, whitish, silky fibrils when young, soon glabrous or with scattered small bumps, moist to dry, at times with water spots, typically zonate, dark purplish brown or purplish gray when young, becoming dark red-brown at the center with age; margin a paler pinkish brown to pinkish buff.

GILLS: attached to slightly decurrent, narrow, often forked, close, white to whitish with pink tints, becoming cinnamon, staining orangey cinnamon with age.

STALK: 1⅛–5½" (4–14 cm) long, ¼–⅜" (5–10 mm) thick, equal or slightly enlarged at the base, solid, becoming hollow, dry, covered with a layer of tiny, whitish, silky fibrils when young, becoming colored like the cap and darkening progressively toward the apex as specimen matures.

FLESH: pale pinkish buff; odor sweet, fragrant, often like burnt sugar, or rarely not distinctive; taste mild then slowly becoming weakly acrid.

LATEX: white on exposure in young specimens, soon watery as specimens mature; taste mild then slowly becoming weakly acrid.

SPORE DEPOSIT: pinkish buff.

MACROCHEMICAL TESTS: cap surface staining pale olive with the application of KOH; flesh in stalk base staining grayish with the application of $FeSO_4$.

MICROSCOPIC CHARACTERS: spores 6.5–9.0 × 5.0–7.5 µm, elliptic, ornamented with warts and ridges that sometimes form a partial reticulum, prominences up to 0.6 µm high, hyaline, amyloid; cap cuticle a layer of tangled tubular hyphae giving rise at the surface to projecting clavate hyphal end cells.

OCCURRENCE: scattered or in groups on the ground under oaks; August–December; reported from eastern Canada south to New York, Michigan, and Mississippi; distribution limits and frequency yet to be determined.

EDIBILITY: unknown.

COMMENTS: *Lactarius mutabilis* is similar, but it has mild-tasting latex and a whitish to cream or dull creamy yellow spore deposit, and it grows on the ground under conifers or in mixed woods.

Lactarius repraesentaneus Britzelmayer *sensu* Neuhoff Illus. p. 113

Die Milchlinge (1956), 111

Northern Bearded Milky, Northern Milk Cap, Purple-staining Milk Cap

CAP: 2⅜–7" (6–18 cm) wide, convex to broadly funnel-shaped; margin conspicuously bearded on young specimens; surface azonate to faintly zoned, with a thin layer of matted fibers, often becoming scurfy with age, dry to somewhat sticky, light yellow to orange-yellow, sometimes with rusty tints when older.

GILLS: attached, moderately broad, close to crowded, sometimes forked near the stalk, cream to pale ochraceous, staining dull lilac to purple when bruised.

STALK: 2–4¾" (5–12 cm) long, ⅜–1⅛" (1–3 cm) thick, nearly equal or enlarged downward, hollow at maturity, sticky to dry, scrobiculate, pale yellow to orange-yellow, staining dull lilac to purple.

FLESH: firm, brittle, white, staining dull lilac to purple when cut; odor sometimes faintly fragrant or not distinctive; taste mild to slightly acrid or somewhat bitter.

LATEX: copious, white to cream, unchanging, staining all tissues dull lilac to purple; taste mild to slightly acrid or somewhat bitter.

SPORE DEPOSIT: yellowish.

MICROSCOPIC CHARACTERS: spores 8–12 × 6.5–9.0 µm, broadly ellipsoid to ellipsoid, ornamented with warts and ridges that do not form a reticulum, prominences up to 0.8 µm high, hyaline, amyloid; cap cuticle an ixocutis.

OCCURRENCE: scattered or in groups on the ground under spruce; August–September; northern United States and southern Canada where spruce is present, also reported from Alaska, California, and the Rocky Mountains; occasional to fairly common.

EDIBILITY: poisonous.

COMMENTS: The bearded yellow to orange-yellow cap, cream to pale ochraceous gills, yellow scrobiculate stalk, and conspicuous staining reactions are this species' distinctive features.

Lactarius resimus var. **resimus** (Fries) Fries Illus. p. 114

Epicr. Syst. Mycol. (1838), 336
Lactarius resimus var. *intermedius* A. H. Smith
Yellow-staining Bearded Milk Cap

CAP: 2⅜–6" (6.0–15.5 cm) wide, deeply depressed with an arched margin, becoming funnel-shaped with age; margin bearded with coarse hairs, at least on young specimens; surface viscid to glutinous, finely tomentose to nearly glabrous, azonate to faintly zoned on young specimens, sometimes conspicuously zoned on old specimens, milky white overall or with ochraceous zones.

GILLS: decurrent, crowded, often forked near the stalk, white when young, becoming pinkish buff at maturity, staining dingy yellow when bruised.

STALK: 2–3½" (5–9 cm) long, ⅜–1" (1.0–2.5 cm) thick, tapered downward, sticky or dry, hollow, white to whitish or pale yellow, inconspicuously scrobiculate or lacking scrobiculations.

FLESH: thick, not brittle, white, staining yellow when cut; odor not distinctive; taste slowly acrid.

LATEX: scant, white on exposure, quickly changing to sulfur yellow; taste slowly acrid.

SPORE DEPOSIT: whitish to pale pinkish buff.

MICROSCOPIC CHARACTERS: spores 6–8 × 5–6 µm, broadly ellipsoid, ornamented with warts and ridges that usually form a partial reticulum, prominences up to 0.5 µm high, hyaline, amyloid; cap cuticle a thick ixocutis.

OCCURRENCE: scattered on the ground under mixed conifers and hardwoods; August–October; widely distributed in North America; occasional.

EDIBILITY: unknown.

COMMENTS: *Lactarius resimus* var. *regalis* Peck (edibility unknown) is nearly identical but has larger spores that measure 7–10 × 6–8 µm.

Lactarius rimosellus Peck Illus. p. 114

Bull. N.Y. State Mus. 105 (1906), 37
Lactaria flocculosaceps Burlingham
Lactarius obnubiloides Thiers

CAP: ¾–3⅛" (2–8 cm) wide, convex, becoming depressed and typically papillate or umbonate at maturity; margin incurved at first, becoming uplifted and often wavy with age; surface dry, azonate, somewhat wrinkled, becoming rimulose-areolate especially toward the margin, dull ferruginous to rusty brown at first, soon becoming dull vinaceous pink to pinkish cinnamon, fading to pale vinaceous cinnamon with age.

GILLS: decurrent, narrow, close, sometimes forked near the stalk, whitish then somewhat yellowish or ochraceous, finally colored like the cap.

STALK: 1⅛–3⅛" (3–8 cm) long, ⅛–⅜" (3–10 mm) thick, nearly equal overall, sometimes with a pinched base, dry, becoming hollow with age, nearly glabrous, colored like the cap or paler.

FLESH: thin, brittle, colored like the cap or paler; odor fragrant, often sweet; taste mild or sometimes disagreeable.

LATEX: white to whey-like or watery on exposure, unchanging, not staining tissues; taste mild.

SPORE DEPOSIT: whitish to yellowish.

MICROSCOPIC CHARACTERS: spores 7–10 × 6.5–8.0 µm, ellipsoid, ornamented with isolated warts that are occasionally connected by fine lines or bands that do not form a reticulum, prominences up to 1 µm high, hyaline, amyloid; cap cuticle a zone of irregularly shaped cells that bear scattered mounds of cylindric, ventricose, or ovoid cells that at maturity adhere in groups.

OCCURRENCE: scattered or in groups on the ground among mosses, on decaying logs and stumps in conifer woods, or in deep pine needle humus; July–December; eastern Canada south to Florida, west to Michigan and Texas; fairly common.

EDIBILITY: unknown.

COMMENTS: *Lactarius areolatus* is very similar, but its spores have warts and short bands, and it grows on the ground under oak. *Lactarius sublacustris* is also very similar, but it has slightly smaller spores, and its cap cuticle is an ixolattice.

Lactarius riparius Methven — Not Illustrated

Mycologia 77 (1985), 476

CAP: ⅝–1½" (1.5–4.0 cm) wide, convex, becoming plane, with a depressed disc; margin incurved at first, becoming decurved, striate to translucent-striate; surface subviscid to viscid, glabrous, azonate, brownish orange to brown or reddish brown.

GILLS: attached to subdecurrent, narrow, close to subdistant, not forked, pale orange to light orange, then grayish orange, not staining when bruised.

STALK: ¾–2" (2–5 cm) long, ¼–⅜" (5–10 mm) thick, nearly equal or slightly enlarged toward the base, dry to moist, glabrous, hollow, not scrobiculate, grayish orange or brownish orange to grayish red.

FLESH: pale orange, unchanging when cut; odor not distinctive; taste mild.

LATEX: white to whey-like on exposure, unchanging, not staining tissues; taste mild.

SPORE DEPOSIT: white.

MICROSCOPIC CHARACTERS: spores 7.0–9.5 × 5.5–7.0 µm, broadly ellipsoid, ornamented with warts and ridges that form a partial reticulum, prominences up to 0.5 µm high, hyaline, amyloid; cap cuticle an ixocutis.

OCCURRENCE: scattered to gregarious in duff in seepage areas in montane conifer forests, under fir, alder, and willow; August–September; reported only from California; common.

EDIBILITY: unknown.

COMMENTS: *Lactarius luculentus* var. *luculentus* has a tawny to ochraceous tawny or ochraceous buff cap, flesh that tastes slightly bitter then slowly acrid, and a buff spore deposit. *Lactarius subflammeus* has a scarlet cap when young that soon becomes orange and finally duller with age and white latex that tastes acrid. *Lactarius lanceolatus*, reported only from Alaska, has an orange-brown cap and white flesh that tastes bitter.

Lactarius rubidus (Hesler and A. H. Smith) Methven Illus. p. 114, 115

Mycotaxon (in press)
Lactarius fragilis var. *rubidus* Hesler and A. H. Smith
Candy Cap

CAP: 1⅛–3⅛" (3–8 cm) wide, convex, soon becoming nearly plane or slightly depressed, sometimes umbonate; margin incurved at first, becoming decurved; surface dry or moist, glabrous, typically wrinkled, azonate, dull dark orange-brown over the disk to yellowish rusty brown at the margin.

GILLS: attached to subdecurrent, narrow, close to subdistant, rarely forked, light orange, not staining when bruised.

STALK: ¾–3½" (2–9 cm) long, ¼–⅝" (5–15 mm) thick, nearly equal, dry, becoming hollow with age, brownish orange to light brown, with a white to light orange basal tomentum.

FLESH: thin, distinctly brittle, light orange; odor not distinctive when fresh, becoming aromatic and resembling maple sugar when dried; taste mild.

LATEX: watery to whey-like on exposure, unchanging, not staining tissues; taste mild.

SPORE DEPOSIT: pale pinkish buff.

MICROSCOPIC CHARACTERS: spores 6.0–8.5 × 6–8 µm, globose to subglobose, ornamented with warts and ridges that form a partial reticulum, prominences up to 1 µm high, hyaline, amyloid; cap cuticle a cellular zone of clavate to vesiculose cells arranged in short chains.

OCCURRENCE: scattered, gregarious, or cespitose on the ground under oak, sometimes on decaying conifer wood; September–February; along the Pacific Coast; common.

EDIBILITY: edible; however, some people are allergic to them.

COMMENTS: *Lactarius fragilis* var. *fragilis* (Burlingham) Hesler and A. H. Smith (edibility unknown), reported from North Carolina and Tennessee, has yellowish gills, a dull yellowish brown cap, and globose spores. *Lactarius camphoratus* occurs in the northeastern United States and Canada, grows on the ground in conifer and mixed woods, usually with pine or hemlock, and has a dark red-brown cap, usually with a small, pointed umbo.

Lactarius rubrilacteus Hesler and A. H. Smith Illus. p. 115

North American Species of Lactarius (1979), 76–79
Bleeding Milk Cap

CAP: 1½–4¾" (4–12 cm) wide, broadly convex with a depressed center at first, becoming broadly vase-shaped with age; margin inrolled when young, becoming decurved and remaining so well into maturity; surface viscid, glabrous, distinctly zonate with alternating bands of orange to brownish orange and paler zones in between, developing greenish stains or flushes with age or when bruised.

GILLS: attached to short-decurrent, moderately broad, close, light pinkish cinnamon when young, becoming reddish to dark dull purplish red or sometimes tan, often staining green with age.

STALK: ¾–2⅜" (2–6 cm) long, ⅜–1⅛" (1–3 cm) thick, usually tapered downward but sometimes nearly equal or enlarged near the base, dry, becoming hollow with age, colored like the cap or paler, often stained green when older, sometimes scrobiculate.

FLESH: thick, brittle, dingy yellowish white, stained greenish when older; odor slightly aromatic or not distinctive; taste mild.

LATEX: scant, in young caps dark blood red to purplish red, in mature caps often paler and dingy orange-red; taste mild.

SPORE DEPOSIT: cream-colored.

MICROSCOPIC CHARACTERS: spores 7.5–9.0 × 6.0–7.5 µm, broadly ellipsoid, ornamented with warts and ridges that form a partial reticulum, prominences up to 0.7 µm high, hyaline, amyloid; cap cuticle a cutis of narrow, appressed, interwoven hyphae.

OCCURRENCE: scattered or in groups on the ground under conifers, especially Douglas fir and pines; July–January; the Pacific Northwest south to California and New Mexico; fairly common.

EDIBILITY: edible.

COMMENTS: The dark blood red to purplish red latex and the green staining reaction of the cap, stalk, and flesh are this species' distinctive features. Other similar species, including *Lactarius deliciosus,* have orange latex.

Lactarius rufulus Peck Illus. p. 115

Bull. Torrey Bot. Club 34 (1907), 346

CAP: 2–4" (5–10 cm) wide, broadly convex, becoming shallowly funnel-shaped; margin incurved to decurved; surface moist or dry, glabrous, azonate, brownish red at first, fading to orange-brown with age.

GILLS: attached to subdecurrent, close to subdistant, not forked, pruinose, pinkish yellow, becoming darker with age, not staining when bruised.

STALK: 1½–3⅛" (4–8 cm) long, about ¼" (5–6 mm) thick, nearly equal or enlarged downward, dry, glabrous, stuffed or hollow, reddish brown.

FLESH: thick, white to pinkish orange, not staining when cut; odor not distinctive; taste slightly acrid.

LATEX: scant, yellowish white on exposure, unchanging, not staining tissues; taste acrid.

SPORE DEPOSIT: white to creamy yellow.

MICROSCOPIC CHARACTERS: spores 7–9 × 7–9 µm, globose to subglobose, ornamented with a partial to complete reticulum, prominences up to 0.5 µm high; cap cuticle a poorly formed layer of inflated cells with scattered filamentous pileocystidia.

OCCURRENCE: scattered or in groups on the ground under oak; January–March; reported only from California; uncommon.

EDIBILITY: edible.

COMMENTS: *Lactarius rubidus* is similar, but it has watery to whey-like latex and develops a strong maple sugar odor when dried. *Lactarius thiersii* is also similar, but it has a smaller cap and stalk and has mild-tasting flesh and latex. The flesh and latex of *Lactarius rufus* has a strongly acrid taste.

Lactarius rufus var. **rufus** (Fries) Fries Illus. p. 116

Epicr. Syst. Mycol. (1838), 347
Lactarius boughtoni Peck
Lactarius rufus var. *boughtoni* (Peck) Kauffman
Red Hot Milk Cap, Red-hot Milky

CAP: 1⅝–4¾" (4–12 cm) wide, convex and often umbonate when young, becoming broadly convex to nearly plane with a depressed center and finally broadly funnel-shaped when older; margin incurved at first, becoming uplifted, sometimes ribbed; surface often coated with a whitish bloom when young, becoming dull, dry, dark brownish red to dark bay red, sometimes zoned with slightly darker bands.

GILLS: attached to slightly decurrent, narrow, crowded, whitish, becoming vinaceous buff to vinaceous tan with age, *not* staining when bruised.

STALK: 2–4⅜" (5–11 cm) long, ⅜–1¾" (9–18 mm) thick, equal, stuffed, dry, with a whitish bloom at first, then colored like the cap, whitish at the base.

FLESH: dingy pale vinaceous, odor not distinctive; taste intensely acrid.

LATEX: copious in young specimens, white on exposure, unchanging, not staining tissues; taste intensely acrid.

SPORE DEPOSIT: cream to pale yellow.

MACROCHEMICAL TESTS: flesh slowly staining olive-gray with the application of $FeSO_4$.

MICROSCOPIC CHARACTERS: spores 8.5–12.0 × 6–8 µm, broadly ellipsoid, ornamented with warts and ridges that form a partial reticulum, prominences up to 0.5 µm high, hyaline, amyloid; cap cuticle a layer of appressed more or less radial hyphae, 2–5 µm wide.

OCCURRENCE: solitary, scattered, or in groups on the ground under pines or among sphagnum mosses in bogs; August–October; widely distributed in North America; fairly common.

EDIBILITY: poisonous.

COMMENTS: *Lactarius rufus* var. *parvus* Hesler and A. H. Smith (edibility unknown), reported only from Upper Priest River, Idaho, has a smaller cap, scant latex, smaller spores that measure 7–9 × 5.5–6.5 µm, and a white spore deposit.

Lactarius ruginosus Romagnesi *sensu* Hesler and A. H. Smith Illus. p. 116

Bull. Soc. Mycol. France 72 (1956), 335
North American Species of Lactarius (1979), 135–137
Lactarius fuliginosus var. *clitocyboides* A. H. Smith and Hesler

CAP: 2⅜–5⅞" (6–15 cm) wide, broadly convex to nearly plane, often with an obscure umbo; margin incurved at first, becoming decurved, elevated, scalloped, or lobed when older; surface dry, glabrous and dull, azonate, often distinctly wrinkled when immature, becoming somewhat granulose under a hand lens at maturity, olive-brown to buff-brown, margin slightly paler.

GILLS: decurrent, broad, distant, sometimes forked near the stalk, whitish to pale olive-buff, staining reddish when bruised.

STALK: 2⅜–4" (6–10 cm) long, ⅜–¾" (1–2 cm) thick, nearly equal or enlarged downward, dry, solid or hollow, dull, whitish when young, colored like the cap or paler at maturity.

FLESH: moderately thick, fragile, whitish, staining red when cut; odor not distinctive.

LATEX: white on exposure, unchanging, staining injured tissues red; taste slowly acrid in young specimens, but mild in older specimens.

SPORE DEPOSIT: dull buff.

MICROSCOPIC CHARACTERS: spores 7–9 × 7–9 µm, globose to subglobose; ornamented with a nearly complete reticulum, prominences up to 2.5 µm high, hyaline, amyloid; cap cuticle a modified trichoderm.

OCCURRENCE: scattered to gregarious under beech; July–August; reported from Mississippi, North Carolina, and Tennessee; distribution limits and frequency yet to be determined.

EDIBILITY: unknown.

COMMENTS: Hesler and Smith's description of North American material differs considerably from the European collections that Romagnesi described. *Lactarius fumosus* var. *fumosus* is nearly identical but has crowded gills.

Lactarius salmoneus var. **salmoneus** Peck Illus. p. 117

Bull. Torrey Bot. Club 25 (1898), 369

CAP: 1–3⅛" (2.5–8.0 cm) wide, convex, becoming nearly plane and depressed at the center; margin inrolled to incurved at first, becoming decurved and remaining so well into maturity; surface dry, subvelvety, azonate, at first white, becoming orange nearly overall as the white layer wears away with age, staining orange when bruised.

GILLS: attached to decurrent, narrow, close to subdistant, typically not forked, light orange at first, becoming paler orange to ochraceous buff with age, staining dark orange when bruised.

STALK: ½–1" (1.2–2.5 cm) long, ¼–½" (6–13 mm) thick, tapered downward, dry, glabrous, becoming hollow with age, white at first, becoming light orange overall as the white layer wears away with age or sometimes retaining white areas, usually not scrobiculate.

FLESH: moderately thick, firm, light orange, staining darker orange when exposed, especially near the gills; odor slightly fragrant or not distinctive; taste slightly peppery or mild.

LATEX: scant, dark orange on exposure, staining gills dark orange; taste slightly peppery or mild.

SPORE DEPOSIT: creamy white.

MICROSCOPIC CHARACTERS: spores 7.5–9.0 × 5–6 µm, ellipsoid, ornamented with warts and ridges that form a partial reticulum, prominences up to 0.4 µm high, hyaline, amyloid; cap cuticle a layer of repent interwoven hyphae, many of which are erect.

OCCURRENCE: solitary, scattered, or in groups on the ground or in wet areas under pine or in mixed oak and pine woods; July–September; South Carolina south to Florida, west to Texas; occasional.

EDIBILITY: unknown.

COMMENTS: *Lactarius salmoneus* var. *curtisii* (Coker) Hesler and A. H. Smith (edibility unknown) is very similar if not identical, grows on moist low-lying areas under pine or mixed pine-hardwood forests from Tennessee and North Carolina south to Florida and west to Texas. It differs from var. *salmoneus* in that the cap surface of old specimens stains bluish green, the gills readily stain green when injured, and the stalk stains green when bruised.

Lactarius salmonicolor R. Heim and Leclair Illus. p. 117, 118

Rev. Mycol. (Paris) 18 (1953), 221–224
Lactarius salmoneus R. Heim and Leclair
Lactarius subsalmoneus Pouzar
Lactarius thyinos A. H. Smith

CAP: 1⅛–4¾" (3–12 cm) wide, convex, becoming broadly convex to nearly plane with a depressed center, sometimes broadly funnel-shaped; margin incurved at first, becoming decurved and remaining so well into maturity; surface viscid when fresh, glabrous overall or sometimes finely striate at the margin, faintly to distinctly zonate especially near the margin, salmon orange to ochraceous orange or peach, not forming green spots or only rarely so on very old specimens.

GILLS: attached to subdecurrent, medium broad, close to subdistant, sometimes forked, pale yellowish orange to pale pinkish orange or pinkish buff, staining orange then slowly wine red to brownish vinaceous when bruised.

STALK: ¾–3⅛" (2–8 cm) long, ¼–1" (5–25 mm) thick, nearly equal or tapered downward, viscid when fresh, glabrous, hollow at maturity, pale salmon orange to salmon peach, sometimes with a silvery sheen, typically with darker orange scrobiculations, sometimes with greenish tinges at the base.

FLESH: fairly thick, firm, white to cream, quickly staining orange when exposed, then slowly becoming coral to wine red or brownish vinaceous, especially in the stalk base; odor usually sweet but sometimes unpleasant; taste mild then slowly astringent to disagreeable.

LATEX: abundant, reddish orange on exposure, very slowly changing to wine red or brownish vinaceous; taste mild then astringent to disagreeable.

SPORE DEPOSIT: pale pinkish buff.

MACROCHEMICAL TESTS: cap surface and flesh negative with the application of KOH, NH_4OH, or $FeSO_4$.

MICROSCOPIC CHARACTERS: spores 9.5–12.0 × 7.0–9.5 µm, broadly ellipsoid to ellipsoid, ornamented with warts and ridges that form a partial reticulum, prominences up to 0.5 µm high, hyaline, amyloid; macrocystidia abundant on the gill edges, fusiform with a moniliform apex; cap cuticle an ixocutis.

OCCURRENCE: scattered to densely gregarious on the ground or in grassy areas under fir trees or among sphagnum mosses in bogs or wet woodlands; September–November; eastern Canada and the northeastern United States, west to Minnesota; occasional to fairly common.

EDIBILITY: edible.

COMMENTS: In their key to species of the subgenus *Lactarius,* Hesler and A. H. Smith state that the stalk base of *Lactarius salmonicolor* does not stain vinaceous (1979, 67), a character that is inconsistent with the original description of this species by R. Heim and Leclair. In addition, we have observed coral to vinaceous stains in the stalk base of specimens of *Lactarius salmonicolor* we collected under balsam fir in upland forests. In all respects except for habitat, *Lactarius thyinos* and *Lactarius salmonicolor* are identical, so we have placed them in synonymy. *Lactarius deliciosus* var. *deliciosus* and *Lactarius deterrimus* are similar but develop conspicuous green to grayish green stains.

Lactarius sanmiguelensis Hesler and A. H. Smith — Not Illustrated

North American Species of Lactarius (1979), 265–266
Lactarius subvillosus Hesler and A. H. Smith

CAP: 3⅛–6" (8.0–15.5 cm) wide, nearly plane with a depressed center, becoming broadly vase-shaped; margin incurved at first, when older expanding with a heavy roll of soft felt that is pale pinkish buff or nearly so; surface glabrous except for the margin, zonate, cinnamon buff zones on a pinkish buff ground color.

GILLS: attached, narrow, close to crowded, often anastomosed, pinkish buff or nearly so, not discoloring where injured.

STALK: 2⅜–3⅛" (6–8 cm) long, 1–1⅜" (2.5–3.5 cm) thick, clavate, scrobiculate, pinkish buff.

FLESH: thick, hard; odor not distinctive.

LATEX: milk white on exposure, unchanging, not staining tissues; taste instantly becoming very strongly acrid.

SPORE DEPOSIT: not obtained.

MICROSCOPIC CHARACTERS: spores 6.5–8.0 × 5–6 µm, ellipsoid, ornamented with warts and ridges that form a partial reticulum, prominences up to 0.5 µm high, hyaline, amyloid; cap cuticle an ixocutis over the disc or a poorly delimited cutis over the marginal area.

OCCURRENCE: cespitose at the edge of a field near cottonwood trees; August; reported only from Placerville, Colorado; distribution limits and frequency yet to be determined.

EDIBILITY: unknown.

COMMENTS: We have placed *Lactarius subvillosus* in synonymy with *Lactarius sanmiguelensis* because of the absence of significant differentiating characteristics.

Lactarius scrobiculatus var. **canadensis** (A. H. Smith) Hesler and A. H. Smith

Illus. p. 118, 119

North American Species of Lactarius (1979), 297–299
Lactarius payettensis var. *canadensis* A. H. Smith
Pitted Milk Cap

CAP: 1½–4¾" (4–15 cm) wide, convex to nearly plane, with a depressed disc; margin incurved to decurved, typically bearded at first with coarse hairs or rarely merely pubescent, becoming glabrous at maturity; surface viscid but soon dry, somewhat fibrillose, azonate, typically yellow from young to older stages, but sometimes whitish to olive-buff when young, becoming yellow when older.

GILLS: subdecurrent, narrow to somewhat broad, crowded, sometimes forked near the stalk, whitish to yellowish or pale orange-yellow, staining yellowish to grayish brown when bruised.

STALK: 1⅛–4¼" (3–11 cm) long, ⅜–1¼" (1–3 cm) thick, nearly equal, dry, stuffed or hollow, scrobiculate, white to yellowish with brownish yellow spots, bruising yellow to rusty brown.

FLESH: thick, white, firm, quickly changing to yellow; odor faintly fragrant; taste slightly acrid or not distinctive.

LATEX: scant, white on exposure, rapidly changing to sulfur yellow; taste slightly acrid or not distinctive.

SPORE DEPOSIT: white to cream-colored.

MICROSCOPIC CHARACTERS: spores 7–9 × 5.5–7.0 µm, ellipsoid, ornamented with warts and branched ridges that do not form a reticulum, prominences up to 0.5 µm high, hyaline, amyloid; cap cuticle an ixocutis with fascicles of fibrils.

OCCURRENCE: solitary to gregarious in conifer forests; July–October; widely distributed in northern and mountainous areas of North America, reported from Alaska south to Idaho, California, and Colorado, east to Nova Scotia, south to Michigan, New England, and New York; fairly common.

EDIBILITY: possibly poisonous.

COMMENTS: *Lactarius scrobiculatus* var. *montanus* Methven (edibility unknown), reported only from California, has a subviscid to viscid cap that stains brownish orange when bruised, white flesh that tastes mild to slightly acrid, white latex that quickly turns light yellow and tastes slightly acrid, and a semihypogeous habit. *Lactarius scrobiculatus* var. *pubescens,* reported from Michigan and Quebec, has a moist to subviscid cap that is distinctly yellow when young and cinnamon buff over the center with orange-yellow along the margin when older, slightly acrid white latex that very quickly becomes pale lemon yellow, and smaller spores that measure 6.0–7.5 × 4.5–6.0 µm. *Lactarius scrobiculatus* var. *scrobiculatus* Fries (edibility unknown) is a European species that has not been documented from North America.

Lactarius scrobiculatus var. **pubescens** A. H. Smith Illus. p. 119

Brittonia 12 (1960), 323

CAP: 3⅛–4" (8–10 cm) wide, shallowly funnel-shaped, smooth, viscid in the depression, with an obscure agglutinated tomentum near the margin; surface azonate, distinctly yellow when young, becoming cinnamon buff over the center with orange-yellow along the margin when older; margin minutely downy to bearded when young.

GILLS: attached, close, narrow, sometimes forked near the stalk, whitish to pale yellow.

STALK: ⅝–1³⁄₁₆" (1.5–3.0 cm) long, about ⅜" (10 mm) thick, somewhat tapered downward or nearly equal, dull, hollow, hard, white.

FLESH: up to ⅜" (10 mm) thick over the disc, white, changing to yellow on exposure; odor and taste not distinctive.

LATEX: white on exposure, quickly changing to yellow, staining flesh and gills light brown; taste slightly acrid or not distinctive.

SPORE DEPOSIT: white.

MICROSCOPIC CHARACTERS: spores 6.0–7.5 × 4.5–6.0 µm, ellipsoid; ornamented with irregular lines forming a broken to partial reticulum with isolated warts, prominences from 0.2 to 0.5 µm, wall nonamyloid, prominences amyloid; cap cuticle a thick ixocutis.

OCCURRENCE: scattered or in groups in duff in mountain coniferous forests; June–September; reported from Quebec, Michigan, and California; uncommon.

EDIBILITY: unknown.

COMMENTS: *Lactarius scrobiculatus* var. *canadensis* is widely distributed in North America. It has a yellow cap from young stages to maturity, a conspicuously bearded margin, and larger spores that measure 7–9 × 5.5–7.0 µm. *Lactarius scrobiculatus* var. *montanus* Methven (edibility unknown), reported only from California, has a subviscid to viscid cap that stains brownish orange when bruised, white flesh that tastes mild to slightly acrid, white latex that quickly turns light yellow and tastes slightly acrid, and a semihypogeous habit.

Lactarius similis Hesler and A. H. Smith Not Illustrated

North American Species of Lactarius (1979), 215–216

CAP: 1½–3⅛" (4–8 cm) wide, convex, depressed; margin entire; surface dry, subtomentose to pruinose, azonate, pale vinaceous cinnamon, often fading to pale yellow.

GILLS: attached to subdecurrent, narrow, close, pale yellow, staining greenish.

STALK: ¾–1⅛" (2–3 cm) long, ⅜–⅝" (1.0–1.5 cm) thick, tapered downward to nearly equal, dry, solid, subtomentose or pruinose, white.

FLESH: not stated in the original description.

LATEX: white on exposure, unchanging, staining the gills greenish; taste mild.

SPORE DEPOSIT: not stated in the original description.

MICROSCOPIC CHARACTERS: spores 7–10 × 5.5–7.5 µm, ellipsoid, ornamented with fine lines that sometimes form a partial reticulum, prominences up to 0.1 µm high, hyaline, amyloid; cap cuticle a mass of interwoven hyphae bearing a dense turf of hypoid, colorless pileocystidia.

OCCURRENCE: on soil in hardwoods; June; reported only from Ramsey Springs, Mississippi; distribution limits and frequency yet to be determined.

EDIBILITY: unknown.

COMMENTS: *Lactarius allardii* is very similar, but it has a larger pinkish cinnamon to brick red cap that does not fade to pale yellow and acrid latex. In our opinion,

Lactarius similis could easily be considered a variety of *Lactarius allardii* rather than being classified as a separate species.

Lactarius speciosus Burlingham Illus. p. 119

Mem. Torrey Bot. Club 14 (1908), 34
Lactaria speciosa Burlingham

CAP: 1⅛–4" (3–10 cm) wide, broadly convex, becoming nearly plane with a depressed center when older, often broadly funnel-shaped; margin inrolled and bearded with coarse hairs when young, becoming expanded to uplifted and glabrous with age; surface sticky when young, becoming dry, covered with a thin layer of fibrils, pale cinnamon or orange-brown, conspicuously zonate with bands of pinkish tan and cinnamon brown.

GILLS: attached to slightly decurrent, close, cream to pinkish buff, staining dull lilac when cut or bruised.

STALK: 1⅛–2" (3–5 cm) long, ⅜–1" (1.0–2.5 cm) thick, equal, hollow, dry, whitish to buff, scrobiculate with reddish brown and yellowish spots and streaks.

FLESH: thick, firm, whitish; odor not distinctive; taste mild to slightly bitter or acrid.

LATEX: white on exposure, unchanging, staining the gills and flesh dull lilac; taste mild to slightly bitter or acrid.

SPORE DEPOSIT: white.

MICROSCOPIC CHARACTERS: spores 10.0–13.5 × 9–11 µm, broadly ellipsoid, ornamented with warts and ridges that form a partial reticulum, prominences up to 2 µm high, hyaline, amyloid; cap cuticle a thin ixocutis.

OCCURRENCE: scattered or in groups in hardwoods and mixed woods; July–December; eastern Canada south to Florida, west to Texas; occasional.

EDIBILITY: unknown.

COMMENTS: *Lactarius dispersus* is similar but has a yellowish spore deposit and smaller, less-reticulate spores.

Lactarius splendens Hesler and A. H. Smith Illus. p. 120

North American Species of Lactarius (1979), 453–454

CAP: ¾–2⅜" (2–6 cm) wide, broadly convex, becoming nearly plane, often depressed at the center; margin inrolled at first, becoming decurved to uplifted with age; surface viscid, glabrous, shiny, bright orange to bright pinkish orange.

GILLS: attached, narrow, close to crowded, often forked near the stalk, pale dull yellow.

STALK: ¾–3⅛" (2–8 cm) long, ¼–⅜" (5–10 mm) thick, nearly equal, lubricous, shiny, becoming hollow with age, sometimes scrobiculate, orange-buff overall or paler at the apex.

FLESH: pale buff, unchanging when cut; odor not distinctive; taste mild.

LATEX: scant, milk white or in old caps a watery cream color on exposure, unchanging, not staining tissues.

SPORE DEPOSIT: yellowish.

MICROSCOPIC CHARACTERS: spores 7–9 × 6–7 µm, ellipsoid, ornamented with warts and ridges that form a partial reticulum, prominences up to 0.4 µm high, hyaline, amyloid; cap cuticle an ixolattice.

OCCURRENCE: scattered to gregarious under conifers, usually among sphagnum mosses; August–November; eastern Canada and New England west to Minnesota; occasional.

EDIBILITY: unknown.

COMMENTS: The name *splendens* means "splendid," an appropriate descriptor for this beautiful species. Mycologist Richard L. Homola (1934–1999) collected the type specimen in Maine.

Lactarius subflammeus Hesler and A. H. Smith Illus. p. 120

North American Species of Lactarius (1979), 451–452

CAP: 1¼–2¾" (3–7 cm) wide, convex, becoming shallowly depressed over the disc; margin incurved then arched, with short translucent striations at maturity; surface slimy-viscid, glabrous, azonate, scarlet when young, becoming orange to yellow orange and duller when older.

GILLS: attached to decurrent, moderately broad, close to subdistant, whitish or colored like the cap but paler.

STALK: 1½–3½" (4–9 cm) long, 3⁄16–⅝" (5–15 mm) thick, enlarged toward the base, moist or dry, hollow, fragile, glabrous, colored like the cap.

FLESH: thin, fragile, pale pinkish buff to dull orange-buff; odor not distinctive; taste slowly acrid.

LATEX: white on exposure, unchanging, not staining tissues; taste acrid.

SPORE DEPOSIT: white.

MICROSCOPIC CHARACTERS: spores 7.5–9.0 × 6.5–7.5 µm, ellipsoid, ornamented with warts and short ridges that do not form a reticulum, prominences up to 1.0 µm high, hyaline, amyloid; cap cuticle a modified ixotrichoderm.

OCCURRENCE: scattered to gregarious under conifers or in mixed conifer-hardwood forests; August–December; Washington south to Idaho, California, and Colorado; common.

EDIBILITY: unknown.

COMMENTS: *Lactarius luculentus* var. *luculentus* is similar, but it has an ochraceous tawny to ochraceous buff cap and stalk, flesh that tastes slightly bitter then slowly acrid, white latex that tastes mild to somewhat astringent, and a buff-colored spore deposit. *Lactarius luculentus* var. *laetus* is also similar, but it has a brownish orange to light brown or reddish brown disc and an orange margin, a light orange to grayish orange stalk, and mild-tasting latex. Also compare with *Lactarius substriatus,* which has white latex that slowly changes to yellow, and *Lactarius subviscidus,* which has similar coloring but white latex that changes to yellow.

Lactarius subgerardii Hesler and A. H. Smith Illus. p. 120

North American Species of Lactarius (1979), 107–108

CAP: ⅝–3⅛" (1.5–8.0 cm) wide, convex, becoming nearly plane with a depressed center, sometimes with a low, broad umbo; margin incurved at first, becoming decurved and remaining so well into maturity, even to finely scalloped; surface dry, minutely velvety, azonate, finely wrinkled, pale gray-brown to pale smoky brown, blackish on the wrinkles.

GILLS: attached to subdecurrent, narrow to medium broad, subdistant or nearly close, not forked, white at first, becoming creamy yellow, not staining when bruised.

STALK: ⅝–3⅛" (1.5–8.0 cm) long, ⅛–⅜" (3–10 mm) thick, nearly equal or slightly tapered downward, dry, minutely velvety, colored like the cap but usually paler, often with a white basal mycelium.

FLESH: thin, whitish; odor not distinctive; taste slowly to quickly acrid.

LATEX: white on exposure, unchanging, not staining tissues; taste quickly acrid.

SPORE DEPOSIT: white.

MICROSCOPIC CHARACTERS: spores 7–9 × 6.0–7.5 µm, ellipsoid to subglobose, ornamented with warts and ridges that form a partial reticulum, prominences up to 0.6 µm high, hyaline, amyloid; cap cuticle a cellular layer of irregular to barrel-shaped or vesiculose cells.

OCCURRENCE: scattered or in groups on soil or among mosses under hemlock or in mixed woodlands with pine, hemlock, poplar, and birch; July–September; reported from eastern Canada, New Jersey, Tennessee, and West Virginia; distribution limits and frequency yet to be determined.

EDIBILITY: unknown.

COMMENTS: *Lactarius gerardii* var. *gerardii* is similar, but it has a dull yellowish brown cap that typically has a pointed umbo and a crenate to wavy margin, a dark, dull yellowish brown stalk, and subdistant gills that become distant at maturity.

Lactarius subisabellinus Murrill — Not Illustrated

Lloydia 11 (1948), 93
Lactarius burkei A. H. Smith and Hesler
Lactarius subisabellinus var. *murrillianus* (A. H. Smith and Hesler) Hesler and A. H. Smith

CAP: 1⅛–2⅝" (3.0–6.7 cm) wide, convex-depressed, becoming broadly vase-shaped; margin incurved at first, becoming decurved to arched; surface dry, dull, subvelutinous, sometimes finely wrinkled over the disc, azonate, pale pinkish buff overall or slightly darker especially over the disc, drying whitish.

GILLS: attached to subdecurrent, narrow, close to crowded, sometimes forked, cream-colored or slightly darker, not staining when bruised.

STALK: 2–2¾" (5–7 cm) long, 5⁄16–½" (8–12 mm) thick, nearly equal or tapered downward, dry, glabrous to obscurely striate, becoming hollow with age, white or colored like the cap disc.

FLESH: thick, whitish, unchanging when cut; odor somewhat fragrant at first or not distinctive; taste mild.

LATEX: copious, white on exposure, unchanging, not staining tissues; taste mild.

SPORE DEPOSIT: yellowish.

MICROSCOPIC CHARACTERS: spores 7.0–9.5 × 6–9 µm, globose to subglobose, ornamented with warts and ridges that form a partial reticulum, prominences up to 1.5 µm high, hyaline, amyloid; cap cuticle a poorly defined layer of short-celled hyphae giving rise to versiform, stubby pileocystidia.

OCCURRENCE: on the ground in mixed woods or hardwoods, usually with oak present; July–September; Tennessee and North Carolina south to Florida, west to Mississippi; distribution limits and frequency yet to be determined.

EDIBILITY: unknown.

COMMENTS: We have placed *Lactarius subisabellinus* var. *murrillianus* in synonymy with *Lactarius subisabellinus* Murrill because of the absence of significant differentiating characteristics.

Lactarius sublacustris Hesler and A. H. Smith — Not Illustrated

North American Species of Lactarius (1979), 489–490

CAP: 1⅛–2" (3–5 cm) wide, convex, soon depressed and finally funnel-shaped; margin striatulate at maturity when moist; surface lubricous to viscid when wet, glabrous, pinkish cinnamon to reddish cinnamon or pecan brown, often darker on the disc.

GILLS: attached to decurrent, moderately broad, crowded, pinkish cinnamon when young, spotting reddish cinnamon and finally becoming reddish cinnamon overall with age.

STALK: 1⅛–2⅜" (3–6 cm) long, ⅛–¼" (3–7 mm) thick, nearly equal, dry, glabrous, colored like the cap on the lower portion and paler on the upper portion, gradually darkening to reddish cinnamon from the base upward.

FLESH: thin, colored like the cap surface and fading to pale vinaceous buff; odor not distinctive; taste mild.

LATEX: copious, milk white on exposure, unchanging, staining gills darker vinaceous cinnamon; taste mild.

SPORE DEPOSIT: white.

MICROSCOPIC CHARACTERS: spores 7–8 × 5–6 µm, ellipsoid, ornamented with warts and ridges that form a partial reticulum, prominences up to 0.5 µm high, hyaline, amyloid; cap cuticle a compact ixolattice.

OCCURRENCE: scattered at the edge of a woodland pool; August; reported from Winnawana Lake, Michigan; distribution limits and frequency yet to be determined.

EDIBILITY: unknown.

COMMENTS: *Lactarius areolatus* and *Lactarius rimosellus* are similar but have rimulose-areolate caps, flesh with a fragrant and often sweet odor, and slightly larger spores with ornamentation that does not form a partial reticulum.

Lactarius subolivaceus Hesler and A. H. Smith Not Illustrated

North American Species of Lactarius (1979), 462–463

CAP: 1⅛–2¼" (3–6 cm) wide, convex to nearly plane, disc slightly depressed, sometimes with a small umbo; margin incurved to decurved, at times striate; surface viscid, glabrous, azonate, light pinkish cinnamon with a distinct olive tint.

GILLS: subdecurrent, medium broad, close, sometimes forked near the stalk, white to pinkish cinnamon.

STALK: 1½–2¾" (4–7 cm) long, ¼–½" (4–11 mm) thick, nearly equal, dry, spongy to solid, glabrous, colored like the cap.

FLESH: thin, firm, white, unchanging when cut; odor slightly pungent; taste acrid.

LATEX: white to whey-like on exposure, unchanging, not staining tissues; taste acrid.

SPORE DEPOSIT: yellowish buff.

MICROSCOPIC CHARACTERS: spores 7.5–10.0 × 6.0–7.5 µm, ellipsoid, ornamented with warts and bands that form a partial to complete reticulum, prominences up to 1.0 µm high, hyaline, amyloid; cap cuticle a tangled ixotrichoderm to an ixolattice.

OCCURRENCE: on soil in pine woods; October; reported only from Tennessee; distribution limits and frequency yet to be determined.

EDIBILITY: unknown.

COMMENTS: The distinct olive tints, southern range, and viscid cap separate this species from a similar species, *Lactarius hepaticus.*

Lactarius subpaludosus Hesler and A. H. Smith Not Illustrated

North American Species of Lactarius (1979), 286–288

CAP: ¾–2" (2–5 cm) wide, convex, becoming nearly plane with a depressed center; margin inrolled and bearded with fine strigose hairs; surface dry, matted-fibrillose, light buff overall or ochraceous buff on the disc, becoming brownish ochraceous with age (lacking any pink or vinaceous tints).

GILLS: attached to subdecurrent, narrow, crowded, whitish to yellowish or light ochraceous buff at first, becoming pinkish buff with cinnamon buff stains over time.

STALK: ⅜–2" (1–5 cm) long, ⅛–⅝" (4–15 mm) thick, nearly equal, dry, glabrous, solid, whitish to yellowish or light ochraceous buff, becoming pinkish buff with cinnamon buff stains when specimen older.

FLESH: thin, white, slowly becoming brownish ochraceous; odor not distinctive; taste instantly acrid.

LATEX: milk white on exposure, slowly changing to creamy yellow and drying slightly darker yellow, viscous, drops very quickly becoming solid; taste acrid.

SPORE DEPOSIT: pale pinkish buff.

MACROCHEMICAL TESTS: latex staining orangey ochraceous with the application of KOH.

MICROSCOPIC CHARACTERS: spores 6–8 × 4.5–6.0 µm, broadly ellipsoid to subglobose, ornamented with warts and ridges that form a partial reticulum, prominences up to 0.3 µm high, hyaline, amyloid; cap cuticle a loosely tangled layer of hyphae and fascicles of hyphae.

OCCURRENCE: subcespitose to gregarious near birch species in wet swampy places; September–October; reported from Michigan and New York; distribution limits and frequency yet to be established.

EDIBILITY: unknown.

COMMENTS: *Lactarius pubescens* var. *betulae* is very similar and has white latex that soon becomes pale yellow, but its cap has pink tints, and it has a white spore deposit. *Lactarius pubescens* var. *pubescens* is also similar, but it has white latex that does not change after exposure. Also compare with *Lactarius subtorminosus,* which has mild-tasting latex.

Lactarius subpalustris Hesler and A. H. Smith Illus. p. 121

North American Species of Lactarius (1979), 334–336

CAP: 4–8" (10–20 cm) wide, broadly convex to nearly plane with a depressed center; margin incurved at first, becoming decurved and remaining so well into maturity; surface slimy to viscid, glabrous, azonate to obscurely zonate, dingy pinkish gray with ochraceous tones, with orangey olive to dingy yellow-brown spots and often developing a dingy gray cast overall with age.

GILLS: decurrent, broad, close to subdistant, creamy buff at first, becoming pinkish buff to cinnamon buff with age, readily staining lilac where injured.

STALK: 2–4" (5–10 cm) long, ⅝–1" (1.5–2.5 cm) thick, viscid but soon dry, firm, becoming hollow with age, glabrous, colored like the cap but paler, typically scrobiculate.

FLESH: thick, watery buff, soon staining bright lilac; odor not distinctive; taste mild.

LATEX: whey-like, pale dingy buff on exposure, unchanging, staining tissues lilac; taste mild to somewhat bitter.

SPORE DEPOSIT: pinkish buff.

MACROCHEMICAL TESTS: cap surface negative with the application of KOH; flesh and latex staining purple with the application of $FeSO_4$ and negative with KOH.

MICROSCOPIC CHARACTERS: spores 8–11 × 7–9 µm, subglobose to broadly ellipsoid, ornamented with bands and warts that do not form a reticulum, prominences up to 2 µm high, hyaline, amyloid; cap cuticle a thick ixocutis of interwoven hyphae.

OCCURRENCE: scattered or in groups in low, mixed hardwoods; July–October; reported from Michigan, Tennessee, West Virginia, and Texas; distribution limits and frequency yet to be determined.

EDIBILITY: unknown.

COMMENTS: *Lactarius maculatus* is similar but has a conspicuously zonate cap and white latex that tastes acrid. *Lactarius uvidus* var. *uvidus* is also similar, but it has white latex that soon becomes dingy pale cream and stains tissues dull lilac, and its cap surface stains green to olive with the application of KOH. *Lactarius maculosus* has white latex that soon becomes dingy pale cream-colored on exposure and does not stain tissues.

Lactarius subplinthogalus Coker

Illus. p. 121, 122

J. Elisha Mitchell Sci. Soc. 34 (1918), 50
Lactarius marylandicus A. H. Smith and Hesler

CAP: 1¼–2" (3–5 cm) wide, nearly plane, becoming broadly funnel-shaped with age; margin uplifted and conspicuously plicate; surface nearly glabrous when young, becoming finely wrinkled when older, whitish when young, becoming yellowish buff to pale tan and finally brownish yellow with age.

GILLS: attached to slightly decurrent, broad, distant, colored like the cap, staining rosy salmon when cut and bruised.

STALK: 1¼–3⅛" (3–8 cm) long, ¼–⅝" (7–15 mm) thick, equal or tapered slightly downward, solid, becoming hollow, glabrous, dry, cream-colored, developing orangish or orange-brown stains with age.

FLESH: whitish, staining rosy salmon when cut or bruised; odor not distinctive; taste acrid.

LATEX: white on exposure, unchanging, but staining gills and flesh rosy salmon; taste acrid.

SPORE DEPOSIT: pinkish buff to cinnamon buff.

MICROSCOPIC CHARACTERS: spores 7.5–9.5 × 7–8 µm, subglobose to broadly ellipsoid, ornamented with warts and ridges that do not form a reticulum, prominences up to 2.5 µm high, hyaline, amyloid; cap cuticle a thin layer of short, ascending hyphal cells.

OCCURRENCE: solitary to scattered on the ground under oak or in oak-pine woods; July–September; Maryland south to Florida, west to Texas; occasional.

EDIBILITY: unknown.

COMMENTS: *Lactarius sumstinei* is similar but has white latex that does not stain tissues. *Lactarius subvernalis* var. *cokeri* is also similar and has white, unchanging latex that stains gills and flesh pinkish to pinkish orange, but its gills are crowded.

Lactarius subpurpureus Peck

Illus. p. 122, 123

Ann. Rep. N.Y. State Mus. 29 (1878), 43
Variegated Milky

CAP: 1⅛–4" (3–10 cm) wide, convex-depressed at first, becoming nearly plane and depressed or funnel-shaped; margin incurved at first, becoming decurved, sometimes very faintly short-striate on mature specimens; surface moist, glabrous, reddish pink to vinaceous pink zoned with paler pink, sometimes more spotted than zonate, the zones fading with age but remaining darker along the margin, sometimes spotted with emerald green.

GILLS: attached to subdecurrent, moderately broad, subdistant, sometimes forked near the stalk, colored like the cap or paler, usually retaining their color longer than the cap does.

STALK: 1⅛–3⅛" (3–8 cm) long, ¼–⅝" (6–15 mm) thick, nearly equal or enlarged downward, moist and lubricous when fresh, becoming hollow with age, glabrous down to a tomentose base, colored like the cap but duller and usually with darker red scrobiculations.

FLESH: whitish to dull pale pink, staining red when cut, especially next to the gills, and eventually greenish; odor not distinctive; taste mild or slightly bitter.

LATEX: scant, wine red to dark vinaceous red; taste mild to faintly acrid.

SPORE DEPOSIT: cream.

MICROSCOPIC CHARACTERS: spores 8–11 × 6.5–8.0 µm, ellipsoid, ornamented with warts and ridges that form a partial reticulum, prominences up to 0.5 µm high, hyaline, amyloid; cap cuticle an ixocutis.

OCCURRENCE: scattered or in groups on the ground in conifer or mixed woods, usually with pine or hemlock; July–October; eastern Canada south to Florida, west to Michigan and Texas; occasional.

EDIBILITY: unknown.

COMMENTS: *Lactarius incarnatozonatus* is similar, but it has a vinaceous pink cap that is usually zonate, white flesh that has an astringent and disagreeable taste, white latex that changes to yellow, and smaller spores that measure 6.5–8.0 × 6–7 µm.

Lactarius subserifluus Longyear — Not Illustrated

Rep. Michigan Acad. Sci. 3 (1902), 57

CAP: ¾–2¾" (2–7 cm) wide, convex-depressed, becoming funnel-shaped with age, usually with an umbo or papilla; margin incurved at first, becoming decurved, often crenate to wavy with age; surface dry, glabrous, orange-brown, becoming paler with age.

GILLS: decurrent, narrow to broad, subdistant, yellowish, soon stained vinaceous cinnamon, becoming orange-cinnamon overall or tinted vinaceous when older.

STIPE: 2–4¾" (5–12 cm) long, ⅛–¼" (3–7 mm) thick, nearly equal, moist, hard, glabrous, orangey cinnamon on the upper portion, dark rusty brown below, orangey cinnamon hairs on the base.

FLESH: thin; odor not distinctive; taste mild or faintly acrid.

LATEX: watery on exposure, unchanging, staining the gills vinaceous cinnamon; taste mild.

SPORE DEPOSIT: pinkish buff.

MICROSCOPIC CHARACTERS: spores 6.0–7.5 × 6–7 µm, globose to subglobose, ornamented with warts and ridges that form a partial reticulum, prominences up to 1.5 µm high, hyaline, amyloid; cap cuticle not sharply distinct from the trama, consisting of a zone of inflated variable cells three to five layers deep.

OCCURRENCE: solitary to scattered or rarely cespitose under oak and hickory; July–September; reported from Michigan, Tennessee, and Florida; distribution limits and frequency yet to be determined.

EDIBILITY: unknown.

COMMENTS: The orange-brown cap, orangey cinnamon to rusty brown stalk, decurrent yellowish subdistant gills that are soon stained vinaceous cinnamon, and the small spores are this species' distinguishing features.

Lactarius substriatus A. H. Smith — Illus. p. 123

Brittonia 12 (1960), 326

CAP: 1⅛–2¾" (3–7 cm) wide, broadly convex to nearly plane, disc shallowly depressed; margin inrolled to incurved, becoming slightly elevated with age, glabrous, translucent-striate when moist; surface slimy-viscid but soon dry, glabrous, azonate, scarlet to orange-red at first, becoming brownish red to brownish orange or rusty orange with pale yellow along the margin, becoming paler overall with age.

GILLS: attached to subdecurrent, narrow, crowded, forked near the stalk, pinkish cinnamon to pale pinkish tan, staining grayish orange where bruised.

STALK: 1⅛–2⅜" (3–6 cm) long, ⅜–⅝" (9–15 mm) thick, nearly equal, moist or dry, hoary-canescent at first, becoming glabrous with age, solid, fragile, apricot buff to dull reddish orange.

FLESH: thin, brittle, light pinkish cinnamon; odor not distinctive; taste slowly becoming mildly acrid.

LATEX: white on exposure, slowly becoming straw yellow; taste bitterish then slowly acrid.

SPORE DEPOSIT: cream-colored.

MICROSCOPIC CHARACTERS: spores 6.5–9.0 × 6–8 µm, subglobose to broadly ellipsoid, ornamented with isolated warts and broad bands that form a partial reticulum, prominences up to 1.0 µm high, hyaline, amyloid; cap cuticle an ixotrichoderm.

OCCURRENCE: gregarious on the ground under conifers, especially in coastal forests; September–December; California, Oregon, and Washington; common.

EDIBILITY: unknown.

COMMENTS: *Lactarius subflammeus* has similar cap colors, but its latex is white and unchanging. *Lactarius subviscidus* is similar, but it has a white spore deposit, and its margin is not translucent-striate when moist. *Lactarius duplicatus*, reported from Alaska and eastern Canada, has a bright orange to copper orange cap and a white spore deposit.

Lactarius subtestaceus Murrill — Not Illustrated

Bull. Torrey Bot. Club 66 (1939), 31
Lactaria subtestacea Murrill

CAP: 2¾" (7 cm) wide, convex to slightly depressed; margin indistinctly striate; surface viscid, glabrous, azonate, ochraceous tawny to reddish ochraceous.

GILLS: attached, medium broad, subdistant, not forked, pale dull yellow, staining brown when bruised.

STALK: 2" (5 cm) long, ¾" (2 cm) thick, nearly equal, glabrous, pale pinkish yellow, not scrobiculate.

FLESH: whitish, not staining when cut; odor not distinctive; taste slowly and distinctly acrid.

LATEX: white on exposure, unchanging; taste not stated in the original description.

SPORE DEPOSIT: not stated in the original description.

MICROSCOPIC CHARACTERS: spores 5–6 × 5–6 µm, globose to subglobose, ornamented with warts and ridges that form a partial reticulum, prominences up to 0.5 µm high, hyaline, amyloid; cap cuticle a thick ixolattice.

OCCURRENCE: solitary on soil in a high hammock; September; reported only from Gainesville, Florida; distribution limits and frequency yet to be determined.

EDIBILITY: unknown.

COMMENTS: *Lactarius hysginus* var. *americanus* Hesler and A. H. Smith (edibility unknown) is similar, but it has a dark vinaceous brown cap, a darker stalk that is often scrobiculate, and larger spores that measure 6.5–8.0 × 6–7 µm.

Lactarius subtomentosus Berkeley and Ravenel *apud* Berkeley and Curtis
Not Illustrated

Ann. Mag. Nat. Hist., 3rd ser., 4 (1859), 293

CAP: 2–3" (5.0–7.5 cm) wide, convex; surface dry, densely and minutely velvety under a hand lens, dark yellowish brown.
GILLS: decurrent, broad to medium broad, distant, white.
STALK: 1" (2.5 cm) long, ½" (1.2 cm) thick, dry, hollow, minutely velvety, colored like the cap, with a white base.
FLESH: firm.
LATEX: white on exposure, turning to yellowish; taste acrid.
SPORE DEPOSIT: not stated in the original description.
MICROSCOPIC CHARACTERS: spores 8.5–12.0 × 7–10 µm, ellipsoid, ornamented with warts and ridges that form a partial to complete reticulum, prominences up to 0.6 µm high, hyaline, amyloid; cap cuticle a turf of brownish, erect pileocystidia.
OCCURRENCE: on soil in swamps; September; reported only from North Carolina; distribution limits and frequency yet to be determined.
EDIBILITY: unknown.
COMMENTS: *Lactarius gerardii* var. *gerardii* and *Lactarius sumstinei* are similar, but they both have white latex that does not turn yellowish.

Lactarius subtorminosus Coker Not Illustrated

J. Elisha Mitchell Sci. Soc. 34 (1918), 18
Tan Wool Milk Cap

CAP: 2–2⅜" (5–6 cm) wide, irregular; margin involute; surface coarsely tomentose, whitish with creamy or honey-colored zones.
GILLS: narrow, crowded, a few forked, cream-colored at maturity, staining pink then light smoky brown where cut.
STALK: ⅝" (1.5 cm) long, ⅜–⅝" (1.1–1.5 cm) thick, tapered downward, hollow at maturity, densely and minutely tomentose overall, white, with a few cream-colored scrobiculations.
FLESH: odor not distinctive; taste like cypress wood.
LATEX: very sparse, white, unchanging, staining gills pink then light smoky brown; taste mild.
SPORE DEPOSIT: not stated in the original description.
MICROSCOPIC CHARACTERS: spores 5.5–7.0 × 5.5–6.5 µm, globose to subglobose, ornamented with warts and short ridges that sometimes form a partial reticulum, prominences up to 0.5 µm high, hyaline, amyloid; cap cuticle an ixocutis.
OCCURRENCE: on soil; July; reported only from Chapel Hill, North Carolina, and western Canada; distribution limits and frequency yet to be determined.
EDIBILITY: unknown.
COMMENTS: *Lactarius pubescens* var. *pubescens*, *Lactarius pubescens* var. *betulae*, and *Lactarius subpaludosus* are similar, but they all have acrid-tasting latex.

Lactarius subumbrinus Hesler and A. H. Smith Not Illustrated

North American Species of Lactarius (1979), 458–459

CAP: ¾–1⅛" (2–3 cm) wide, broadly convex, becoming nearly plane with a slightly depressed center when older; margin even; surface viscid, glabrous, azonate, date brown.

GILLS: attached, narrow, close, whitish, not staining when bruised.

STALK: 1⅛–1½" (3–4 cm) long, about 3/16" (4–5 mm) thick, enlarged slightly downward to nearly equal, dry, becoming hollow with age, glabrous, colored like the cap but paler.

FLESH: dingy whitish; odor not distinctive; taste slightly acrid.

LATEX: sparse, white on exposure, unchanging, not staining tissues; taste slightly acrid.

SPORE DEPOSIT: cream-colored.

MICROSCOPIC CHARACTERS: spores 7.5–9.0 × 6–8 µm, broadly ellipsoid with a distinct plage, ornamented with a partial reticulum of nodulose ridges and isolated ridges and warts, prominences about 1 µm high; cap cuticle a short ixotrichoderm composed of branched, septate, thin-walled elements that measure 3–8 µm wide.

OCCURRENCE: scattered on soil and in deep humus in a pine planting; August; reported only from Highlands, North Carolina.

EDIBILITY: unknown.

COMMENTS: Similar species include *Lactarius imperceptus, Lactarius fusco-olivaceus* var. *fusco-olivaceus,* and *Lactarius fusco-olivaceus* var. *graveolens.*

Lactarius subvellereus var. **subdistans** Hesler and A. H. Smith Illus. p. 124

North American Species of Lactarius (1979), 203–207

CAP: 1⅞–6" (5–15 cm) wide, convex, depressed to funnel-shaped; margin even or sometimes plicate, becoming uplifted with age; surface dry, azonate, with fibrils especially at the margin, velvety to tomentose, white with yellow tinges or grayish.

GILLS: adnate to subdecurrent, close to subdistant, growing distant with age, narrow, some forking, with numerous lamellulae, white, becoming yellowish, often with hyaline droplets, staining brownish to pinkish where injured.

STALK: ¾–2" (2–5 cm) long, ½–1⅜" (12–35 mm) thick, equal to tapered downward, solid, dry, velvety, white with yellowish or brownish tinges.

FLESH: compact, hard, medium thin, white becoming yellowish or sordid when cut; odor not distinctive; taste acrid.

LATEX: white, changing to dull yellow on exposure, drying creamy yellow to ivory yellow, staining gills brownish to pinkish brown; taste strongly acrid.

SPORE DEPOSIT: white.

MACROCHEMICAL TESTS: flesh staining reddish orange with the application of $FeSO_4$ and orange with KOH.

MICROSCOPIC CHARACTERS: spores 7.5–9.0 × 5–7 µm, ellipsoid to broadly ellipsoid, ornament with low warts, prominences up to 0.2 µm high, hyaline, amyloid; cap cuticle a thin zone of interwoven hyphae giving rise to a turf of thick-walled, cylindric pileocystidia.

OCCURRENCE: on the ground in mixed forests; July–September; widely distributed in eastern North America; fairly common.

EDIBILITY: edible.

COMMENTS: *Lactarius subvellereus* var. *subvellereus*—reported from eastern Canada, New England, Michigan, West Virginia, and Alabama—is very similar but has crowded gills, white flesh, and white to pale creamy white and unchanging acrid latex that stains gills tawny.

Lactarius subvellereus var. **subvellereus** Peck Illus. p. 124

Bull. Torrey Bot. Club 25 (1898), 369

CAP: 2–5⅝" (5–15 cm) wide; broadly convex, becoming nearly plane with a depressed center when older; margin incurved when young, often remaining so well into maturity; surface dry, felty to somewhat velvety, whitish, developing pinkish buff or yellowish tints with age.

GILLS: attached to slightly decurrent, narrow, crowded, often forked, pinkish buff to pale yellow, staining tawny when bruised and drying cinnamon tan.

STALK: ¾–2" (2–5 cm) long, ½–1" (1.2–2.5 cm) thick, short, equal or tapered downward, solid, dry, white-downy, whitish with pinkish buff tints.

FLESH: firm, whitish; odor not distinctive; taste acrid.

LATEX: abundant, whitish to pale creamy white on exposure, unchanging, staining gills tawny; taste acrid.

SPORE DEPOSIT: white.

MICROSCOPIC CHARACTERS: spores 7.5–9.0 × 5.5–7.0 µm, ellipsoid, ornamented with warts and fine ridges that sometimes form a partial reticulum, prominences up to 0.2 µm high, hyaline, amyloid; cap cuticle a layer of narrow interwoven hyphae giving rise to a tangled turf of more or less erect elements.

OCCURRENCE: scattered or in groups on the ground in mixed woods; July–October; reported from eastern Canada, New England, Michigan, West Virginia, and Alabama; distribution limits and frequency yet to be determined.

EDIBILITY: edible.

COMMENTS: *Lactarius subvellereus* var. *subdistans* is very similar, but it has subdistant to distant gills at maturity, white flesh that stains reddish cinnamon with the application of $FeSO_4$ and orange with KOH, and acrid white latex that changes to creamy yellow and dries creamy yellow on the gills, and it is widely distributed throughout eastern North America.

Lactarius subvelutinus Peck Not Illustrated

Bull. N.Y. State Mus. 75 (1904), 18

CAP: 1–2" (2.5–5.0 cm) wide, convex, becoming nearly plane with a depressed center; margin incurved at first, becoming decurved; surface dry, minutely velvety, sometimes wrinkled, ochraceous orange to bright golden orange-brown.

GILLS: attached to slightly decurrent, narrow, close, sometimes forked, whitish then cream-colored, becoming darker with age, not staining when bruised.

STALK: ⅝–1⅛" (1.5–3.0 cm) long, ¼–⅜" (5–10 mm) thick, nearly equal or tapered slightly at the base, dry, solid, slightly velutinous, colored like the cap or paler.

FLESH: white, not staining when cut; odor not distinctive; taste mild.

LATEX: white on exposure, unchanging; taste mild.

SPORE DEPOSIT: white.

MICROSCOPIC CHARACTERS: spores 7–9 × 6.5–7.5 µm, ellipsoid, ornamented with warts and ridges that form a partial to complete reticulum, prominences up to 0.8 µm high, hyaline, amyloid; cap cuticle a zone of irregular brownish cells bearing a turf of cylindric to subulate or aciculate pileocystidia.

OCCURRENCE: on soil in woods and open places; July–September; reported from New York and Tennessee, distribution limits and frequency yet to be determined.

EDIBILITY: unknown.

COMMENTS: *Lactarius volemus* var. *volemus* is similar, but it has a darker-colored cap, white latex that changes to creamy white then brownish or grayish and that stains gills and flesh tawny brown, broad gills, and whitish flesh that has a fishy odor at maturity.

Lactarius subvernalis var. **cokeri** Hesler and A. H. Smith Illus. p. 124, 125

North American Species of Lactarius (1979), 144–146
Lactarius cokeri A. H. Smith and Hesler, *Brittonia* 14 (1962), 425

CAP: ¾–2⅜" (2–6 cm) wide, broadly convex to plane and becoming shallowly depressed with age, with or without an umbo; surface dry, unpolished to powdery, becoming naked and finely wrinkled with age, azonate to faintly zonate at the margin, whitish when young, buff-tinged to pale smoky brownish when older; margin lobed or wavy, sometimes arched.

GILLS: broadly adnate to short-decurrent, crowded, narrow, forking near the stalk, whitish to pinkish buff, spotting pinkish where injured.

STALK: 2–2¾" (5–7 cm) long, 5⁄16–⅝" (8–15 mm) thick, equal to slightly enlarged at the base, stuffed to hollow, dry, white, covered by whitish bloom when young, pallid when bloom is gone, staining pinkish where bruised.

FLESH: fairly thick, white, staining onion skin pink when cut; odor not distinctive; taste acrid.

LATEX: white, unchanging, staining gills and flesh pinkish where cut, taste acrid.

SPORE DEPOSIT: yellow.

MICROSCOPIC CHARACTERS: spores 7–9 µm in diameter, globose to subglobose, ornamented with a complete reticulum of coarse and fine ridges, prominences from 0.6 to 1.5 µm high, hyaline, amyloid; cap cuticle a cellular layer without a well-developed turf above it.

OCCURRENCE: on the ground in groups or scattered under hardwoods; June–October; reported from Massachusetts south to Florida and west to Texas; fairly common in wet seasons.

EDIBILITY: unknown.

COMMENTS: *Lactarius subvernalis* var. *subvernalis* is similar, but it has a pale tan to pinkish tan or yellowish cap that becomes darker yellow over the disk and latex that is milk white on exposure and changes to yellow-ochre.

Lactarius subvernalis var. **subvernalis** Hesler and A. H. Smith Not Illustrated

Brittonia 12 (1960), 340

CAP: ¾–1" (2.0–2.5 cm) wide, convex, becoming nearly plane with age; margin incurved at first, becoming decurved and remaining so well into maturity; surface dry, dull, velvety-tomentose, azonate, with a few irregularly spaced water spots, pale tan to pinkish tan or yellowish, becoming darker yellow on the disc.

GILLS: short-decurrent, narrow, close, pale buff to yellowish, unchanging when bruised.

STALK: 1⅛–1½" (3–4 cm) long, ¼–5⁄16" (5–8 mm) thick, slightly tapered downward, dry, pruinose, dull, solid, pinkish tan, staining yellow when bruised.

FLESH: thick, white or concolorous with the cap surface, staining pale lavender to vinaceous buff when exposed; odor not distinctive; taste acrid.

LATEX: milk white on exposure, changing to yellow-ochre; taste acrid.

SPORE DEPOSIT: not obtained.

MICROSCOPIC CHARACTERS: spores 6.5–9.0 × 6.5–8.5 µm, globose to subglobose, ornamented with warts and ridges that form a partial reticulum, prominences up to 1.5 µm high, hyaline, amyloid; cap cuticle consisting of a basal layer of isodiametric cells with an upper turf of cylindric, aciculate, fusoid-ventricose, or clavate cells.

OCCURRENCE: gregarious on humus in a dense pine-hardwood forest; May; reported only from the Sam Houston National Forest, Texas; distribution limits and frequency yet to be determined.

EDIBILITY: unknown.

COMMENTS: *Lactarius subvernalis* var. *albo-ochraceus* Hesler and A. H. Smith (edibility unknown), reported from Tennessee and Florida, is similar but has a whitish to buff cap and white, acrid latex that dries red and fades to yellowish shade. *Lactarius subvernalis* var. *cokeri*, reported from Massachusetts south to Florida, west to Texas, is also similar, but it has a whitish cap that becomes buff or smoky brown at maturity, crowded gills, and white, unchanging, acrid latex that stains gills and flesh pinkish to pinkish orange on cut or broken surfaces.

Lactarius subviscidus Hesler and A. H. Smith Illus. p. 125

North American Species of Lactarius (1979), 474–476

CAP: ⅜–1½" (1–4 cm) wide, convex and shallowly depressed over the disc, expanding and becoming shallowly funnel-shaped; margin arched and incurved, becoming wavy; surface subviscid to thinly slimy, glabrous, soon dry and conspicuously wrinkled, hygrophanous, azonate, dark mahogany red to brick red, becoming onion skin pink, margin fading first.

GILLS: decurrent, narrow, crowded, occasionally forked, pinkish cinnamon, becoming darker with age, pruinose, not staining where bruised.

STALK: 1¼–1½" (3–4 cm) long, 3/16–5/16" (4–8 mm) thick, nearly equal or enlarged downward, moist or dry, hollow, glabrous, colored like the cap.

FLESH: thin, colored like the gills; odor not distinctive; taste slightly acrid.

LATEX: scant, white on exposure, unchanging; taste slightly acrid.

SPORE DEPOSIT: dull white to yellowish.

MICROSCOPIC CHARACTERS: spores 8–10 × 7–8 µm, broadly ellipsoid, ornamented with isolated warts and ridges that form a partial reticulum, prominences up to 1.5 µm high, hyaline, amyloid; cap cuticle a modified ixotrichoderm consisting of a lower zone two to four layers of inflated cells that give rise to a turf of upright hyphal proliferations.

OCCURRENCE: scattered or in groups on the ground or on decaying conifer wood, especially spruce, in conifer or mixed conifer-hardwood forests; September–December; California, Oregon, and Washington; uncommon.

EDIBILITY: unknown.

COMMENTS: *Lactarius subflammeus* is very similar, but it has a scarlet cap when young that becomes orange to yellow-orange at maturity, crowded gills, and a glabrous cap surface when dry, and it is associated with pine. *Lactarius substriatus* is also very similar, but it has a scarlet to orange-red cap when young that becomes brownish red to brownish orange or rusty orange, white latex that slowly changes to straw yellow and tastes bitterish then slowly acrid, and a cap margin is translucent-striate when moist.

Lactarius sumstinei Peck Illus. p. 126

Bull. Torrey Bot. Club 32 (1905), 78

CAP: 1½–3⅛" (4–8 cm) wide, convex, becoming broadly convex and depressed; margin even or plicate; surface dry, azonate, glabrous or faintly radiately rugulose, pinkish buff to pale pinkish cinnamon.

GILLS: attached to decurrent, broad, distant, pinkish buff.

STALK: 2–3½" (5–9 cm) long, ⅜–½" (9–12 mm) thick, nearly equal, firm, dry, glabrous, pinkish buff.

FLESH: thin, whitish; odor not distinctive; taste acrid.

LATEX: white on exposure, unchanging, not staining tissues; taste acrid.

SPORE DEPOSIT: not stated in the original description.

MICROSCOPIC CHARACTERS: spores 8.5–11.0 × 9–11 µm, globose to subglobose, ornamented with prominent spines and ridges that form a partial to complete reticulum, prominences up to 2 µm high, hyaline, amyloid; cap cuticle a modified trichoderm of more or less inflated cells.

OCCURRENCE: grassy places in open woods; July–August; reported from Pennsylvania and Tennessee; distribution limits and frequency yet to be determined.

EDIBILITY: unknown.

COMMENTS: *Lactarius gerardii* var. *gerardii* is similar, but it has a dark brown cap with a small umbo, white to pale cream gills, and somewhat smaller spores. *Lactarius subplinthogalus* is also similar but has white latex that stains tissues rosy salmon.

Lactarius tephropeplis Hesler and A. H. Smith — Not Illustrated

North American Species of Lactarius (1979), 390–391

CAP: 1⅛–2¾" (3–7 cm) wide, convex, becoming nearly plane; margin incurved at first, becoming decurved; surface viscid, somewhat shiny, azonate, matted-fibrillose, grayish brown to purplish brown, appearing frosted, becoming pale gray when dried.

GILLS: subdecurrent, broad, close, pale yellowish buff, not staining when bruised.

STALK: 1⅜–2½" (3.5–6.3 cm) long, ½–⅝" (1.2–1.5 cm) thick, tapered downward, slightly viscid or dry, becoming hollow with age, pale pinkish gray, appearing frosted.

FLESH: taste mild; no additional information provided in the original description.

LATEX: white on exposure, unchanging, not staining the gills; taste mild.

SPORE DEPOSIT: pale yellowish buff.

MICROSCOPIC CHARACTERS: spores 7–8 × 6–7 µm, broadly ellipsoid, ornamented with warts and ridges that form a partial reticulum, prominences up to 1 µm high, hyaline, amyloid; cap cuticle a poorly delimited ixocutis.

OCCURRENCE: on soil in mixed woods; September; reported only from South Conway, New Hampshire; distribution limits and frequency yet to be determined.

EDIBILITY: unknown.

COMMENTS: The dark viscid cap and grayish stalk that appear frosted, mild white latex, and nonstaining gills are this species' distinctive features.

Lactarius texensis (A. H. Smith and Hesler) Hesler and A. H. Smith — Not Illustrated

North American Species of Lactarius (1979), 118–119

Lactarius lignyotus var. *texensis* A. H. Smith and Hesler

CAP: ⅝–1½" (1.5–4.0 cm) wide, obtusely conic to convex, becoming nearly plane and somewhat plicate; surface dry, dull, pruinose to velvety-tomentose, uneven to distinctly rugulose, dark brown to nearly black.

GILLS: attached to short-decurrent, narrow, subdistant to distant, dark to pale tan with dark brown edges.

STALK: ⅝–1⅜" (1.5–3.5 cm) long, 3/16–5/16" (4–8 mm) thick, nearly equal, obscurely plicate at the apex, dull, moist, glabrous to finely tomentose, dark brown.

FLESH: moderately thick, brittle, white, not staining when exposed; odor not distinctive; taste mild.

LATEX: scant, white on exposure, unchanging; taste mild.

SPORE DEPOSIT: yellow.

MICROSCOPIC CHARACTERS: spores 7.0–9.5 × 7–9 µm, globose to subglobose, ornamented with warts and ridges that form a partial reticulum, prominences up to 1.5 µm high, hyaline, amyloid; cap cuticle a poorly formed hymeniform layer of clavate to odd-shaped cells.

OCCURRENCE: in groups under hardwoods in a pine forest; May; reported only from Texas; distribution limits and frequency yet to be determined.

EDIBILITY: unknown.

COMMENTS: *Lactarius lignyotellus* is very similar, but its cap cuticle is a trichoderm, it has whitish to pale cream gills, and its spore ornamentation forms an inconspicuous partial reticulum. Also compare with *Lactarius lignyotus.*

Lactarius thejogalus (Fries) S. F. Gray *sensu* Hesler and A. H. Smith Illus. p. 126, 127

Nat. Arr. Brit. Pls. 1 (1821), 624

Lactarius isabellinus Burlingham

CAP: ¾–3⅛" (2–8 cm) wide, obtuse to convex, becoming nearly plane with a slightly depressed center, often with a low acute umbo; margin incurved at first, becoming decurved, sometimes faintly striate at maturity; surface moist, glabrous, azonate or sometimes faintly zoned, brownish orange to apricot orange or orangey cinnamon, fading to pinkish cinnamon and finally orange-buff or dull pale orange.

GILLS: decurrent, narrow, close to crowded, pale pinkish buff, becoming darker orangey cinnamon with darker spots when older.

STALK: 1½–2⅜" (4–6 cm) long, ¼–⅝" (6–15 mm) thick, nearly equal or enlarged downward, dry, becoming hollow with age, glabrous, usually with a conspicuous white strigose base, colored like the cap or paler, sometimes with a sheen.

FLESH: firm, brittle, dull white to pale vinaceous, usually staining yellow quickly when cut; odor not distinctive; taste slowly becoming slightly acrid.

LATEX: white on exposure, usually changing to yellow slowly (taking a much longer time than the flesh does); taste slowly becoming slightly acrid.

SPORE DEPOSIT: whitish to yellowish.

MICROSCOPIC CHARACTERS: spores 7–9 × 6.0–7.5 µm, broadly ellipsoid to subglobose, ornamented with isolated warts or irregular ridges that do not form a reticulum, prominences up to 1 µm high, hyaline, amyloid; cap cuticle a distinct layer of inflated to clavate or irregular cells.

OCCURRENCE: scattered or in groups on the ground or among sphagnum mosses under hardwoods or in mixed forests, usually with birch and often with beech present; July–November; widely distributed from Alaska to Nova Scotia and the northern United States, south to North Carolina; fairly common.

EDIBILITY: unknown.

COMMENTS: *Lactarius carbonicola* is very similar, but it has a distinctly arched margin, vinaceous hairs at its stalk base, a gregarious to subcespitose habit, and slightly smaller spores with different ornamentation, and it typically grows in dried-up woodland pools. *Lactarius badiopallescens* is similar, but it has a radiately rugulose-tuberculate cap surface, milk white and mild-tasting latex that does not change on exposure, pale vinaceous pink gills with vinaceous red edges at maturity that stain or discolor dull vinaceous red overall with age, and an vinaceous orange to vinaceous red stalk with an inconspicuously strigose base.

Lactarius thiersii Hesler and A. H. Smith — Not Illustrated

North American Species of Lactarius (1979), 510–512

CAP: 3/8–1 1/8" (1–3 cm) wide, broadly convex to nearly plane, sometimes deeply or shallowly depressed, rarely obscurely papillate-umbonate; margin irregular in outline and undulating; surface dry, glabrous or sometimes rimose or scaly, cinnamon to ochraceous tawny.

GILLS: subdecurrent, very narrow and thin, fragile, close to subdistant, pale dull yellow or with reddish tones.

STALK: 3/8–3/4" (1–2 cm) long, 1/8–1/4" (3–5 mm) thick, nearly equal, dry, dull, colored like the cap.

FLESH: cinnamon to ochraceous tawny, not staining when bruised; odor not distinctive; taste mild.

LATEX: whey-like to watery on exposure, unchanging, not staining tissues; taste mild.

SPORE DEPOSIT: not stated in the original description.

MICROSCOPIC CHARACTERS: spores 7.5–10.5 × 7.5–9.0 µm, subglobose to broadly ellipsoid, ornamented with warts and ridges that form a partial to nearly complete reticulum, prominences up to 0.5 µm high, hyaline, amyloid; cap cuticle a poorly delimited layer of tubular hyphae and some greatly inflated cells.

OCCURRENCE: gregarious in humus in open pine woods; April; reported only from California; distribution limits and frequency yet to be determined.

EDIBILITY: unknown.

COMMENTS: *Lactarius subdulcis* (Fries) S. F. Gray (edibility unknown), reported from Europe and not known to occur in North America, has an azonate, umbonate, reddish brown then vinaceous cinnamon to vinaceous brown cap; white and unchanging latex that tastes slowly bitter then slightly acrid; and a creamy yellowish spore deposit. It grows on the ground under hardwoods, especially beech.

Lactarius tomentosomarginatus Hesler and A. H. Smith — Illus. p. 127

North American Species of Lactarius (1979), 195–197

CAP: 1 1/2–3 1/2" (4–9 cm) wide, convex-depressed, becoming vase-shaped; margin incurved and long remaining arched; surface dry, appressed-fibrillose to silky, white at first, becoming flushed dull grayish pink and finally pale, dingy orange-brown.

GILLS: decurrent, narrow, crowded, often forked especially near the stalk, white when young, becoming pinkish buff then cinnamon buff and darkening to dull brown with age.

STALK: 1 1/8–2" (3–5 cm) long, 1/2–1 1/8" (1.3–3.0 cm) thick, nearly equal or narrowed downward, dry, solid, firm, somewhat velvety, white.

FLESH: thick, hard, white, slowly darkening to more or less pinkish buff where cut; odor not distinctive; taste acrid.

LATEX: scant, white on exposure, unchanging, staining tissues cinnamon buff; taste acrid.

SPORE DEPOSIT: not obtained.

MACROCHEMICAL TESTS: cap surface negative with the application of KOH; flesh staining vinaceous cinnamon with the application of $FeSO_4$ and negative with KOH.

MICROSCOPIC CHARACTERS: spores 9–11 × 7.0–8.5 µm, ellipsoid, ornamented with isolated warts and indistinct lines that do not form a reticulum, prominences up to 0.7 µm high, hyaline, amyloid; cap cuticle a layer of thin-walled hyphae.

OCCURRENCE: solitary, scattered, or in groups on the ground among hardwoods or mixed woods, usually with oak; July–November; New England south to Florida, west to Michigan and Texas; fairly common, especially in the southern part of its range.

EDIBILITY: unknown.

COMMENTS: *Lactarius deceptivus* is similar, but it has a larger cap and stalk, a conspicuous cottony and inrolled margin on young specimens, and larger spore prominences that measure up to 1.5 µm high.

Lactarius torminosus var. **nordmanensis** Hesler and A. H. Smith Illus. p. 128

North American Species of Lactarius (1979), 277–278
Lactarius nordmanensis A. H. Smith, *Brittonia* 12 (1960), 308

CAP: 1⅝–3⅞" (4–10 cm) wide, convex, becoming broadly convex to nearly plane with a depressed center; surface moist to dry, not viscid, covered with conspicuous radiating appressed hairs, azonate, vinaceous cinnamon to light pinkish cinnamon, sometimes rosy pink in areas; margin incurved and distinctly bearded.

GILLS: short-decurrent, crowded, narrow, often forked near the stalk, pale cinnamon pink or pinker, spotting pale yellow.

STALK: 1¼–2⅜" (3–6 cm) long, ⅜–1" (10– 25 mm) thick, nearly equal, dry, firm, hollow, smooth, obscurely spotted, colored like the cap.

FLESH: thick, brittle, pallid to pinkish; odor not distinctive; taste extremely acrid.

LATEX: abundant, white, slowly changing to pale yellow or spotting gills pale yellow; taste extremely acrid.

SPORE DEPOSIT: white.

MICROSCOPIC CHARACTERS: spores 8–11 × 6.5–8.0 µm, broadly ellipsoid, ornamented with bands and branches that often form a partial reticulum, prominences from 0.3 to 0.5 µm high, hyaline, amyloid; cap cuticle a layer of compactly arranged, radially oriented hyphae becoming loosely tangled inward.

OCCURRENCE: on the ground under a mix of aspen, birch, and conifers; August–September; reported from Idaho, eastern Canada, Michigan, California, and Wisconsin; occasional.

EDIBILITY: unknown.

COMMENTS: *Lactarius torminosus* var. *torminosus*, widely distributed in North America, is nearly identical, but its strongly acrid latex does not change color or stain tissues. Its cap has dull reddish orange to orange-brown concentric zones over a pale pinkish ground color, and it grows on the ground under birch. Compare with *Lactarius pubescens* var. *pubescens*, which has a paler cap and smaller spores.

Lactarius torminosus var. **torminosus** (Fries) S. F. Gray Illus. p. 128

Nat. Arr. Brit. Pls. 1 (1821), 623
Woolly Milk Cap

CAP: 1½–4¾" (4–12 cm) wide, convex, becoming broadly convex to nearly plane with a depressed center; margin incurved and distinctly bearded when young, becoming decurved with age; surface viscid and glabrous on the disc and dry toward the margin, covered with conspicuous radiating, appressed hairs that extend as the bearded margin, with dull reddish orange to orange-brown concentric zones over a pale pinkish ground color, becoming paler with age, marginal hairs whitish.

GILLS: attached to short-decurrent, narrow, crowded, often forked or anastomosing at the stalk, pale pinkish buff to pale cinnamon pink.

STALK: 1⅛–2⅜" long, ⅜–1" (1.0–2.5 cm) thick, nearly equal or tapered downward, dry, firm, becoming hollow with age, glabrous, pale pinkish buff to pale cinnamon pink or with salmon orange tints, often with a coral pink zone at the apex, sometimes with a white basal mycelium.

FLESH: thick, brittle, whitish to pale pinkish buff, unchanging when cut; odor not distinctive; taste strongly acrid.

LATEX: abundant, white on exposure, unchanging, not staining tissues; taste strongly acrid.

SPORE DEPOSIT: whitish to pale cream.

MICROSCOPIC CHARACTERS: spores 7.5–10.0 × 6.0–7.5 µm, ellipsoid, ornamented with warts and ridges that form a partial reticulum, prominences up to 0.5 µm high, hyaline, amyloid; cap cuticle an ixocutis of densely interwoven hyphae.

OCCURRENCE: solitary, scattered, or in groups on the ground under birch; July–October; widely distributed in North America wherever birch is present; fairly common.

EDIBILITY: unknown.

COMMENTS: *Lactarius torminosus* var. *nordmanensis*—described from Nordman, Idaho, and reported from eastern Canada, Michigan, Wisconsin, and California—is nearly identical, but its strongly acrid, white latex slowly changes to pale yellow on the gills or the gills become spotted pale yellow when cut. It has a vinaceous cinnamon to light pinkish cinnamon cap that sometimes has rose pink or salmon orange tones, and it grows on the ground under aspen, birch, willow, and conifers including fir or hemlock. Compare with *Lactarius pubescens* var. *pubescens,* which has a paler cap and smaller spores.

Lactarius trivialis (Fries) Fries

Illus. p. 129

Epicr. Syst. Mycol. (1828), 337

CAP: 1½–6" (4.0–15.5 cm) wide, convex, becoming broadly convex to nearly plane or centrally depressed; margin incurved at first, becoming decurved and finally uplifted with age; surface viscid to slimy, glabrous, azonate to obscurely zonate, pinkish gray to light vinaceous gray when young, developing cinnamon to pale brick red tones at maturity, often spotted with cinnamon or brownish tints.

GILLS: attached to subdecurrent, broad, close to subdistant, sometimes forked, creamy white to dull creamy white at first, gradually darkening with age, not spotting appreciably.

STALK: 1½–4¾" (4–12 cm) long, ⅜–1" (1.0–2.5 cm) thick, nearly equal, viscid or dry, glabrous, becoming hollow with age, whitish to cream or pale grayish tan, developing brownish tints with age, typically with a white basal mycelium or a white strigose base.

FLESH: thick, firm, whitish; odor not distinctive; taste mild then slowly acrid.

LATEX: abundant, whitish to pale cream on exposure, unchanging, drying olive-buff to pale olive-gray; taste mild then slowly acrid.

SPORE DEPOSIT: pinkish buff.

MACROCHEMICAL TESTS: latex turning orange-yellow with the application of KOH.

MICROSCOPIC CHARACTERS: spores 7–10 × 6–8 µm, broadly ellipsoid, ornamented with warts and ridges that form a sparse partial reticulum, prominences up to 1 µm high, hyaline, amyloid; cap cuticle an ixocutis or ixotrichoderm.

OCCURRENCE: solitary, scattered, or in groups on the ground under conifers or in mixed woods; July–November; reported from eastern Canada south to West Virginia, as well as from Alaska, Idaho, and Washington; distribution limits and frequency yet to be determined.

EDIBILITY: unknown.

COMMENTS: Much confusion exists in the literature regarding the interpretation of this species in North America. It is likely that what has been called *Lactarius trivialis* in North America is in fact a species different from the one described here.

Lactarius turpis (Weinmann) Fries Illus. p. 129

Epicr. Syst. Mycol. (1838), 335
Lactarius necator Fries
Lactarius plumbeus (Bulliard : Fries) Gray
Lactarius sordidus Peck

CAP: 1¼–5½" (3–14 cm) wide, convex, becoming broadly convex to nearly plane and slightly to distinctly depressed; margin incurved to inrolled at first, becoming decurved, velutinous to tomentose when young, becoming shiny and nearly glabrous at maturity; surface moist to slightly viscid especially over the disc, finely velutinous, often finely wrinkled, azonate, pale brownish yellow or olive-brown to brown with ochraceous tints, typically darker brown or dark green to blackish on the disc.

GILLS: attached to subdecurrent, narrow to medium broad, close, some forked, whitish to yellowish, staining dull brown to olive-brown when bruised.

STALK: ⅝–2½" (1.6–6.5 cm) long, ⅜–1" (1.0–2.5 cm) thick, nearly equal or tapered downward, sometimes compressed, subviscid, solid or hollow, glabrous, usually scrobiculate, pale brownish yellow or pale olive to brownish olive or grayish olive.

FLESH: firm, whitish; odor not distinctive; taste mild at first then very acrid.

LATEX: white to whitish on exposure, unchanging, staining the gills dull brown to olive-brown; taste very acrid.

SPORE DEPOSIT: pale cream-colored.

MACROCHEMICAL TESTS: cap surface staining reddish purple with the application of KOH.

MICROSCOPIC CHARACTERS: spores 6.3–8.8 × 4.8–6.5 µm, ellipsoid, ornamented with warts and ridges that form a partial reticulum, prominences up to 1 µm high, hyaline, amyloid; cap cuticle an ixocutis with slightly ascending hyphae.

OCCURRENCE: solitary, scattered, or in groups on the ground under conifers, especially spruce and balsam fir; also scattered to gregarious on lawns and among horticultural plantings in California in association with birch species introduced from Europe; August–December; eastern Canada west to Alaska, across the northern United States, south to California and North Carolina; occasional to fairly common.

EDIBILITY: unknown.

COMMENTS: *Lactarius olivaceoumbrinus* is similar, but it grows on the ground under conifers, especially spruce, and it has a zonate cap, white latex that rapidly or slowly turns greenish gray, and larger spores. *Lactarius turpis* has often been confused and misidentified as *Lactarius necator, Lactarius plumbeus,* and *Lactarius sordidus,* all of which Basso (1999) now recognizes as synonyms.

Lactarius umbrinopapillatus Hesler and A. H. Smith Not Illustrated

North American Species of Lactarius (1979), 486–487

CAP: ⅝–1⅜" (1.5–3.5 cm) wide, convex to nearly plane with an acute small central papilla; margin incurved, becoming decurved and remaining so well into maturity; surface viscid, glabrous, striate, azonate, dull yellowish brown on the disc, becoming dingy tan over the marginal area.

GILLS: decurrent, subdistant, dingy tan overall except where stained yellow by the latex.

STALK: ¾–1½" (2–4 cm) long, ⅛–¼" (3–7 mm) thick, nearly equal or slightly enlarged downward, subviscid, pinkish tan on the upper portion, becoming dull yellowish brown on the lower portion.

FLESH: thin, pinkish tan; odor and taste not determined.

LATEX: white on exposure, unchanging, staining cut surfaces yellow in a few minutes; taste not determined.

SPORE DEPOSIT: white.

MICROSCOPIC CHARACTERS: spores 7.5–9.0 × 6.0–7.5 µm, ellipsoid, ornamented with warts and fine lines that form a partial reticulum, prominences up to 1 µm high, hyaline, amyloid; cap cuticle a poorly defined mixture of tubular hyphae, not forming a well-defined cutis or trichoderm.

OCCURRENCE: on the ground under pine; October; reported only from Prince George's County, Maryland; distribution limits and frequency yet to be determined.

EDIBILITY: unknown.

COMMENTS: *Lactarius oculatus* is similar, but it has a dark reddish brown cap and scant whey-like latex that does not stain cut surfaces yellow, and it grows among sphagnum mosses in bogs or on the ground among needles in conifer woods.

Lactarius uvidus var. **montanus** Hesler and A. H. Smith Illus. p. 130

North American Species of Lactarius (1979), 340–341

CAP: 1³⁄₁₆–5" (3–13 cm) wide, convex-depressed to nearly plane; margin even at first, becoming wavy with age; surface powdery when young, smooth, viscid, azonate to faintly zonate, purplish umber to grayish vinaceous or dark vinaceous brown.

GILLS: adnate, close, narrow, pallid to pale vinaceous buff to creamy, staining pale lilac to vinaceous brown where injured.

STALK: 1⅛–3⅞" (3–10 cm) long, ⅜ –⅝" (10–15 mm) thick, club-shaped then becoming equal with age, dry and downy when young, brittle, pallid to vinaceous buff, staining lilac vinaceous, often stained ochraceous at the base.

FLESH: pallid, staining vinaceous brown where injured; odor slight but not distinctive; taste strongly resinous but not acrid.

LATEX: abundant, white to cream, unchanging, staining gills pale lilac to vinaceous brown; taste resinous but not acrid.

SPORE DEPOSIT: not reported.

MACROCHEMICAL TESTS: flesh staining vinaceous buff with the application of $FeSO_4$; cap and stalk staining green with KOH.

MICROSCOPIC CHARACTERS: spores 9–12 × 7–9 µm, ellipsoid, ornamented with a broken to partial reticulum with scattered warts and ridges, prominences up to 0.5 µm high, hyaline, amyloid; cap cuticle an ixolattice to an ixocutis.

OCCURRENCE: on the ground under conifers; July–September; reported from California, Colorado, and Idaho; occasional.

EDIBILITY: unknown.

COMMENTS: This species' distinguishing characteristics are the cap's vinaceous coloration, flesh that stains reddish brown and has a resinous taste, and a dry stalk. *Lactarius uvidus* var. *uvidus* is similar, but it has a pale pinkish lilac to lilac-brown cap with lilac spots, a sticky to slimy stalk, and mild-tasting flesh that slowly becomes bitter then faintly acrid.

Lactarius uvidus var. **uvidus** (Fries) Fries Illus. p. 131

Epicr. Syst. Mycol. (1838), 338

Common Violet-latex Milky, Purple-staining Milk Cap

CAP: 1⅛–4" (3–10 cm) wide, convex to nearly plane, sometimes with a low umbo or shallowly depressed; margin incurved at first; surface sticky to slimy, glabrous, typically azonate, pale pinkish lilac to lilac-brown with lilac spots.

GILLS: attached to decurrent, close, creamy white, staining dull lilac when bruised.

STALK: 1⅛–3⅛" (3–8 cm) long, ⅜–⅝" (1.0–1.6 cm) thick, equal, sticky to slimy when fresh, shiny when dry, whitish to pale buff, typically becoming ochraceous near the base with age, not scrobiculate.

FLESH: whitish, staining dull lilac then slowly tan to darker brown when cut; odor not distinctive; taste mild then slowly bitter and finally faintly acrid.

LATEX: white on exposure, soon changing to a dingy cream color, staining tissues dull lilac; taste mild at first, then bitter.

SPORE DEPOSIT: pale yellow.

MACROCHEMICAL TESTS: cap surface staining grass green to olive with the application of KOH and negative with NH_4OH, and $FeSO_4$; flesh negative with the application of $FeSO_4$.

MICROSCOPIC CHARACTERS: spores 7.5–11.0 × 6.5–8.5 µm, broadly ellipsoid to subglobose, ornamented with ridges, bands, and isolated particles that do not form a reticulum, prominences up to 1 µm high, hyaline, amyloid; macrocystidia 40–80 × 6–10 µm, obtuse at first, becoming tapered to an acute apex, prominently projecting; cap cuticle a thick ixocutis to ixolattice.

OCCURRENCE: scattered or in groups on the ground, usually in mixed woods with aspen, birch, and pine; August–October; eastern Canada south to Tennessee, west to Wisconsin, also reported from California; occasional to fairly common.

EDIBILITY: unknown.

COMMENTS: *Lactarius uvidus* var. *acystidiosus* Hesler and A. H. Smith (edibility unknown), reported only from Nova Scotia, Canada, is very similar, but it has white, unchanging latex that stains tissues dull lilac and long-decurrent gills; it grows on the ground under conifers; and it lacks macrocystidia. *Lactarius uvidus* var. *montanus*—reported from California, Colorado, and Idaho—is similar, and its latex stains tissues dull lilac, but its cap is pale grayish purple to grayish purple or dark purplish brown and fades to vinaceous cinnamon with age, and its stalk is dry; its flesh stains reddish brown; it has a strong resinous taste; and it grows on the ground under conifers. *Lactarius maculatus* has a distinctly zoned cap and acrid-tasting flesh. *Lactarius subpalustris* has whey-like milk, and its cap surface does not stain green with the application of KOH.

Lactarius vellereus var. **virescens** Hesler and A. H. Smith Not Illustrated

North American Species of Lactarius (1979), 201–202

CAP: 1½–4¾" (4–12 cm) wide, convex, becoming broadly convex with a depressed center; margin incurved at first, becoming decurved and remaining so well into maturity, uneven and lobed or wavy; surface dry, unpolished to velvety, milk white overall at first, soon flushed or stained ochraceous and finally darkening to dingy cinnamon buff.

GILLS: decurrent, narrow, close to crowded, dull white with a greenish flush near the stalk, soon stained cinnamon buff to pinkish cinnamon where bruised.

STALK: 1⅛–2⅜" (3–6 cm) long, ⅝–1⅛" (1.5–3.0 cm) thick, tapered downward, dry, solid, dull white, covered overall by a dull whitish pubescence, slowly staining dingy ochraceous when bruised.

FLESH: thick, brittle, white, slowly staining cinnamon buff; odor not distinctive; taste acrid.

LATEX: scant, milk white on exposure, unchanging, staining tissues dingy ochraceous; taste acrid.

SPORE DEPOSIT: dull white.

MACROCHEMICAL TESTS: flesh staining pinkish cinnamon then slowly dull pinkish brown with the application of $FeSO_4$ and negative with KOH.

MICROSCOPIC CHARACTERS: spores 7.5–10.0 × 7.5–9.0 µm, broadly ellipsoid to subglobose, ornamented with warts and ridges that form an obscure partial reticulum, prominences up to 0.2 µm high, hyaline, amyloid; cap cuticle a zone of more or less compactly interwoven hyphae that give rise to a dry turf of thick-walled pileocystidia.

OCCURRENCE: gregarious on a stream bank under mixed hardwoods and conifers; August; reported only from Tahquamenon Falls State Park, Michigan; distribution limits and frequency yet to be determined.

EDIBILITY: unknown.

COMMENTS: *Lactarius vellereus* var. *vellereus* (Fries) Fries (edibility unknown), reported from Europe and not known to occur in North America, has a white, velutinous, larger cap up to 12" (30 cm) wide, moderately crowded narrow gills, white acrid latex, and spores that measure 7.5–12.0 × 6–10 µm.

Lactarius vietus (Fries) Fries

Illus. p. 131

Epicr. Syst. Mycol. (1838), 344
Lactarius parvus Peck
Lactarius trivialis var. *gracilis* Peck
Lactarius varius Peck

CAP: ⅜–3⅛" (1–8 cm) wide, broadly convex, becoming plane with a depressed center when older; margin wavy and sometimes becoming finely scalloped or pleated with age; surface dry, slightly sticky when wet, glabrous, moist, azonate, dark vinaceous brown to reddish brown when young, fading to pale grayish brown or pale lilac-gray.

GILLS: attached to slightly decurrent, broad, close, pinkish white to cream, soon staining dingy brown when bruised.

STALK: 1¼–2⅜" (3–6 cm) long, ⅜–¾" (8–18 mm) thick, equal, fragile, dry or moist, pale pinkish brown overall.

FLESH: whitish to pinkish buff; odor not distinctive; taste acrid.

LATEX: white on exposure, changing to or drying olive-gray, staining gills gray to olive-gray or grayish brown; taste acrid.

SPORE DEPOSIT: white to cream.

MACROCHEMICAL TESTS: flesh slowly staining grayish with the application of $FeSO_4$.

MICROSCOPIC CHARACTERS: spores 7.5–9.0 × 6.0–7.5 µm, ellipsoid to broadly ellipsoid, ornamented with warts and ridges that sometimes form a partial reticulum, prominences up to 0.4 µm high, hyaline, amyloid; cap cuticle an ixocutis.

OCCURRENCE: scattered or in groups or clusters on decaying conifer or hardwoods, or sometimes on the ground, usually with birch present in the vicinity; August–October; widely distributed in North America; occasional.

EDIBILITY: unknown.

COMMENTS: The dark brown cap that fades to pinkish brown or lilac-gray, acrid white latex that changes to olive-gray, pinkish buff gills that soon stain dingy brown when bruised, fairly small spores, and typical growth habit on wood are this species' distinctive features.

Lactarius vinaceopallidus Hesler and A. H. Smith

Illus. p. 132

North American Species of Lactarius (1979), 425–427

CAP: 2–2¾" (5–7 cm) wide, convex-depressed, becoming broadly vase-shaped; margin inrolled and cottony on very young specimens, soon becoming decurved and glabrous; surface viscid, glabrous, azonate to subzonate, whitish to pale grayish vinaceous, zones darker when present.

GILLS: short-decurrent, moderately broad, close, whitish at first, becoming pale pinkish cinnamon, slowly spotting brownish.

STALK: 1⅛–1½" (3–4 cm) long, about ⅜" (1 cm) thick, nearly equal or tapered downward, usually with a narrowed base, dry or slightly viscid, especially on older specimens, solid, dull, colored like the cap.

FLESH: whitish to pale vinaceous buff; odor peculiar and disagreeable or not distinctive; taste mild at first then slowly slightly acrid.

LATEX: white on exposure, unchanging, slowly spotting the gills brownish; taste mild at first, then slowly becoming slightly acrid.

SPORE DEPOSIT: pinkish buff.

MICROSCOPIC CHARACTERS: spores 7–9 × 6–8 µm (some up to 15 × 9 µm), broadly ellipsoid, ornamented with warts and ridges that form a partial or complete reticulum, prominences up to 1 µm high, hyaline, amyloid; cap cuticle an ixocutis or ixolattice.

OCCURRENCE: gregarious under conifers; August–October; reported from Michigan and Quebec; distribution limits and frequency yet to be determined.

EDIBILITY: unknown.

COMMENTS: The pale grayish vinaceous and viscid cap, white and unchanging latex that is mild then slowly becomes slightly acrid, pinkish buff spores, and the dry stalk of fresh specimens are this species' distinctive features.

Lactarius vinaceorufescens A. H. Smith

Illus. p. 132

Brittonia 12 (1960), 334

Lactarius vinaceorufescens var. *fallax* Hesler and A. H. Smith,

Yellow-latex Milky, Yellow-staining Milk Cap

CAP: 1⅝–4¾" (4–12 cm) wide, convex then becoming broadly convex to nearly plane; margin incurved at first, expanding and becoming somewhat uplifted and uneven with age; surface glabrous, pale pinkish cinnamon with pinkish buff at the margin when young, becoming darker pinkish cinnamon to orangey cinnamon when older, faintly zoned with bands or water spots of nearly the same color.

GILLS: attached to slightly decurrent, narrow, close, often forked near the stalk, whitish to pinkish buff, soon spotted vinaceous to pinkish brown or dark reddish brown.

STALK: 1⅝–2¾" (4–7 cm) long, ⅜–1" (1.0–2.5 cm) thick, nearly equal or enlarged slightly downward, hollow, nearly glabrous, with white to brownish stiff hairs at the base, pinkish white overall, darkening with age;

FLESH: moderately thick, white to pinkish, staining bright sulfur yellow when cut; odor not distinctive; taste acrid.

LATEX: white on exposure, rapidly changing to bright sulfur yellow; taste acrid.

SPORE DEPOSIT: white to yellowish.

MICROSCOPIC CHARACTERS: spores 6.5–9.0 × 6–7 µm, subglobose to broadly ellipsoid, ornamented with warts and ridges that sometimes form a partial reticulum, prominences up to 0.8 µm, hyaline, amyloid; cap cuticle a thin ixocutis.

OCCURRENCE: scattered or in groups on the ground under pine; August–October; widely distributed in North America; fairly common.

EDIBILITY: poisonous.

COMMENTS: *Lactarius xanthogalactus* is nearly identical and is microscopically indistinguishable, but it lacks the reddish vinaceous stains that develop on the cap, gills, and stalk of *Lactarius vinaceorufescens*, and it grows on the ground under oak. *Lactarius colorascens* is very similar, but it has a smaller fruiting body, a whitish cap that becomes brownish red with age, whitish gills that become yellowish with age and do not spot vinaceous or brown, bitter to faintly acrid latex, and slightly smaller spores. *Lactarius chrysorrheus* is similar, but it has a whitish to pale yellowish cinnamon cap with slightly darker spots and grows on the ground under hardwoods especially oak, and its gills do not discolor or spot vinaceous or brown.

Lactarius vinaceosporus Hesler and A. H. Smith Illus. p. 133

North American Species of Lactarius (1979), 305–306

CAP: 2⅜" (6 cm) wide, convex, becoming deeply depressed; margin entire; surface viscid, glabrous, distinctly zonate with watery spots, pale buff.

GILLS: subdecurrent, moderately broad, close, sometimes forking near the stalk, ochraceous buff, staining yellowish.

STALK: 1⅛" (3 cm) long, ¾" (2 cm) thick, tapered downward, solid, becoming hollow with age, scrobiculate, white, staining yellow when bruised.

FLESH: white, staining yellow on exposure; odor and taste not stated in the original description.

LATEX: white on exposure, very quickly changing to yellow; taste acrid.

SPORE DEPOSIT: pale grayish pink.

MICROSCOPIC CHARACTERS: spores 6–8 × 5.0–6.5 µm, subglobose to ellipsoid, ornamented with warts and ridges that sometimes form a partial reticulum, prominences up to 1 µm high, hyaline, amyloid; cap cuticle a thick ixocutis.

OCCURRENCE: on soil; August; reported from Cades Cove, Smoky Mountains National Park, Tennessee; distribution limits and frequency yet to be determined.

EDIBILITY: unknown.

COMMENTS: *Lactarius albolutescens* is similar, but it has pale grayish pink to pale lavender gills.

Lactarius volemus var. **flavus** Hesler and A. H. Smith Illus. p. 133

North American Species of Lactarius (1979), 165–166

CAP: ¾–3½" (2–9 cm) wide, plano-convex becoming depressed; an uplifted, even margin; surface dry, velvety, azonate, ivory yellow to orange-yellow, brownish where bruised.

GILLS: adnate, whitish to cream, close, narrow to somewhat broad, forked near the stalk, lamellulae present, staining brown from the latex.

STALK: 1⅛–4" (3–10 cm) long, ⅛–⅝" (4–16 mm) thick, equal, solid, dry, velvety, cream-colored to pale yellow.

FLESH: firm, whitish to ivory, staining brownish from the latex; odor strong and fishy to nondistinct; taste mild.

LATEX: white, unchanging, staining all parts brown, sticky; taste mild.

SPORE DEPOSIT: not reported.

MICROSCOPIC CHARACTERS: spores 6.5–9.0 × 6–8 µm, globose to subglobose, ornamented with broad to narrow bands forming a partial to complete reticulum, prominences from 0.2 to 0.5 µm high, hyaline, amyloid; cap cuticle two to three layers of inflated cells bearing a sparse turf of pileocystidia.

OCCURRENCE: on the ground in deciduous or mixed woods; July–September; occurring in the southeastern United States from South Carolina to Florida, west to Texas; rare.

EDIBILITY: edible.

COMMENTS: *Lactarius volemus* var. *volemus* is nearly identical, but it has a dark orange-brown to cinnamon brown cap, pale orange-brown to dull orange stalk, white to creamy white to brownish or grayish latex that stains gills and flesh tawny brown, and a mild taste, and it is widely distributed throughout eastern North America and has been reported from western Canada and California. Also compare with *Lactarius subvelutinus.*

Lactarius volemus var. **volemus** (Fries) Fries Illus. p. 133, 134

Epicr. Syst. Mycol. (1848), 344
Lactarius lactifluus (L.) Quélet
Apricot Milk Cap, Bradley, Voluminous-latex Milky,
Weeping Milk Cap

CAP: 2–4" (5–10 cm) wide, broadly convex, becoming nearly plane with a depressed center to broadly funnel-shaped when older; margin incurved at first, expanding and becoming uplifted with age; surface dry, pruinose to velvety when young, becoming glabrous to finely wrinkled at maturity, dark orange-brown to cinnamon brown at the center, paler orange-brown toward the margin, fading with age to pale orange-brown then honey yellow.

GILLS: attached to slightly decurrent, broad, close, often forked, whitish to cream, slowly bruising tawny brown.

STALK: 2–4½" (5–11.5 cm) long, ¼–¾" (5–20 mm) thick, nearly equal or tapered at the base, solid, sometimes becoming hollow with age, nearly glabrous, pale orange-brown to dull orange.

FLESH: thick, brittle, white, staining brownish when cut or bruised; odor not distinctive in very young specimens, soon becoming fishy as the mushroom matures; taste mild.

LATEX: copious, white on exposure, becoming creamy white then brownish or grayish and staining gills and flesh tawny brown; taste mild.

SPORE DEPOSIT: white.

MACROCHEMICAL TESTS: flesh instantly staining dark blue-green with the application of $FeSO_4$.

MICROSCOPIC CHARACTERS: spores 7.5–10.0 × 7.5–9.0 µm, globose to subglobose, ornamented with warts and ridges that form a reticulum, prominences up to 1 µm high, hyaline, amyloid; cap cuticle a turf of clavate, cylindric, flask-shaped, or subfusoid pileocystidia, typically with a slender neck.

OCCURRENCE: solitary, scattered, or in groups on the ground under hardwoods or mixed woods; June–September; widely distributed throughout eastern North America, also reported from California and western Canada; fairly common.

EDIBILITY: edible.

COMMENTS: *Lactarius volemus* var. *flavus* (edible) is nearly identical, but it has a yellow to orange-yellow cap, cream to pale yellow stalk, and mild-tasting, white, unchanging latex that stains all tissues brown, and it occurs in the southeastern United States from South Carolina to Florida, west to Texas. *Lactarius subvelutinus* is similar, but it has an ochraceous orange to bright golden orange-brown cap, white latex that is unchanging and does not stain tissues, and narrow gills, and lacks the fishy odor.

Lactarius westii Murrill Not Illustrated

Bull. Torrey Bot. Club 67 (1940), 59
Lactaria westii Murrill

CAP: 2–2¾" (5–7 cm) wide, convex to broadly convex with a slightly depressed center; margin incurved, even; surface dry, glabrous or nearly so, azonate, white to pale pinkish brown.

GILLS: attached to slightly decurrent, narrow, close to subdistant, yellowish to dingy brownish yellow.

STALK: ¾–1½" (2–4 cm) long, 5⁄16–½" (8–13 mm) thick, nearly equal or tapered downward, pruinose near the apex, dry, white.

FLESH: white, not staining when cut; odor not distinctive; taste acrid.

LATEX: white on exposure, unchanging, not staining tissues; taste acrid.

SPORE DEPOSIT: not stated in the original description.

MICROSCOPIC CHARACTERS: spores 9–11 × 8–10 µm, globose to subglobose, ornamented with warts and ridges that form a partial reticulum, prominences up to 1.5 µm high, hyaline, amyloid; cap cuticle a trichoderm of clavate to subcylindric pileocystidia.

OCCURRENCE: solitary, scattered, or in groups on the ground under oak; July–August; reported only from Florida; distribution limits and frequency yet to be determined.

EDIBILITY: unknown.

COMMENTS: The white to pale pinkish brown cap, yellowish to dingy brownish yellow gills, white and acrid-tasting flesh and latex, and association with oak in Florida are this species' distinctive features.

Lactarius xanthogalactus Peck *apud* Methven Illus. p. 134

The Agaricales (Gilled Fungi) of California 10. Russulaceae 2 (1997), 55

CAP: ¾–4" (2–10 cm) wide, convex, becoming nearly plane with a depressed center; margin incurved at first, becoming decurved; surface moist to subviscid, glabrous, azonate, often water-spotted and obscurely zonate, grayish orange to grayish red or brownish orange, finally becoming light brown to reddish brown.

GILLS: attached to subdecurrent, narrow to moderately broad, close to subdistant, forked near the stalk, pale yellow to pale orange or light orange, not staining when bruised.

STALK: ¾–4" (2–10 cm) long, ¼–1" (7–25 mm) thick, nearly equal or slightly enlarged downward, dry to moist, glabrous, becoming hollow with age, lacking scrobiculations, pale orange to light orange or grayish orange, finally becoming grayish red, not staining, with a white to pale orange tomentum at the base.

FLESH: white, quickly staining yellow; odor not distinctive; taste mild to slightly bitter or slightly acrid.

LATEX: white on exposure, quickly turning yellow, not staining the flesh and gills; taste mild to slightly astringent or slightly acrid, often with a bitter aftertaste.
SPORE DEPOSIT: pale yellow to light yellow.
MICROSCOPIC CHARACTERS: spores 7–9 × 5.5–7.0 µm, broadly ellipsoid to ellipsoid, ornamented with warts and ridges that form a partial reticulum, prominences up to 0.5 µm high, hyaline, amyloid; cap cuticle an ixocutis.
OCCURRENCE: scattered to gregarious in duff in coastal and montane mixed woods under oak; September–January; reported from California, distribution limits and frequency yet to be determined.
EDIBILITY: unknown.
COMMENTS: *Lactarius vinaceorufescens* is nearly identical and microscopically indistinguishable, but its cap, gills, and stalk develop reddish vinaceous stains, and it grows on the ground under pine.

Lactarius xanthydrorheus Singer Illus. p. 135

Mycologia 37 (1945), 426

CAP: ⅜–1" (9–25 mm) wide, broadly convex to nearly plane and sometimes shallowly depressed at maturity; margin arched, sometimes short-sulcate; surface dry, subglabrous, papillate, conspicuously rugose-venose over the disc, dingy yellowish olive or more brownish, especially on the disc.
GILLS: arcuate-decurrent, narrow, subdistant, cream-colored, unchanging and not staining when bruised.
STALK: ½–⅞" (11–22 mm) long, ⅛" (3 mm) thick, nearly equal, dry, glabrous, subglabrous, solid at first, becoming hollow with age, colored like the gills, with a whitish basal mycelium.
FLESH: fragile, white, not changing when cut; odor not distinctive; taste mild.
LATEX: watery on exposure, instantly changing to yellow, not staining tissues; taste mild.
SPORE DEPOSIT: not stated in the original description.
MICROSCOPIC CHARACTERS: spores 7.5–9.0 × 6.0–7.5 µm, ellipsoid to broadly ellipsoid, ornamented with spines and ridges that form a partial reticulum, prominences up to 1.5 µm high, hyaline, amyloid; cap cuticle a well-delimited cellular zone three to five layers deep.
OCCURRENCE: scattered or in groups on the ground under hardwoods, especially oak; July–October; reported from Florida west along the Gulf Coastal Plain to Texas; occasional.
EDIBILITY: unknown.
COMMENTS: *Lactarius louisii*, reported only from Pennsylvania, is similar, but it has cream-colored flesh that tastes bitter and scant, watery, unchanging latex, and it grows on buried wood or among sphagnum mosses in wet areas of deciduous woods that are predominantly oak and maple.

Lactarius yazooensis Hesler and A. H. Smith Illus. p. 135

North American Species of Lactarius (1979), 264–265

CAP: 2–6" (5.0–15.5 cm) wide, convex, becoming broadly convex with a depressed center then broadly funnel-shaped; margin inrolled and minutely pubescent at first; surface viscid, glabrous, conspicuously zonate, the darker zones orangey ochraceous to rusty orange or dull orange-red, gradually becoming paler and more ochraceous, with alternating cinnamon buff and paler zones when older.
GILLS: attached, becoming decurrent, moderately broad, crowded, pallid to pale vina-

ceous cinnamon at first, becoming vinaceous cinnamon to dull vinaceous or light pinkish brown, slowly staining brownish.

STALK: ¾–2⅜" (2–6 cm) long, ⅜–1" (1.0–2.5 cm) thick, nearly equal, dry, glabrous, whitish to pallid or somewhat discolored when older.

FLESH: firm, pallid, unchanging when cut; odor not distinctive; taste excruciatingly acrid.

LATEX: copious, milk white on exposure, unchanging, not staining tissues; taste exceedingly acrid.

SPORE DEPOSIT: buff-yellow.

MICROSCOPIC CHARACTERS: spores 7–9 × 6.0–7.5 µm, subglobose to broadly ellipsoid, ornamented with warts and ridges that do not form a reticulum, prominences up to 1.5 µm high, hyaline, amyloid; cap cuticle an ixocutis.

OCCURRENCE: gregarious to cespitose in grassy areas under hardwoods, especially oak; July–November; Florida west along the Gulf Coastal Plain to Texas; occasional.

EDIBILITY: unknown.

COMMENTS: The conspicuously zonate cap, excruciatingly acrid-tasting flesh, and the gills' color change from pallid to dull vinaceous or light pinkish brown are this species' distinguishing features.

Lactarius zonarius var. **riparius** Hesler and A. H. Smith Illus. p. 135

North American Species of Lactarius (1979), 252–254

CAP: 2–4" (5–10 cm) wide, convex at first, soon depressed, then broadly funnel-shaped; margin incurved at first, becoming arched and finally uplifted; surface viscid when fresh, glabrous, azonate when young, becoming obscurely zonate with age, dull white at first, slowly flushed very pale buff to yellowish and finally pinkish buff, stained dingy ochraceous over time.

GILLS: decurrent, close to crowded, narrow, white, soon creamy yellow then bright ochre-yellow, staining tawny brown when bruised.

STALK: ¾–2" (2–5 cm) long, ⅜–¾" (1–2 cm) thick, nearly equal or tapered downward, solid, becoming hollow with age, glabrous, white, becoming pale ochre-yellow and bruising tawny orange.

FLESH: flesh firm, white, unchanging; odor faintly fragrant; taste acrid.

LATEX: creamy white on exposure, unchanging; taste slowly and distinctly acrid.

SPORE DEPOSIT: pinkish buff.

MACROCHEMICAL TESTS: flesh negative with the application of $FeSO_4$; cap surface staining salmon with the application of 30 percent KOH; injured gills staining somewhat dingy vinaceous with the application of 30 percent KOH.

MICROSCOPIC CHARACTERS: spores 7–9 × 6.0–7.5 µm, broadly ellipsoid, ornamented with warts and ridges that sometimes form a partial reticulum, prominences up to 1 µm high, hyaline, amyloid; macrocystidia lacking; cap cuticle a thick, distinct ixocutis.

OCCURRENCE: scattered on rich, wet humus along small streams in hardwood forests; September; reported from the Highlands Recreation Area near Pontiac, Michigan, and from eastern Canada; distribution limits and frequency yet to be determined.

EDIBILITY: unknown.

COMMENTS: *Lactarius luteocanus* is similar, but it has a white spore deposit and numerous conspicuously projecting macrocystidia. *Lactarius zonarius* var. *zonarius* (St. Amans) Fries *sensu* Neuhoff (edibility unknown) is a European species that has yet to be documented from North America.

Genera and Species Related to *Lactarius*

ZELLEROMYCES

Singer and Smith erected the genus *Zelleromyces* in 1960 to accommodate hypogeous fungi with gasteroid fruiting bodies that exude latex when cut. Species in this genus have globose to ellipsoid basidiospores with amyloid ornamentation and typically lack a distinctive stipe-columella at maturity. They also have lactiferous hyphae present in their hymenophoral trama.

In North America, seven species were originally assigned to the genus *Zelleromyces*. They were collected and described primarily from the Pacific Northwest and the southeastern regions of the United States. Miller and Lebel (1999) recently described two new species from the southeastern United States. They also synonymized *Zelleromyces ravenelii* with *Zelleromyces cinnabarinus*. We have included a description and color illustration of *Zelleromyces cinnabarinus* as our representative of this genus.

Zelleromyces cinnabarinus Singer and A. H. Smith Illus. p. 136

Zelleromyces ravenelii (Berkeley and Curtis) Singer and A. H. Smith

FRUITING BODY: 3/8–1½" (1–4 cm) wide, subglobose to turban-shaped, typically somewhat flattened, often lobed or furrowed to the base, sometimes fused with other fruiting bodies, lacking a stalk.

PERIDIUM: dry, tomentose at first, becoming nearly glabrous with age, attached to the substrate by a conspicuous knob-like pad of mycelium, pale orange at first, becoming brownish orange to reddish brown at maturity, often mottled dark reddish brown on the upper portion, sometimes dark brown overall and lacking reddish tinges.

GLEBA: arranged in scattered, conspicuous, and irregular compartments, pale orange-white to buff at first, becoming brownish at maturity; stipe-columella distinctive in immature specimens, arising from a small sterile base, branched like a tree, becoming inconspicuous with age; odor aromatic or pungent, sometimes like bread dough when fresh, resembling rubber in older specimens; taste not distinctive.

LATEX: abundant, thick, white on exposure, becoming thin and watery.

MICROSCOPIC CHARACTERS: spores 13–18 × 11–16 µm excluding ornamentation, globose to broadly ellipsoid, thick-walled, ornamented with spines and ridges that form a complete reticulum, prominences up to 3 µm high, hyaline, amyloid; clamp connections lacking.

OCCURRENCE: scattered or in groups hypogeous to subhypogeous under pines; widely distributed in the southeastern United States, also reported from the region bordering the Gulf of St. Lawrence; August–February; common.

EDIBILITY: unknown.

COMMENTS: According to Miller and Lebel (1999), *Zelleromyces cinnabarinus* is the most common gasteroid member of the Russulales in the southeastern United States.

BONDARZEWIA

Kotlaba and Pouzar erected the family Bondarzewiaceae in 1957 to accommodate a single genus, *Bondarzewia,* that has many of the features of the genus *Lactarius,* both of which are classified in the suborder Russulineae. Species of *Bondarzewia* form large overlapping clusters of flattened fused caps, or sometimes a solitary cap, attached to a solid central stalk arising from an underground sclerotium. They have thick, corky to fibrous-tough flesh and tubes with pores on their undersurfaces. Species of *Bondarzewia* have lactiferous hyphae and exude abundant white, milk-like latex when cut. They also have spores with amyloid ornamentation. We have included the following description of *Bondarzewia berkeleyi* as our representative of this genus.

Bondarzewia berkeleyi (Fries) Bondarzew and Singer Illus. p. 136

Berkeley's Polypore

FRUITING BODY: a large overlapping cluster of flattened fused caps, or sometimes a solitary cap, attached to a solid central stalk arising from an underground sclerotium.

CAP: 2⅜–10" (6.0–25.5 cm) wide, fan-shaped, laterally fused and typically forming a rosette, sometimes lobed, fleshy-tough; surface densely matted and wooly or nearly smooth, dry, radially wrinkled and pitted, obscurely to conspicuously zoned, variously colored whitish to grayish, pale yellow to yellow-brown; margin blunt, wavy.

FLESH: up to 1⅛" (3 cm) thick, corky to fibrous-tough, white; odor not distinctive when fresh; taste mild, becoming bitter with age.

LATEX: abundant, milk-like, white on exposure, unchanging.

PORE SURFACE: white to creamy white; pores angular, frequently torn and irregular, 0.5–2.0 per millimeter.

STALK: above-ground portion 1¾–4¾" (4.5–12.0 cm) long, 1⅛–2" (3–5 cm) thick, central, roughened, dingy yellow to yellowish brown.

SPORE DEPOSIT: white.

MICROSCOPIC CHARACTERS: spores 7–9 × 6–8 µm, round, with prominent amyloid ridges, hyaline.

OCCURRENCE: solitary or scattered on the ground at the base of hardwood trees, especially oak; July–October; widely distributed throughout eastern North America, also reported from the Pacific Northwest; occasional.

EDIBILITY: edible when young and easily sectioned, becoming fibrous-tough and bitter with age.

COMMENTS: Mature specimens may be more than 40" (102 cm) wide.

A HYPOGEOUS SPECIES OF *LACTARIUS*

A species of hypogeous *Lactarius* first discovered in June 1982 in Yosemite National Park, California, was again discovered in June 2001 at the Cold Creek Campground approximately 130 miles farther north in the Sierra Nevada of California. When first collected, this fungus was thought to be a new species and temporarily named *Zelleromyces rubriviridis.* After collecting fresh material of this fungus in 2001, however, Dennis Desjardin observed several features that were not consistent with *Zelleromyces* and later named the new species *Lactarius rubriviridis.* It differs from *Zelleromyces* species by having ovoid to ellipsoid basidiospores that are forcibly discharged, by lacking a peridium, and by having a well-developed branching stipe-columella. The following description is based on Desjardin's (2003) publication of this new species.

Lactarius rubriviridis Desjardin, Saylor and Thiers Illus. p. 137

Mycologia 95 (2003), 148–155

FRUITING BODY: gasteroid, hypogeous, 1–2⅜" (2.5–6.0 cm) long, ¾–1¾" (2.0–4.5 cm) broad, ⅝–1¼" (1.5–3.0 cm) thick, irregularly globose to ovoid or ellipsoid, sometimes lobed; surface distinctly ridged and pitted; ridges reddish brown to dark brown, staining deep greenish gray to bluish green or dark green where bruised.

GLEBA: contained in many small irregular to elongated cavities, up to ⅛" (5 mm) long or wide, filled with yellowish white to orangish white or cream-colored spores at maturity; trama firm, waxy, white to yellowish white, but becoming reddish brown when cut and stained by the exuded latex; stipe-columella rudimentary to well developed, composed of radiating branched veins arising from a central main veil, 1⁄32–⅛" (1–4 mm) wide, white at first, staining grayish white to grayish green over time when cut.

LATEX: scant, deep red, staining tissue dark brownish red; odor not distinctive; taste mild.

MICROSCOPIC CHARACTERS: spores ovoid to ellipsoid, densely ornamented with a complete to partial reticulum, prominences 0.5–1.0 µm high, deeply amyloid, forcibly discharged, producing an orangish white to yellowish white or cream deposit.

OCCURRENCE: solitary to scattered, hypogeous, buried under needle duff of conifers; reported only from the Sierra Nevada, California; June; uncommon.

EDIBILITY: unknown.

COMMENTS: The name *rubriviridis* means "red and green," a reference to the red latex and green stains. The diagnostic features of *Lactarius rubriviridis* include a gasteroid hypogeous fruit body that lacks a peridium, red latex, green-stained tissues, a stipe-columella, and reticulate spores.

ARCANGELIELLA SPECIES

The genus *Arcangeliella* was erected in 1900 by Cavara from material collected in Italy. To date, five species of *Arcangeliella* have been reported from the western United States, especially from California and Oregon. The fruiting bodies have a distinct cap and stalk as well as irregularly oriented, branching gill-like plates that are covered by a peridium when young. The peridium may or may not break free from the stalk at maturity to expose the gill-like plates. Species of *Arcangeliella* may be hypogeous, subhypogeous, or epigeous, and their latex is white to watery-white and sometimes stains the gill-like plates brownish or reddish.

Arcangeliella crassa Singer and A. H. Smith Illus. p. 137

Mem. Torr. Bot. Club 21 (1960), 74

Arcangeliella tenax A. H. Smith and Wiebe

FRUITING BODY: subepigeous to epigeous, with a distinct cap and stalk as well as irregularly oriented, branching gill-like plates that are crossveined and pitted; the gill-like plates are covered with a peridium when young and become exposed at maturity.

CAP: 1–3⅛" (2.5–8.0 cm) wide, convex when young, becoming broadly convex or shallowly depressed at maturity, often highly irregular or uneven in outline; surface dry to moist or sometimes subviscid, dull, typically smooth, pale pinkish buff to pinkish buff to pinkish cinnamon or darkening to reddish brown with age, unchanging when bruised.

GLEBA: composed of gill-like plates covered by a peridium when young and usually fully exposed at maturity, irregular in orientation with numerous branches, crossveined, pitted like a honeycomb or with elongated indentations, white when very young, becoming pale yellow and finally ochraceous buff to pinkish buff, unchanging when bruised.

STALK: 3⁄16–⅝" (5–15 mm) long, 3⁄16–7⁄16" (5–10 mm) thick, often eccentric, dry, smooth, solid or hollow at maturity, colored like the cap.

FLESH: ⅜–¾" (1–2 cm) thick over the disc, thinner toward the margin, firm, white to cream-colored to pale pink, unchanging on exposure; odor not distinctive or unpleasant; taste immediately and strongly acrid.

LATEX: white when exposed, unchanging, not staining gill-like plates; taste strongly acrid.

MICROSCOPIC CHARACTERS: spores 7.5–10.6 × 5.5–8.1 µm, ellipsoid, ornamented with a complete or partially broken reticulum, hyaline, amyloid; cap cuticle a sometimes gelatinous layer of closely appressed, more or less repent interwoven hyphae.

OCCURRENCE: solitary, scattered, or in groups on soil associated with red fir at higher elevations; fall and spring; California and Oregon; occasional.

EDIBILITY: unknown.

COMMENTS: *Arcangeliella saylorii* Thiers has similar color but is much smaller (3⁄16–5⁄16" [4–7 mm] wide), is totally hypogeous, has smaller spores (5.7–8.2 × 4.9–5.8 µm), and a peridium that does not break free from the stalk at maturity.

Arcangeliella desjardinii Thiers Illus. p. 138

Sydowia 37 (1984), 300–301

FRUITING BODY: epigeous, with a distinct cap and stalk as well as irregularly oriented, branching gill-like plates that are crossveined and pitted; the gill-like plates are covered with a peridium when young and become exposed at maturity.

CAP: 1½–2" (4–5 cm) wide, convex when young, becoming broadly convex to nearly plane, or more typically shallowly depressed at maturity, sometimes with an umbo over the disc, often becoming uneven and irregular in outline with age; margin incurved; surface dry, often pruinose, somewhat wrinkled, and often undulating or lobed on the margin, dark brown to olive or olive-buff to olive-brown, not changing when bruised.

GLEBA: composed of gill-like plates covered by a peridium when young and usually fully exposed at maturity, irregular in orientation with numerous branches, crossveined, pitted like a honeycomb or with elongated indentations, pale yellow to buff, unchanging when bruised.

STALK: 1⅛–1¾" (3.0–4.5 cm) long, ⅜–⅝" (1.0–1.5 cm) thick, nearly equal overall, solid, dry, colored like the cap or somewhat paler.

FLESH: about ⅛" (2–3 mm) thick, solid, firm, white, unchanging on exposure; odor not distinctive; taste mild.

LATEX: copious, white, unchanging on exposure, typically staining gill-like plates brownish to reddish upon drying; taste developing a tingling sensation on the tongue after a few minutes.

MICROSCOPIC CHARACTERS: spores 7.6–10.5 × 6.5–9.5 µm, globose to subglobose, ornamented with a complete or broken reticulum, hyaline, amyloid; cap cuticle a layer of tangled hyphal tips, ochraceous in Melzer's and pale buff in KOH.

OCCURRENCE: solitary, scattered, or in groups on soil in woodlands under Douglas fir; fall and spring; reported only from California; distribution limits and frequency yet to be established.

EDIBILITY: unknown.

COMMENTS: *Arcangeliella variegata* Thiers occurs in the same type of habitat and has similar coloration, but has a variegated cap and acrid-tasting flesh, and its gill-like plates do not stain brownish or reddish.

Arcangeliella parva Thiers

Illus. p. 138

Sydowia 37 (1984), 301–302

FRUITING BODY: completely hypogeous during all stages of development, with a distinct cap and reduced stalk as well as irregularly oriented, branching gill-like plates that are crossveined and pitted; the gill-like plates covered with a peridium that remains attached at maturity.

CAP: ¼–⅞" (7–22 mm) wide, convex, becoming broadly convex to nearly plane; margin permanently attached to the stalk; surface moist, smooth, white to off-white to pale yellow to cream-colored, unchanging or staining grayish orange to brownish orange when bruised.

GLEBA: composed of highly crowded gill-like plates covered by a peridium that remains attached at maturity, irregular in orientation with numerous branches, crossveined, pitted like a honeycomb or with tiny chambers, white, unchanging when bruised.

STALK: 3/16–7/16" (5–12 mm) long, ⅛–¼" (3–6 mm) thick, nearly equal overall, dry, smooth, colored like the cap.

FLESH: about ⅛" (2–3 mm) thick, white on exposure, unchanging; odor not distinctive; taste immediately acrid.

LATEX: white to somewhat watery white, very slowly (after one-half hour or more) changing to pale yellow, not staining gill-like plates; taste acrid.

MICROSCOPIC CHARACTERS: spores 7.5–9.6 × 5.5–7.0 µm, ellipsoid to ovoid, ornamented with a complete to sometimes broken reticulum; ornamentation 0.25–0.5 µm high, hyaline, amyloid; cap cuticle a compactly woven trichoderm with scattered free hyphal tips, not gelatinous.

OCCURRENCE: solitary, scattered, or in groups buried in soil under conifers at higher elevations; June; California; distribution limits and frequency yet to be determined.

EDIBILITY: unknown.

COMMENTS: *Arcangeliella saylorii* Thiers has about the same stature and is also hypogeous, but it is pale orange to orange-brown and has smaller spores that measure 5.7–8.2 × 4.9–5.8 µm.

Hyperparasites of the Genus *Lactarius*

Hyperparasites, or fungicolous fungi, are fungi that grow on other fungi. Hyperparasites that grow on gilled mushrooms are called "agaricicolous fungi," and at least ten species are known to occur on members of the genus *Lactarius.*

Rogerson and Samuels (1995) have documented the occurrence of thirteen species of the Ascomycetes genus *Hypomyces* on gilled fungi. According to their findings, most are found on members of the Russulaceae. Eight species of *Hypomyces* are known to occur on *Lactarius,* including *Hypomyces camphoratus,* which attacks *Lactarius camphoratus,* and *Hypomyces lithuanicus,* which occurs on *Lactarius torminosus* and *Lactarius pubescens.* The best-known example of a species of *Hypomyces* that attacks gilled mushrooms is *Hypomyces lactifluorum,* which occurs on several species of milk mushrooms, including *Lactarius deceptivus, Lactarius piperatus,* and *Lactarius subvellereus* var. *subdistans.* It also attacks several *Russula* species, including *Russula brevipes.* We give a description and color illustration of this interesting and colorful hyperparasite.

Hypomyces lactifluorum (Schweinitz : Fries) Tulasne Illus. p. 139

Lobster Fungus, Lobster Mushroom

FRUITING BODY: orange to reddish orange, sometimes with whitish areas, roughened like sandpaper, growing over the surface of funnel-shaped to irregular caps, stalks, and deformed gills of host mushrooms; parasitized caps are typically dense, often partially buried in conifer debris, 2–7⅞((5–20 cm) wide, white and firm within.

MICROSCOPIC CHARACTERS: spores 35–40 × 4.5–7.0 µm, spindle-shaped, 2-celled, prominently warted, hyaline.

OCCURRENCE: solitary, scattered, or in groups on several species of *Lactarius* and *Russula;* July–October; widely distributed in North America; infrequent to fairly common.

EDIBILITY: edible, choice.

COMMENTS: *Hypomyces lactifluorum* is a very popular edible mushroom even though the identity of the host species is usually undetermined. No asexual stage is known.

Two species of Basidiomycetes, *Asterophora lycoperdoides* and *Asterophora parasitica* are agaricicolous fungi known to occur on species of *Lactarius* and *Russula.* We give a description and color illustration of *Asterophora lycoperdoides* as our representative of this group.

Asterophora lycoperdoides (Bulliard : Mérat) Ditmar : Fries Illus. p. 139

Powder Cap

CAP: 3/8–3/4((1–2 cm) wide, rather round, dry, cottony, becoming covered with dense brown powder; odor and taste farinaceous.

GILLS: typically malformed, attached, distant, narrow, thick, often forked; whitish.

STALK: 3/4–1 1/4((2–3 cm) long, 1/8–3/8((3–10 mm) thick; white, becoming brownish; minutely hairy or silky; stuffed, becoming hollow.

SPORE DEPOSIT: white.

MICROSCOPIC CHARACTERS: basidiospores 3–6 × 2–4 µm, elliptic to oval, smooth, hyaline, inamyloid; cap surface also produces chlamydospores that are strongly warted or have blunt spines, oval to subglobose, 13–20 × 10–20 µm (excluding ornamentation), thick-walled, pale brown, inamyloid.

OCCURRENCE: in clusters on decaying species of *Lactarius* and *Russula;* July–November; widely distributed in North America; occasional to common but often overlooked.

EDIBILITY: unknown.

COMMENTS: *Asterophora parasitica* (Bulliard : Fries) Singer (edibility unknown) is similar, but it has well-developed gills, a white to grayish or pale tan cap that is silky, not powdery, and only smooth, elliptic basidiospores.

GLOSSARY

REFERENCES

INDEX TO COMMON NAMES

INDEX TO SCIENTIFIC NAMES

PHOTO CREDITS

Glossary

aciculate: superficially marked as if scratched with a pin
acrid: peppery, producing a burning sensation in the mouth
acute: narrowed or somewhat pointed
adnate: attached to the stalk without a notch
agglutinated: firmly attached as if glued together
allantoid: curved and sausage-shaped
amyloid: staining grayish to blue-black in Melzer's reagent
anastomosed: fused together
apex: the uppermost portion of the stalk or the terminal portion of a hypha
apical: pertaining to the apex
apiculate: having one or more short projections
apiculus: a short projection at or near the apex of a spore
appressed: flattened onto the surface
appressed-fibrillose: having fibrils that are flattened onto the surface
appressed-pubescent: having short, soft, downy hairs that are flattened onto the surface
appressed-tomentose: coated with a thick covering of hairs that are flattened onto the surface
apud: meaning "in"; indicates a name published by one author in the work of another
arcuate-decurrent: turned upward near the stalk, then descending along a portion of the stalk
areolate: marked out into small areas by cracks or crevices
areolate-scaly: having scales that are marked out into small areas by cracks or crevices
asci: sac-like cells in which ascospores are formed
Ascomycetes: a major group of fungi that includes those species that produce ascospores in asci
ascospores: sexual spores formed within asci
astringent: causing the mouth to pucker by contraction of the membranes
attached: joined to the stalk
azonate: lacking zones
basal: located at the base
base: the lowest portion of the stalk
basidium (pl. basidia): a club-shaped cell on which spores are formed
basidiospore: a spore formed on a basidium
bearded: adorned with hairs
bloom: a dull, thin coating that is typically whitish
buff: pale creamy gray to pale creamy yellow
canescence: a whitish to grayish dust-like bloom
canescent: having a whitish to grayish dust-like bloom
cap: the upper part of a mushroom, which supports the gills
capitate: having a small knob at the apex
caulocystidia: cystidia found on the stalk
cellular: composed of more or less rounded cells
cespitose: occurring in groups
cheilocystidia: cystidia that occur on the edge of a gill; compare with pleurocystidia
chlamydospores: thick-walled asexual spores that are often subglobose
clavate: club-shaped
close: spacing that is halfway between crowded and subdistant
concentric: having rings or zones
conic: shaped more or less like an inverted cone
convex: curved or rounded like the exterior of a circle
convex-umbilicate: curved or rounded with a small central depression
corrugated: coarsely ridged or folded
cottony-tomentose: like densely matted cotton

crenate: finely scalloped
crenate-plicate: finely scalloped and deeply grooved
crenulate: very finely scalloped
crossveined: having tiny veins that connect adjoining gills or vein-like ridges
crowded: almost touching
cuneiform: shaped like a wedge
cuticle: the outermost tissue layer of the cap or stalk
cutis: the outermost tissue layer of the cap or stalk
cylindric: having the same diameter throughout its length
cystidia: sterile cells that project between and usually beyond the basidia
cystidioid: resembling cystidia
decumbent: having the lower portion lying down
decurrent: descending or running down the stalk; a form of gill attachment
decurved: bent downward
delimited: marked out or defined
depressed: sunken
dextrinoid: staining orange to orange-brown or reddish brown in Melzer's reagent
disc: the central area of a mushroom cap's surface
distal: farthest away from the point of origin
distant: spaced widely apart
eccentric: away from the center
ectomycorrhizae: thin layers of fungal hyphae on the surface and between the outermost layers of tree roots
elevated: raised upward above the plane
ellipsoid: resembling an elongated oval with similarly curved ends
elliptic: pertaining to an elongated oval with similarly curved ends
entire: even; not broken, serrated, or lacerated
epigeous: developing above the ground
equal: having the same thickness over the entire length
even: stopping at the distal portion of the gills, not projecting as a band of sterile tissue
expanded: somewhat elevated
expanding: becoming somewhat elevated
farinaceous: having the odor of fresh meal or cucumber
fascicles: small bundles
ferruginous: rust-colored
$FeSO_4$: iron sulfate, usually a 10 percent solution
fetid: having a heavy, offensive odor, like rotten, decayed, or fecal material
fiber: a hair-like structure present on the cap or stalk
fibril: a tiny fiber
fibrillose: composed of fibrils
filamentous: composed of filaments
flesh: the inner tissue of a mushroom
flexuous: having turns or windings; curves or curving
fruiting body: a mushroom or other spore-producing macroscopic fungus
fulvous: reddish cinnamon; colored like a red fox
fuscous: dark brownish gray to brownish black
fusiform: spindle-shaped and narrowing at both ends
fusoid: somewhat spindle-shaped
fusoid-ventricose: swollen in the middle and somewhat spindle-shaped, with the apex rounded or acute
gasteroid: resembling puffballs or having a gleba consisting of branching plates that are irregularly oriented
gelatinized: having a jelly-like consistency
gelatinous: jelly-like
gill edge: the vertically oriented thin lower surface of a gill
gill faces: the horizontally oriented broad surfaces of a gill
gills: thin to thick knife blade–like structures on the undersurface of the cap
glabrous: bald and smooth
glaucous: covered with a thin, whitish bloom that is easily rubbed off
gleba: spore-bearing tissue of puffballs and other stalked or stalkless gasteroid fungi that lack true gills
globose: round
gluten: a sticky, glue-like, pectinous material
glutinous: having gluten
gregarious: closely scattered over a small area
hammock: a fertile area that is higher than its surroundings and characterized by hardwoods and deep humus
hoary: having a whitish to grayish sheen
humus: decaying organic material, mostly of plant origin, in soil
hyaline: transparent; clear and nearly colorless
hygrophanous: appearing water-soaked when

fresh, fading to a paler color as water is lost
hymeniform: made up of erect club-shaped to pear-shaped cells arranged more or less perpendicularly to the surface
hymenophoral trama: tissues in the gills that support the basidia
hyperparasite: a fungal parasite that attacks other fungi
hypha (pl. hyphae): thread-like filaments of fungal cells
hyphoid: resembling a hypha
hypogeous: occurring below the ground surface and sometimes protruding above ground level
incrustations: affixed particles that give a roughened appearance
incurved: bent inward toward the stalk
inrolled: bent inward toward the stalk and upward
intervenose: having veins on the gill faces that often extend between the gills or from gill to gill
interzonal: between zones
isodiametric: having equal diameters in all directions
ixocutis: a gelatinized layer of hyphae lying parallel to the cap surface
ixolattice: a cap cuticle consisting of branching, ascending, entangled hyphae in a gelatinous matrix
ixotrichoderm: a gelatinized cap cuticle in which the distal portion of the filiform elements is different lengths and the elements themselves are arranged perpendicular to the surface
KOH: potassium hydroxide, usually made up in a 3-5 percent concentration in water; used to test color reactions
lactifer: hyphal element that contains a milk-like fluid
lactiferous: composed of lactifers
latex: a watery or milk-like fluid that exudes from some mushrooms when they are cut or bruised
lobed: having rounded divisions
longitudinal: oriented along the vertical axis
lubricous: smooth and slippery
macrochemical: pertaining to the application of reagents to various tissues of a mushroom and the observation of reactions without the use of a microscope
macrocystidia: very long cystidia
margin: the edge of a mushroom cap
marginate: having gill edges that are darker-colored than the faces
matted-fibrillose: having fibrils that are somewhat flattened toward the surface
matted-tomentose: a thick coating of hairs that are somewhat flattened toward the surface
Melzer's reagent: a solution containing iodine, potassium iodide, and chloral hydrate that is used for testing fungal spores for color reactions
moniliform: arranged like a string of beads
multizonate: having many zones
mycelium: a mass of hyphae visible to the unaided eye
mycophagist: a person who eats mushrooms
mycorrhizal: having a mutually beneficial relationship with a tree or other plant
NH_4OH: ammonium hydroxide; used to test color reactions on mushroom tissues
nodulose: having very small knot-like projections
oblong: longer than wide and with somewhat flattened ends
ochraceous: pale brownish orange-yellow
ocher: brownish orange-yellow
palisade: a perpendicular arrangement of elongated cells
papilla: a small nipple-like projection
papillate: having a small nipple-like projection
papillate-umbonate: having a pointed elevation at the center of the cap
peridium: one or more layers of the spore case of puffballs or other gasteroid fungi
pileocystidia: cystidia located on the surface of the cap
plage: a smooth area near the apiculus on the surface of a spore
plane: flat
plano-convex: convex but somewhat flattened
pleurocystidia: cystidia that occur on the gill faces; compare with cheilocystidia
plicate: deeply grooved, sometimes pleated or folded
plicate-striate: having deep grooves that are more or less parallel
pruinose: appearing finely powdered
pubescent: having short, soft, downy hairs
pungent: sharp and piercing
radial: pointed away from a common central point, like the spokes of a wheel
refractive: bent sharply from the base;

appearing somewhat differently colored when viewed at various angles
repent: prostrate
reticulated: covered with a net-like pattern of ridges
reticulation: raised, net-like ridges
reticulum: a system of raised, net-like ridges found on the spores of some mushrooms
revolute: rolled up toward the disc, then toward the margin; opposite of *inrolled*
ridges: elevated, laterally elongated projections
rimose: having distinct cracks or crevices
rimulose-areolate: marked out into small areas by very fine cracks
rivulose: marked with lines like a river system on a map
rugose: coarsely wrinkled
rugose-areolate: coarsely wrinkled and marked out into small areas by cracks
rugose-venose: coarsely wrinkled and vein-like
rugulose: finely wrinkled
rugulose-tuberculate: finely wrinkled and warted
scale: an erect, flattened, or recurved projection or torn portion of the cap or stalk surface
scaly: having scales
sclerotium: a rounded to irregular body composed of dormant hyphae; typically found below ground level
scrobiculate: pitted or smeared; having depressed or flat shiny areas
scrobiculation: a depressed or flat shiny area
scurfy: roughened by tiny flakes or scales
semihypogeous: partially buried in soil
sensu: in the sense of or according to
septate: divided by crosswalls
slimy-viscid: slimy and sticky or tacky
spermatic: resembling the odor of semen
spore: a microscopic reproductive cell with the ability to germinate and form hyphae
spore deposit: a deposit of mushroom spores on a piece of paper or glass, dropped from the gills
squamules: minute scales
stalk: the structure that arises from the substrate and supports a mushroom's cap or spore case
stipe-columella: a sterile stalk-like structure inside the fruiting body of some gasteroid fungi
striate: having small, more or less parallel lines or furrows
striatulate: having very fine, more or less parallel lines or furrows
strigose: coated with long, coarse, stiff hairs
stuffed: containing a soft tissue that usually disappears with age, leaving a hollow space
subapical: located just below the apex
subcespitose: more or less occurring in groups
subcutis: a layer of tissue just below the cutis
subcylindric: nearly cylinder-shaped
subdecurrent: extending slightly down the stalk
subdistant: spacing that is halfway between close and distant
subfusoid: somewhat spindle-shaped; tapered slightly at both ends
subglobose: nearly round
subhygrophanous: appearing water-soaked when fresh, fading to a slightly paler color when dry
subhypogeous: partially buried
subochraceous: slightly pale brownish orange-yellow
subplicate: somewhat grooved or pleated
subpruinose: appearing somewhat finely powdered
subscrobiculate: somewhat pitted or smeared
substrate: the food source on which a mushroom is growing
subtomentose: coated with a somewhat thick, matted covering of hairs
subulate: awl-shaped
subviscid: slightly sticky or tacky
subzonate: more or less arranged in concentric bands of different colors
sulcate: grooved; deeper than striate, shallower than plicate
tawny: dull yellowish brown
tomentose: coated with a thick, matted covering of hairs
tomentose-areolate: densely matted like wool and marked out into small areas by cracks or crevices
tomentum: a covering of soft hairs
trama: supporting tissue
translucent-striate: appearing striate when gill edges are viewed through moist and nearly transparent cap tissue
trichoderm: a cap cuticle in which the distal portion of the filiform elements is different lengths and the elements themselves are arranged perpendicular to the surface

tuft: a cluster closely held together
turf: superficial mycelial growth
umbilicate: having a small central depression
umbo: a pointed or rounded elevation at the center of a mushroom cap
umbonate: having an umbo
uplifted: elevated toward the plane
velvety-tomentose: densely matted and velvety
velutinous: coated with fine, short, soft hairs
ventricose: swollen in the middle and tapering to somewhat of a point
versiform: having variable shape depending on maturity
vesiculose: bladder-like or somewhat spherical
vinaceous: pinkish red to pale purplish red
violaceous: resembling violets in color; bluish purple
viscid: sticky or tacky
viscous: thick and slimy
warts: blunt to somewhat pointed projections on a spore's surface
zebroid: resembling the markings on a zebra
zonate: arranged in zones
zoned: having zones
zones: concentric bands of different colors on the surface of the cap or stalk of some mushrooms

References

Basso, M. T. 1999. *Lactarius persoon.* Fungi Europaei VII. Mycoflora. Massimo Candusso, Alassio, Italy. 845 pp.

Beardslee, H. C., and G. S. Burlingham. 1940. Interesting Species of *Lactariae* from Florida. *Mycologia* 32: 575–586.

Bessette, A. E. 1988. *Mushrooms of the Adirondacks: A Field Guide.* North Country Books, Utica, N.Y. 145 pp.

Bessette, A. E., A. R. Bessette, and D. W. Fischer. 1997. *Mushrooms of Northeastern North America.* Syracuse Univ. Press, Syracuse, N.Y. 584 pp.

Bessette, A. E., O. K. Miller, A. R. Bessette, and H. H. Miller. 1995. *Mushrooms of North America in Color—A Field Guide Companion to Seldom-Illustrated Fungi.* Syracuse Univ. Press, Syracuse, N.Y. 188 pp.

Bessette, A. E., W. C. Roody, and A. R. Bessette. 1999. *North American Boletes—A Color Guide to the Fleshy Pored Mushrooms.* Syracuse Univ. Press, Syracuse, N.Y. 395 pp.

Bessette, A. E., and W. J. Sundberg. 1987. *Mushrooms: A Quick Reference Guide to Mushrooms of North America.* Macmillan, New York. 17 pp.

Bills, G. F. 1985. Ecological and Taxonomic Studies of the Russulaceae and Other Ectomycorrhizal Basidiomycetes in High-Elevation Forests of the Southern Appalachians. Ph.D. diss., Virginia Polytechnic Institute and Virginia State University.

———. 1986a. Distribution of *Lactarius* in the High-Elevation Forests of the Southern Appalachians. *Mycologia* 78 (1): 80–85.

———. 1986b. Notes on *Lactarius* in the High-Elevation Forests of the Southern Appalachians. *Mycologia* 78 (1): 70–79.

Burlingham, G. S. 1907. Some *Lactariae* from Windham County, Vermont. *Mem. Torrey Bot. Club* 34: 85–89.

———. 1908. A Study of the *Lactariae* of the United States. *Mem. Torrey Bot. Club* 14: 1–109.

———. 1910a. *Lactaria. Pers. North American Flora* 9: 172–200.

———. 1910b. The *Lactariae* of North America—Fascicles I and II. *Mycologia* 2: 27–36.

———. 1913. The *Lactariae* of the Pacific Coast. *Mycologia* 5: 305–311.

———. 1932. Two New Species of *Lactaria. Mycologia* 24: 460–463.

———. 1936. New or Noteworthy Species of *Russula* and *Lactaria. Mycologia* 28: 253–267.

———. 1940. Interesting Species of *Lactariae* from Florida. *Mycologia* 40: 575–586.

Coker, W. C. 1918. The *Lactariae* of North Carolina. *J. Elisha Mitchell Sci. Soc.* 34: 1–61.

Desjardin, D. E. 2003. A Unique Ballistosporic Hypogeous Sequestrate *Lactarius* from California. *Mycologia* 95 (1): 148–155.

Giltrap, N. J. 1982. Production of Polyphenol Oxidase by Ectomycorrhizal Fungi with Special Reference to *Lactarius* Spp. *Trans. Brit. Mycol. Soc.* 78: 75–81.

Heilmann-Clausen, J., A. Verbeken, and J. Vesterholt. 1998. *The Genus* Lactarius *(Fungi of Northern Europe)*. Vol. 2. Danish Mycological Society, Copenhagen. 287 pp.

Hesler, L. R. 1960. *Mushrooms of the Great Smokies.* Univ. of Tennessee Press, Knoxville. 289 pp.

Hesler, L. R., and A. H. Smith. 1960a. Studies on *Lactarius.* I. The North American Species of Section *Lactarius. Brittonia* 12: 119–139.

———. 1960b. Studies on *Lactarius.* II. The North American Species of Sections *Scrobiculus, Crocei, Theiogali,* and *Vellus. Brittonia* 12: 306–350.

———. 1979. *North American Species of Lactarius.* Univ. of Michigan Press, Ann Arbor. 841 pp.

Homola, R. L., and M. M. Czapowskyj. 1981. *Ectomycorrhizae of Maine. 2. A Listing of* Lactarius *with Associated Hosts.* Bulletin no. 779. Life Sciences Agricultural Experiment Station, Univ. of Maine, Orono. 19 pp.

Knudson, H., and T. Borgen. 1982. Russalaceae of Greenland. In *Arctic and Alpine Mycology,* ed. G. A. Laursen and J. A. Ammirati, 216–243. Univ. of Washington Press, Seattle.

Kobayasi, Y., N. Hiratsuka, K. Aoshima, R. P. Korf, M. Soneda, K. Tubaki, and J. Sugiyama. 1967. Mycological Studies of the Alaskan Arctic. *Ann. Rep. Instit. Fermentation* 3: 1–138.

Korhonen, M. 1984. *Lactarius hysginoides,* a New Boreal Agaric. *Karstenia* 25: 62–65.

Laursen, G. A., and J. A. Ammirati. 1982. *Lactarii* in Alaskan Arctic Tundra. In *Arctic and Alpine Mycology,* ed. G. A. Laursen and J. A. Ammirati, 245–281. Univ. of Washington Press, Seattle.

Methven, A. S. 1985. New and Interesting Species of *Lactarius* from California. *Mycologia* 77 (3): 472–482.

———. 1992. An Introduction to the Infrageneric Classification of *Lactarius. McIlvainea* 10 (2): 29–40.

———. 1993. Contributions to a Study of the North American Species of *Lactarius. McIlvainea* 11 (1): 26–34.

———. 1997. *The Agaricales (Gilled Fungi) of California 10. Russulaceae 2.* Lactarius. Mad River Press, Eureka, Calif. 78 pp.

Miller, O. K., Jr. 1983. Ectomycorrhizae in the Agaricales and Gasteromycetes. *Can. J. Bot.* 61: 909–916.

Miller, O. K., Jr., G. A. Laursen, and B. M. Murray. 1973. Arctic and Alpine Agarics from Alaska and Canada. *Can. J. Bot.* 51: 43–49.

Miller, S. L. 1999. A Field Key to Common Genera of Hypogeous and Gasteroid Basidiomycetes of North America. *McIlvainea* 14 (1): 8–29.

Miller, S. L., and T. Lebel. 1999. Hypogeous Fungi from the Southeastern United States. II. The Genus *Zelleromyces. Mycotaxon* 72: 15–25.

Murrill, W. A. 1938. New Florida Agarics. *Mycologia* 30: 359–371.

———. 1939. Additions to Florida Fungi. I. *Bull. Torrey Bot. Club* 66: 29–37.

———. 1940. Additions to Florida Fungi. II. *Bull. Torrey Bot. Club* 67: 57–66.

———. 1948. Species of Florida *Lactarius* Fr. *Lloydia.* 11: 86–98.

Peck, C. H. 1870. Report of the State Botanist. *Annual Rep. N.Y. State Mus.* 24: 41–108.

———. 1872. Genus *Lactarius* Fr. In Report of the State Botanist (for 1869). *Ann. Rep. N.Y. State Cab.* 23: 114–120.

———. 1876. Report of the State Botanist. *Annual Rep. N.Y. State Mus.* 28: 31–88.

———. 1885. New York Species of *Lactarius.* In Report of the State Botanist (for 1884). *Ann. Rep. N.Y. State Mus.* 38: 111–133.

———. 1907. New Species of Fungi. *Bull. Torrey Bot. Club* 34: 345–349.

Rapior, S., F. Fons, and J. M. Bessière. The Fenugreek Odor of *Lactarius helvus. Mycologia* 92 (2): 305–308.

Redhead, S. A., and A. H. Smith. 1983. *Lactarius neotabidus* nom. nov. for *Lactarius canadensis* Smith. *Mycotaxon* 17: 521–522.

Ridgway, R. 1912. *Color Standards and Nomenclature.* R. Ridgway, Washington, D.C. 43 pp., 53 pl.

Rogerson, C. T., and G. J. Samuels. 1995. Agaricicolous Species of *Hypomyces. Mycologia* 86 (6): 839–866.

Singer, R. 1975. *The Agaricales in Modern Taxonomy.* 3rd ed. J. Cramer, Vaduz, Liechtenstein. 912 pp.

Singer, R., and A. H. Smith. 1960. Studies on Secotiaceous Fungi. IX. The Astrogastraceous Series. *Mem. Torrey Bot. Club* 21: 1–112.

Smith, A. H. 1949. *Mushrooms in Their Natural Habitats.* Vol. 1. Sawyer's, Portland, Ore. 626 pp.

Smith, A. H., and L. R. Hesler. 1962. Studies on *Lactarius.* III. The North American Species of Section *Plinthogali. Brittonia* 14: 369–440.

Sundberg, W. J., and J. M. Trappe. 1975. Notes on *Zelleromyces cinnabarinus* (Hydnangiales). *Trans. Br. Mycol. Soc.* 66: 533–536.

Thiers, H. D. 1984. The Genus *Arcangeliella* Cav. in the Western United States. *Sydowia* 37: 296–308.

Trappe, J. M. 1962. Fungus Associates of Ectotrophic Mycorrhizae. *Bot. Rev. (Lancaster)* 28: 538–606.

Weber, N. S., and A. H. Smith. 1985. *A Field Guide to Southern Mushrooms.* University of Michigan Press, Ann Arbor. 280 pp.

Wells, V. L., and P. E. Kempton. 1975. New and Interesting Fungi from Alaska. *Beih. Nova Hedwigia* 51: 347–358.

Index to Common Names

Index to Scientific Names

Page number in *italic* denotes illustration.

PHOTO CREDITS

All photographs other than the ones listed here were taken by Alan E. Bessette, David B. Harris, and Arleen F. Bessette. The authors extend their sincere appreciation to the individuals who provided photographs that contribute immensely to this book.

Harley Barnhart: *Lactarius hygrophoroides* var. *hygrophoroides* (B), *Lactarius indigo* var. *indigo* (C), *Lactarius luculentus* var. *luculentus* (A), *Lactarius mucidus* var. *mucidus, Lactarius olivaceoumbrinus, Lactarius rufulus, Lactarius subplinthogalus* (A), *Lactarius subpurpureus* (A)

Michael Beug: *Lactarius alpinus* var. *mitis, Lactarius fallax* var. *concolor* (B), *Lactarius fallax* var. *fallax, Lactarius luculentus* var. *laetus, Lactarius occidentalis, Lactarius pallescens* var. *pallescens* (C), *Lactarius pseudomucidus* (B), *Lactarius torminosus* var. *nordmanensis*

Robert Chapman: *Lactarius alnicola* var. *alnicola* (A), *Lactarius barrowsii, Lactarius rubrilacteus, Lactarius uvidus* var. *montanus* (C)

Dennis Desjardin: *Arcangeliella desjardinii* (B), *Arcangeliella parva, Lactarius argillaceifolius* var. *megacarpus* (B), *Lactarius colorascens* (A), *Lactarius fumosus* var. *fumosoides, Lactarius manzanitae* (B), *Lactarius substriatus*

Vera Evenson: *Lactarius caespitosus*

Dan Guravich: *Lactarius agglutinatus* (A), *Lactarius argillaceifolius* var. *argillaceifolius* (A), *Lactarius chrysorheus* (A), *Lactarius fumosus* var. *fumosus, Lactarius hygrophoroides* var. *hygrophoroides* (C), *Lactarius imperceptus* (A), *Lactarius indigo* var. *indigo* (D), *Lactarius peckii* var. *peckii* (B), *Lactarius subvernalis* var. *cokeri* (B), *Lactarius sumstinei* (A, B), *Lactarius thejogalus* (B), *Lactarius yazooensis*

Roy Halling: *Lactarius manzanitae* (A), *Lactarius pallidiolivaceus*

Richard Homola: *Lactarius camphoratus* (scanning electron micrograph [SEM]), *Lactarius carbonicola* (A,B), *Lactarius cinereus* var. *fagetorum* (B), *Lactarius deceptivus* (SEM), *Lactarius eburneus, Lactarius fragilis* var. *fragilis, Lactarius frustratus, Lactarius fumeacolor, Lactarius gerardii* (SEM), *Lactarius gerardii* var. *fagicola, Lactarius gerardii* var. *subrubescens* (B), *Lactarius highlandensis* (A, B), *Lactarius louisii* (A, B), *Lactarius minisculus, Lactarius neotabidus, Lactarius obscuratus, Lactarius pseudomaculatus, Lactarius resimus* var. *resimus* (SEM), *Lactarius scrobiculatus* var. *canadensis, Lactarius uvidus* var. *montanus* (SEM), *Lactarius vinaceopallidus*

Emily Johnson: *Lactarius gerardii* var. *gerardii* (C, D), *Lactarius hibbardae* var. *hibbardae* (A, C), *Lactarius hygrophoroides* var. *rugatus* (A), *Lactarius maculatipes* (A), *Lactarius peckii* var. *peckii* (C), *Lactarius scrobiculatus* var. *canadensis* (C), *Lactarius subplinthogalus* (C, D), *Lactarius subvernalis* var. *cokeri* (C), *Lactarius volemus* var. *volemus* (B, C)

David Lewis: *Lactarius angustifolius* (A, B), *Lactarius caeruleitinctus*

Andy Methven: *Lactarius colorascens* (B), *Lactarius vinaceosporus*

Orson K. Miller: *Lactarius lanceolatus*

John Plischke III: *Lactarius badiopallescens, Lactarius gerardii* var. *subrubescens* (A)

Bill Roody: *Lactarius camphoratus* (A), *Lactarius chelidonium* var. *chelidonioides* (B), *Lactarius chelidonium* var. *chelidonium, Lactarius chrysorheus* (B), *Lactarius controversus, Lactarius croceus* (C), *Lactarius deliciosus* (Rovellons) in Spain, *Lactarius floridanus* (A, B), *Lactarius furcatus, Lactarius hygrophoroides* var. *hygrophoroides* (A), *Lactarius indigo* var. *indigo* (B), *Lactarius lignyotellus, Lactarius maculatus* (A), *Lactarius neuhoffii* var. *neuhoffii, Lactarius pallescens* var. *pallescens* (A), *Lactarius petersenii* (A, B, C), *Lactarius proximellus* (A, B), *Lactarius psammicola* f. *glaber* (A), *Lactarius psammicola* f. *psammicola* (A, B), *Lactarius pseudodeliciosus* var. *pseudodeliciosus, Lactarius purpureoechinatus, Lactarius pyrogalus* (A), *Lactarius subpalustris, Lactarius subvernalis* var. *cokeri* (A), *Zelleromyces cinnabarinus* (A, B)

Kit Scates-Barnhart: *Lactarius fallax* var. *concolor* (A), *Lactarius olympianus* (cover photo), *Lactarius pseudomucidus* (C)

Walt Sturgeon: *Lactarius aspideoides* (A), *Lactarius chelidonium* var. *chelidonioides* (A), *Lactarius croceus* (A)

Walt Sundberg: *Lactarius duplicatus*

Harry Thiers: *Arcangeliella crassa, Arcangeliella desjardinii* (A), *Lactarius gossypinus* (A, B), *Lactarius hepaticus* (A), *Lactarius payettensis, Lactarius scrobiculatus* var. *pubescens*

Steve Trudell: *Lactarius affinis* var. *affinis* (B), *Lactarius alnicola* var. *alnicola* (B), *Lactarius argillaceifolius* var. *argillaceifolius* (C), *Lactarius argillaceifolius* var. *megacarpus* (A), *Lactarius circellatus* var. *borealis, Lactarius olympianus* (A, B), *Lactarius pallescens* var. *pallescens* (B), *Lactarius subflammeus, Lactarius subgerardii, Lactarius subpurpureus* (C), *Lactarius subviscidus, Lactarius uvidus* var. *montanus* (A, B)

Nathan Wilson: *Lactarius pubescens* var. *betulae*

Michael Wood: *Lactarius rubriviridis* (A, B)

Alan E. Bessette is a mycologist and emeritus professor of biology at Utica College of Syracuse University. He has published numerous professional papers in the field of mycology and has authored or coauthored nineteen books, including *Mushrooms of the Adirondacks, Mushrooms: A Quick Reference Guide to Mushrooms of North America, Edible Wild Mushrooms of North America, Mushrooms of Northeastern North America, Mushrooms of the Southeastern United States,* and *North American Boletes—A Guide to the Fleshy Pored Mushrooms.* He has presented numerous mycological programs, was the scientific advisor to the Mid-York Mycological Society, and served as a consultant to the New York State Poison Control Center for more than twenty years. He has been the principal mycologist at national and regional forays, and was the recipient of the 1987 Northeast Mycological Foray Service Award and the 1992 North American Mycological Association Award for Contributions to Amateur Mycology.

David B. Harris is a mycologist and botanical photographer who has collected and studied the genus *Lactarius* in North America for more than ten years. His photographs have won several awards in the North American Mycological Association's photo contests. He was president of the Mid-York Mycological Association and has presented several lectures on the genus *Lactarius.*

Arleen R. Bessette is a mycologist and botanical photographer who has been collecting and studying wild mushrooms for more than fifty years. She has authored or coauthored eleven books, including *Taming the Wild Mushroom: A Culinary Guide to Market Foraging, Mushrooms of North America in Color, Mushrooms of Northeastern North America,* and *Mushrooms of Cape Cod and the National Seashore.* Her most recent book is *Common Edible and Poisonous Mushrooms of New York.* She has won several national awards for her photography and teaches introductory courses in mycology as well as mushroom-dyeing workshops for the North American Mycological Association and other organizations.